THE
AMERICAN
BOMBER BOYS

THE
AMERICAN
BOMBER BOYS

THE US 8th AIR FORCE AT WAR

MARTIN BOWMAN

AMBERLEY

This edition first published 2012

Amberley Publishing
The Hill, Stroud
Gloucestershire, GL5 4EP

www.amberley-books.com

British Library Cataloguing in Publication Data.
A catalogue record for this book is available from the British Library.

ISBN 978-1-4456-0858-7

Typesetting and Origination by Amberley Publishing.
Printed in Great Britain.

Contents

1

Rites Of Passage

Come and join the Air Corps
It's a grand bunch so they say,
We never do no work at all,
Just fly around all day!
While others work and study hard
And so grow old and blind,
We take to the air, without a care,
And you will never mind.

8am, December 7 1941

I had just returned from 7 o'clock Mass at St Patrick's in the Kaimuki district of Honolulu when I noticed the black puffs of anti-aircraft shells over Pearl Harbor. Our house faced the harbor and was on high ground. Thinking it odd for the Navy to be holding maneuvers of some sort on a Sunday morning, I went into our house and turned the radio set to KGMB. I waited but nothing happened – the station seemed to be off the air – then in a minute or so a highly excited announcer broke the silence with words to the effect that we were under sporadic air attack by unidentified aircraft. It was some minutes before the attackers were identified as Japanese. I watched the bombing of Pearl Harbor from our front porch. Japanese high-level bombers formed up in vics (in "Vee" formation) at about 8,000 feet above my house for the return to what proved to be their carriers – and they headed north.

The only good news was that twenty-nine enemy aircraft were downed, more than a third by Army Air Corps pilots flying obsolete P-36s and P-40s. None of our fighter pilots had any combat experience yet they managed to shoot down several Mitsubishi "Zero"-type fighters along with the dive and torpedo bombers they bagged that morning.

That same evening the skies of Pearl Harbor were lit up by hundreds of anti-aircraft trajectories and exploding shells – a most spectacular display. The "enemy" proved to be US Navy carrier-borne aircraft returning to Pearl from our two carriers at sea.

The next morning, I was up early enough to watch the anti-aircraft batteries at Fort Ruger open fire on a formation of three of our B-18s heading east at only 3,000 feet. No one had any idea what a Japanese airplane looked like.

A pall of black smoke hovered over Pearl Harbor for weeks. At the Hawaiian Pineapple Company where I worked as an apprentice machinist, we began working ten hours a day, six days a week. We repaired and reconditioned dozens of huge electric motors and other types of machinery salvaged from our damaged and sunken naval vessels. I spent many hours on a lathe making parts for ships' intercom systems. Work was all we had time for. Martial law imposed a 10pm curfew and anyone caught outdoors in the blackout after that time risked being shot on sight – no questions asked. Fishing was banned and the beaches were barricaded with barbed wire. In a matter of weeks my island had become a huge fort, a supply dump, a trap perhaps.

Martial law allowed the US Coast Guard to confiscate my father's year-old thirty-foot fishing boat. This entitled Dad to membership in the Coast Guard temporary service, which he declined and sent me in his place.

I was glad to attend the training program. Beginning in January I attended night classes in navigation, Morse code, signals, meteorology, among other sea-going subjects, taught by a young ensign who had cut his teeth on the famed American sailing vessel *Yankee*. All of this learning helped me pass the Army Air Corps aviation cadet test program which I took May 17 at Hickam Field.

Abe L. Dolim, who after washing out in flight school in March 1943, became a navigator, graduating on 16 October 1943. By November he was part of a B-17 crew at Drew Field, Florida

There were "distractions when the love bug got to us". Sergeant Kelch married the "girl back home." Sergeant Long remarried his ex-wife, and our co-pilot, 2nd Lieutenant Harvey Brown, married his South Carolina sweetheart at the base chapel. Then it was my turn when my cousin Hank's wife, Virginia, arranged a blind date for me with the baby sitter for their two-year-old son. There was no doubt I was smitten on meeting Mary Frances Nuzum, a real sloe-eyed brunette beauty. This eighteen-year-old cadet nurse led me a merry chase, but it was fun all the way, until she turned me down when I asked her to marry me. She was the only girl I ever considered for marriage, my true soul mate, so I was not about to give up on her. On March 12 I kissed my ladylove, the unobtainable Mary Frances, good-bye and headed back to Drew to gear up for the big move.

The Love Bug, Abe Dolim. The 22-year-old B-17 navigator and the rest of the crew sailed aboard the Queen Elizabeth for England and assignment to the 94th Bomb Group

Things were to change for every American, Pearl Harbor Day was an event that angered everyone. From a peace-loving nation we became a nation of enraged patriotic citizens. Everyone was for America and the young men all asked the same question, "Where do I enlist?" Just before entering the Army I met Rose Mandel, my first real serious romance and the girl that I wanted to be waiting for me when my service was over. We only had about six months of dating before I entered the Air Corps. My military service began 16 October 1942 and little did I know that I would volunteer in the near future for flying duty as a B-17 radio operator. In September 1943 we were on our way overseas and sailed on the *Queen Mary* from New York along with 15,000 other Army Air Corps personnel. Needless to say this was a very crowded ship, but after five days we arrived safely and disembarked in Scotland. With twenty-nine other crews we were assigned to a replacement pool and after five days we were rushed to a bomb group as replacement crews for those lost. When we entered our barracks on a cold dreary night all we saw were empty beds. We were told that these were the beds of men who had been shot down a few days before. A very sobering thought for us as a group. Suddenly flying status was not that appealing. Someone said out loud, "And we volunteered for this?"

Larry Goldstein, who was born in Brooklyn, 10 February 1922. Goldie completed his 25-mission tour on 4 March 1944 and, after returning home, married Rose on a hot summer's day in New York on 4 July 1944

They came out of the wheat fields, the factories in the cities. They were guys just off the street. Some I them only had a few weeks' training, a few months' at the most. As soon as the commander said, "I think I can make it," they sent him out.

General Lewis Lyle

Two Royal Navy ships were in dock at Mare Island Naval shipyard for repairs to damage sustained in the battle for Crete. One ship still had sixty men sealed into the bow. The bodies were later removed. A short time after that I decided that I was not going to be just another shipyard worker and I took examinations for pilot training in the Air Corps.

Carl L. Anderson

Our squadron loved to sing as we marched, so we made up a song about Squadron "H" to the tune of "Mademoiselle from Armentières, Parlez-Vous". It went thusly:

> Squadron H is always late, Parlez-vous?
> Squadron H is always late, Parlez-vous?
> Squadron H is always late
> They lay in bed and masturbate

Hinky Dinky Squadron, Parlez-vous?

John W. McClane Jr,
AAF Aviation Cadet, Squadron G, Nashville AAF Classification Centre

Before being shipped off to the various kinds of flying officers' schools, the Ellington cadets were sent to gunnery schools, I to Harlingen Army Gunnery School, on the Texas Gulf Coast near the Mexican border, to take a few intensive weeks of instruction ... Harlingen was the first station for me and thousands of other cadets ... Matamoros was at the end of the bridge that spanned the Rio Grande River from Brownsville, Texas. The regular Army enlisted men who operated the Harlingen base, whether PE aides or dollopers of mashed potatoes in chow line, would ask if we had visited Rosita yet in Matamoros. "Oh, you simply must go see her," they said with smirks. "She's much better than anything you ever saw at your county fair back home!"

Of course, we all did go see Rosita and she was much better. But we did not just go for her benefit but to taste the romance of Old Mejico. With each new group of cadets, the camp emptied out on the first Sunday and filled the streets of Matamoros. What streets! Apart from the main drag, they were dry, dusty, unpaved streets littered with trash and horse manure. Flies were everywhere and the smell of horse manure permeated the air. Cheap shops, restaurants and bars lined most of the streets. Each bar must have had its own Baja Marimba band, or a good nickelodeon, because the gayest of lilting Mexican music wafted to the street from behind the swinging saloon doors.

One street had an elevated boardwalk, beyond which were small rooms, one after another, exhibiting a single window each and either an open door or closed door. If the door were open, a dark-skinned friendly señorita stood in a tight-fitting brightly colored dress from which protruded plenty of leg and breast. The señoritas as a group weren't particularly pretty, their complexions commonly revealing unhealthy or unclean upbringings or smallpox scars. But, my oh my, those sexy petite bodies! If the Matamoros' Chamber of Commerce had bothered to clean up the aroma and flies a bit, say by removing all that horse shit, who knows how many additional cadets might have added tax rakeoffs to the C. of C. treasury, courtesy of those sexy petite bodies.

Indeed, as cadets got off the bus or parked their rented cars in Matamoros and began their adventure in twos and threes, they were approached by young Mexican boys: "You wanna fuck my seester?"

To see the real pièce de resistance, Rosita, it was necessary to hire a Mexican cab. Back in Harlingen, there seemed to be only one Rosita in Matamoros. But of course there may have been two-dozen Rositas and the taxi driver had some way of knowing just which Rosita was not giving an audience at the moment he arrived. If a Rosita was engaged, on to the next possibility went the cab.

My particular Rosita operated in a small room with a double bed, a washstand and pitcher of water and room for perhaps six or eight US servicemen to stand around the bed. Rosita did have a male accomplice, but he disappeared through the curtained doorway into the back room. She operated completely in the nude – no reason to be ashamed of that body – and was far less modest about her perfect body than any trollop at the home county fair was – and her price was much more reasonable to boot!

Rosita did various burlesque types of things with sashes, her breasts and her behind, but her main entertainment was In what she put into her behind and her vagina, either one orifice at a time or both at once, especially silver dollars and eggs. Could she have handled five eggs at once? I think that was her claim. Once the eggs were assimilated, all done in plain sight, she then flipped the eggs out, one at a time, no hands, with cute little gyrations of her pelvis. In the example of silver dollars, she balanced herself, nearly prone, on two bended and spread legs and one arm and with one hand and an inserted finger she flicked the coins toward the cadets, who scrambled to get out the way.

For one moment, Rosita disappeared behind the curtains momentarily, then resumed the above-described posture and proceeded to squirt water at the now more intently scrambling cadets, who somehow didn't think it was innocent maiden's water.

Show over, Rosita invited any adventuresome soul who dared to come with her behind the curtains. I recall that no one went, nor did anyone stoop to pick up the silver dollars.

All About Harlingen, Rosita and Machine Guns, Bob Shaver

We never did much on pass to San Antonio. There were many base activities to substitute, including dances and movies. We did see glimpses of glamour in the Air Corps. Occasionally, Roy Ruhge, I and one or two others went to San Antonio, rented a car at an exorbitant cost and drove to the Saturday-night dance in New Braunfels, or we tooled around San Antonio. I had one date with a San Antonio girl whose name was very forgettable because she got lipstick all over me and she was a heavy smoker. The combination of red lipstick spread with a knife and the strong odor of Camel cigarette smoke was just too much for me. Rosita of Matamoros didn't seem all bad in comparison.

New Braunfels was a German-dominated community thirty miles on down the road from San Antonio. The dances were almost like Oktoberfests, largely family affairs, with traditional German waltzes and polkas, gaiety and sumptuous eating. We servicemen were welcome to everything, including the first – or second – generation fräuleins. That did not necessarily mean hog heaven for us, however, because the fat Hausfrau mothers kept wary eyes out from their seats along the wall.

Still, it wasn't entirely a protective matter for all the fräuleins, who reputedly, along with Japanese women, were said to understand and enjoy their roles as housewives, mothers and servers of men better than all other national groups of women. I did have two unprotected dates with a Virginia Siegfried, who wasn't from New Braunfels originally, but who lived on an isolated ranch with her father near Seguin, Texas.

I never quite understood the New Braunfels connection for her or her relationship with her strict (as she said) father, but I did come to understand that she was an emotionally disturbed girl. She looked fine, with Cybil Shepherd kind of eyes and a body to be fully respected. She knew what to do with that body, up to a point, and how to give sensational lingering kisses. It was as if the world and her body were mine, but she began to tremble and her suggestive motions were a bit jerky or uncontrolled. She suddenly pulled away at the hotter moments, only to return for more up to that point. All ended in frustration and additionally, for her part, in tears, so emotional she was, not because I persisted.

I must have represented something much more to her than a good time and a male body, up to a point. A Prince Charming perhaps? One who would take her away from an isolated existence with a strict (or abusive) father? Perhaps, but I had had only two dates with her. I was thrilled but not in love; she was in love, she said. When I graduated from Hondo and was shipping out of San Antonio on a bus or train in early January 1944, she somehow knew the time and place – she may have pried it out of me. She wanted to see me and it would have to be an afternoon meeting at the station – I remember that I had my packed B-4 bag where we met. She was indeed emotional, intermittently in tears, wanted to marry me and "Will I ever see you again?" The situation was impossible, of course.

Poor Virginia, she never did see me again, nor did we correspond. I never thought that I was that devastating; I thought that much of my attraction for her was in her need to escape from something and that I had treated her decently. I still feel sympathy to this day.

Love, Texas Style, Bob Shaver

While training in the States, my pilot's wife, Donis Campbell, a tall nice-looking girl and four other pilots' wives, followed their husbands from base to base in an old beat-up car loaded down with what possessions they could get in. They were at the gate the morning we left the States to tell their husband's good-bye. Donis Campbell was the only one of the five to have her husband return.

Howard H. Hernan

Pvt. John Doe, after a long and tiresome journey, the last part of which was across "No Man's Land" (the Great Salt Lake desert), arrives at a railroad station at the west extremity of Utah, at perhaps 9am. He glances curiously out of the coach and it's not the train that makes him wonder, "What in hell have I done to deserve this?"

Sergeant Marshall F. Baker, squadron clerk, 306th Bomb Group

Despite the intensive training at Wendover, there was still an occasional moment for recreation. Some relaxed at the State Line Hotel, where half the bar was in Utah and half in Nevada. When midnight closed Utah, the bar patrons simply moved a few steps west. There were nurses to be impressed in Elko, Nevada. (In those days a buzz-job in a B-17 had a way of attracting a lady's attention!) Those unmarried and in search of excitement had to travel the 120 miles to Salt Lake City, or go west to Kimberley, Nevada.

Russell A. Strong

He was flying a light bomber somewhere in the States and had a forced landing outside Syracuse. This time he allowed the mechanics to work on the trouble and went into town for a meal. While he was there he suddenly remembered he once knew a girl in an office nearby, so he called her up. In exactly 90 minutes he had proposed to her and they were married. He saw his bride for exactly eight hours! After that he flew away and before he could return, his Liberator group was heading across the North Atlantic for Britain – and the war. He didn't mind that. He figured that night that with any luck he would soon complete his operational war missions and get a chance to go home for instruction work.

Arch Whitehouse, writing about Captain John B. McCormick, 389th Bomb Group pilot

In January 1944 we wallowed in latrine rumours about what theatre we would go to – England or Italy, or, some said, Norway ... Satisfied with the formation flying, the POM inspectors gave the go-ahead signal and in a few days all planes were on the way to Morrison Field, West Palm Beach, Florida, which was the shoving-off base ... Many crews added weight to their planes by loading on cases of the plentiful native rum and the not-so-plentiful Scotch and bourbon ... After crossing the Equator, right on the banks of the Amazon River, the next stop was Belem, Brazil, where all personnel below the grade of field officer were restricted to the base. From Belem, some of the planes flew to Fortaleza and others to Natal where most crew members acquired a pair of the well-known Natal boots and bought stockings to be mailed home to wives and girl friends ... From Marrakech to Prestwick, Scotland; Valley, Wales; and Mawgan, Wales, crews kept guns loaded and maintained a sharp watch for German planes as they skirted Portugal and Spain and passed by the Brest Peninsula.

Allan Healy, 467th Bomb Group

The 467th picked me up at Herington, Kansas, when their chief operations clerk washed out on the overseas physical. I flew over with one of the combat crews in old 5-2-5. Our flight to West Palm, Trinidad, Belem, Forteleza, Dakar and Marrakech was eventful. We lost an engine over Brazil, blew a supercharger out of Forteleza and fractured a nose wheel landing at Dakar. But the big foul-up came at Marrakech! The ATC guys said we could go into town. We did. Oh boy, did we ever. When we got back at midnight we were told that our plane was scheduled to take off in 30 minutes. We made the deadline but the navigator was somewhat the worse for wear. Somehow we got lost – bad lost. The next morning we wondered about those black puffs of smoke. Back in the waist, where I was, a gunner said, "We must be over Spain or Portugal."

Spain, hell! Old 5-2-5 was over France near Le Mans. Eleven green flyboys and the German AA had our range and altitude. Those puffs were flak. Over the intercom the first pilot said we had screwed up again. He said he didn't think we had enough gasoline to get to England and we had battle damage. I was scared. The bombardier came back to the waist and told us to throw out stuff – but not the rum we got in Brazil. Out went the 50s. The pilot said we probably would have to ditch. They were transmitting Mayday! Mayday! Everyone was excited. I was thinking about how cold the Channel would be. What a way to go. As if by magic, an RAF Beaufighter appeared and led us to RAF Station Exeter. The engines were sputtering as we landed poorly downwind. There was a lot of screeching and then blam! Somebody helped me out. We straggled out of the plane, pondering how angry Colonel Albert Shower would be. No lie.

A British Customs official asked the pilot to make out a declaration. Soon an RAF lorry took us to a rather barren building. We were herded into a room with no furniture. A British sergeant told us to strip naked. Then he took all our clothes. I was scared, cold and slightly bruised. Some of my teeth were broken. Soon a rather businesslike RAF officer came in with a WAAF. She ignored our nakedness. We resented the off-hand manner. Then our ball-turret gunner whispered, "They think we are Germans. No stuff."

The officer asked me to pronounce several words. He asked me the capital of Maryland. I said Baltimore; then corrected myself to Annapolis. He grunted. The WAAF took notes. Finally the first pilot got through on the telephone to Rackheath, home of the 467th. They vouched for a missing bunch of Eightballs. The serial number of our aircraft was, indeed, one of theirs. Our most recent delay had been Dakar, they thought. I gathered that the pilot thought it might have been easier to take the rap as German intruders, rather than face Colonel Shower at Rackheath.

Later an RAF sergeant told me he knew we were *real* Yanks when we started asking about passes into town.

We got the passes and an RAF guide. I knew I was going to like England and I did.

> Tom Swint, pilot, B-24 42-52525 *Six Bits*, 789th Bomb Squadron, 467th Bomb Group. Six Bits failed to return on 21 June 1944 when 2nd Lieutenant Edward F. Rudowska was forced to land at Bulltofta in Sweden

The crew came together at MacDill AFB, Tampa, Florida and we went to Savannah, Georgia, to pick up a brand new B-17. After picking up all the kit in an assembly-line process, we took off at 2am. We went to Bangor, Maine, stayed there a day and then on to England via Labrador. A tremendous storm at Goose Bay set in. Winds blew at 100kt and blew two B-17s into the sea. Then on to Bluey West 3 at Greenland. At the end of the runway abutted a 1,000ft glacier. We stayed there a week until the storm abated.

We played poker, slept and ate. We had to use a rope between our barracks and the mess hall in order to stop us being blown away. We then flew on to Keflavik, Iceland, on to Valley, Wales, and our plane was taken from us. The crew was assigned to various bomb groups.

John A. Holden, navigator

March 7 1944: All set to fly to England. We were to fly up past Spain, Portugal and France and into England. Take-off was at 23:45hr. At altitude it soon became colder as we neared the northern climes, so out came our woollies. The navigator had to make sure he stayed on his meridian. Too far east and Jerry might come up and give us a going over. Too far west and we are liable to run out of fuel.

Philip H. Meistrich, 453rd Bomb Group

The day we brought our *Snoozy II* in, the English tower master said on open radio: "I say there, American aircraft, this is your field; you are cleared to land." Lord Haw Haw must have been listening, for that night on radio he said: "Welcome to England, 306th Group!"

Al La Chasse, bombardier

Arriving over Valley at the northwest tip of Wales, we signaled our friendly nature by firing the colors of the day from our Very pistol. "Welcome to the Old World," came back the reply. We landed in daylight. Before I was fifty feet beyond the plane, a Welsh lad walked up to me and asked, "Got some gum chum?" We had also been briefed about that and it thus proved to be far more accurate information than had been the North Atlantic weather data.

For us, Valley was only a gathering station, as it also was for the never-ending stream of bombers rolling off the American assembly lines and tolling the doom of the German war effort. Even before arriving at Valley, we had orders to continue on to the American base at Alconbury, near Cambridge. The next day, July 6, we left for Alconbury but in formation with several other newly arrived planes, both B-17s and B-24s, led by a B-24 from the Air Transport Command. Apparently, the British didn't trust green Americans to fly over their densely populated Midlands by themselves.

Along the way, the B-17 pilots bitched at the B-24 leader to hold down his speed so that they could keep up, which was a note for future reference for me that the B-24 could fly faster and higher and carry greater tonnage than could the B-17. More interesting than that, however, were the vistas slipping past below. The heavily industrialized cities of Liverpool and Stoke-on-Trent were covered by a haze of smoke or smog. The British had completely rebuilt whatever factory capacity the Germans had knocked out a few years earlier.

The English countryside and the cities looked much different from American counterparts. Nothing was regular. There were no one-mile road grids or neatly square city blocks; rather, road networks lacked pattern and city streets looked as though they could have been planned by a drunken spider. The most unifying characters seemed to be the irregular but beautiful patchwork of fields and red tile-roofed villages and cities.

Alconbury was a special training station in advanced radar navigation. I was the critical factor, therefore, in the orders that brought my crew and plane there. Neither would stay and within a couple of days, I said goodbye to the second crew with whom I thought I would fly combat ... I went temporarily to a base at Bovingdon, near Watford, west of London, for indoctrination to the European Theater of Operations, including how to get along with the English people.

About the latter, I remember that we should never, never say "bloody" in polite company unless one wanted to achieve the same effect that "shit" would back home. They did not prepare me, nevertheless, for what I soon saw in the park at Watford during evening hours: there, several couples were lying on the grass and engaging in rather more than casual bloody love making – with double British Summer Time it didn't get dark until after 11pm, which just happened to be the time when personnel carriers left town with their loads of servicemen returning to base. Nor did they tell me at Bovingdon how to ask an English girl politely if she wanted to make love. That remained for a new Alconbury acquaintance of mine, Lieutenant Tversky. After our first outing to a dance in Cambridge, he advised that the proper words a girl had told him were, alternatively: "I say, let's 'ave a go", and "'ow about an on?"

My God, I thought, don't the English speak American? The English ancestry was supposed to be even closer to Olde Germany and its common vernacular than was American ancestry. I think that Tversky fibbed in using that cockney accent. Cambridge was not in cockney land. Besides, the East Anglia girl that I married within the year never talked like that, not bloody likely!

Valley, Wales, Robert H. Shaver

The old men of the village were standing around the pubs, hands up to their mouths: "The Yanks are coming, have you heard?" "I suppose you've heard them old Yankees are coming," and similar comments punctuated their games of darts, skittles or pints of beer. "They'll be after our women – they are all oversexed." The men seemed despondent ... First came the GI trucks and jeeps and then we started seeing the Americans themselves, good-looking men in uniforms. "What will life be like now?" I thought. "Maybe I'll marry one of them when I grow up and go to live in America." They were good to us then, as we were the "Chewing Gum Kids". One of the Americans used to come to my home for dinner and my mother did washing for them.

Connie Richards, Bedfordshire teenager

All our past errors, all our omissive sins,
Must be wiped out. This war no nation wins.

Remember that when you are over here.

Lines to An American officer, Noël Coward

When we arrived at our Quonset hut at Deopham Green, so many officers had been killed there was no room to hang our clothes. One door was blocked with piles of uniforms. In the interim, our crew borrowed a wheelchair from supply and moved clothing and footlockers out. It took us two days to empty the barracks.

John A. Holden, navigator, 731st Bomb Squadron, 452nd Bomb Group

We arrived April 11 with three other crews. Later in the mess hall we learned that four crews failed to return on this day from Poznan, Poland. Such news to hear on arrival. For the month of April, twenty-five crews were lost. What would our fate be?

Wilbur Richardson, gunner, 94th Bomb Group

The weather is going to be very hard to get used to. It's very damp and you seldom see the sun ...

USAAF Sergeant in a letter to his wife in California, October 1944

We were treated like long-lost relatives. They didn't have much, but they cooked eggs and toast and made a pot of tea. The teakettle hung on a hook over a raised stone hearth, which contained a peat fire ... There used to be a gnome-like Irishman who came around to the barracks with fresh eggs for sale. One night he appeared with a bottle of Jameson's Irish whiskey, which he sold us for $10. After he had gone, we poured ourselves a drink in our mess cups and, to our chagrin, found out it was cold tea. Needless to say we never saw the little Irishman again.

George M Collar, 445th Bomb Group

I traveled to Aberdeen, Scotland, on a three-day pass to see my grandparents, whom I had not seen since I was four. How their eyes lit up when I had unpacked five pounds of sugar, a large tin of Spam and three pounds of butter – through the courtesy of a friendly mess sergeant. They hadn't seen food like that since wartime rationing started in 1940.

Douglas D. Walker, *Carpetbaggers*

On 6 December 1944, the crew was entitled to a three-day pass. Most of the crew went to London. I stayed around the base. I had no desire to go to

London anymore. I heard that if you were going on pass that you could be issued a ration coupon for the days you would be gone, if you were going to visit English people. I thought it might be of some help to 'Rene's mom and dad. So I applied. What a shock! For a three-day pass, I received one slice of bacon, one sausage, a "patty" of butter, the equivalent of a teaspoon of sugar and flour and some other items I cannot remember, all of which could be put in a small paper bag, about 2" by 6." I was almost ashamed to take it with me. I never knew what little the English were existing on.

Time on My Hands. George E. Kistner, extra gunner and radio operator, 388th Bomb Group, Knettishall. George Kistner married Irene on 31 March 1945

Malcolm Smith the maltster, who had been bombed out of his house in East Dereham, invited us for dinner almost every Saturday night. We would bring oranges and butter, etc. He would always have Scotch salmon, partridge and other un-rationed food. He had a plentiful supply of Scotch and a unique cellar of old wines. He loved to talk. He lived in a house near the airfield at Attlebridge.

Lieutenant Colonel George H. Parker, Station Engineer

The drinks weren't too good. The only whisky we had was after a mission at the debriefing table. The English had several beers (no good). They called them mild, mild and bitter and half and half (pronounced by the English *holf and holf*). They had cola but that was for the ladies. Once in a while you could catch one of the pubs with gin. At the officer's club you could get gin and orange or Scotch and coke. After a while, you would get a taste for it.

John Belingheri

Early in the mornings we would hear the drone of the planes overhead as they assembled, layer upon layer, ready for their attack on the enemy. When they returned, often shot to pieces and limping home with sometimes only one engine left functioning, our thoughts would be with those men.

May Ayers

Remember I'm a Britisher.
I know my country's faults. It's rather slow,
Superior assumptions; its aloof
Convictions in its destiny. The proof
Of its true qualities. I also know –
This lies much deeper. When we stood alone,
Besieged for one long agonising year,
The only bulwark in our hemisphere
Defying tyranny, in this was shown

> The temper of our people. Don't forget
> That lonely year. It isn't lease or lend,
> Or armaments, or speeches that defend
> The principles of living. There's no debt
> Between your land and mine except that year.
>
> *Lines to An American Officer,* Noël Coward

We flew to Europe in a B-24 Liberator fresh off the assembly line. They told our crew often that she was ours and never did an airplane have more affection bestowed upon it. Down from Florida to Brazil, across the South Atlantic to Africa and up to Wales we went with her and we babied her all the way.

I'll always remember that ship, 29511, because I named her after my wife, *Sweet Eloise*. And, I paid a GI seven bucks in Marrakech to paint the name along her nose. It was just before our last hop to Wales. For the moment we set foot on ground again, they took her from us.

We were just a replacement crew.

Late winter and early spring was a tough time in 1944 for bomber crews – especially replacement crews. The only good airplanes were those ferried over by replacements and they went to the old crews who were most apt to get the most good out of them. The battle-damaged wrecks that were left went to the green crews.

On the field of the 44th Bomb Group, oldest B-24 outfit in England, the plane supply was at an especially low ebb. Many of those remaining were in sad shape, war-weary and battle-scarred. New planes and new crews were needed badly.

Some of the new "24"s we had ferried were already in use by the time our gang piled off the trucks at the site of the 44th. We represented ten brand new complete bomber crews: forty officers and sixty noncoms. But none of us was destined to get many flights in new airplanes for a long time to come.

After losing the only new bomber we had ever flown, the one that had been given to us in Topeka, Kansas, it was quite a letdown to see what was offered on the base of the 44th Bomb Group. One of a cluster of airfields in England's East Anglia, our concrete pasture was located near the village of Shipdham, not far from Norwich, in Norfolk County, south of The Wash. The base was an ugly sprawl of Nissen huts and stucco buildings with airplanes to match.

The 44th had staggered up from Africa after being mauled at Ploesti and a few other choice targets. It had literally been wiped out several times over when numbers of planes lost were compared to the normal complement on the field. It was putting aloft about thirty-six planes to a mission when we arrived. Four didn't make it back that day. It was early March 1944.

They were glad to see us at the 44th, I guess. At least the CO of the 66th Bomb Squadron to which my crew was assigned seemed glad to see us. But we were a long way from combat despite an attack by the Germans somewhere south of us that first night on the field.

As we entered the Nissen hut reserved for us, we wondered about the empty cots so stark in the damp coldness. The sergeant who greeted us turned back to the chest of drawers he was emptying.

"Here, lieutenant. You might as well have this."

I caught the half-empty bottle and saw that it was aftershave lotion. Again the sergeant turned, several packs of cigarettes in his hand.

"There is no point in sending stuff like this back," he explained half apologetically. "If you don't take it, the vultures over at headquarters will get it." He turned back to the chest, picked off a picture of a girl, glanced briefly at it, then dropped it into a large bag. "I'll be out of here in a minute."

Larry, Dale, Jack and I exchanged glances. None of us knew who had been in the hut before. But suddenly it seemed much larger and much more empty. The same thought made the rounds. Would someone be collecting soon to send our belongings back to the United States – a pitiful pile of secondhand hairbrushes, underwear, souvenirs and maybe a few Short Snorter bills picked up on the way over – as evidence that we, too, fought the war in Europe?

A replacement crew was a lonely entity. It was accepted to take over a spot which might have belonged to one of the old gang who had earned a certain affection and respect. Either the old crew was on the way home, rotting in prison camps, or scattered in charred chunks of flesh and bone somewhere east. In any event, it had left a void that no replacement crew could possibly deserve until it earned it. Unless, of course, the missing crew was also a new replacement. In that case, it wouldn't be particularly missed except by people like the girl behind the picture that went so unceremoniously into the bag. There were only a few men on the base of the 44th Bomb Group who had completed their twenty-five missions to earn an overseas pass to home.

"Well, where do we go from here?" Jack broke the uncomfortable stillness as we started to sort out our belongings. It was more an expression than a question, but an answer came from an unexpected source.

"You Macs will see plenty of action. Just take it from old Mac."

The announcement came from an armload of wood staggering through the door ahead of a Latin type topped by a shock of curly black hair. As the wood tumbled in a heap beside the potbellied stove, somewhat swarthy features revealed themselves behind a nose that wandered decisively to the left. "There's a lot of war left. I'm Mac." He offered his hand around our little circle of officers.

"You just gotta take your turn. Me, I ain't in no hurry. My wife at home is just waitin' to get at me."

It didn't take much prying to learn that Mac also had an English wife. "I got me a kid, too. Just too bad it had to be a goddamned Limey." After what he apparently considered a proper tirade against the British, he filled us in on current events.

Whatever the truth of his marital affairs, he seemed to the military situation. It didn't take long to realize that everyone was "Lieutenant Mac" to Mac. We were never to be around long enough to learn his real name. He lamented the last crew who had occupied the hut.

"He sat right where you're sittin' Lieutenant Mac. "Only had two more missions to go. They didn't count any chutes."

We were to become accustomed to Private Mac's straightforwardness. Maybe his pugilistic training, mentioned in passing and obvious in appearance, taught him to hit straight from the shoulders. Each night he disappeared only to return with all the news and always on time. Frequently he would bring a hatful of fresh eggs from what was probably the only source within mile of the base. We never questioned his methods or his motives. The eggs, fried over the potbelly at odd hours, beat anything from the cans in the mess hall. Further, there was always fuel to keep the stove cherry red most of the time and hold back the heavy dampness.

Already we had become somewhat accustomed to this dampness that shrouded the English countryside much of the time. At a placement center where we had awaited our assignment to the 44th, there was time to get the feel of both the weather and the countryside. Green fields and fence rows much like Pennsylvania made it an easy transition for me. And I enjoyed the quiet villages with their pubs and churches that vied for the restive part of men's souls.

We thought that our final assignment would *bring* the action for which we had waited and trained over what had been nearly a year and a half for the officers. But in terms of waiting, we were a long way from combat. Already we had been in England for nearly three weeks with nothing more exciting than a link trainer flight to liven things up.

My only form of entertainment had been censoring mail. Little things like, "I miss your warm belly against my cold back at night," as some GI pined for his wife. Or maybe it would be a grimacing form of humor such as, "I received your picture; it is very good. Ha, ha."

Rounds of classes, more link trainer followed by practice flights and test flights gave my co-pilot, Jack Emerson, a chance to find out what the '24 was all about. Jack was the boy who had joined the crew only days before we left Casper, Wyoming, to pick up our new airplane in Topeka. He didn't get much dual time at Topeka. Swinging the compass was our only flying chore before heading for Florida and points east. It took my experience to hold headings while the navigator checked his directions to eliminate as much error as possible. So, during the practice sessions over England, I let Jack handle the plane as much as possible.

It gave me a chance to think back to the emergency leave I had risked while we ground our teeth in Topeka. Thinking back took my thoughts to the new picture on the chest of drawers and to February 11. A telegram had come from my mother-in-law. "Eloise went into the hospital today." The next morning came the second telegram. "You're the father of a boy."

At 9am I was at headquarters. "My wife went to the hospital yesterday. Today I'm a father," I told the CO.

I didn't have the nerve to *ask* for a leave. We were on alert for overseas. In fact, officialdom held it over our heads that any infraction of the rules to stay close to quarters would result in losing our airplanes and we would be shipped by boat. Nothing could be more degrading at this point. I might have been tempted to sneak away, but there were nine men depending on me. Consequently, I stood nervously in front of the CO, my situation in his lap. He looked at me steadily for several long moments. Finally, he glanced at his wristwatch.

"Lieutenant, it is now nine o'clock. Your leave begins at one o'clock this afternoon. Be back in thirty-six hours." I had a round trip of 2,600 miles to go.

It was my first inkling that the Army Air Force had a heart. I ran to the Red Cross building, for I didn't have money for a train ticket. After a wasted fifteen minutes I finally convinced the RC official that I didn't have to get twelve signatures to prove that I was: (1) alive; (2) broke, (3) an officer and a gentleman. He assured me that this was roughly the minimum requirement to borrow $100 for three days. Finally, I changed the rules.

"Look, suppose I make out a check for the money. I have it in my savings account at home, but my check won't be good until I get there. Just wait until I get back and I'll cash it."

He mulled this over in his mind while muttering objections. I kept checking my watch, watching the precious minutes disappear. At last and quite reluctantly, he accepted my bum check and handed me the money.

"Whatever you do, don't cash that check," was the last thing I said as I rushed from the building. Apparently he deposited it before I hit the gate.

There was a train leaving for Chicago at one o'clock. I was on it with a so-called, second-class priority. Ostensibly, this meant I would be able to get a train east out of Chicago. But the ticket agent actually laughed at me when I presented it at the window. There were only minutes to spare.

"Look, Lieutenant, everybody has priorities. There's just no seat available."

I found my gate and squeezed through with the crowd. Whether the weary gateman noticed or not, he didn't even call after me. Running down along the many coaches, I jumped up the first set of empty steps and worked my way forward. When the train finally began to move, it was certain to take me closer home. How close, I wouldn't know until the conductor found me. It *was* surprisingly easy. He accepted my proffer of money and handed me a ticket for Harrisburg, Pennsylvania.

It was a long night, with snatches of sleep in a seat, when a seat was available. At Harrisburg, I headed for the nearest highway. In the time it would take to find a bus, if one was available, I could be on my way. And, I was on my way. I rode my thumb. It was nine o'clock, thirty-two hours from Topeka, when I ran up the steps of Geisinger Hospital in Danville.

She didn't know I was coming. But, waiting for me the girl who dared to marry me six months ahead of schedule two years before, so that we could have a few in before I enlisted. It *was* the same girl who had followed me from base to base around the country. A cadet married to the lowest rank in the service. But now she was an officer's wife and a very sick one – though I did not know it then.

It was the last tenderness I was to know for a long time to come. We broke every rule in the hospital, the one where she learned to become a nurse, wife and mother. And finally, one of the nurses sneaked a bundle from the nursery. She informed me that the tiny creature inside the blanket was our son.

Babies had always looked about alike to me. This one didn't look much different. Gazing at that fragile, new person, I suddenly felt that the war was much less grim. Here was a part of me that would continue on regardless of what happened. He even had my name over my protests. I was suddenly glad that everything was exactly as it was. I ran down the hospital steps with tears of happiness streaming down my face. Even then, the incongruity of it all insisted that I was a fool I was running away from everything I had wanted out of life to that point, but I was supremely happy and so proud.

Berwick is only twenty-two miles from Danville. The folks at home explained that Eloise was dangerously ill. My leave was already too far gone. The next morning I talked to the doctors. The head obstetrician was gentle with me, too gentle.

"There is something we can't define at this point," he explained. 'But I think Eloise will be all right."

I suspected more than they were telling me. After explaining my situation, I asked, "Do you think I should still ask for an extension of my leave?" The answer was affirmative.

Topeka said no. Get back at once. I rushed to the bank to pick up money to cover my bad check and made air reservations to prolong my visit as much as possible. But bad weather again forced me to take the train and I was a day late getting back. Fortunately, nothing was said. Then we sat around Topeka for another fourteen days before heading overseas. It was time enough to learn that my wife would recover. It was also time enough to discover that I would have to wire back the money to cover my still bad check.

And now, in England, we were playing the old army game again. Each day we would rush to the bulletin board to see if we were scheduled for combat. Jack was ready. So was Dale Raushcher, my navigator and Larry Davis, the bombardier. Just as ready was the rest of the crew. We were not much different from the average crew of a B-24 bomber. Each had his own reason for being there. In the main, we had the average desire to serve out country in a time of obvious need. We sought the glamour of the flying war, the excitement. Maybe we had a little more than average crew esprit de corps; maybe we were a little more eager than the average. But, for all crews there could be no doubt of the need to do a job.

Aside from those reasons, which I shared, I had three personal purposes. First, I thought that flying offered an easy way to a commission. I was wrong. Secondly, I wanted to come back in one piece or not at all. I thought the Air Force provided the way until I saw what a 20mm, burning gasoline, a chunk of flak, or a sprinkling of 30-caliber bullets could leave alive of a kid who flew. Finally, I was married and wanted a job that would support a wife while I was in service. This it did.

But now, as March slid into April, all the previous training, the pent-up energy and the desire to test our fighting skills made each hour drag. We had developed a healthy respect for the vagaries of the weather and a little fear, but we were combat-ready. So we thought.

It was the weather that held us up as much as anything. Too thick to breathe and too thin to drink, fogs wrapped the base in a milky package that even the Germans didn't often try to penetrate in the daytime. Night was different.

As the infrequent sun splashed down somewhere beyond the mist, the British would roar out to battle. Singly, they rumbled out over the tops of ground clouds to admit the gaze of curious stars. We shuddered for them, wondering where they found the courage to take on the enemy in the black of night. And, we were told that they shuddered for the fool Yanks. Crazy Americans, who took over in the mornings to crawl across fields of flak with their bellies exposed to hot steel from below while painting stark targets against the blue canvas for the *Luftwaffe*.

Somehow, this morbid sympathy for the seeming stupidity of others drew us to these magnificent Britishers. They had held the line somewhere out over the water before the Americans came. But all of their warm blood so freely spilled had failed to raise the frigid temperature of the clutching North Sea that was both their defense and their enemy ...

Elusive Horizons, Keith C. Schuyler

2

'We're Here To Win The War For You'

These lines are dedicated to a man
I met in Glasgow, an American.
He was an Army officer, not old,
In the late twenties. If the truth were told
A great deal younger then he thought he was
I mention this ironically because,
After we'd had a drink or two, he said
Something so naïve, so foolish, that I fled.
This was December, Nineteen-Forty-Two.
He said: "We're here to win the war for you."

Lines to An American officer, Noël Coward

It was mid-afternoon when we finally made fast to our dock and we hung over the rails and out of portholes to talk with the men on the quay. British soldiers stood below and joined in the sport of jumping for apples, oranges and cigarettes that we tossed down. We didn't know that these would be the last oranges we would see for more than a year.

We were in good spirits now and we looked at the British soldiers curiously. Strange uniforms ... strange caps ... strange shoes. For a time we were silent, for we did not know what to say to them.

"Where are we?" someone called.

"Glazzga," answered a native.

"How are the women?" someone shouted tentatively.

The soldier smiled. "Yew'll soon find oot," he returned, in a voice that had been dragged through a bed of thistle.

"When does the next boat sail for America?" shouted Johnny Ludwig.

"Canna taell ye thot," replied the Scottie. "Bu' ah can taell ye thus ... yew'll no' be on ut!"

Robert S. Arbib Jr

Most GIs were surprised by the great variation in British accents and the fact that some were so heavy they could not understand what was being said. When we docked at Glasgow we were taken by lighter to a railroad station. While the troops waited for a train a woman came along dispensing tea; she kept calling, "Gay yer cunten coups oot" and GIs kept asking each other, "What she say?"

Having lived among the Scots community in New York I could translate her request as "Get your canteen cups out."

Arthur 'Art' Swanson, 357th Fighter Group

Upon arriving at Prestwick, Scotland, we turned over our new B-17, changed our money for British pounds and were bussed to Glasgow to await our train for our new base. There was a pub at the station where some of us went for a brew. Upon being served we were examining the coins in our change out of curiosity when an old lad seated at a nearby table came over to us. He inquired as to what we had given the waitress. He then asked to see our change. When we showed him he said, "You've been done for thrupence lads."

Bill Sullivan

My first taste of austerity travel on the railways of Britain came the day following our arrival in Scotland. The date was 18 August and the newspapers were full of the first American air raid on France. Late that evening we marched down from Bellahouston Park and loaded our duffle into a long, dirty troop train. We did not know how long the journey was to be, or where we were going but we did know that we would be sitting up eight men to a compartment throughout the night.

As the train pulled out of the station the sky was growing dark and we looked out of the windows curiously, noting with interest each feature of the hilly, quiet countryside of Lanarkshire. But it soon blackened and as we strained our eyes through the windows we could see nothing, not even a single light. It was like a continuous ride in an endless tunnel and it was vastly impressive. This was our first experience with the blackout. We marvelled at its completeness.

The compartment became hot and uncomfortable and sprawled, snoring bodies soon made it almost unbearable. One by one the men moved out into the passage and lay down on the arty floor to sleep. I found that the next car forward was an empty baggage car and spread my shelter-half on the floor. When I awoke the next morning, stiff and bruised, I found the floor of the car covered with other sleeping soldiers. We were at Ely – high up on a hill overlooking the flat farmland stood the ancient cathedral.

"Ely! Where the hell is that?" someone asked. I drew back in my memory and scrawled a rough map of England on an envelope.

"It's just about here," I said "and I can't figure out why we are going though Ely. I thought we were headed for the south of England."

The countryside flew past and more familiar names of unfamiliar places flashed by. Newmarket, Bury St Edmunds – Ipswich! We stopped at Ipswich for some time and then moved off again. Finally the train drew into a little country siding and the sign said Wickham Market! Here we were then. Who ever heard of Wickham Market? New York, Halifax, Glasgow, Wickham Market! That was probably the first train in the history of England that had gone non-stop from Glasgow to Wickham Market, Suffolk, but trains were doing many strange things in those memorable days. And we were to experience even stranger things than that during the following two years.

Is Your Journey Really Necessary? Robert S. Arbib Jr

We were assigned to the 44th Bomb Group, nicknamed "Flying Eightballs", a few miles north of Norwich by a small town called Shipdham. Arriving over our base, I noticed how pretty it was, surrounded by green grass and trees. We were met by an officer who welcomed us to the base. While the officer was talking to Spencer, his driver came over to us and asked, "Who's the tail gunner on this crew?"

I told him I was.

He said, "See that bomber over there?" pointing to a bullet-ridden plane on the runway. "It got a direct hit in the tail today and they're sucking out what's left of the tail gunner."

Some welcome, I thought, but they're not going to do it to me!

The next day as we walked into the Groups Headquarters Building, we saw this big sign that read:

"Good Morning! One more day closer to victory."

Eddie S. Picardo

I was detached from the FANY to act as a driver for officers of the US Army Services Supply at Cheltenham. Stayed with them three years. They were enormous fun to be with, very friendly, clued up, yet there was a simple naturalness about them. I think most were still civilians at heart.

While they did not expect you to take their remarks at face value, it was important to know that one should never make jokes about their flag or national institutions. On the other hand, some were not too careful in what they said about us. On one occasion the officer I was driving actually said they had come over to win the war for us. I was so cross I stopped the car and ordered him out. He got out, but by then I had calmed down enough to appreciate the situation of having ordered a US officer out of a US vehicle. Fortunately, he apologized and I relented and let him resume his seat!

Daphne Chute

Some time was allowed for my first look around a little of London. On a stroll up Regent Street a rather touching minor event occurred. Of course, I was in uniform and a rather small, neatly dressed lady of probably some seventy years young accosted me with, "You're American, aren't you?"

I replied in the affirmative.

"You don't realize how happy we are to see you, you have been missing since the last war and we really do need you!"

Tom Morrow, Ordnance Officer

One English lady I got into conversation with when I was walking down town was very enthusiastic about the United States. She said she had told her children that after the war America was where they should go; there was a better future in the colonies!

I said nothing.

Elenor Fredericks, first WAC increment to arrive in England

Perhaps it was just a coincidence, perhaps it was a touch of clairvoyance but the only book I brought with me from America – a book hastily purchased in New York City for shipboard reading – was Dickens's *Pickwick Papers*. I had space in my duffle for just one book; I wanted one that was amusing, lengthy and yet compact and concerned with England, which my hunch told me was our destination ... It was a happy choice, for I found myself lying in the cramped stateroom or on the crowded deck rediscovering half-forgotten treasures in the adventures of Pickwick and his company in London, Bath, Bury St Edmunds and Ipswich. It was even more apropos, I decided a week after our arrival in England, when I found myself walking down the streets of that same Ipswich and stopping at a hotel for a beer – a hotel named the Great White Horse – the very same hotel, I recalled with delight, where transpired that epic incident of the Lady with the Yellow Curl Papers.

I will not remember Ipswich, I am afraid, because of Pickwick. No city could have been farther removed from that Dickensian world than Ipswich in the autumn and winter of 1942. Dirty, crowded, noisy, evil smelling, it was then a composite of the smaller English provincial metropolis at war. Though it retained to some degree its basic East Anglian character, it was now in addition a roaring industrial town, a busy port and an amusement centre for troops of a dozen Allied nations. Nine miles from our camp at Debach, it became the destination for most of us on our weekly twenty-four-hour leaves and the source of many an evening's adventure. We thronged it, we criticized it and we admired it. We changed its life considerably.

The evening liberty truck left camp promptly at seven o'clock, overflowing with soldiers dressed up in their only suits of clean, pressed clothes. The truck was designed to carry fourteen men but usually there were more than twice that number crowded in the dark interior, squatting on the floor, sitting three-deep on each other's lap, hanging over the edge of the tail-gate and standing stooped under the low tarpaulin hood. We were allowed 15 per cent of the company each night, which was thirty men but we were also allowed one truck, for gasoline economy. But we didn't mind. We were on our way to town. We bounced and careened over the winding road to Ipswich, a trip that often took forty minutes in the unfamiliar blackout.

The truck parked in Princes Street and the human cargo spewed forth into the street, breaking up into little groups of two, three or four. These were hard-driving engineers, men who had been working from dawn to dark all week under the worst possible physical conditions; men who were homesick and longed for companionship that was not circumscribed by an olive-drab uniform, men to whom being overseas meant a release from the inhibitions that would naturally bind them in their own home communities. They wanted relaxation, they wanted release and they wanted a change from the gruelling drudgery of the job.

... Our first stop was the YMCA where we could shave and wash in that greatest of luxuries – hot water. Then we went upstairs and had breakfast for a few pennies. Coffee and hot buttered toast, with jam and a few pleasant words from the girl in slacks who worked behind the counter ... If we had errands in Ipswich we would attend to them. The dry cleaners usually, for we always had a load of filthy clothes. Vera at the shop ... could do the impossible and rush our most urgent orders through in not the usual ten days but in two – or if we spoke nicely – perhaps even one! And there was always the beautiful girl walking up the hill to work – who always smiled and waved to us.

There were the motion picture palaces – but often the films which were being shown were old ones that we had already seen in America. Then, too, the evening performances had already begun before our truck arrived in town. There was an occasional concert at the Public Hall but the number of devotees to classical music within our midst was a definite minority. What was there to do?

The obvious and most convenient answer was the public house. Ipswich boasted nearly two hundred of these; if the beverage served was not exactly to our tastes, at least the pub was a place to escape the rain and to sit down and often to meet people. You had to imbibe a truly impressive quantity of the beer to acquire a degree of inebriation but strangely enough a number of soldiers found that it was indeed feasible. There were all types of public houses in Ipswich. The most popular of these were the ones where girls congregated – "The Cricketers", "The Great White Horse", "The Mulberry Tree" and these were usually bedlams of sound and excitement while the beer lasted. There were the more sedate places like "The Crown and Anchor" and "The Golden Lion" and "The Unicorn" where the American would occasionally enjoy a quiet hour in less frantic surroundings. There were the less-imposing pubs like "The Fox", "The Plough", "The Blue Boy" and "The Waggon and Horses" where there was less formality and which were "Off Limits" to our troops at various times. There were others – family pubs, workers' pubs, railway pubs, seaport pubs, large and small ones, clean and dirty ones; with names like "The Queen's Arms" and "The Welcome Sailor", "The Running Buck" and "The Spotted Cow", "The Griffin" and "The Saracen's Head" and we explored most of them. As we grew to know Ipswich each of us had his favourites where he knew the barkeeps, the regular customers and the local traditions.

A popular alternative among the younger soldiers was dancing. There was a dance at Ipswich almost every night in the week, either at the Co-operative Hall or St Lawrence's Church Hall. At both these halls soldiers came in groups and the girls came unescorted and paid their own way, which resulted in a somewhat variegated choice of partners, ranging from pretty children of not more than fourteen to middle-aged spinsters and offering an equally wide range of dancing styles. The music was loud, the dance floors were crowded and in deference to British custom and to the mixed ages and nationalities of the dancers, there was a master of ceremonies, who announced each dance. Many of these dances were unfamiliar to us; at first we stood aside and watched with interest group dances such as the "Palais Glide", the "Hokey-Cokey", the "Boomps-a-Daisy" and "St Bernard's Waltz". Many of us were frankly terrified by the prospect of a "Ladies' Invitation Slow Fox Trot", when the girls had the opportunity to pick partners, an experience that we had never suffered before. We found later that the "Ladies' Invitation" was apparently a measure arising out of the surplus of women, enabling the least attractive of these to dance with a male partner at least part of the time; all-girl dancing couples were prevalent here, a practice frowned upon at home. But we never quite liked the "Ladies' Invitation" dances; male vanity will not suffer the popularity contest in which the woman has willingly competed since time began, and many a soldier who fancied himself as a Don Juan must have forsworn English dances forever the first time he found himself, unwillingly, a wall flower.

Perhaps the chief attraction of Ipswich was the girls. It seemed to us then a town of girls, with a high proportion of young and pretty ones and their behaviour was nothing like that of girls we had known at home. In the evening they walked along the pavements in pairs, smiling, swinging their supple hips in short skirts, looking after the soldiers, whispering "Hi, Yank!" or whistling a phase from "Yankee Doodle." Many were young – fourteen, fifteen or sixteen, though we could not judge how old they were and they always said they were eighteen at least. They had beautiful flowing hair, they wore tight sweaters and flat-heeled shoes and they spoke that sing-song Suffolk dialect that often we could not fathom. They went unescorted to the dance halls and to the public houses and it was there that we met them.

Early in the evening it was pairs of girls and pairs of soldiers in the streets but by nightfall the pairs were usually then a soldier and a girl. But sometimes it was still a pair of girls and you would be bumped in the darkness and hear a peal of laughter, a snatch of song, or a whispered, "Hi Yank." It was not quiet on the Ipswich streets after dark. At ten o'clock, when the public houses closed, there would be singing, laughing crowds in the streets, shouts and now and then some scuffling or a fight.

It was a dirty, smelly, crowded old town after dark, this Ipswich of the war. Little streams of urine ran down from doorways into the gutter and in some doorways there were the dark forms of a boy and a girl pressed close together. The night air had a musty, old, stale smell; the smell of fried fish, of coal smoke, of horse manure and of fog and the sea. It smelled of beer and rain and aged, mouldy stones. The flat-paned windows were gaping and vacant, the streets narrow, cobble-stoned and dark. It was not until midnight that they became silent and empty and you could hear again the echo of your own footsteps and far down by the River Orwell the clanking and screaming of the trains.

The trucks left the parking lot in Princes Street at eleven and here were soldiers and girls saying good night and other soldiers loudly calling the names of their friends, trying to locate their own company truck. Occasionally a bellyfull of bitter played tricks and a soldier would awaken the next morning in a strange bed at the wrong aerodrome and sometimes not at an aerodrome at all but in an even more unfamiliar bed at the Ipswich Police Station.

The truck ride home was an ordeal; the same thirty men were on board but it was eleven o'clock now and not seven and there was shouting and laughter and singing and loud, violent arguments about nothing and occasionally a scuffle and always a few men asleep. The truck roared though the silent villages of Suffolk, leaving a bellowed wake of "Bell-bottomed Trousers," or "God Bless America" – and the persistent monologue of one raucous soldier, describing to a disinterested world the details of a probably imaginary doorway romance.

There was nothing restful in these nights in town; there was little relaxation; there was little inspirational and nothing of beauty. They served merely for an escape, a blowing off of steam, a release from confinement and they were the only diversion that the world could offer us at the time.

Many of us and certainly many people of Ipswich were disturbed by what they saw and heard and by the easy familiarity of the young girls that roamed the streets and frequented the public houses. We had many a long and serious discussion on this topic in Hut Seven but we never came to any conclusions. Was it wartime excitement and the ever-present threat of death from the sky that had induced this "gather ye rosebuds" attitude? Was it a relaxation of parental influence caused by the absence of fathers, by working mothers and the lack of family life? Was it the sudden presence of a crowd of strange and carefree men in uniform? Or was it all these things that, summed up, were the impact of war on this town and inevitably brought with it new and lowered, standards?

Was it happening in other towns in England and in other countries in war? Was it happening at home, in our own land, in our own hometown?

We hoped that it wasn't but we feared in our hearts that it was.

Ipswich Evenings, Robert S. Arbib Jr

I made the acquaintance of "Iris Harding" the way many an American soldier met many an English girl – at a public house. Iris was the first English girl I met, not counting the fickle Miss Polly of Woodbridge and the first one to give me a glimpse of what English women were doing to help win the war.

I met Iris one evening, not long after our arrival at Debach, in the tiniest room of the liveliest pub in Ipswich, "The Cricketers". It was a little room where four persons could stand with some crowding – a room accessible by the back entrance, where the more modest members of the female sex could enter, have a drink and retire without parading though the noisy, jam-packed front rooms. Iris was there that night with a friend and ... we got acquainted as most people get acquainted at bars – by breaking into a conversation with a casual remark and we continued our acquaintance by offering cigarettes, a drink. Iris was not a beautiful girl, but had a clever look about her and a nice smile that crinkled her nose and curled the corners of her mouth. Whatever it was I said to her, she had a quick answer and one that made us laugh – and from then on we were friends.

When "The Cricketers" sounded the inevitable tocsin at ten o'clock, we were hungry – and Iris knew a place to go. The only place in Ipswich it was possible to eat after closing time – the Rainbow. "Would you like a spot of fish and chips at the Rainbow?"

We would.

So we stumbled out into the blackness, holding hands so that we wouldn't lose each other and Iris led the way to the Rainbow. It was a crowded restaurant, empty five minutes before ten o'clock and crowded five minutes afterwards. Here, for a few shillings, they brought us a heaping plate of tender, crisp fish, surrounded by a mountain of "French fried" potatoes – chips. We stuffed ourselves. And over the fish and chips I learned that Iris was a factory worker – that she operated a huge machine which punched holes of various sizes in sheets of steel, in Ipswich's largest industry, the Ransomes, Simms & Jefferies farm-machinery plant …

Any Old Weather, Robert S. Arbib Jr

To the 92nd's personnel, the physical appearance of Bovingdon was something of a disappointment. The barracks required strenuous cleaning, the sanitary facilities were poor and those for bathing almost non-existent. The sites on which the various squadrons lived did not have bathhouses and the communal site with its one bathhouse was sadly overtaxed. Food upon the Group's arrival and or about four weeks was strictly British and the menus monotonously featured mutton, potatoes and Brussels sprouts. On the other hand it *was England – the* England of the schoolbooks, of King Arthur and Robin Hood and Cromwell and for practically every member of the Group the first foreign country ever visited. It was also the beginning of the great adventure. Morale was buoyed up by an excitement that neither mud nor minor discomforts could dispel.

John S. Sloan

I liked Wattisham for several reasons. This was even more beautiful countryside than that about Debach and it was closer to Sudbury and the girl Joan … I discovered that if I walked cross-country two miles to Bildeston I could catch a bus Saturday evenings that wandered through the lovely valleys to Brent Eleigh, to Lavenham, to Long Melford and finally to Sudbury. Or I could try to hitchhike to Sudbury by the road that went down through Chelsworth and Waldingfield. Or I could go from Chelsworth across to Hadleigh and pick up my old Ipswich–Sudbury bus there. Or I could ride my bicycle all fourteen miles. This was perhaps the most enjoyable method and I came to know every twist and turn and every landmark along this sheltered, picturesque road.

Here there was a long hill that gave a view across ten miles of rolling countryside where you could count eight church steeples. There was a stump where a little owl liked to perch in the late evening hours. Around that bend was a bean field in full bloom, its heavy, sweet fragrance pervading the air from thousands of waxy white blossoms. And at Chelsworth, one of the loveliest small villages in England, there was a small child standing at the gate who would smile and wave as I passed. It was a long, hard ride and three hills that I must walk up but in the end I managed to cover the distance in just over an hour and came down that last long hill into Sudbury in a whirl of speed. Swifts were screeching in the air, people were standing in their yards or clustered around "The Pheasant" at Chelsworth or "The Swan" at Little Waldingfield and cars were few and far between. Three airfields were being built on that fourteen-mile stretch of road between Wattisham and Sudbury.

Coming back was more difficult. By bicycle it was uphill most of the way and a long and lonely plod late at night, with only the hoot of tawny owls or the scream of lapwings in the fields for company. But the only other way home was to catch the evening train to Marks Tey, change for the Ipswich train and then board the last liberty truck back to the camp. Roundabout – four hours for the fourteen miles – but then most of my travels to and from Sudbury were involved and complicated and dependent on several modes of transport. Somehow, miraculously, I always made it back on time.

... We were given a day off a week – sometimes and the men could go in to Ipswich evenings for a short session with the beer or the girls. Apart from the fact that we were far from home and could look ahead to many months more of separation and harder days of actual war ahead, we had few complaints.

I remember with pleasure the back road that meandered across country from just behind our row of flats. Several evenings I walked along that road, enjoying the June evenings, exploring again the Suffolk lanes. Down the road I found a little parish church, set back among fields on the side of a hill and here I would sit on a wooden bench on the church porch and write letters. Here I was shown through the church by the sexton and was taken to the cemetery, where in a lonely corner of the field there was a row of graves set apart. Seven white crosses and on them German names – a bomber crew that had come down in flames the year before. Like all soldiers' graves in foreign fields, they seemed lost and desolate in this poppy strewn English meadow.

Wattisham Days, Robert S. Arbib Jr

The English cities weren't that much different from home but out in the real rural areas, oh boy! It was arranged for my friend Elinor and myself to go down to a little village near Salisbury and stay for a short vacation. This was all so strange and quaint to us. I stayed with the local postmaster, whose wife warmed our bed with hot smoothing irons. The place was like an old world picture postcard with a duck pond in the middle and quaint old houses. The local accents were so strong it was like a foreign language to us. We found the village blacksmith. I had always imagined him to be a big man, but this one was a real small guy. When we called in, he took a red-hot iron bar from the fire, lit his cigarette and then put the iron back before talking to us.

"Oh, you're Americans are you. Do you know my cousin in Chicago?"

I think he honestly thought Chicago was a little place like his village.

Helen Maravell

It was no secret that many of the British didn't like us, even though we were helping win the war for them. After all, the British were in a helluva more dangerous situation with Hitler than the Americans were. I think they probably needed us more than we needed them, but they were terrific fighters, our most loyal allies before and after the war.

Eddie S. Picardo

A lady from Suffolk wrote to the local US base commander and invited six servicemen for Sunday lunch, adding in brackets at the end of the invitation ('no Jews'). Around 1pm the following Sunday the lady answered a knock on the door and was faced by six black American servicemen. She said.

"I invited six servicemen; surely there must be some mistake?"

"No ma'am", replied one of the black GIs. "Colonel Cohen don't make no mistakes."

… In the twilight of that evening almost at midnight, we heard a low throb begin in the sky above and grow to a mighty crescendo. In the bar, when the sound began, the song stopped a moment. We listened and someone said, "The RAF's out again. God bless 'em." I walked outside to see, but against the darkening sky the big black airplanes, Halifaxes and Lancasters, scarcely showed up at all. They were evidently going over at medium altitude and they flew in a peculiar manner not at all like our formations. Still, it was a discernable pattern with distances of about half a mile between airplanes. Sometimes I could pick out a ship, but not many. I felt intense gratitude to those hardy lads going out just as we were having a final beer before going to bed. They were fighting a tough war and had been for a long time. Theirs was a beautiful country and one could understand their determination to defend it.

Philip Ardery

Romances got started in a vapor of boasts. Americans boasted of toilets that flushed, sinks that drained, clean kitchens and sunlight. The English girls chided the "Yanks" for their boastfulness – then boasted of their own modesty! The Americans were at first given to slurring the British currency, belittling the wagon-sized freight cars (goods wagons), moaning about the weather and groaning about the insipid beer – a generally raucous, tiresome bunch of visiting firemen who had forgotten Lieutenant General Ira Eaker's classic: "Until we've done more fighting, we won't do much talking. We hope that after we're gone, you'll be glad we came." But as time went on, the soldiers lost their sense of being strangers; they adapted themselves to British customs and folkways as no other army could have and blended easily and naturally into the civilian mass. When months later newly arrived soldiers conducted themselves as they had done in the beginning. The veterans frowned on them as foreigners. After the war the Limeys debated whether the Yanks had not influenced the '45 Labour Party landslide. They never became completely reconciled or at ease in the face of American boisterousness and gritty impatience with formalities, but neither were they completely reconciled to the Americans leaving their country. After the war, one English town, Baldock, had been without GIs for two weeks. When others came in, publicans held on to their raincoats to make sure they would return next night. As I saw it, Americans generally felt like shaking Englishmen by the neck to rout them out of what was seen as their "rut", they refused to give England a full measure of credit for its wonderful war role, but they answered "nobody" when asked: "Well, if you don't like England as an ally – then what country would you choose in her place?"

The American Male At Debden, Grover C. Hall Jr

Dear Family

I'm sorry I can't tell you ... when we first arrived, how we travelled and where we are. However, I can say that England is really beautiful – everything is so neat and orderly. The trains are just like in the movies – only no sleeping accommodations except luxury trains, no dining cars. Sunday we visited Cambridge which is quaint – no buildings are over 3 storeys. The streets are cobblestone and run in every damned direction! The lower class English rather resent us, however, the middle class and upper bend over backwards being nice to us.

We are at one of the finest Airdromes; the accommodations are excellent. In fact they beat those of my former station. Virginia creeper, ivy and honeysuckle grow on many of the structures and there are lawns, roses and poplars. A few observations on the customs. We're taking to 'tea' wonderfully ... the Bank of England (Lloyds?) representative changed our money. I can't make change yet, they have a god awful system.

The Scotch people we have met are really swell, more like Yanks.

We have to watch our slang. Have already had a few misunderstandings that way.

The British version of toilet tissue is equivalent to the rotogravure section of the Sears Roebuck catalogue. There are no oranges. We will soon be eating American food tho' I like English food, but they have tried to cook our dishes and have flopped so far. But their hospitality extended that far!

The English people have taken a terrible beating in the air raids and many people show it. When they play they play hard, though they have very high spirits and rarely speak of the war except in passing, or else of the end of it. They have no doubts as to an English victory.

The British WAAFs (Womens Army Air Force [sic]) are taken very seriously and do a good job. We palled up with a few at a pub and they knew our latest songs and some slang ... the English seem to feel that our high pay will buy up everything in the way of luxuries; one British Major said to me that if we kept drinking at the rate we were (really very little on American standards) all the Scotch in England would be gone in a month. So you can see, we are rightly called 'crazy Yanks' (they call us Yanks whatever we are).

The blackouts are terrific, 100% all over. I've bumped into lamp posts a hundred times and said politely 'beg your pardon'.

In conclusion, I'm well, I'm happy ... I like the country, the people and a fraction of the customs.

If you send a package make it the size of a shoe box. I'd like some pine nuts, stamps and airmail stationery. I'll write soon again.

All my love Sam

Sergeant Sam E. Frisella

The British advertising, on posters and in magazines and newspapers, strikes you as a masterpiece of negation. "Pardon us for mentioning it," the ads seem to say, "but we think you'll like our product." "Sorry to intrude on your privacy, old fellow, but if by any chance you need sausages, why we've been making them for four hundred years." "We don't want to influence you in any way, of course but we make beer, too."

This combination of innate modesty and dislike of ostentation and boasting and the need for advertising one's wares results in a highly confused and often amusing state of affairs and gives the American visitor the impression that British advertising is about thirty years behind the times. Where modesty overrules everything else, advertising is likely to degenerate merely to an announcement of the name, without even a clue as to the nature of the product. Thus the American Lids himself wondering what is the meaning of such slogans as "What We Want is Watneys!" "You are now in the Strong Country." "Players Please," "Ah, Bisto!" not to mention Hovis, Virol and the other non-committal names.

Even when there are slightly more hints as to the nature of the product (with pictures or descriptions) the same old inhibitions lead to confusing results. Possibly the gems of these are the signs in the non-smoking cars of the London Underground which say, "No Smoking – Not Even Abdullahs," by which the Abdullah people accomplish two feats: they suggest that Abdullahs are really something less than bona-fide cigarettes and then they advertise this product in one of the few places in London where non-smokers can segregate themselves!

I suppose it is a sign of civilization but in Britain only in a rather distasteful type of medical advertising is modesty thrown aside. A product with the lovely name of Bile Beans is a prominent feature of the landscape and up in Suffolk there is a medicine (for animals?) advertised by the name of Constitution Balls. But my favourite was always the highly-evocative product for "Arteries, Blood, Veins and Heart" called Elasto, which boasts, "Take it and stop limping!" – immediately bringing visions of a liquid which turns one's blood to chewing gum and sends the crutches flying while the patient does handsprings on the wall.

The great majority of billboards and posters and car-cards, however, are of war-time origin and are simple commands from the various governmental agencies and other public services to "Keep on Saving", to "Dig for Victory", to "Stagger Working Hours and Save the Rush", to "Shop Between 10 and 4" and "Is Your Journey Really Necessary?" These are usually modest, polite and clever and seem, too, unusually successful ...

Thoughts On British Character, Robert S. Arbib

During the war years they were often called "the Bloody Yanks", for initially there was a general disapproval of the exuberant young men who began to appear in our towns and countryside. Not so much personal disapproval, but a reflection of the prevalent British attitude that the Yanks were all talk and hadn't much stomach for a fight; this itself having something to do with big prosperous cousin taking over the Allied direction of the war effort. As a 14-year-old I was not immune from this unfair view and, with my school chums, was quick to dismiss the high claims of enemy aircraft shot down by the Fortress and Liberator aerial gunners as typical Yank exaggeration. Nevertheless, as an aeroplane-mad youth I was soon to relish the American presence in the East Anglian sky.

Like many of my generation, before 1939 the most desired occupation when one "grew up" was on the footplate of an express locomotive. Within a year the fascination for steam locomotives had been abandoned for the dream of being a fighter pilot. Young eyes were frequently turned skywards at the ever-mounting activity. Late in 1942 an RAF officer uncle, who had the task of opening up new airfields, arranged for my cousin and myself to inspect one of the USAAF A-20 Havoc light bombers based at Horham. This was a great thrill for we boys although we were somewhat astonished to find this particular aircraft filled with canned candies, cigarette cartons and toilet rolls! Our disdain was reflected in our speculation as to the need for the latter. What we did not know was that this aircraft was about to set off to operate from North Africa where the crew knew conditions would be primitive and that there would be few luxuries.

In June 1943 the airfield that had been carved out of farmland only a mile from my home was ready for occupation. We boys longed for RAF Spitfires. In the event sixty-four Martin B-26 Marauder medium bombers and two-and-a-half thousand young Americans arrived. Their coming quickly provided a new dimension to our interest. Nearly all the aircraft had nicknames painted on their noses in addition to comic motifs or quite revealing nudes. Unbeknown to the aviators, several Marauders were "adopted", their fortunes followed from vantage points on the neighbouring public road through regular appraisals of the symbols painted on nose sides – for combat missions flown and enemy fighters claimed shot down. My Marauder was called *Privy Donna* and carried a motif featuring a winged "outhouse" dispensing bombs. Its selection had nothing to do with the lavatorial leanings of a schoolboy but rather the proximity of the aircraft's parking place to a gap in the roadside hedge. At first the American MPs endeavoured to keep locals moving along the public road bordering the western side of the airfield. Curiosity brought people from nearby villages and towns to view the then novelty of locally based aircraft, although I fancy the large number of young girls in attendance were more interested in the men who flew and serviced the Marauders. No doubt appreciating it was a pointless exercise, the base authorities eventually withdrew the regular MP Jeep patrols that tried to keep people moving and spectators were no longer barred.

What was seen at the local airfield was soon to change our opinion of the Yanks. Perhaps summed up by the local butcher's son, once an ardent critic who, watching a combat mission return one evening pronounced: "No-one is going to tell me the Yanks can't fly and fight".

Certainly the activity on our doorstep brought home the grim reality of the air war, most notably the empty parking places when a bomber failed to return. There were specific incidents that left lasting impressions, none more so than a warm July day in 1943 when a badly shot-up Fortress staggered into the landing pattern. One could literally see daylight through holes in the wings and tailplane. The ambulances in attendance indicated casualties – seven wounded of the ten men on board was the rumour. Those BBC news reports of the bomber offensive over Hitler's empire were suddenly given substance. No one disagreed with the butcher's son. The Marauders, Liberators and Fortresses had become just as much "our" aircraft as the Halifaxes, Stirlings and Lancasters.

The Marauders at our airfield were eventually replaced by fighter squadrons with aircraft carrying even more flamboyant decor. There was the occasion when the youthful "plane watchers" at the roadside were approached by a pilot, Lieutenant Richard Heineman, who wanted to know if we would like to look at his Thunderbolt. An unbelievable invitation from a real fighter pilot! We were through the boundary hedge and barbed wire like greased lightning. Had we any sisters? My friend had three (old enough to be of interest) and immediately received most attention from our host. My friend was even allowed to sit in the cockpit! I only had a brother and would dearly have liked to arrange a sex change for him at that moment. A few days later Richard Heineman's colourful Thunderbolt was no longer to be seen at its usual place. We assumed it was in the hangar or had been relocated to another part of the base. Unbeknown to us in those war days, Richard Heineman had been shot down and killed in an air fight, probably an incident recorded as a victory symbol on some Luftwaffe pilot's Messerschmitt.

Having left school to meet the need for extra agricultural labour, my prime indulgence received a boost when my father was asked to farm fields taken over for the air base but left unused. Equipped with a pass, I could actually enter onto the flying field itself – ostensibly in pursuance of farming duties. Here the generosity of the GI was encountered: "Say kid, would you like some candy?" The sweets were welcome but the fact that they were given to me by the head mechanic of fighter ace Fred Christensen's Thunderbolt was the real accolade.

Then there was the evening after haymaking near the perimeter track when through the hedge from the road a very large sergeant appeared. "Hey Pop", he addressed my father, "any chance of a lift to the other side of the airfield?" My father said we were just leaving and invited the sergeant to enter our large Talbot saloon. He was, to say the least, surprised when the sergeant called back to the hole in the hedge from whence he had come: "Okay you guys, we ain't got to foot it back to camp after all." There appeared another GI, then another and another; they kept coming. "I don't think we are going to be able to squeeze you all in," my father said diplomatically. To no avail; the throng was already squeezing into the Talbot. The air was heavy with beery breath and it was evident that there were some very happy men present. The happiest was the large sergeant and I ended up riding on his lap. He held a yellow rose in his right hand, which he periodically jammed under my father's and my nose, with the joyous explanation: "The lady at The Fox gave me this real English rose out of her garden. Don't that smell just cute? A real English rose!" We agreed it did smell cute, although its fragrance was drowned by the overpowering beery atmosphere in the overloaded car. The old Talbot slowly but safely made the other side of the airfield, despite the rear tyres occasionally rubbing the mudguards. As they disembarked the GIs cascaded coins onto the rear seat despite my father's protestations that it was unnecessary. After the thirteen GIs – yes thirteen – staggered away, I gathered up over £5, a fortune to a boy earning fifteen shillings a week. Unfortunately, my father decided it was far too large a sum for me and pocketed it himself.

The average Britisher did not appreciate the nature of the US populace. After an evening's harvesting or haymaking the farm workers would be treated to a pint at the local hostelry. Here shoulders were rubbed with GIs and conversations pursued. After one bout of refreshment, Willie, an Essex stalwart, emerged somewhat troubled. "That Yank I bin talking to. He's really a bloody Germin! His father and mother were Germins and he was born in Germiny!" The fact that the GI concerned was undoubtedly as true to the USA as its founding fathers would have been difficult for Willie and many like him to comprehend in those parochial days. On another occasion when imbibing at "The Crown", a GI asked about our farming practices and said he was previously a cowboy. Detecting scepticism he took a cart rope from a tractor and trailer parked outside, twirled the rope above his head and lassoed old Horry, who was standing thirty feet away. Horry was not amused; we were all amazed.

There was no doubt about the attraction American servicemen had for a large proportion of local womanhood. Many girls had amorous liaisons with them (I plead guilty to being a witness in some cases) and several became GI brides, including a land girl on our farm. A benefit which

I derived from this match was copies of *The Stars and Stripes*, the US forces' daily newspaper, which her husband passed on after he had read them. The feature, which drew my attention (and also my father's) was the cartoon strips. The adventures of *Li'l Abner*, *Dick Tracy* and *Terry and the Pirates* being far more entertaining than anything that appeared in British publications. And in those days or shortages and clothes rationing other pass-downs were a boon. For years I wore the lightweight GI shoes, which had rubber soles in contrast to our usual studded heavy leather and GI cotton caps which were washable. Fortunate were the locals who had a friendly GI benefactor. We got to know their genuine generosity they gave and expected nothing in return. When our farm grass mower broke down on the airfield a sergeant from the nearby machine shop took it in and effected repairs in his free time.

By the summer of 1944 the Yanks had become an accepted part of life in East Anglia and the East Midlands. The sky rarely failed to hold one of their aircraft and hundreds were not uncommon. The throb of aero engines seemed incessant. The familiar "OD" uniforms were rarely absent from our towns and villages where a Yank leaning against a wall watching the world go by, or pedalling his bike down the middle of the road, was a familiar sight. They were to leave a considerable impression on those who knew them, which did not easily fade when they departed. In the immediate post-war years a flock of home-going rooks might for an instant be mistaken for a formation of returning Fortresses; a tractor starting in a winter's dawn could momentarily be the life-burst of an unsilenced aero engine on the nearby airfield. But even now there are times when the far off burble of young voices raises the ghosts of North American laughter floating through the leafy English lanes as of long ago.

Remember the Yanks, Roger A. Freeman

As the district police sergeant I was informed by Divisional Office to expect Americans at King's Cliffe railway station and to go along and see that there were no problems. It was a cold January afternoon in 1943. I drove up and was surprised to find a number of American soldiers already in the station yard. They turned out to be members of a brass band who had been driven up from some headquarters to provide welcoming music for the troops arriving by train. I hadn't been there long when another American vehicle arrived with a doughnut-making machine on board. I'd never seen anything like this. The operators immediately set about turning out doughnuts and handing them around to the bandsmen and the villagers who had come to see what was going on.

It was dark before the troop train finally arrived. These fellows had only been in this country a few hours, having come straight off a ship in the Clyde. A very strong wind was blowing and as it passed under the station building, which was raised on stilts, it made a howling noise. One of the newly arrived officers asked how close we were to the sea and I said "not far", meaning about thirty miles. Then I realized that he and the others thought the noise made by the wind was the sea; they thought that with a name like King's

Cliffe they were somewhere right on the coast. These fellows may have been tired but they cannot have been that tired because the following morning I received a call and was told two cases of Scotch whisky had been stolen from the station. It was arranged for me to meet a railway policeman and together we went to the airfield. To our surprise the administrative officer we were taken to see was walking around wearing his medals. He had obviously seen service elsewhere and wanted us to know. We did recover a few empty bottles from the camp cinema but that was all. I suspect the Americans weren't particularly anxious to find the guilty party, probably thinking the warming celebration of their arrival at King's Cliffe was justified.

Jack Neasham

We were told by the brass that a formal introduction would be necessary in order to meet English girls and that the English were more straight-laced then us broad-minded Yanks. We found both to be untrue. Whoever researched this information must have seen a lot of old British movies. It was obvious on our first visit to town (Huntington) that boy meet girl routines were not very different from those back home.

We met a couple of girls and invited them for a drink but the pubs were closed at the time. I asked them if they could take us to where we could get something to eat and they did. We came to a darkened entranceway protected by a double set of blackout curtains. Bending our heads we angled into the store and found ourselves in a poorly stocked green grocer (fruit & vegetable store) and our guide said we could buy some apples. I was about to laugh but choked it realizing that this was my first experience with a war economy ... it wasn't funny and we had a lot to learn. Our first visit to a pub was further enlightening. I requested a scotch and was told there were no spirits. I then requested rye whiskey and was again told the same thing ... I learned the word "spirits" covered all hard liquors so I ordered a beer. The bar keep looking rather bored at this time asked if I wanted bitters, light ale larger or brown ale. I ordered a pint of bitters, as it appeared other Yanks were drinking it. I poked my partner, "This beer tastes like it's watered down ... there's no head!" I learned later on that the higher the alcohol content the less carbonation ergo the flat taste. No wonder it was so damn hard steering those English bikes after only two or three pints of the stuff.

There were shortages of all kinds except sandy potatoes, Brussels sprouts and mutton. Mutton cooked army-style in huge pots was about the worst I ever tasted. Now sandy boiled potatoes and Brussels sprouts I could handle out mutton would make me gag. When they had it in the mess hall I would have to skip chow altogether. I could detect it a mile away. I wasn't able to eat any of the other junk cause the mutton smell would make me sick. I guess my tastes hadn't caught up with the reality. They say mutton is the closest to human flesh. We figured it out, the English kept these old sheep who were going bald and when they did they slaughtered them for food.

An English airman heard me bitching about powdered eggs and spam. "'Ere Yank and where do you think we get the bloody stuff? It's coming from the US."

When there were mutton meals we'd amble over to the NAFFI ... the equivalent to the Red Cross and have a cup of tea and a spam sandwich. I know water boils and becomes steam at 212 degrees Fahrenheit, but English tea is hotter and don't steam off. And watch out for English mustard cause if the tea don't get you the mustard will ... third-degree burns. Thank God for fish and chips.

Merry Ole England, W.J. 'Red' Komarek

It was our first 48-hour pass from Rougham. Roy and I decided to hitch a ride into London. We hadn't heard about any big raids going on lately and we were looking forward to a good time in the big town! We caught a ride on a lorry and saw the country from our perch on the top of a stack of lumber. After a long ride the driver pulled over somewhere and said "I'm turning right here, London's that way", pointing a finger ahead, "It's not far, you're on the outskirts, you can probably get another ride into the bright lights of London". He laughed when he said it because everyone knew that London, like everywhere else, was in total blackout. He dropped us off outside a pub. I forget what it was called – somebody's arms I think. I remember thinking that arms and heads were Britain's favourite parts of the anatomy when it came to naming pubs.

Doyle Coppinger

Odd these British pubs. They seemed to think that a pub wasn't worth walking into unless it was at least a century old and nearly every Britisher would boast that his father, grandfather and great grandfather had drunk ale in the same chair. Too, all the British smoke, from little brother and sister to grandpa and grandma, so that after an hour, many of the fellows claimed they needed a radar set to find their way through the fog to the bar. Practically all the ale was one kind or another of Tolly. A fellow didn't dare enter a pub without a good supply of cigarettes because he would be hit up at least a dozen times an evening by "Gotta American cigarette chum?" any time one was offered, it was always accepted.

Diarist in the 493rd Bomb Group stationed at Debach in Suffolk where the favourite watering holes on 'pubbing missions' were 'The White Hart', the 'Dog' at Grundisburgh, 'The Turk's Head' at Hasketon and the 'Greyhound' at Wickham Market

... It was at "The Dog" that we were officially welcomed to England ... When we entered the little pub, it was almost empty. We found three or four small, plain rooms with wooden benches and bare wooden tables. Each room connected somehow with a central bar – either across a counter or through a tiny window. One of the rooms had a dartboard and another had an antique upright piano. We went into the room with the dartboard and ordered beer. "What kind of beer?" asked the man behind the counter, a ruddy, pleasant man whose name was Mr Watson.

"Oh just beer," we said. "Is this American money any good?" We conferred about the money and Mr Watson finally decided to accept it after counsel with his wife, at the rate of four shillings to the dollar. He agreed to repay us later if the exchange proved to be higher and he did.

We tried the mild beer. It was weak, watery and warm. "Haven't you anything stronger?" we asked.

"They're all about the same now," he answered. "War-time quality, you know. Pretty weak." We tried the bitter. It was weak, sweet and warm. We tried the brown ale. We tried the stout. We tasted the Guinness. We ended by drinking the light ale, which was the only variety that seemed strong enough to put a foam on the glass. Later we came to like or at least became accustomed to, the other types of English brew and would sit like the natives and talk over our pints of mild, or bitter, or 'aff and 'aff.

Someone must have seen us go into "The Dog" for soon the villagers began to arrive. By ones and twos they came and sat themselves down in their accustomed seats. The front room with the dartboard filled with the younger men – the farm workers in their rough clothes, talking their musical dialect that puzzled us. In Norfolk they call it "Norfolk canary." But in Suffolk it is a twittering close-lipped sing-song too.

The back room filled with the old gaffers and their evil-smelling pipes filled the room with blue smoke and the smell of burning seaweed. Here the conversation was slower – in fact it bordered on paralysis in social intercourse. A remark was made at one side of the table. Then would follow a long silence. Finally from the other side of the room would come the answer. A chuckle, glasses would be lifted slowly, quaffed, carefully set down, the pipes would be sucked and then the third comment would come from deep in the corner. There was no need for these old men to hurry. Decades of hard work had brought them a deserved time for relaxation. Here was contentment, companionship, a time for thinking and for the slow exchange of ideas. For years they had occupied the same chairs, drank the same pint of bitter from the same silver mugs, talked about the crops, the weather, the latest village gossip and now another war. Mr Watson could set his old clock by their entrances. He handed them their brimming mugs of "the usual" with the expected and customary greeting and took their coppers with a nod. These were his "regulars."

The other two rooms – the front room or "saloon bar" and the back room with the piano – were for family groups, for casuals, for young couples and for the women. There was plenty of high-pitched chatter here; there was music and the beer disappeared faster, with less philosophy.

But this Saturday evening there was excitement and a high tempo in every room in "The Dog". The Yanks have arrived! There are seven of them in "The Dog" right now! People came in from all the farms and cottages and they filled the old public house with a carnival spirit. By eight o'clock there was standing room only and by nine o'clock even the dark narrow hall between the rooms was full and you could hardly turn around. The smoke was thick and the conversation excited.

The Yanks have arrived! The work on our aerodrome is about to begin at last! It has begun already! Right here, in changeless old Grunsbra we are going to have a great new bomber aerodrome and thousands of American soldiers and airmen! And bombers flying right over Berlin to pay those Jerries back! Surely the tide of war is turning today!

And so they flocked in and they questioned us and answered our questions and we listened to stories about the Blitz and heard about Dunkirk from men who had been there and we sat in the little back room with the piano and bought a round of drinks for everyone who joined the group.

First there were seven of us and then ten and then twenty-one drinks to the round and then twenty-eight. We started to sing and a girl named Molly tried to play the piano but she wasn't very good and the piano was very old. Nobody asked her to stop.

We all sang the songs we knew and the people of Grunsbra joined in, humming when they didn't know the words. Johnny Ludwig was grinning at a tall, cross-eyed girl sitting across the room, who smiled back at him. But the old lady sitting almost in Johnny's lap warned him. "Stay away from that hussy," she confided. "She's got a bad name and a bad reputation. Went bad almost the day her husband went away to the Middle East. I know, I'm her mother-in-law." The cross-eyed girl didn't quite look like the siren type and Johnny Ludwig was feeling good enough to roar with laughter at her coy glances, so the warnings were needless.

The last round we bought from the harassed Mr Watson was for forty-seven drinks. There had never been anything like it before in the long history of "The Dog". Everyone was shouting, everyone was singing and milling about, holding bands full of glasses over their heads as they pushed though the crowd. The word "Yanks" was on everyone's lips and if you turned away from someone it was to answer someone else shouting in the other ear.

The last act, just before closing time, was a speech by Tom Stinson, who by that time was feeling no pain. Tom jumped up on a table, held his hand over his head for silence and then addressed the crowd. I don't remember what he said, except that he started off "Friends, Britons and countrymen!" There was a little bit of Julius Caesar in it, a smattering of Macbeth, a dash of W.C. Fields, a touch of Hamlet and a slice of pure ham. It was a speech of thanks, I believe and a speech welcoming these people to England. It was greeted by roars of approval and Tom managed to stay on his feet, which was more than many of us expected; though he did kick over three of Mr Watson's precious beer-glasses in his descent.

Just about that time Mr Watson raised his closing-time chant and a powerful call it was to cut though the din that rocked the rollicking old "Dog" that night. "Time, please, Gentlemen!" rang though the house like a brass gong and I suddenly realized with surprise what those lines in T.S. Eliot's "Waste Land" poem meant. "Hurry up, please. It's Time!" I heard that line a hundred times in dozens of public houses after that first night in "The Dog" and I never quite got over the feeling that the publicans were quoting the poem and not the other way around.

That was our first welcome to England. We said goodnight to our new friends many times inside the pub and many times outside – and how we got home up the pitch-black country lanes to our tents in the Maze, I cannot quite recall.

We were the first of many American soldiers to spend a friendly evening with the light ale in the Grundisburgh "Dog". But 'none of the nights quite equalled the enthusiasm and abandon of that first visit of our gang. Mr Watson told me that himself many months later.

That was Saturday night ... that welcome at "The Dog". On Tuesday night "The Dog" went dry – stone dry and Mr Watson hung out a sad little sign on his door – "No Beer" – and closed his inn for the evening – the first time in 450 years of "The Dog's" history.

The Yanks had come to England.

Welcome At 'The Dog', Robert S. Arbib Jr

Some day you should go over the hills to Lavenham, Bob – there's the most beautiful little Elizabethan village in England. The old Guildhall, the beautiful lath-and-plaster houses, all bright pink and yellow, the wool church. And there's one man left of the old wool-weavers, one man who carried on the trade that made Lavenham rich and famous! You can still buy from him (if you could get the coupons and if he has the material) the real English home-spun tweeds – and there's none finer in the world Bob, none finer in the world! Some Sunday we'll go out to Lavenham on our bicycles and I'll show you around the town and we'll have a drink at "The Swan" – there's a real old English inn for you!"

Here We Are Together, Vivian Goodman

The country of East Anglia is well endowed with historic old inns and most of them have preserved the Olde Englishe Quaintnesse one expects to find nowadays only on Christmas cards and in antique prints.

In the little region of Suffolk that I knew best, the tourist guides undoubtedly point out as rare treasures "The Bull" at Long Melford, the Lavenham "Swan", the Thetford "Bell" (across the line in Norfolk) and the Martlesham "Red Lion", the Woodbridge "Crown" and the Bury St Edmund's "Angel". In all of these and many more, you can find the low-beamed ceilings, the capacious fireplaces, the polished copper saucepans on the wall, the hunting prints, the winding, uneven staircases and the leaded diamond windows that are so dear to British hearts and the LNER poster artists.

But my favourite Suffolk inn had few of these attributes. True, it had a winding staircase and it had old oak beams and a copper saucepan or two. But I liked it for other reasons – for warmer, more human things. I liked it for its personality ... The little inn I loved was Gainsborough House, in Sudbury. The personality and the hospitality of the place centred mainly about Winnie Offord, the twenty-three-year-old girl who ran it, who acted as manager, chief cook, chief steward, cashier, hostess and even upstairs maid. Winnie Offord was too busy to be seen about the streets of

Sudbury much, except for a morning sortie for provisions and perhaps a quick evening run across the street to "The Christopher" for an ale. Winnie was not in Sudbury "society" either. But she certainly was one of Sudbury's most important people and although she had constant alerts and warnings from the National Labour Service Board, their deferment of her transfer to a factory was one of the wisest decisions that august body ever made. I like to think of Winnie as one of the thousands of English girls who coped with a job big enough for several men during the war and always had time for fun and laughter. Many times, many of us were boundlessly glad that Winnie was there, doing cheerfully an amazingly big job.

Winnie's domain, Gainsborough House, stood on Gainsborough Street, which wound down to the river from Market Hill, where stood the statue of Sudbury's most famous native son. Gainsborough himself was born in this house in 1727, you were told by a plaque on the wall. The house was an old one; it had been a home and then an inn long before Gainsborough's father, a minister, had moved in. And now the full cycle had come round and the home was now an inn again. The front had been modernized and it was only from the garden side that you could admire the old and pleasant proportions of the house.

The rooms in the Gainsborough House interested me for two reasons. First, because they were all on different levels, with two steps up or three steps down to each one. And second, because they were each named after one of the master's paintings ...

Robert S. Arbib Jr

It was at "The Unicorn" that I met Joe and Elsa Clode and Mervyn and Bessie Loverock and Jim and Alice Simmons, who were among the finest and most loyal friends I made in England. We did our most serious thinking here on Allied problems, on the course of the war, on the social problems of Great Britain, on politics and education, economics and music, on books and art and in fact the whole range of the world's interests from coarse humour to theology. I later visited these friends at their homes, ate at their tables, slept on couches in their parlors, went to parties and dances with them and walks and rides; took baths in their tubs and made myself as completely at home as I ever was in someone else's house. But it was in the reeking blue atmosphere of the middle bar of "The Unicorn" that we met and where we spent many of our friendliest hours.

And though there will be many things about England that I will forget and others that memory will soften or distort, I will never forget Jimmy's closing-time chant, accompanied by flickering lights, ribald comment and an extreme reluctance on the part of the clientele to depart. It went like this:

"Ladies and Gentlemen: 'Tis now the grim grey hour! Come along now, everybody, it's *time*. Time, please. Everyone! Come along, you ropey types; get along home with you. Come along, Bessie; come along, Joe; come now, my young correspondent, let's be on off home to our beds. Time, please! Oh, please, good people, will you go *home*!

Come along now, you odds and sods, come along there, young Alice,
think of our licence! Oh, what will we do if we lose our licence! It's way past
time now, please. Please go home, everyone. *Time*! Not one more drink will
you have, my good Freddie, Not even one tiny little wee drink. I said *time*!
Must I throw you all out into the night! Get along home there, everyone ...
You've had your fun, we've had your mun', now *bugger off!*"

"*'Tis The Grim, Grey Hour!*" Robert S. Arbib Jr

Two days after our first mission we made the first of many trips into
Norwich (pronounced Nor'ich) a city of probably 100,000 people. As
one who always had a keen interest in history I found the city with its
narrow, winding streets (some with centuries-old cobblestones) 900-year-
old Norman cathedral with the second tallest spire in England, eleventh-
century Norman castle and large open-air market to be a fascinating place.
Even though it was winter, I was surprised to see fresh meat hanging out in
the open in the market place. The supply of warm English beer was rationed
daily and did not last long after the pubs opened their doors each evening. I
bought my first fish and chips wrapped in newspaper from a street vendor
and was surprised to find that the chips were not like our potato chips but
rather were French fries.

Staff Sergeant Dale R. VanBlair.

As a gesture towards promoting Anglo-American goodwill the mayor of
Peterborough arranged for me to spend a weekend at the Marlborough
Head Inn at a picturesque place called Dedham near Colchester. While there
I met Edgar Cooper and his wife, farmers from a nearby village, with whom
I became lifelong friends. I subsequently made other visits to Dedham when
I had leave and the Coopers introduced me to many of their friends. One
evening a couple, relatives of the Coopers, were present. I enjoyed their
company and hoped to expand on the friendship at a later date. With this
in mind, when the couple came to leave, instead of wishing them good night
I tossed an American flip: "I'll see you later." Unfortunately they took this
to mean that I was going to visit them later that night in their home. After
sitting around until 3.00am they went to bed, probably with some pretty
hard thoughts about Americans who said they would visit but didn't show
up. When I heard about this I bought an American to English and English to
American dictionary but I was a long time getting their friendship back!

Nelson Matthews

After partaking of various beverages over the course of the evening it was
necessary to make use of a facility euphemistically called a "water closet".
A closet it certainly was not. It was outside in the back of the building and
consisted of a partially enclosed slate wall with a diagonal trough at the
base. There was no lighting because of blackout requirements and overcast
clouds limited any natural light. It was not quite pitch black, but it was

close to it. Two or three local customers were occupying the available space, facing the wall, while I waited my turn. Then one of the Englishmen spoke to another beside him, showing forbearance impossible for an American. What he said was, "Pardon me old chap but you're urinating on my leg."
                                    Lieutenant Jack Bryant, stationed at Sudbury, Suffolk

We marvelled at the numbers and the cleverness of the camouflage of the pillboxes. Some were disguised as farm buildings, with thatched roofs and painted sides. Some were made to look like brick outbuildings; some to look like workmen's shacks. One near Ipswich was painted black, covered with tarpaper, for all the world like a construction-foreman's shack by the roadside. In big white letters on the walls were painted the words, "A. Mole, Tunnel Contractor, Deepdownham, Suffolk." Another large pillbox near Woodbridge looked like a triangular billboard. One side had the inviting advertisement for the "Hotel Continental – Warm Reception Guaranteed for Visiting Troops." Some others had grass growing on the roof; many looked like haystacks and water-tanks. They were everywhere. Each main crossroad had at least one – some had two, thee, or four. They lined the main roads, the railways, the river valleys, the easiest routes for an invasion force into the heart of England. Some were deep in groves and copses – others were out in the middle of fields. Their fire overlapped, interlocked and covered the landscape with a lacework of death. Everywhere scattered between the concrete pillboxes were the little dugouts in the hedges, lined with sandbags, concealed with bushes and vines and weeds. In the towns, garden walls were pierced with slits and reinforced with concrete and ready for the defenders' guns. Even the Market Hill in Sudbury had its sunken and reinforced machine-gun pits. The defences were everywhere. And the men were there to man them – the barber, the butcher, the banker. Trained in the use of new weapons. Familiar though life-long intimacy with every field, every hedge, every sunken gulley and wooded cover, vantage points, observation posts, the obstacles, the traps, the ambushes.
                                    In Defence Of England, Robert S. Arbib Jr

I was still caught up in the adventure of war and could equate many things with stories I had read. As a kid I was an avid reader of anything on WWI and the flying aces. By now most of us had at least one mission in so we had been initiated in combat and entitled to a little swagger. Although not quartered in a battle-scarred French château we did have a bomb-damaged roof in the shower building, a combat crew club and within a couple of miles there were two pubs. One was "The Red Fox" and the other "The Black Swan" wherein the Packer Crew had a Christmas dinner including roast pheasant and champagne, vintage 1913.

Even closer was an estate converted billet for twenty-three bonnie Land Army girls, all of whom are spoken for. We met them the second night at the Nissen hut next to the road. Several of the girls were cycling to their quarters. We chatted a moment and they continued onto their billet. I yelled after them or I should say after this blonde beauty, "We'll meet ya at the choich at seven thoity" in my best New Yorkese.

They showed up and I began a romantic interlude with Jeannie with the light blonde hair. The girls worked in the surrounding fields and used to wave as we taxied out to the runways. They confided that they knew when we were going on a mission by either the early takeoff or the length of runway it took to get off the ground.

What a war ... mission in the morning ... dating in the evening ... bed and blankets at night, that was our theme song. The only danger at night was a bike and bitters sortie to the local pub.

December, W.J. 'Red' Komarek

Conveniently located a couple of miles from our airdrome in Flixton, we cycled over there every chance we had and met with the Land Army Girls (there were twenty-three girls stationed one mile from our Nissen hut) and other locals. The hours were from 6–10pm, four hours away from the cares of the day and time to write corny verse as appears in Merle's diary. Occasionally the Germans would bomb the city of Yarmouth where there were Naval installations. Standing outside the Red Fox we watched several of these raids in the distance.

One night we were treated to a special performance of the English ack-ack and searchlight batteries, a direct hit on one of the Jerry bombers, which went down flaming all the way.

Another favorite pastime was to swap stories while quaffing pints of Bitters. We heard of ghost stories from the locals and we would listen with veiled amusement and usually make the comment, "The natives were really restless tonight", when out of earshot of the storyteller.

One night was different. At closing time I asked Harry Ahlborn, our engineer who was at least six foot tall, not to pedal too fast, as I had no flashlight on my bike. It was dark with no moon and I needed to follow him closely.

Due to Harry's long legs and the winding road he soon out distanced me and was out of sight. I could see little and noted a figure ahead of me. I knew it wasn't Harry; it appeared to be an elderly man or woman pedaling laboriously and having no bike light. I thought of the local Constable and his repeated warnings to us to put lights on our bikes, but since he had no jurisdiction, could not ticket us. This was a different situation; this party could be in violation.

Since I knew many of the civilians in this small rural community, I pulled to the right and abreast of the figure and was about to bid them the time of day, when the figure disappeared! There was no turn off path (hedges paralleled the road), no shadows and no logical explanation as far as I could determine.

I soon learned that if you tell an Englishman a ghost story, he won't laugh at you, he'll come back with one of his own.

There was another incident locally that was shared by both Americans and English. The pubs closed at 10pm and the Land Army Girls had to be in at 11pm so there was this extra hour for what we used to call a little hallway time. The hallway in this case was the church grounds, which included the cemetery. I wasn't there at the time so you can't accuse me of delirium. Bud and several of the other guys, even level-headed Jack Lang, were and all experienced the same happening. Each couple was in a different part of the church grounds when suddenly there was Christmas carol singing coming from the church. In the sharing of this incident all agreed, the men that is, it did not seem unusual. It was dissimilar with the girls; they were alarmed, as they all knew the church was dark and empty. I'm aware that sounds can carry a great distance from the source on a still clear night, but even so, the English at 11pm would not be at church, except for possible refuge during an air raid.

The Red Fox, W.J. 'Red' Komarek

At first English people seemed reserved and to avoid contact with us, but once the ice was broken they could not have been more friendly and helpful. Introductions were the problem. Mine came when we were putting on a show and wanted some civilian clothes for our girls and boys to wear on the stage. There was a canteen run by a women's voluntary organization at Blackfriars Hall, Norwich and I went down with the hope that someone could help me. The middle-aged lady I approached said she had a trunk at home full of old clothes and if there was something there we could use she'd be pleased to let us have it. So I got my driver to take us to her house. Evelyn Thwaits became a good friend and thereafter I was often invited to her home. Our relationship lasted until she died.

Hathy Veynar, one of the first WACs (Women's Army Corps) to reach the UK

On my first visit to the cinema in Ipswich I was surprised to find people smoking inside. This was not allowed in the US. Another surprise I had was the reaction of the audience when an air raid warning was flashed on the screen. Nobody moved; they just carried on watching the film. Even when the "red alert" was flashed on the screen nobody left. I sat tight, all be it somewhat nervous. Fortunately no bombs were dropped near the cinema. After going to see a film or just spending some time in Ipswich, hot fish and chips, wrapped in a newspaper English style, were good eating.

Raymond G. Dozier, Assistant engineering Officer, 829th Engineer Aviation Battalion during the construction of airfields in East Anglia in summer 1942

The two buddies hear about the Marx Brothers movie in downtown Bury St Edmunds and can't wait to get there, but it's too early so they get fish and chips at the local mom and pop stand – a rolled-into-a-cone London *Times* – chips under, cod deep fried in a batter on top – doused with malt vinegar, it's the best meal off base – but it doesn't taste just right unless it's packed up in the London *Times*. The movie is a gas! The Marx Brothers have the pair in stitches till it dawns on them that they are the only people in the theater who are laughing. They notice the local folk all staring at them like they've lost their minds.

We have a light-hearted attitude about money. I send home a third of my pay to my parents who buy war bonds for my nest egg if I make it in one piece. The rest I spend fast enough so that by my second 48-hour pass of the month, I am so broke I stay on station or visit the Bury St Edmunds Corn Exchange to dance the "hokey pokey" with some of the local girls, or take in a cinema.

Slapstick 1944, Abe Dolim

All in all, I liked England. It was disagreeable at times, the hoarfrost for one thing. When it came, it just covered everything. You had to get up on an airplane wing. First we'd take a crew chief's stand and we'd slide it up to the wing and we'd take isopropyl de-icing fluid and brooms to de-ice it and get the hoarfrost off. Sometimes it'd be an inch thick. Things like this were kind of disagreeable and it rained quite a bit, but not near as much as I thought it would. In the summer time England was just beautiful!

My first contact with a real Englishman was when this old man come ridin' along on his bicycle one day. He stopped and said, "Heyo 'ere, mite." we could hardly understand him. It was different learnin' to speak his language. He was a real funny old guy. He wanted to know if we'd like him to do our laundry. All we had was a shower room where we did our laundry. We were just tickled to death to let him do our laundry. He'd come around once a week and pick up our laundry and take it home. His wife did it, I'm sure. It was a very nominal fee, just a few shillings, for a bundle of laundry. It was wonderful, better than doing it ourselves.

There was a farm off the base and a real nice old lady worked on the farm. She didn't have any sugar and we couldn't hardly ever get any fresh eggs so we'd trade her sugar for eggs. One Christmas her fourteen or fifteen-year-old boy brought us a cake. She'd saved her sugar and made us a cake.

Our leave time was spent mostly in the little town of Attlebridge and it was quite an experience. There was a hill as you went down into town. We'd ride our bikes and park outside the pub and go in just like we were English. When we first started going there we would order "half and half" and they'd give it to us but we didn't know how much money, so they'd just take whatever they wanted. Same with fish and chips. Oh, they were good. Of course, we were always hungry. It didn't take us long so we could count their money pretty good. You know there was a funny thing about those English bicycles. You could go to the pub on one of them and if you went down to Attlebridge and had fish and chips and rode back home you had to walk up that hill; but if you stayed in the pub long enough when you got back out on your bicycle, you could jut ride up the hill!

Sergeant Robert 'Bob' S. Cox, mechanic, 466th Bomb Group

... I managed to draw a bicycle from the supply office. The base was so spread out it was difficult to get around without a Jeep or a bike. The English summer was at its height, though it never really got warm enough according to my idea of summer. The air was fresh and cool, like a day of spring at home and the woods which were scattered all over our airdrome were beautiful. Through the woods small lanes were cut leading to the various living sites. I found in those first days in England many of the acquaintances of my early years: there were rooks and jackdaws flying overhead and grouse, plover and pheasants in great numbers just off the runways.

The second afternoon I was in England, I rode my bike into the small village of Wymondham (pronounced Windum) near the field and was impressed by its picturesqueness. The lane leading into the village was narrow and winding, with hedgerows on either side and well-kept fields over the hedgerows. There were haystacks in the fields that were so perfectly formed they looked like loaves of gingerbread.

On the edge of the village was a little pond with ducks on it. Farther on the streets were narrow with brick buildings almost to the edge of the pavement. They seemed particularly incongruous when an occasional tremendous American Army truck lumbered through. At the far end of the town was a very old church that looked as if it might have been started as a Stonehenge in pagan times and continued having parts added down through successive ages of Christianity. The whole scene had a kind of beauty strange to me.

Philip Ardery

With the extended daylight hours provided by double British summertime, airmen from the B-24 bomber base at Wendling took off on what came to be known as "low-level missions." These occurred when there was no combat alert for the following day.

Scores of Wendling inhabitants mounted their trusty bicycles and headed for pubs in such villages as Castle Acre and Swaffham. A few pints consumed by the riders often had a definite effect on the GI's sense of balance. There were numerous casualties from these missions.

My buddy from Powell Station, Tennessee, was mounted on a most unruly vehicle. After several spills, he picked up the bike, carried it down a hill and tossed it into a stream. He then started on the five-mile hike back to the base.

Stanley White

... Podington in the extreme northwest corner of Bedfordshire ... had been built for the RAF but never used to any extent. The field, once a portion of peaceful countryside (the country of Cromwell and Bunyan) had originally been the property, on its western end, of the Orlebar family, whose splendid old mansion, Hinwick House, stood on the road intersection just outside the gate. The eastern end of the airdrome had originally been the property of Lord Luke ... Although Wellingborough was the nearest town into which a liberty run might be sent, it was also the home of a rather sizable detachment of colored troops and Northampton, about eighteen miles away, was chosen. Bedford, the county seat of Bedfordshire, was slightly closer than Northampton but was being used as a recreational town for another Group. The Group's bicyclists, however, rapidly discovered every village within a fifteen to twenty-mile radius and Wollaston, Podington, Rushden, Bozeat, Sharnbrook, Harrold and Olney, among others, received the attentions of the GI's.

John S. Sloan

I was heading for "The Dog" pub one evening. Hadn't met any traffic so, not thinking, was riding my bike on the right-hand side of the road as if I was back in the States. Suddenly a lorry comes round a corner, head-on towards me. I dodged out of the way by pedalling off the road, finishing up in a bramble bush.

Ivan Brown, Halesworth

My first impression of England was that it was a nice place to be; a beautiful country. The people that I came in contact with were extremely pleasant. They were family people. I was married and was invited to some of the homes.

1st Lieutenant F.E. 'Phil' Arbogast, co pilot, B-17, 398th Bomb Group

October 15:
Last night was dull. A dance in the Aero Club proved no different than the others they hold there. Drab looking WAAFs. The music wasn't bad though, played by some GIs.

February 1, Tuesday.
... Saturday night Ken Buchner and I went to a dance in Shipdham and what a dance it was. At a dance of similar size in the states there would be at least six pretty girls. This had only one fairly pretty girl ...

Jacob T. Elias, 14th Bomb Wing Operations Clerk, Shipdham. In April 1944 Elias was transferred to the 44th Bomb Group as a gunner. He finished thirty missions early in January 1945

The first thing the Debden soldier did was to make for the local at the Rose and Crown to order a scotch and soda.

"Sorry", the barmaid would answer, "you've had it."

"Had it, did you say? I just got here."

Somebody would then explain that "had it" is RAFese for you're out of

luck, or it's all gone – there ain't no more.
                                    The American Male At Debden, Grover C. Hall Jr

My first impression of the English, I couldn't hardly understand most of 'em; the cockneys anyway. But they were very nice people and they really appreciated us being there. I was there about nine months or a little over. So help me God, there was only two days in about September when it didn't rain. And I don't think it ever got any warmer the whole time I was there. It rained at least once every day and sometimes two or three times. It's just unbelievable. We had to wear our winter uniforms all the time.
            1st Lieutenant James 'Jim' H. Royer Jr, pilot, 446th Bomb Group

An American Air Force fighter base, England – After having taken board and room in several different bomber stations I thought I ought to get around to a fighter base and see how the other half lives ... A slightly alcoholized bombardier recently put the prevailing sentiment: "Every time I see a fighter pilot I want to kiss him. A lot of us wouldn't be here if it wasn't for those babies."

There are photographs and drawings of their former officers on the walls, some long dead, some happily alive and thriving. A famous British artist has his studio in one of the mess hall rooms. The first shot in the Battle of Britain was fired from this post ... I did not expect the additional comforts this station offers ... You can have your breakfast as late as 8:30 in pleasant contradistinction with the infantry's stoic 7am and if you sneak in at 9 o'clock you still have a good chance of being fed. The food is superior to that offered by some de luxe London hotels. It was the first time I had looked an egg in the eye for the several months I have been in England. For the first time on a visit to an air force station I was able to sleep without shivering in the usual sleeping garments ...
            Debden, William F. McDermott of *The Cleveland Plain Dealer*

The quality of food at the combat officers' mess reflected the price we paid. Not that the food was non-nourishing or skimpy – it was in rather too ample supply. There was more of it than the quality of preparation warranted eating. This lack of tasteful quality may have been partly due to the form in which the food arrived to be subjected to the tender mercies of the men who prepared it ... There were no fresh eggs at breakfast time; the only eggs available were powdered. These were prepared by being whipped into a great sticky emulsion, then apparently fried in axle grease left over from the needs of the motor pool; the result was a well-vulcanised, plastic lump of lukewarm goo. Milk also was available only in powdered form. We were warned in lectures by the flight surgeon's staff never to drink local milk in England, but only to consume the GI powdered product. I found it unthinkable that a modern, civilised nation like Great Britain did not regulate the pasteurisation of milk but such seemed to be the case. I never did have the nerve to find out if the medicos were wrong.

Jackson Granholm

The ground crews lived together so long, we became family, sharing everything, the good, bad and in between. Working long hard hours, we still had lots of fun together. Each cot was put in the same general area in the barracks. The barracks walls were well decorated with pin-up girls such as Betty Grable, Rita Hayworth, Lana Turner, Alexis Smith and Vargas calendar girls. Popular dance bands heard on Armed Forces Radio helped relaxing after the day.

Free time for the troops was available once your plane was secured for the day. We had permanent passes to use when we were off. They just required you to sign out in the orderly room before leaving. A big 6 x 6 GI truck left the base at 6:00pm for Cambridge and picked up between 11:00 and 12:00pm for return to the base. Favorite GI haunts on base were The Sergeant Club, Duffy's Tavern, NAAFI-Red Cross Aero Club, Church Army and Betty and Bunty's Cafe. Just adjacent to the base were The Plough and John Barleycorn pubs in Duxford village, The Brewery and the Waggon and Horses pubs at Whittlesford Station and the Flower Pot in Little Abington. Towns farther afield were Hinxton, Sawston, Harston, Shelford, Thriplow Fowlmere, Great Chesterford, Foxton, Melbourne and Ickleton. Establishments the GIs were fond of in Cambridge proper included the Red Lion pub on Trumpington Road, Bull Hotel (Red Cross club), Dorothy Cafe, American Bar, the Criterion and the Rex Ballroom.

There we congregated with many of the bomber crews and hashed out the missions of the day, drank Mild & Bitter, threw darts and sang. The bars closed at 10:00pm and after singing "God Save the King", many of us queued up for fish and chips wrapped in newspapers at places that sold them. It was the best fish and chips I have ever eaten.

Three-day passes were available every two or three months and most went to London on these occasions, where it was popular to stay at the various Red Cross clubs at Rainbow Corner, Hans Crescent and the Mostyn.

A few humorous incidents involved the time our whole flight was quarantined in our barracks for three or four days with measles or something. We couldn't go to town or Duffy's Tavern, so some of our buddies filled up the bathtub with beer so we could enjoy our restriction. Another time, a British truck loaded with kegs of beer had a flat tire close to the flight line. While the driver was gone to get help, some "C" Flight characters stole a keg of his beer, took up the floor in the flight shack and stashed the keg under the floor. The MPs looked everywhere and questioned many people after the driver reported his keg missing, but it was never found. We enjoyed it for many days.

James Tudor, crew chief, 78th FG at Duxford

We landed and it was just pouring with rain. It had been light rain just shortly before and we got on the ground and got over to our dispersal area and I mean it just opened up about three faucets; it just came down in buckets. I didn't know what to think of it. The buildings were so unusual; most of 'em were Quonset huts. We were there two days before we got our pass to go into town. Of course, we were briefed on the money situation and so on. We were briefed on what to expect and went into town the first time and thought it was great. I thoroughly enjoyed myself all the time, really. We had an attitude; "Here today, Gone tomorrow and the devil may care".

I don't think that some of the guys used good judgment in their dealings with the English people. A man would go and buy something and hand out a fistful of money, take what it is, take what you need. 'Course we made much more money than the English servicemen and that caused some bad feelings in some places and rightly so. As a whole, I thoroughly enjoyed it.

Technical Sergeant Walt Hagemeier Jr, radio operator, 306th Bomb Group

The English people were the friendliest I ever met. They were always ready with a cup of tea. We also had parties for the kids. They always preferred Milky Way candy bars. We used to load up on them but when they were gone, they would take any kind. They would repay us by putting on stage plays. They were all about the history of England.

Rocky Starek, gunner

Our narrow roads were busy with convoys of supplies and there were many young and so-friendly Yanks who stopped to ask the way. They were very good to the children and we were invited to the camp for special occasions for a party.

Patricia Everson, schoolgirl

Well, I'm here at last. Looks like a good outfit and I hope I stay here as long as I'm in Europe ... Times are pretty hard over here. In fact, just one look at conditions will make you glad to be an American. Folks in the States don't know what rationing really is. But in spite of it all I've never seen a healthier bunch of kids than the English kids are. The food we get here isn't quite as good as the States but the bread is better I think ... I read in Yank that the war is all but over as far as the people back home are concerned. Or so all the politicians say. They don't know about the 5 empty bunks in our barracks. Neither do the strikers in Detroit and Lockland, Ohio. After all, it's nothing, absolutely nothing, to their selfish feelings. After all, it happens every day ... I've been around enough now to know that it's not just a privilege, or a "good deal", it's a plain luxury to live in the United States under wartime conditions. I don't see how we can have so much and the rest of the world so little, when the average American doesn't realise it in the least. Strikers show by their actions that they wouldn't even work in England such less fight here.

Sunday 13th August: '*had a chicken dinner when we got back today. Ice cream too ... Things look better every day, don't they? I don't think it will last too much longer. In fact, a lot of fellas expect to be home for Christmas ...*

William Y. 'Bill' Ligon Jr was born on 9 August 1922. He graduated from Sunset High School in 1940. He was a member of the high school baseball team for two years. He was once a route carrier for *The News*. After leaving school hen worked for the Walgreen Drugstores until he enlisted in the AAC in Dallas, Texas, in 1943 and trained as a bombardier and then Staff Sergeant gunner on B-17s. He and his crew were ordered to England in July 1944 where he joined the 548th Bomb Squadron, 385th Bomb Group, at Great Ashfield, Suffolk. All through training and in combat, Bill wrote a series of letters home to his 'folks' – to Mum and Dad, Minnie and William, brothers John R. and Jimmy, sisters Lucy and Anne and Mrs Delia Ligon, his grandmother, all of Dallas. After their mother's death in 1980 Anne Ligon Morton became the custodian of her brother's letters and in 1983 she compiled them in a small book called *Bill's Letters*.

Muhlmeister's name finally came up and we had been assigned to the 487th Bombardment Group (Heavy). It was part of the 3rd Divison and based at Station 137, located just outside of the village of Lavenham in Suffolk ... It was into the 6 x 6s with our bags and off to the railroad station from the Repo-Depo. The train traveled northeast into the area called East Anglia. We were met by 6 x 6s at Bury St Edmunds, the closest railroad station to Lavenham. The area is primarily agricultural, mostly small farms. During our stay at Lavenham, we would see farmers working the fields and I was amazed at the methods they were using. On one farm near the airfield, one man led the horse while the other man handled what appeared to be a cultivator. It seemed very inefficient. We would also see the Land Army girls working in the fields using hoes and other hand tools. It may have been inefficient but everyone appeared to be involved in the war effort in some fashion.

Upon arrival at the base, we were assigned to the 837th Bomb Squadron. The base was five or six miles from Lavenham and surrounded by farmland. It consisted of the usual triangular runway and taxiway system with the maintenance facilities, the tower and operations office located on the southeast point. The aircraft were all parked on hardstands and were connected to the runway by a network of taxi strips, each squadron's aircraft was located in their own area of the field.

The personnel assigned to each squadron were housed in their own area, surrounded by farms and connected to the mess halls, base theater, officers' club, the flight line and other administration buildings by a series of narrow asphalt roads. About twenty yards south of the officers' club was a fence separating the base from a farm. Just across the fence was a shed that housed an old steam tractor and threshing machine. They were obviously still in use, as the brass was kept polished on the steam tractor but to me they looked like they belonged in a museum.

We were given our housing assignments and moved into our new quarters, which consisted of the standard Quonset hut. The officers had their area and shared a separate latrine and shower building. The enlisted personnel were located close by in their own area. The squadron operations office and supply building were next to the road and bus stop. The senior officers had separate quarters and were assigned jeeps but the rest of the troops either rode the bus (6 x 6 trucks) or walked. Many of the permanent personnel had bicycles. The officer's mess was located in the officers' club. This was also the officers' central social facility on the base; it included a bar with the ever-present crap table and poker tables.

Four crews (sixteen officers) were housed in each hut. There was no running water, only two or three hanging light fixtures and one small coal stove (about twelve inches in diameter and twenty-four inches high) in the center of the building for heat. Our ration was one twenty-quart bucket of coke each week. Needless to say, the hut was seldom heated to a comfortable level. We each had a space to hang our clothes; a footlocker, which we had brought with us, and a standard army cot. Arrangements were made with civilians to do our laundry and cleaning which we paid for. The latrine and shower building was mostly unheated and about twenty yards away. At least it had running water, both hot and cold. I had been raised on a farm in central Kansas where we did not have running water or electricity so this was not all bad. At home, the shower was a fifty-gallon drum on the roof of the garage. In the winter, we used a galvanized tub in the kitchen by the wood fired cook stove. The hot water came out of the reservoir built at the end of the stove. The Quonset hut was unheated most of the time, but we didn't have central heat on the farm either, just an oil-fired stove in the living room. We were still a lot better off than many of the other troops who were fighting the same war.

We arrived at Lavenham in mid-January. The winter of '44–'45 was the worst in decades. The Battle of the Bulge was winding down but the weather was still lousy; fog almost every morning and lots of clouds and drizzle. We flew several practice missions over England before we were ready for our first mission.

A typical mission started by being awakened by an orderly at between 3:00 and 4:00am. The Quonset hut was cold, the latrine was cold and so were we. The weather was damp and it was tough to get out of bed in the middle of the night. Then it was into 6 x 6s to the officers' mess (Club) for breakfast and on to the flight line. Briefing was at 6:00 to 7:00, with take-off a short time later. The briefing was theater at its best (or worst). When everyone was assembled, the briefing officer would call everyone to attention and the base commander would enter. He was a Bird Colonel (Colonel William K. Martin) and was seated on the front row with the officers of the lead crews. A purple velvet curtain was hung across the back of the well-lighted stage. With no more ceremony, the briefing officer would go to the left end of the velvet curtain and slowly draw it back revealing a wall-mounted map, starting from England on the left, across Holland, Belgium, Germany into Poland and Russia. It covered the area from the Baltic Sea to southern France. The flight path of the bomber stream for that day would be marked with bright red yarn starting from the forming point over England, across the North Sea and into the heartland of Germany, tracing our route in to the target and our route home. The flight path was very carefully prepared. First, it was supposed to keep us away from the major "Flak" areas. It was also designed to not let the enemy know what the target was for the day. At different points along the flight path, various groups would leave the bomber stream and attack their assigned target. Briefing information included the target of course, the number and placement of the Anti-Aircraft batteries in the vicinity and the location of enemy fighter bases as well as the likelihood of enemy fighter action. We were also assigned alternative targets in the event we could not to bomb the primary target due to the cloud cover. Weather conditions were also included in the briefing. The meteorologist assigned to the group would invariably forecast scattered clouds over our base for the time of our scheduled return. However, he also never went anywhere on or off of the base without his umbrella.

Lavenham was a typical, quaint old English village. It was just a small place with a "White Swan" pub, a few merchants, an old stone church and many of the homes had thatched roofs. The church is a beautiful old stone building with its tall bell tower dating back to the 1600s. I attended services there one Sunday and felt welcomed by the congregation. The permanent party personnel looked upon the village as "theirs". After all, they had been there a long time before we arrived and we were just passing through. I didn't spend much time in Lavenham. Our off-duty hours were spent at the base, or, if we had a three-day pass, we would go to London.

Dean M. Bloyd

We were appalled at the barracks. It was an un-insulated tarpaper hut with only one entrance door. This led to a small 4ft-long vestibule with a second door. The wooden structure, one of many huts, was falling apart. Inside were cots for the gunners of five crews – thirty men. There were a few double-decked bunks as extra beds. The hut was full except for six empty cots. The crew quickly claimed their spaces and were widely separated from each other. We were not prepared for the sinister silence, which greeted us. No one yelled the usual, "I see they've lowered the standards again." Not a soul announced, "Here comes the fresh meat!" No one made a sound or looked at us. Looking around the hut I was disturbed to see an old and torn die-cut sign which proclaimed, "Merry Christmas". In May?

I looked closely at the men in the cots. I wasn't prepared for the green-tinged faces, the tired, listless eyes. Our crew looked out of place, in their best uniforms and bright expectant faces. Strangely dressed reclining figures, one more outrageous than the next, allowed themselves to be scrutinized and took no notice. They wore rumpled fatigues, assorted parts of summer and winter uniforms. Some had hats on, the knitted infantry wool cap, fatigue hats with the brims snapped up, fleece-lined leather caps. My God! There was one guy wearing a steel flak helmet.

The whole picture was disturbing. The rest of the crew got it. I could see them tip-toeing around trying not to upset anybody. It was difficult moving around the narrow cots in the three-foot space between each bed. I felt my confidence slowly ooze away. What a bunch to live with – all in each other's laps. These men were all insane.

The afternoon wore on. The new crew unpacked and stowed their gear as best they could on pipe racks above the cots and in the blessed footlockers. Much of the gear went under the bed. At evening chow, the men drifted out of the hut singly and returned to their cots quietly within a half-hour. Our crew did what everybody else did. We tried to blend in and be invisible until we could get the lay of the land.

At 6pm the double doors burst open. I raised myself up to see a tall angry man dressed in a field jacket, spotted fatigues and no hat or insignia. Every pure white hair in his head stood straight up in the air. He began to shout. "All right you fish eaters, you better come to mass! I want to see all you fish eaters at confession and Sunday services! Are you a Catholic son? No. That's all right, I'll talk to you anyway. God is going to take care of you and I'm going to help him! The guys all call me 'White Flak'. I don't care what you call me – just come to services. Come to confession and get rid of that load of sin I know you're carrying around. I know you boys, you've got lots of sin. If you'll come to confession you'll shoot straighter and kill more Krauts. That's what the Lord wants. Me too!"

The room was still silent. "White Flak" continued, still shouting: "No Catholics at all? OK, OK. You know none of you are going to heaven unless you see me first. Anyone who wants to get converted can find me any time." With that he exited, slamming doors hard enough to shake the whole hut. A voice in the cot next to me said, "Don't pay any attention to 'White Flak'. He does that performance for all new crews. He's crazy but he's a good guy."

Staff Sergeant Robert H. Sherwood, top turret gunner part of a
replacement crew at Hethel

November 11:
Got up late for breakfast again today. Bed feels good in the cold barracks. I started two fires but with these stoves you could keep the fires going red hot for 24 hours a day and it wouldn't be warm.

Jacob T. Elias

3

Target-For-Today

As I lay there in my bunk, waiting for the squadron clerk's call, I found myself staring at my watch. The circular motion of the luminous sweep secondhand reminded me of the hunk of flak that ricocheted round the shattered nose of our aircraft just two short months ago – and the apprehension mounted.

"All right you guys, hit the deck. Breakfast at three, briefing at four!" yelled the clerk in a voice that sounded like a buzz bomb. At least now maybe my apprehension would ease up because there was always a lot of work for me to do between briefing and take-off time. I had to get the guns loaded in the chin turret of our new B-17G, check the arming wires and safety pins in the bombs and make a last-minute review of the target photos.

I always filled my flak helmet with water the night before and left it on the pot belly stove near my bunk so I could have a hot water shave before breakfast. My shave took three minutes and my cold water shower in the little house out back took even less time.

Breakfast in the combat crew mess hall was the typical breakfast-before-a-mission type: hot cakes and syrup, one fresh egg on top, a glass of real milk and the ever-present Sulphur pills. That type of breakfast must have been considered a fringe benefit for flying combat. On the days we didn't fly, we had either powdered eggs or S-O-S with biscuits and powdered milk. When we wrote home about it we referred to S-O-S as "same old stuff," but among the troops it was well known as "same old shit."

'Breakfast at three, briefing at four!' (21st December 1944, Battle of the Bulge mission), Lieutenant William L. Cramer Jr 351st Bomb Group

The excitement of my first mission over enemy territory crowded out almost all thoughts except an expectation of seeing fiery Messerschmitt fighters flashing past with cannons blazing. But all my expectations were in vain. Nothing exciting happened. No fiery fighters, no flashing cannon, no exploding anti-aircraft shells nearby. Frankly, I was disappointed. At approximately 15:00hr I was swinging my B-17 about the circular concrete hardstand and the big ship halted in its sharp arc. As the engines were being cut, I could already see my crew chief, Sergeant Jim Haley, racing down the taxi strip in a Jeep, heading towards our Fort. I believe he got his Jeep training at Le Mans! The Jeep stopped just short of the No.1 engine propeller arc, just as the props were coming to rest and Jim was coming to meet me as I swung down through the bomber's forward escape door, seven feet to the concrete below.

"Boy," I yelled at him, "If all my missions are like this 'milk-run', I've got it made."

Jim was a veteran. He had already wet-nursed six Fortress crews, efficiently keeping their ships running smoother than any in the group. I detected a rather incredulous look on Jim's face. He said, "Lieutenant, let me show you something." Then he methodically guided me on a tour around the Fort.

Before we were finished, he had shown me no less than twenty-seven jagged shrapnel holes in my ship, all from enemy anti-aircraft fire!

Jim added, "It's the ones you don't see that get you."

Lieutenant Bob Browne, pilot

Flak is an ugly word. Sitting on the ground during a raid and hearing the flak go up toward the raiders high above, you know why they call it flak. The guns spit it up and they go flak, flak, flak. The Germans named it and somehow the guttural tongue of our enemies reproduces in a word the whole sound of anti-aircraft fire.

From the air, as the Fortresses sweep in on their target, there is little sound. The roar of the big engines and the trip-hammer percussions of the machine guns tend to drown out the sound of the flak. But you can see it.

First it comes up in single bursts, specking the sky with ugly yellowish-brown mushrooms of smoke. Then, as the gunners on the ground below start to lay their box barrage in anticipation of the bombing run, you finally can hear the noise of the explosives. It sounds something like the smothered roar of the underwater exhaust of a speedboat.

Sixty flying seconds from the bomb target the whole sky is brown and yellow with smoke from the guns. The barrage is shaped exactly like an oblong shoe box, or a coffin. The bombers plow into it, their speed cut as they come into the wind. The big planes are targets the like of which an anti-aircraft gunner never hoped for. They cannot take evasive action; they cannot twist and turn to make themselves hard to hit. They must go straight.

They must give the bombardier the forty seconds necessary to aim and release his deadly cargo. Then, with the bombs away, the pilot once more can take evasive action that may make the difference of life and death to the ten men in the crew and to the magnificent fighting machine called the Flying Fortress.

For that forty seconds above the target the bombardier is the Army Air Force.

Every effort all along the line has been funneled down to him. General Henry H. (Hap) Arnold in his office in Washington, the cares of an entire air force on his shoulders; Lieutenant General Brehon Somervell, working with the problems of supply and distribution; the vital pools of man power, the men who make the airplanes; the test pilots at Wright Field working out the fine details of the great machines; the men in the arsenals making the bombs; the school children gathering scrap in the cities; Major General Ira C. Eaker, picking his targets; finally, the pilots, the gunners, the machine guns themselves – all aimed at one objective – to get the bombs and the bombardier with his delicate, precise bombsight over the target for that forty seconds.

The room in the Nissen hut was small, chill. A squat English stove struggled vainly to warm it. Less effective than a fire for display, it was only slightly more useful for heating. A small coal scuttle stood beside the stove. It was partly filled with coal and over the black lumps lay a sprinkling of cigarette butts and burned matches.

A map adorned one wall, a map of the United States with the signatures of flyers scrawled over their home states. Beneath the map was a rickety chair and against the other wall an iron cot. At the foot of the cot stood a foot locker with a water bucket on top of it, for shaving. A flight bag and a musette lay beside the foot locker. On a box built to serve as a desk was a coal-oil lamp for emergency use when the electricity failed during bombing raids.

The one window was carefully blacked out and the room was filled with cigarette smoke.

A second lieutenant, a bombardier, was sitting on the floor, his back against the wall. Bud had sandy hair, a reddish mustache, which failed to give him the added years he affected, and blue eyes. About him was the same air of relaxed ease that is often seen in a basketball player resting during time-out on the gym floor. He talked eagerly, rapidly, the words cutting sharply with a pronounced upstate New York twang.

At Colgate University he played basketball. He tried out for the football team and missed because he was too small.

His companion, a tall Texan, was stretched out on the narrow cot. His speech was slow, drawling and considered. Months spent in Britain had not altered the soft slurring of his r's, the slangy pungency of his words.

"I tell you, Tex," the smaller man said from his place on the floor against the wall, "this war isn't all it's cracked up to be. I've been over six times, six missions in a row. I'd like to go home. I'd like to see my wife."

"I'd like to go home, too, Bud. Shore is a wet, cold country." The Texan drawled the words, "I know how y'all feel, bein' a new pappy and all. Guess I'll feel the same way one o' these days. My wife, back home, she's expectin' too. Worries me a little. She says she feels fine. Expects the bronc' buster next month. Funny setup. She's back there in Texas and I'm here, but it's our kid. Kinda strange."

"Strange? I guess so." Bud contemplated the glowing end of his cigarette before he squashed it on the floor and flipped it toward the coal scuttle.

"Guess you're right. Never gave it much thought before. Just sort of took it for granted, I guess. Wonder if my kid looks like his old man?"

"Probably ain't sprouted a red mustache yet," Tex chuckled. "Don't worry. Even if it does look like you, your wife'll tell you that it's the most beautiful baby in the world."

Bud squirmed to get his hand into his hip pocket. After slapping both sides of his trousers, he fished a worn telegram from his breast tobacco pocket.

"Can't keep my eyes off this thing." He laughed self-consciously. "Just gotta keep reading it."

"Won't hurt yo' none."

"I guess not, Tex. I know the thing by heart. 'You're a father. Five-pound baby boy. Hurry home. I love you.' Sure means something."

"Keep you from hellin' round maybe."

Bud looked up quickly. "You kidding? You know I haven't been running around to speak of. I been pretty good. But I'm getting to feel like a drink right now. I feel like putting one together."

"Not tonight, Bud, even if you feel like it. Got a mission tomorrow. No drinkin' tonight. Maybe you'd better let me get you off, this once. The Old Man'll do it this once if I'd ask him. He knows."

"Not on your life. Sure he knows. But he won't take me off because I don't want off. Someone else go in the *Baby Doll?* Not on your life!"

"Dunno, Bud. You've got six missions now, all right in a row. You got responsibilities too. Maybe you better let me do it."

"No."

"OK, OK, you know what you want to do. But me, I'm goin' to bed and get me some shut-eye. That briefin' time comes awful early:

At six the next morning, orderlies in hobnailed boots were stomping in double time up and down the upper hall banging on doors and bawling loudly. There was the tread of hurrying feet.

By 6.30 the mess was full. At the long tables were the flying officers, pilots, navigators and bombardiers, flanked by armament officers, meteorologists, radio officers and Intelligence men. Red-eyed and weary, the Intelligence officers were easy to spot. They had been up all night preparing the data for this mission.

Outside it was still dark. The ground mist was thick on the field. But above was a promise of clear skies and the "met" men confirmed it.

"This is it. Today we go."

Last-minute checks of the big bombers were being made by the ground crews. They never let a bomber which isn't mechanically perfect leave the field. Those planes, ungainly and hag-like on the ground, are the constant pride of the men who service them. They know better than anyone else that the hag on the ground is a queen in the air.

The briefing room was long and bare. Grouped on the front benches were pilots, navigators and bombardiers.

The Colonel took his place. His "target-for-today" voice was monotonous. His pointer beat a tattoo on the map on the wall. Like a trained thing, the pointer came to rest on the target, tracing the route unerringly.

With the aid of the map and blown-up photographs, he retraced the route, gave the rendezvous at which the bombers were to be joined by fighter support, the bombing altitudes, the bomb load, the take-off time and the estimated time of return.

Then the meteorological officer took over. He had been up all night over his weather charts; his young voice cracked with weariness. The forecast was not too promising but better than the normal English weather.

The mounting tension was felt in the room as more and more details were presented.

The light was turned off for the showing of the pictures and shadowed profiles filled the room, young intent profiles.

A half-hour passed. The lights came on, revealing a group of enlisted men, combat-crew members, gunners, radio men and engineers, grouped together at the rear of the room.

The Colonel held up his hand. "The time …"

There was absolute quiet as crewmen prepared to synchronize their wrist watches. "It is now thirty-five seconds after – thirty-seven seconds – forty seconds …"

This was the moment they had known all their lives, the tensest moment of any operation, the zero hour when men synchronized their watches, not knowing which of them might return a few hours later.

Then the navigators, the pilots and the bombardiers separated to go to their specialized briefings in the corners of the rooms. One man from each combat crew passed a table to pick up the escape kits, paraphernalia designed to prove highly useful in case of a bail-out or a forced landing in enemy-held territory.

There was a general exodus towards the trucks and cars, which were waiting to take the crews out to their respective ships, dispersed on concrete aprons around the field.

The captain of the Fortress *Baby Doll*, the tall Texan who only last night was worrying about his wife and their expected baby, took his place in the plane. Bud, the new father, was the bombardier in the same ship.

The last bomb load had been checked and double-checked.

On the field the bombers were ready; the motors were warming.

Roaring down the runways at thirty-second intervals, the squadrons took off. There was a minor crisis every half-minute, for at the instant of take-off a plane carrying a heavy bomb load is a potential danger. All the pent-up hate in the explosives might suddenly be loosed by some mischance.

Airborne, the bombers swung clean and free, gaining altitude. The big precision bombers need the cold comfort of altitude. Once air-borne and with altitude, they can fight off almost any threat. Their bristling guns and hair-trigger crews can take care of themselves. But they must have altitude.

Like flying dragons they disappeared momentarily into the mist still lying over the lakes at one end of the field. Then they came thundering out, heading for the foe, each plane in its appointed place in the tight Vee of Vees. They disappeared once again, off on their mission.

The Spitfires reached the limit of their range and turned to go back. Ahead was Saint-Nazaire, the German U-boat base. The purpose of the mission was to attack the submarine installations and slow up the turn-around time of the *Untersee* raiders.

The British and American navies have their destroyers and corvettes out surrounding the convoys. Other airplanes, those of the RAF Coastal Command and the Anti Submarine Command of the United States Army Air Forces, attack the subs at sea.

But here at its base the sub is most vulnerable. If the raiding captains cannot get supplies, if the ships cannot get repairs, if the crews cannot get desperately needed relaxation because of the bombing raids, the intensity of their efforts is crippled. For these reasons the bombing missions against the sub bases are highly important and one of the biggest factors in winning the Battle of the Atlantic.

As the bombers approached the target, they wheeled and came into the wind. At an altitude of 23,000 feet, the wind that day was blowing 120 miles per hour. That meant that the bombers' speed for their run would be cut almost in half.

Ugly blotches of yellowish-brown smoke began to dot the sky. Flak. The bombers straightened into position for their run. Sixty seconds from the release point, the sky was filled with smoke and the roar of the explosives, shut out for a time by the drumming guns and engines, became audible.

Its speed cut by the high-altitude hurricane-like wind, the bomber formation swept through the barrage.

The enemy fighters, disregarding their own flak, dived to the attack. Any bomber that dropped out of formation was the immediate concentrated target. The box barrage was all around. The *Baby Doll* straightened out and was in its bomb run.

Under the skilled hands of the Texan, the plane rode straight and true. Crouching over the bombsight like an acolyte at an altar was Bud, the bombardier. First Wing was funneled down to Bud. Blue eyes intent, he aimed. Into the delicate throat disc connecting him with the intercom, he whispered directions – green for right, or starboard and red for left, or port.

"Green a little ... Red ... Red ... Steady on."

His hands were on the bomb release. "Red ... Red ... Steady." The image of the target came on the hairline of his sight. He tripped the bomb release.

"Bombs away! Bombs away!" His voice lifted with excitement.

For a moment Bud was the Army Air Force. He was General Arnold. He was the factory workers in all their millions. He was America at war.

Again he became Bud, the second lieutenant bombardier in First Wing, the earnest youth who was too small to make the football team at Colgate, the father of a newborn son.

Flak. Flak. A gunner far below sighted and trained his gun. He fired. His particular shell, lost in the barrage, found its mark. The *Baby Doll*, victim of a direct hit, staggered.

Its number-four engine trailed flames. A huge hole blossomed in a wing. Wind pressure stripped more of the wing covering. The *Baby Doll* was mortally wounded.

Diving to the kill like jackals after a wounded lion came the Focke-Wulfs.
Their cannon spurted flame and more holes appeared. Another engine died.
Bits began to break off the crippled wing.

Tex was fighting his controls. Every member of the crew stayed at his
place firing the defiant guns. But the *Baby Doll* was doomed. Slowly,
reluctantly, she sagged.

Another dull blow, a whacking sound like the cupping blow of a giant hand
on water. Flak. Again a direct hit and the Fortress spiraled downward.

The *Baby Doll* and her highly trained crew had their forty seconds over
the target, the forty seconds necessary for precise aim to deliver her deadly
cargo. Those forty seconds were the period for which she was built, for which
her crew was trained; the forty seconds for which she was expendable.

Major John M. Redding

We went to Kassel about every three weeks to mess up their railroad
marshaling yards. They rebuilt rather quickly and we destroyed. This was
the very key to the German railway system. On one of these runs to Kassel,
the bomb bay doors would not open. Moisture in the tracks froze them
shut. When bombs-away time came, the bombs tore the doors loose but not
free. The bombs hit the target and we went home with four doors flapping
in the slipstream. Approaching England, we were notified that our home
base was socked in with fog and were diverted to an alternate English base.
Over the base, we executed the standard American procedure of a squadron
of ten birds peeling off in train in the traffic pattern. This was followed by
the second squadron and third, landing thirty birds in fifteen or twenty
minutes. The English allowed only one bird in the traffic pattern at a time.
My ship was the only one showing battle damage with the bomb bay doors
flapping in the breeze. The English base commander saw this and drove up
to my plane and offered any assistance the plane might need to become air
worthy again. I assured him my crew could handle it which they did by
using arming wires, much as we in Texas use baling wire to tie the doors
in place until we returned to home base.

While talking to the base commander, he commented, "Magnificent show,
Yank, thirty bombers orbiting the patch, then five machines on the runway
and five on final approach. You Yanks must be daft."

Landing at an RAF base after a mission, they always fed us fresh farm
eggs and French fried potatoes after we had had a dram or two of spirits.
I always wondered where did they get the eggs; we did not have them on
our base.

This base being a photo-reconnaissance base had a great number of
women photo interpreters with whom we were billeted. Interesting to
say the least, learned that it was vulgar to use the term fanny in mixed
company, but all right to use ass. Next day the fog lifted and we returned
home.

The run to Minden I wanted to see – a canal crossing a river. The bridge
carrying the water in the canal was to be destroyed thereby draining the
canal, making it useless and at the same time flooding the river below

making it useless. We hit it but turned off target in a direction so I could not see. Mission accomplished. That was always the important thing.

Airfields, marshaling yards, submarine pens, industrial plants were our most common targets and well defended. If for some reason we could not bomb the primary target, they always briefed secondary targets, or as a last resort, a target of opportunity could be used. Bielefeld was such a target. To this day, I do not know if the aqueduct at Bielefeld still stands. If you still hadn't gotten rid of your bombs somewhere over the North Sea, they were to be toggled out manually. I toggled out only one load of bombs into the North Sea. That was on my only aborted mission. Had to, they were RDX, very sensitive. Any major jar such as a rough landing might set them off.

This mission was aborted because soon after take-off the No.3 engine started to trail smoke – a constant gray stream, never increasing or decreasing, as reported by the waist gunners. Could see no fire, but where there is smoke, there is fire. Fire is a real concern in the air with all that hundred-octane fuel around. I had the squadron commander flying a P-47 and herding us into formation come over under my wing to take a look, which he did. He reported seeing no fire and told me to continue on the mission as briefed. This didn't sit quite right with me. Fire is fire, respected by every flyer. Trying to analyze the problem, I remembered a similar problem when working on engines while at engine specialist school. The oil line from rocker box to rocker box on the front bank of cylinders had ruptured spewing oil on the hot cylinder behind it in the second bank. This caused the oil to smolder, but seldom flare and burn. This was, then, not a serious fire hazard, but I knew what the loss of all engine oil was and this would take place time wise before we crossed German soil. The engine loss going into combat is serious enough to abort. I reported my analysis to the squadron commander; he did not show concern and threatened me with "Cowardice before the enemy." Decision time, so I offered a deal. If I was right, we would forget the incident; if not, he could do as his conscience dictated. Documented evidence proved I was right. We never had the same relationship again. The crew thought I was terrific.

Long missions, eight hours or longer, were extremely tiring and mentally fatiguing. I recall a long deep mission into southern Germany, flak most of the way, some bad weather and the loss of several aircraft and crews. This was somewhere between my twenty-fifth and thirtieth mission. We came home exhausted and something happened to me after landing. War, death and destruction just didn't make any sense to me anymore. That evening instead of singing and whopping it up at the bar as was my custom, I chose a table off in the corner to be by myself. My friend, Father McDonough, came over with a drink having noticed the change. I told him my problem and asked for help. He was silent for sometime contemplating the drinks and my problem. Then he looked me square in the eye and said, "Tays, all of the major religions of the world have as their primary mission to teach man to live in peace and harmony with his fellow man. When I do not do my job as a man of the cloth, then you will have to do your job as a soldier." His wisdom shocked me into reality and has held me on a meaningful course ever since. Thanks, Father McDonough, wherever you are.

In the fall of 1944, the bombing strategy intensified which frequently called for what was known as "maximum effort" missions. Every aircraft on the base would be scheduled to fly. Maintenance personnel worked around the clock to keep aircraft airworthy. Loaded with maximum fuel and maximum bomb load, off we went. For some the strain was too much and they crashed on takeoff. Others would make target then straggle back landing at many bases. Mechanical failures increase as men and machines are pushed past their limitations, yet strategically, it paid off. The German civilian population was losing its will to fight.

Robert H. Tays

January was a mix of training, scrubbed missions, mistakes and lectures. One in particular was on an air-sea rescue. The guest speaker was a British Merchant Marine sea captain. We were told of the serious exposure in the North Sea and the survival techniques. The captain gave an account of his own experience after being torpedoed in the North Sea. He and several survivors managed to get away in a lifeboat and for the next thirty days fought off the elements and what seemed the inevitable: freezing to death. Some crewmembers succumbed and were buried at sea. Others huddled together for warmth with the exception of one red-headed Scotsman. The captain portrayed him as unusual in what was his daily ritual.

This man each morning would remove his clothes and rub down his body with seawater, wash his clothes, ring them dry and put them back on. He was the most active, bailing, fishing and collecting rainwater. The men felt their survival was mainly due to him and the model seaman he was.

The captain said they were finally rescued and taken to an English hospital where they were examined and hospitalized. That is all except the Scotsman. They could find nothing wrong with him and he wished to leave the hospital. The doctors prevailed on him to at least stay the night; no doubt to give them more time to examine this phenomenon.

The captain ended his talk, which was impressive, but the point could not have been made more emphatic then when the captain picked up two canes as he was leaving the podium on his artificial legs.

He lost his legs to the frigid North Sea.

W.J. 'Red' Komarek

The sky was dotted with fair-weather cumulus cloud piled up like balls of cotton wool, which we swung round or through. It was a wonderful feeling. The knowledge that we wouldn't bounce off them, but punch our way through them increased our confidence. The oxygen was pouring into our faces from our rubber face masks, which also contained our intercom. I controlled the oxygen supply from a tap above my navigation table. I was told later on that it was a sure-fire cure for a hangover, especially when it was turned to emergency. Crews used it for this during night flying tests, which were carried out each day before a night op.

"She flies very well on one engine," Bill said quietly "I'll feather the starboard prop and show you." With that he prodded one of the many buttons on the dashboard in front of him. The starboard motor cut and the prop became rigid, but the airspeed indicator didn't falter as he applied a bit more throttle to the port motor. It was then we spotted a Flying Fortress ahead of us. It also had one of its four propellers feathered. As we dived past him with our wings waggling in greeting, we could see half of his tail was missing and there was a large hole punched in his fuselage. That sobered us up. I supposed it was one of the many I had seen earlier that morning circling East Anglia and getting information before the lot set course on a daylight raid over Germany.

"By God, the Yanks take one helluva beating going over there in daylight, in spite of all the guns they carry," I said. "The formation, I understand, protects them, so the theory goes. Their fire power is terrific, but it is no damned good against predicted flak."

"Unlike us – we have one Very pistol," replied Bill, jerking his thumb upwards. There was one pistol clipped to the perspex roof, to be used for firing off flares in an emergency.

"A fat lot of good that will be against German fighters, not that the Fortress' guns seem to protect them. Let's hope that crew make it back to base." We had left the Fortress well behind us, but our thoughts were very much with them and what lay ahead for us.

One Man's War, Sergeant Johnnie Clark, RAF Mosquito navigator

The Hut

Home for the bomber crew officer personnel in our squadron was a Nissen Hut accommodating twelve crewmembers or four crews, each consisting of a pilot, co-pilot and navigator. The hut was small, approximately twenty by thirty feet, with a concrete floor and the typical corrugated steel hemispherical construction. A small vestibule with double doors (for blackout protection) was supposedly located at one end. A single door provided access at the other end.

Warmth in cold weather (it usually was), was supposedly provided by a small stove located in the center. Government Issue fuel consisted of large chunks of coal, actually coke. Each hut was equipped with a metal bin to accommodate the weekly allotment of 52 pounds of coke. We quickly found that you could consume the whole 52 pounds in one day if you wanted to keep the hut comfortable.

Thus rationing of the fuel became an art form, aimed at providing warmth only when we were all in the hut. Since some were flying when others were not, some at the club when others were not, etc., the periods of heating became the subject of considerable controversy. One time that it was never warm was when we arose at 2 or 3 am to go flying. At those times the place was as cold as outdoors – and just as damp, an English specialty.

What to do? The obvious answer was to augment the coal supply in some fashion. Wood seemed the best solution since the earl's estate on which the base was located included a fair amount of forest. Initially, the wood collectors went for every scrap of fallen wood they could find, until the place was picked clean. Then the axes and hatchets appeared and the night air was filled with cries of "timberrrrrr!" This quickly produced a violent reaction from the earl and the military authorities, threatening all sorts of dire consequences if the practice continued.

The next solution was to augment the small weekly supply of coal by stealing from some of the base supplies, in our case the officer's mess coal pile located about a hundred yards or so from our hut. The coal pile was surrounded by a high barbed-wire fence. The approved procedure was to send a couple of volunteers to the pile equipped with a blanket and burlap sack. The blanket was first thrown over the barbed wire to protect the climber who then went over the fence. Once inside, he proceeded to toss the larger pieces of coal over the fence to his waiting accomplice outside. The accomplice then placed the coal chunks in the sack to be carried by the two thieves back to the hut. The outside man also served as a lookout to watch for the authorities. In short order the authorities caught on to the practice and posted an armed guard on the coal pile. This was only a mild deterrent since a third party would be sent along to distract the guard in some fashion, by engaging him in conversation, causing some commotion on the other side of the pile etc. The coal stealing process to be successful assumed a certain amount of common sense on the part of the thieves who elected to drag the sack back to the hut rather than carry it, oblivious to the fact that it had recently snowed – thus leaving a neat trail from coal pile to the hut. The MPs were at the hut first thing in the morning. We couldn't believe it.

An exquisite solution to the heating problem was finally reached when some inventive soul came up with an oil burner modification to the stove. The contraption consisted of a small can of one or two gallon capacity with a small hole in the bottom to which was brazed a length of copper tubing. The tubing was equipped with a petcock to regulate the flow of oil. The can was then mounted next to the stove with the tubing inserted in the clean-out hole in the bottom of the stove. The can was then filled with used engine oil diluted with a small amount of hundred-octane aviation gas to increase its volatility. The first oil burners were professionally done and used with some care; producing a nice small flame and enough heat to warm a small area, fine for those huts divided into small rooms – not ours unfortunately which was just one large room. Then the amateurs moved in. Everyone started to make them, resulting in all kinds of problems, the most dramatic being when some decided to "richen up the mixture", producing some rather large explosions and resulting crackdowns by the authorities. Fortunately we were ultimately saved from ourselves with the coming of spring and somewhat warmer weather.

Another facet of hut life was the diverse life styles of the various inhabitants. You had the swingers, the club hounds, the pub crawlers, the sack rats who never left their beds except to fly or to eat, the eager beavers who followed every rule and restriction to the letter, the neatniks, the slobs, etc., etc. Conflicts often arose because of the differing personalities. A classic was the midnight snack. One or more of the occupants would return to the hut after a big evening at the club or a pub or in town and want something to eat. Assuming they found something, they would typically want company and rouse or try to rouse the sleepers to join them in the repast. "The Captain", one of our more outrageous hut-mates, was the principal offender. He maintained a seemingly endless supply of biscuits and cheese which you were expected to eat – or else. He was relentless. To this day I can't eat a biscuit without a vision of The Captain sitting on the edge of my bunk trying to stuff a biscuit in my mouth.

During the really cold weather, everyone requisitioned (stole) extra blankets in an effort to keep warm. At one time I had nine as I recall. Almost everyone took to sleeping with their heads under the blankets to keep warm or to block out the light if the lights were on. This made for some interesting activity whenever the party "broke wind" – a muffled rumbling sound followed by a frantic hunt for air. The gastronomic problems were the result of what we typically ate, or more to the point how much we ate. When not flying we usually ate four meals a day – breakfast, lunch and two dinners. We'd line up in the mess hall at about 4:50, ready for the place to open at 5:00. We'd then take a ride on our bicycles or otherwise kill time until just before they closed the doors at 7:00. Each night as we headed for the mess hall at 4:50 we heard the famous battle cry – "They're gonna feed 'em now!"

Then there was Retreat. Every day at 4:30 they lowered the flag at headquarters accompanied by a canned recording of a bugle playing Retreat over the PA system. Everyone not under cover (outdoors) was supposed to then stand at attention and salute in the general direction of headquarters and the flag. Fortunately, there was a short preamble before the actual blowing of Retreat started. Somehow, standing Retreat became something to be avoided at all costs. Thus, when the preamble sounded, everyone outside immediately headed for cover. If we were in the hut we'd invariably open the door to see if anyone were headed for the hut. If they were we would then close the door and hold it so that the culprit couldn't get in. You'd think there was poison gas out there to hear the pitiful cries to "Let me in!" Always a lot of cursing outside and merriment inside.

George, the ex-coal miner, typically used his three-day passes to go to London. Invariably, he would show up just before midnight on the last day – very drunk and very obnoxious. He would noisily come into the hut, turn on all the lights and start hassling the troops. One rainy night with George expected, we decided to teach him a lesson. We short-sheeted his bed, placed several pieces of angle iron under the straw pallets that served as a mattress, then removed all the fuses from the light fuse box. True to form, George came lurching into the hut about 11:30 and tried to turn on the lights. Infuriated finding no lights, he crashed around inside the hut until he finally found his bunk, fell on it amid much clanking from the angle iron. Almost immediately he started snoring, accompanied by much giggling from the rest of us. Periodically during the night he clanked around as he tried to get comfortable on the angle iron. In the morning he wouldn't speak to any of us and remained in a snit for a couple of days. What we didn't know until later was that walking into the base from the bus, he was hit by a guy on a bicycle, knocked down, ripping his uniform and being covered with mud. Thus he was in a pretty foul mood before he ever reached the hut.

One chore of the officers was the censoring of the enlisted men's mail. The censoring was accomplished by removing the offending word or statement using a razor blade. Thus, some of the worst violator's letters looked like a piece of lacework. Woe unto those who foolishly wrote on both sides of the paper! Some of the nastier censors cut out whole innocent sentences out of pure cussedness. Some of the letters were pure pornography, filled with lurid descriptions of what the sender planned to do to the recipient when he got home. These gems were always shared with the others with much profanity and glee. It often livened up an otherwise boring hour or two.

"Hangar flying" while sitting around the hut was the most popular pastime by far, typically aimed at the humorous side of the situation being described. The discussions were usually about something stupid that someone had done – the dumber the incident the funnier. While some more serious types usually describe such behavior as an emotional response to nervousness, I disagree. I think it was just a high-spirited bunch of guys with a sense of humor who managed to find something funny about most situations. I think most would call it gallows humor. In any case, it remains the most memorable part of the whole experience.

Ronald D. Spencer

The crew that we resided with were on their twenty-eighth or twenty-ninth mission and they were all crazy. One in particular would wake up in the middle of the night and shoot his .45 off at mice. A .45 reverberates and makes quite a bit of noise and disturbs your sleep!

John A. Holden, navigator

We had four officer crews in one Nissen hut. The night before a mission I would go over to the barracks and write letters and get some early sleep because you never knew when you would be alerted to fly a mission the next day. One night one of the officer crews packed all their belongings. It made me wonder what insight they must have had when they knew they would not survive the next mission. Sure enough, the next day they went down. We had another crew who went on a bombing mission to southern Germany. After bombing the target we turned around and came home, but this crew took off for Switzerland. When we got back I checked their clothes in the hut. Everything was there except for their Class A uniforms, which they had worn on the raid to prove their identity. They had just given up fighting ... The squadron flight surgeon drank with us and palled around with us but kept a very watchful eye on us. He knew what shape we were in, how many combat missions we had flown and what the crew situation was. He was the one who dispensed the pills. In February-March 1944, I was on pills to put me to sleep and on the morning of a mission

I was on pills to wake me up and get me going. Sleeping at night became so bad that we started taking pills from our escape kits.

Bill Rose, pilot

One of the boys from the Bronx came back and caused quite a disturbance. He got drunk every chance he could, he knew he would get killed the next time out; but this particular night he did not come straight in. He went out to the ship in a stolen Jeep, rounded up the Very pistols, burned up several wheat fields during his riot and finally ended up in our barracks. He opened one door and started firing Very pistol shots into the barracks, setting fire to clothing and bedding. The door on the other end of the barracks had a traffic jam. Because of the firing they got down on their hands and knees and crawled into the ice and snow. I went next door and called the MP. He was interested in the information but said there was no way he could make his appearance until things quieted down.

They still did not send the boy home. They just confined him to barracks and counselling.

Emmett D. Seale

I moved my gear into a barracks and threw it onto one of the lower bunks which was conveniently near one of the two warm "pot-bellied" stoves. One of the men said,

"You can take that bunk if you want but it belonged to our engineer, who got it through the head on a mission a couple of days ago."

With no further words I selected another bunk, farther away from the heat of the stove.

I was a fatalist at the time. I did not keep a diary. After my first mission I made a conscious decision not to write about what happened each day and the only record I kept was a listing of my missions. This I religiously tabulated on a sheet of paper I kept with my writing paper and letters from home. I though that the odds against my making it through the thirty-five missions, required for a complete tour, were slim and I wouldn't really want my family or some Army personnel reading my inner secrets, should the inevitable occur. I was superstitious to the point that I would not go out in a mission without being sure that I had recorded the last one on the sheet. For some reason, I thought that if I did not do this, some dire consequence would take place. I was 19 and I never really expected to make my 20th birthday, which was 28 May 1945.

William C. Stewart, air gunner

Diversion to York

On one of our missions, attempted in very bad weather, we managed to reach the Dutch coast before the decision was made to abort. By the time we got back to England all the airfields in East Anglia were closed in, the decision was made to head for the RAF bases in the Midlands in the area of York [sic]. By the time we arrived in the vicinity of York, it had begun to get dark with extremely poor visibility. In addition we were completely unfamiliar with the area. Somehow in the confusion another B-24 and us became separated from the rest of our group. We were following the other guy who was making a run on a runway with us not far behind. As we neared the runway all set to land, we suddenly spotted another B-24 making a run on the same runway from the opposite direction. One of us gave way, but I don't remember whom at this point. In any case, we landed and followed the other B-24 to a parking area. We got out, compared notes and decided that we had landed at the wrong field since we were the only B-24s there. We later found that the rest the group had all landed at the correct field nearby. Like East Anglia the York area was covered with airfields, all very close together. This was the home of the RAF bomber fleets.

In any event, we were not about to take off and start looking for the proper airfield. We also wisely concluded that we would be part of a mob scene at the other base, while we were visiting celebrities where we now were. At some point a truck arrived and took us into Flight Operations where we explained the situation and requested that we be permitted to put up for the night. They were gracious enough to agree and provided a truck to take the enlisted crewmembers to a barracks and the rest of us to the BOQ. After dinner, we went to their officers' club and spent a very pleasant evening discussing our respective aircraft, tactics, targets, the enemy, etc. They were operating Lancasters so we learned a good deal about that aircraft. The Lanc, as they called it, was a heavy lifter and could carry a 22,000lb bomb, referred to as the "earthquake" bomb and for good reason. We were surprised at the Lancaster's speed, being told that they came home from the target in a shallow glide at about 300mph. They flew individually, not in close formation as we did.

I hadn't mentioned before, but we still had our bombs on board, not having dropped them in the North Sea on the way home. The other B-24 had theirs as well, so we were both pretty heavy even with a minimum fuel load to get back to Rackheath.

At this point we noticed that the Lancasters were making take-offs and landings from a very short 4,000ft runway. Being light, they were all getting off in about 2,000ft or less. We always used 6,000ft runways for all take-offs and landings. Having our bombs on board, we felt that we would have to get them to change the active runway before we could take off. I was delegated to go to the tower and request the runway change. No dice. I was told that they were not about to foul up their operations for us. If they could use a 4,000ft runway, why couldn't we? When I said that it was unacceptable, they referred me to the base commander who had just walked in. I explained at the B-24 had a very critical wing and required a long runway to get off, particularly when carrying a bomb load. He was unimpressed with my explanation and allowed that if his Lancasters could get off in a couple of thousand feet, we ought to be able to make it in four.

When I saw that he wasn't going to give in I returned to our airplanes and said that it was the 4,000-footer or nothing. While Kilar, very conservative pilot, was against it, the other pilot said, "What the hell', he'd give it a try. Kilar then decided to let the other guy try first. If he made it then we'd give it a try. So, we all climbed aboard, fired up and after warming up, taxied down the perimeter track after the other B-24.

By this time everyone on the base had come out to watch the ugly, squatty-looking airplanes take off. Compared to the tall, huge-winged Lancasters, we looked like a couple of dachshunds. The pilot of the other airplane had already decided to make a running take-off, meaning that he would roll down the perimeter track, then without stopping would hit the left brake and have a head of steam up by the time he hit the runway.

With everything fire-walled he rolled down the runway, as usual looking like it was never going to leave the ground. He hit the end of the runway still on the ground. At that point he lurched ungracefully into the air and immediately leveled off to pick up speed, disappearing into the distance at almost zero altitude. The British were all taking it pretty big, obviously thinking that they had just witnessed a near crash. It really looked awful!

We all looked at one another with Kilar saying something like "I guess if he can so can we". So we did the running take-off too and headed down the runway pulling all kinds of power. About 100ft from the grass Kilar yanked back on the wheel and we staggered into the air, immediately leveling off like the other guy to pick up speed. To get a fairly heavy B-24 off in 4,000ft was really stretching things to the limit and violated everything we were supposed to do. I'm sure the base commander had second thoughts about making us use the 4,000ft runway when he saw our performance. We decided that we were the talk of the place for the next day or so.

Ronald D. Spencer

4

Boys Will Be Boys

Our hardstand was right beside the Royston-Cambridge highway. Most mornings girls would cycle past on their way to work. Often we'd be pre-flighting our B-17 *Vertigo* for a mission. When we saw the girls coming we'd have the engines idling. As soon as they reached directly behind the aircraft we'd crack up the power and try to blow up their skirts. Nearly blew two right off their cycles one morning.

Warren Hill at Bassingbourn

Some fool stood up and asked what were the odds. The lecturer responded thusly: "On an average, mission after mission flying against the Nazi Fortress of Europe, the 8th Air Force lost four out of every 100 planes, i.e. 4 per cent." Of course, some would be "milk runs" with no loss, but others would be a disaster due to very aggressive enemy action. Still, on average we could expect a 4 per cent attrition rate. This being the case, he reasoned, a crew that flies twenty-five missions has a 100 per cent chance of being shot down on their last mission. A great quiet fell over the room. For many, including myself, this was the first time it had dawned on us that we were not playing for marbles. Someone could get hurt. Up to now we were just big boys playing with expensive toys, not a care in the world nor a thought of danger. This was a sobering thought. How can anyone expect to survive such odds? I estimated later that one-third would.

Lieutenant John W. McClane Jr, navigator

The modern doughboy is ... a sober, rather pale, normally-built young man of middle height ... Where the nostalgic Briton aboard tends to think of his country as a whole, the doughboy will recall first his own town and house. [He is] slightly homesick, no doubt, but a sound and vigorous soldier ... The doughboys of 1942 are a crosscut of the American Nation. They derive from all grades, all professions, all states. No composite picture can be entirely accurate; but there are qualities, besides enthusiasm, grit and humor that most of these young men share.

Yank magazine, November 1942

Our first introduction to the Yank was his arrival at the pub in the evening, plenty of money to burn and looking for a good time. In summer they used to spend their rest periods in properties along the riverbanks. Lassies and we young lads were welcome to visit them and make use of the dinghies paddling up and down the river. Also, there were special treats, such as sweets, cigarettes and tinned fruit.

Neville Firman

There is a clearly understood working agreement between crew and pilots that permits maximum effectiveness with the least expenditure of work, time and effort. Only crews that gain such ability survive long, for the Nazis are quick to take advantage of any slip.

But how does food affect these things?

Surely food alone doesn't make the difference between a lost crew and a safe one? No, not food alone. Yet it is a fact that the losses in a large group of men will be smaller if they are properly fed. And the phrase, properly fed, deals with more than cooking alone.

The crews of the *Little Beaver* and the *Suzy Q* eat apart from the squadron mess. They have fostered a feeling of oneness among themselves to a point where they not only live together but they eat together, fight together and when the time comes, if it must, they will die together. Part of that feeling, that *esprit*, comes from their crew mess.

The private mess they operate began because of the dislike of these men to "foofaraw." They didn't want to wear their blouses to dinner in the officers' mess. They came to England to fight a war.

When they landed as part of the early contingents of First Wing, they were ready to fight their way into the country. They alighted from their planes at an air-transport base with guns loaded at ready in their holsters.

Lieutenant Chester Lucius Phillips, who through the subtle alchemy of nicknames is called George, phrases it thus: "We thought the war was right here in England instead of two hours flying time across the Channel."

These men wanted to grow beards and wear torn, comfortable uniforms like the men pictured at their posts in the Pacific.

"We didn't want to wear blouses and pinks and get all dolled up. To get away from that we just had to learn to cook, so we did," Phillips explains it.

In the Nissen hut where the crews of the *Little Beaver* and the *Suzy Q* await their dinner, there is a cheery odor of broiling pork. Through the pleasantly smoky atmosphere comes the crackle of spattering grease as the potatoes fry merrily on top of the little stove, behind the broiling meat. Coffee will be prepared later with Nescafé. The men are ready for their meal.

And they are not wearing their blouses. It is important to them, this manner of eating.

Number One Priority, Major John M. Redding & Captain Harold
Leyshon

We fixed up a small open bay at the end of our barracks, which was Building
200, so we called it the "200 Club". It was a place for parties and sitting
around "shooting the bull" when we didn't have anything else to do. A
favourite stunt was to drop .45 calibre ammo' in the little potbellied stove,
secretly of course. That used to stir things up. I once let go a smoke bomb ...
almost ruined our clothes and bedding with the stench. On one occasion I was
definitely the "square" of the group although part of it. It was decided to strip
me of my clothes. The girls thought it was very funny but I got as mad as hell
(this about 3am) and almost had a fistfight with Bob Brown, one of my best
friends. He would have killed me. I was the type who got into trouble trying
to do the right thing ... like getting transportation for the girls at 4am, when
all my buddies went to bed and left them there.

On one occasion I woke old George and "Gentleman" Jim at 5am for the
practice mission ... not realizing they had a couple of girls in the sack with them
... and was met by a barrage of .45 gunshots over my head in the dark ... I hit
the floor of the hallway and crawled out! They were quite a bunch and when
they were gone there was no-one who ever quite took their places.

Lieutenant (later Colonel) William Cameron, 67th Bomb Squadron,
44th Bomb Group, original pilot of B-24D Liberator *Little Beaver*. On
14 May 1943 Captain Chester 'George' Phillips flying *Little Beaver* was
killed leaving the target at Kiel

At Christmas 1943 British people near our base invited individual GIs to go
along to their homes for the day. A Donald Nicoll went all out and accepted
two of us (myself and Kenny Norris, a member of my crew) to share the
holiday with his family. Don and his wife Dorothy were in their forties and
they had a little six-year-old daughter, Cynthia. We knew all about how the
English folks were rationed and the shortages so we were prepared to go easy
on eating and drinking. They couldn't have done more to make us feel at home.
I took along a box of chocolates, which was obviously a special treat. They
made it last for several days; rationing themselves to one each per day. I don't
think "Cindy" had ever seen chocolates before. After dinner I played darts with
the father, who was a prison guard. On that first visit I remember the Morrison
table shelter in the dining room and the threadbare towels which they couldn't
replace because of the rationing. This was the start of a lifetime friendship
and during the rest of my time in England. I accepted the Nicolls' invitation
to use their spare bedroom whenever I had passes. It was an escape from the
military life and the home life atmosphere they provided I feel sure helped me
to survive. I recall making one mistake and that took place on 4 July 1944. I
went out in their backyard and shot off my .45 pistol into the air to celebrate.
That sure upset Don Nicoll because he was the neighborhood warden!

Saul Kupferman, 306th Bomb Group at Thurleigh

In 1941 John Goldsmith was working at Reydon for W.H. Smith, the newsagents, and earning sixteen shillings a week when he was told about jobs that were about to start at Holton airfield, which was to be built. The wages would be £2; more than he could earn in his current job. It was not until 1942, however, that John actually started work at Holton, as a bricklayer's labourer. One morning the runways under construction were machine-gunned. The same afternoon whilst working on the erection of Nissen huts John heard aircraft engines quite close. He recalls, "We saw a Junkers Ju 88 flying very low. It dropped four bombs. The blast from one blew the corrugated sheets away from the concrete base that we had just constructed. We then had to fix them all back again." One of John's working companions was missing from the transport bus one Monday morning. It was learned later in the day that he had been killed on the Saturday night in an air raid on Southwold.

On one of John's inspections of snares he had set for catching rabbits he had his first meeting with an American airman. "Not knowing how to address him I said, 'Hello, welcome to Holton.' I asked him where he came from in the States. He was only too ready to talk to me and I found him very friendly. There was not much happening at the time. We just waited for the aircraft to arrive. One day I had a terrible toothache. Father suggested that I go to the newly finished hospital site to see if there were any dentists there. Finding a dentist I was invited to sit in the chair and have my tooth pulled out. I was the dentist's first customer."

In a very short period of time the number of American personnel arriving at Holton increased. P-47 Thunderbolts of the 56th Fighter Group soon followed. This group soon became famous as "Zemke's Wolf Pack" after their CO, Colonel Hub Zemke. On the day they arrived at Holton John recalls that, "Word was that the aircraft were to be prepared for action but not flown, but contrary to orders they were taken up with the result that five aircraft crashed killing four pilots. One crashed at Wangford and another at Sotherton near Sotherton Hall."

One American officer John got to know had an office near where he worked. Before the war he had worked at the Walt Disney studios. He had painted Disney characters on some of the fighters and he took John to see some of them on the airfield. He had also painted some of these characters on his office wall. John says, "They were still there until after the war but were destroyed when the buildings were pulled down. If only I had had a camera at that time." The fighters moved from Holton in 1944 and there was a transition period before bombers arrived. Most of the civilian work force was laid off but John and his father were needed to carry out maintenance and continued looking after the machinery. One day he came across a strange truck with legs at the corners, spread out like tentacles. The vehicle was probing the concrete, testing for low spots underneath. A few days later American servicemen pumped grout under pressure beneath the runways. In some cases it was as thick as ten inches deep. The runways had to be strong enough to take the weight of fully loaded Liberators of the 489th Bomb Group that were to become residents at Holton.

John's work not only involved working at Holton, but maintenance jobs at the surrounding airfields, He recalls a very amusing incident whilst he and his father were trying to find their way to Thorpe Abbots airfield. They stopped to ask an old man on a bicycle the way.

Father says to the old boy, "Can you tell us the way to the aerodrome?"

The old man replies, "Aerodrome, what aerodrome?"

"Thorpe Abbotts, old man."

"Thorpe Abbotts; where do you come from?"

"Metfield aerodrome"

"Yes but where do you come from?"

"Southwold" say's father.

"How do I know that?" says the old man.

Father showed him his driving licence.

"How do I know that's not a forgery?" says the old man.

Father then said, "How do I know that you are not a spy?"

"Do I look like a spy?" asks the old man.

"Do I look like a spy?" asks father.

The old man replies, "Well no".

So father says, "Then tell us the way to the aerodrome", which the old man then proceeded to do.

An incident John witnessed was the Liberator crash in which Joe Kennedy Jr, John F. Kennedy's older brother, was killed. This was a US Navy "Anvil" operation. These old aircraft were stripped of all their usual equipment and loaded with an explosive known as Torpex. The PBY4-1 carried only two crew who flew the aircraft to the coast and then baled out, leaving the plane to be guided remotely to France where it was supposed to be dived onto an enemy rocket site. Most of all these operations were not successful and some of these aircraft exploded before reaching their target. According to all accounts this is what is supposed to have happened to Kennedy's aircraft. John's account differs considerably from the official accounts. He recalls, "I was sitting on Might's Bridge on the road into Southwold. My attention was drawn to the Liberator by the sound of the engines, which were running very fast. In fact they seemed to be screaming as though the aircraft was trying to climb. It approached us from the Beccles-Wangford direction and flew to the West and South of Southwold before turning left towards the sea up the Blyth estuary. It then turned right again flying towards Dunwich. The aeroplane was some way from me but easily recognizable as a Liberator by its distinctive twin fins. My attention was drawn away from it for a few seconds, when I looked back again. I saw two white puffs of smoke slightly behind it. About four seconds later the aircraft blew up. The explosion was like nothing that I had seen before; tremendous. The puffs of smoke looked just like anti-aircraft fire. Now I maintain that aircraft was shot down, whether by design or accident I cannot say but I am convinced it was shot down."

To back John's claim he says that a friend of his who lived at Westleton also saw this incident. He actually saw something fired from the ground and hit the aircraft. At that time there were anti-aircraft gun and rocket

Ground crew painting the kills on a 354th Fighter Squadron Mustang at Steeple Morden. (Crow)

Ground crew working on a 55th Fighter Group P-51D Mustang at Wormingford. (TAMM)

Above: B-17G *American Beauty* in the 447th Bomb Group, which crashed at Rattlesden on 9 January 1945. (via Ian McLachlan)

Left: Throwing snowballs at Thorpe Abbotts. (TAMM)

Above: General Dwight D. Eisenhower, Supreme Commander Allied Expeditionary Force, presenting the DSC to Captain Don S. Gentile and Colonel Don Blakeslee of the 4th Fighter Group at Debden, Essex on 11 April 1944. (USAF)

Right: HRH Princess Elizabeth meets the crew of *Rose of York* in the 306th Bomb Group at Thurleigh after christening the Fortress on 6 July 1944. (USAF)

Lieutenant Ralph K. 'Kid' Hofer and his Alsatian dog on the wing of P-51D Mustang *Salem Representative* at the 4th Fighter Group base at Debden, Essex. (USAF)

American airmen enjoying a break from the war with their pet dog in the club on the base. (USAF)

Red Durham ground crewman on P-51D Mustang *Cecilia* in the 354th 'Bulldogs' Fighter Squadron in the 355th Fighter Group at Steeple Morden. (Crow)

Carnival at the 100th Bomb Group 200th mission 'Fiesta Party' at Thorpe Abbotts on 30 September 1944. (TAMM)

Base dance. (TAMM)

The launch of 'Salute The Soldier' week on Saturday 25 March 1944 in Trafalgar Square. (Private Alex C. 'Cal' Sloan II)

Trafalgar Square during 'Salute the Soldier' week. One of many Government-sponsored saving drives, the target was £165 million. (Private Alex C. 'Cal' Sloan II)

View of Ludgate Circus and Fleet Street from the top of St Pauls in 1944. (Private Alex C. 'Cal' Sloan II)

St Pauls from Cheapside with bombed buildings on the right. (USAF)

The cleared Blitzed area on each side of Cannon Street viewed from the dome of St Paul's Cathedral. The roof of Cannon Street Station (right) was so badly damaged that it was dismantled. (Private Alex C. 'Cal' Sloan II)

An American officer having a cigarette outside a London club. Dinner at the private Exhibition Club came with drinking, dancing and carousing until well into the night came after a show. Being a private club, it could stay open until 2:00 a.m. with continuous entertainment on three floors. (TAMM)

units in Dunwich woods, manned by the Home Guard and regular army personnel. Like John his friend is of the same opinion that the aircraft was shot down, not by another aircraft, because contrary to all accounts, there were no other aircraft in the vicinity at the time. "Controversial," says John, "but I know what I saw."

John also recalls visiting the bomb dump at Metfield the day after it blew up. "It was just like a volcano had erupted. The earth had been scattered over a large area. I climbed up a large bank of earth which was about fifteen feet high, to look down into the bole. It was one of the biggest holes I had ever seen. It seemed big enough to drop Southwold church lengthways into it." The indentation in the earth is still visible today.

Dick Wickham

I walked into the officers' mess and I heard this horrendous noise. I thought it was some sort of welcome for me. Then a huge lump of shrapnel landed about twenty feet away and that was my introduction to the base.

Lieutenant Calvin Shahbaz, 491st Bomb Group, Metfield

It seemed the explosion was caused by some engineers who were unloading bombs from a truck to the bomb dump. The bombs were not primed and the men were kicking them off the truck and on to the ground. While they were being unloaded in this fashion, one went off. The grass from the bomb dump to the hangar was scorched and the bottom of the hangar ripped out. Sometime later the truck's differential axle was discovered in a village about a mile from the scene of the explosion, thrown there by the blast!

Mr Pye, Chief Foreman of Trades

In a few minutes we were over Metfield. What a mess. For hundreds of yards out from the centre of the blast, a large blackened area of destruction lay before our eyes. Buildings and planes were destroyed everywhere. It seems that ordnance personnel were unloading "high-explosive" bombs when one accidentally detonated. This in turn set off 1,200 tons of other HE bombs and incendiaries. The blast killed six men and was heard for forty miles. Property was damaged as much as five miles away. Five B-24s were wrecked and six others badly damaged.

1st Lieutenant John W. McClane Jr, lead navigator, 44th Bomb Group, describing a flight over Metfield after the bomb dump explosion on 15 July 1944 at 19.30hr

I'll never forget the day I met Joe Kennedy Jr, USN, (oldest brother of President Kennedy). He landed his B-24 at Watton. Lieutenant Kennedy had volunteered for the "Mother" and "Drone" missions over V-1 and V-2 rocket sites and German submarine pens. These missions were code-named "Aphrodite" and "Anvil". I never saw Lieutenant Kennedy again as he was killed on one of these dangerous missions, on 12 August 1944. His plane was filled with highly explosive Nitro starch in boxes with detonators connected to each container. The plane – the baby – was to be headed toward a German secret weapon site at Mimoyecques. Joe Kennedy was to parachute out of the bomber into the sea and be picked up by an RAF high-speed boat. Hopefully, the huge "flying bomb" would strike the submarine pen. Lieutenant Kennedy's plane blew up before he exited, however. One of our "Bluestocking" weather patrol Mosquitoes was flying directly behind the ill-fated bomber and was nearly downed by the debris. Its mission was to photograph the flight and its results.

Joe Capicotta, 8th Combat Camera Unit

It was spring 1943 when I walked from my home in Market Weston toward our school. Two men on a tandem cycle stopped me near the school. I was frightened until I saw they were in uniform. The tall guy in front said, "Hey kid, do you know where we can we get some eggs?" I took them to Mr Ward's farm where they purchased a dozen.

The men asked if I would like to go to the base with them to get some candies. I had no cycle, so I ran alongside them. There they filled a large sack with chocolates, gum and shelled nuts, Baby Ruths and Hershey bars – as much as I could carry. I said, "Thanks a lot!" When I got home to Mum and opened the sack, she cried when she saw all the goodies. We were down to just mini-rations, which was hardly a mouthful, so this was a real feast for the children in my neighborhood.

It was a busy area. For two years a small village became a city. The roads were full of traffic and skies were thundering with aircraft engines. When I saw aircraft in the sky, I used to think the boys were safe up there. In later years I realized they were riding in a death trap if hit by flak or fighters.

There were also terrible accidents on the flight line with planes loaded with gasoline and bombs.

I started going to the base and I'm afraid I missed quite a bit of school, but I loved the military life – especially the Other Ranks Mess Hall and Red Cross, places that were great for eats. They called me Chowhound, but the white goat with "Lend" on one side and "Lease" on the other in red paint was usually the first in line. It would eat nearly everything edible.

In about two months, Pop White, the cycle man down past the fire station, made me a super bicycle. It was really appreciated. I wore shorts then and it was cold on base, especially at the bomb dump and ammunition huts near the old Knettishall church. I used to fill 100-pound practice bombs with sand, which were dropped at Redgrave Fen.

Martin Kozelka, an armoury sergeant, sent back to the US for a uniform for me. It was great! Long pants and warm legs. Really appreciated. In 1944 I made Private First Class and Captain Leo H. Rector presented me with a bolt-action 22mm Mossberg rifle. It was a lovely gun, but one of the local farmers reported me to the police and there were problems. My sister Norma later told me that Dad took the gun and threw it into a big pond near our home. It must still be there.

Roy Torgeson and Ray Sherman used to cycle ten miles to and from the Bury Dance Hall. They were two of the best jitterbuggers in town. Roy and Ray also made bracelets and necklaces with Plexiglas, English silver threepenny pieces and a reel of silver wire. They'd sandwich a threepenny between two sheets of Plexiglas in a wire frame about two to three inches off a heated stove top. They would then cut the heat-sealed Plexiglas into a heart shape and polish it with Duraglit wool polish. Finally they would drill small holes, two at each side of the coin and thread in the silver wiring. The trade in these necklaces and bracelets was very good.

I remember the great movie theatre on the domestic site. The seats came from bombed out theatres in London. We had free movies for all the children.

There was plenty of gambling on base. I once saw Mac, the barber who cut my hair on Site 11 opposite the base hospital, throwing dice. Mac pocketed about £100 that day. The boys really enjoyed their leisure time, which was not too long. They worked very hard around the clock, some of them. We had several boys visit our home; they were very careful with their money and bought War Bonds with it.

One night over the Tannoy system there was a gas warning alert. I was pretty scared. Boys were running around hunting up a spare gas mask for me as mine was at home with Mum and Dad. After about five to ten minutes we got the all clear, thank God. Another night, two Doodlebugs came over the base flying east to west about three minutes apart. The noise was nearly beyond bearing.

We used to watch ships leave for missions and meet the assembly ship. There was plenty of activity on each mission. When we lost planes it was very bad. The day we lost eleven ships was really below the belt; a terrible loss of good men.

Mum was a lovely laundry lady and the day *Skipper an' the Kids* crashed in Scotland killing Captain Littlejohn and all the crew, their laundry had all been washed and pressed, but no one to wear it. All the family cried. We were heartbroken.

The 200th Mission Party Day was great! Plenty of drinks and eats. I had the honor of meeting General James Doolittle, a wonderful man. In the evening we went to the Number One hangar for the big dance. The crystals used to absorb moisture in cargo packaging were scattered on the floor to help the dancers. It was a great night – truckloads of women. They chased me around the inside of the hangar until I climbed up a steel frame where I stayed until the end of the dance.

In wintertime the cold was so severe, I still wonder how the engineers and ground crew worked on that cold metal. The stoves in the huts were a bonus to come home to – glowing red-hot – you could then thaw out. The flyers had problems with their heated suits; there were plenty of malfunctions and bad frostbite. Cold was the number one enemy.

I think we had some 250 dogs on base. After the boys went home the dogs were either destroyed or taken by English families. There was also a massive "grave" not far from Number One Hangar where motorcycles and bicycles had been flattened by a bulldozer and then buried. When VE-Day came all the base went crazy – guns and flare pistols were fired and every truck and Jeep blew their horns in harmony. Peace was here at last. When the trucks lined up on the road in front of Coney Weston Hall near the 562nd Squadron area to go to Thetford Station, it was time to say good-bye. It broke my heart after two years of friendship. I realized later that the boys had wives and families to go home to; then the hurt was not so bad.

I think the 388th was tops in the ETO. They fought and died for the peace we have enjoyed and to all the boys that returned home, thanks fellows, you are my heroes.

It's been a great honor to have such wonderful friends. God bless you all.

You Are My Heroes – Percy Prentice

I was on a short leave in London from my fighter squadron in 1944. While window shopping, I happened by a pet store that had a Scottie pup in the window. Since I had left an aging Scottie at home when I joined the Army Air Force, I went in only to look at the pup and maybe scratch it behind the ears. The lady removed the pup from the window and set it on the floor. It started wagging its tail and ran over to me like I was its long-lost master. I had no intention of buying the dog when I went in but after that greeting I walked out of the pet shop with the puppy under my trench coat and headed for the train back to Colchester and the 55th Fighter Group.

We lived in twelve-man Quonset huts and housebreaking the puppy in such living quarters did present some problems, especially when one of the other pilots stepped in it. Flying combat missions and leaving the puppy locked up in the barracks for five or six hours at a time didn't help the housebreaking but she eventually learned and became the beloved pet of the whole barracks.

One afternoon I was going up for a local test hop in a P-51 and decided to take the dog now named Lassie II for a ride. The cockpit was too cramped to carry her on my lap or on the floor, so I spread my heavy jacket over the flat surface of the radio just behind the armour plate behind the seat and set her on the jacket. After take-off, I looked back at her several times and she appeared to be enjoying the ride. When the time came to land I temporarily forgot about the dog and entered the standard fighter pattern, which was to fly toward the approach end of the runway at tree-top level and when reaching the runway, breaking upward in a steep, left climbing turn to slow for lowering the gear and flaps. Normally the fighter would pull three or four Gs in the initial climbing turn.

Immediately after breaking to the left, I remembered the dog and turned around to look at her. She looked like a bearskin rug, flattened out and spread-eagled by the G forces. I loosened up the turn to allow her to raise her head, and landed. She rode in the P-51 with me on several subsequent local flights but she never made a combat mission – only because we didn't have an oxygen mask to fit her.

There was a Piper L-4 assigned to the group and I was the only fighter pilot authorized to fly it. Every time I went to pick up one of our stranded pilots at surrounding bases, I took Lassie with me in the Cub. She rode in the canvas sling baggage compartment behind the rear seat. One day while I was on a mission over Germany, someone accidentally let her out of the barracks and she headed toward my parking area on the flight line. While crossing the road, she was hit by a GI ambulance and badly injured. The ambulance driver, knowing the dog, picked her up and took her to the base hospital immediately. When I got back, the group flight surgeon, Capt Randolph Garnett, had me hold her while he took X-rays. She had a broken left hind leg near the hip joint. I held her again while he manipulated and set the broken leg. He then wrapped a plaster cast around the leg and also around her middle to immobilize the leg. We also attached an aileron pulley to the end of the cast so she could roll the stiff leg on smooth surfaces. After four weeks we removed the cast and she was as good as new.

After finishing my combat tour, Lassie and I rode a B-17 to a staging base in northern England to begin our homeward journey. Not knowing how the captain of the troop ship would react to a dog on board, I gave her two sleeping pills a few hours prior to boarding and smuggled her up the gangplank in a laundry bag.

I kept her hidden under my bunk until we left port lest she be discovered and possibly put ashore. Safely at sea, I brought her up on deck and happily discovered there were four other smuggled dogs on board plus one that belonged to the ship's crew. Lassie spent most of the time with the other dogs on a big hatch cover just aft of the galley. It was too high off the deck for them to jump off and being near the galley, those dogs ate far better than the troops did.

When we docked in New York, I repeated the sleeping pill routine and smuggled her off the ship to avoid any possible hassle over customs or quarantine. We then boarded a troop train to Saint Louis. From Saint Louis to my home town of Lamar, Missouri, she had to ride in the baggage car of the civilian train.

After Lassie's successful "immigration" to the US I was released from the Air Force, got married and started working as a flight instructor at the Nevada, Missouri, airport. Lassie went with me to the airport every day and at first I assumed she would lie around the office waiting for me while I was flying. I found that wasn't true when shortly after taking off with a student. I looked back and Lassie was pounding down the runway in pursuit of the departing Cub. When I made the left turn in the traffic pattern, Lassie also made a 90-degree left turn and was running on a parallel course with the plane. We landed immediately, picked up the dog and put her in the baggage compartment behind the rear seat as I had done in the L-4 in England. From that time on, she always went along with the students and me and enjoyed the stalls, spins, lazy-eights, an occasional loop and hundreds of landings. She "logged" more than 200 flying hours there, in addition to her military flying time.

At that time I was also in an Air Force Reserve unit at Kansas City flying AT-6s, C-45s and C-47s. She rode in all those planes numerous times. The only place to put her in the AT-6 was the passenger's lap.

Lassie accompanied my wife and me when I was recalled to active duty again in 1951. When we were stationed at Victorville, California, in 1953, Lassie's years began to catch up with her. She developed kidney problems that eventually led to paralysis of her hind legs. The conditioned worsened until it became necessary to put her to sleep. Her final flight was from Los Angeles to Kansas City aboard a Flying Tiger Air Freight DC-4, her body sealed in a metal box. My father drove to the Kansas City airport to receive the box and returned her to Lamar to be buried near the grave of the other Scottie I had left behind in 1943.

Lassie, The Flying Scottie, Walt Konantz, 338th FS, 55th FG

There were several good reasons why the American soldiers devoted so much attention to the children of Britain and got along so famously with them. First, because these were for the most part young men and children figured somewhere in their present lives or in their dreams. The friendship of these handsome children provided a vicarious enjoyment, without the attendant worries and troubles. Then, too, the children of Britain were an unfortunate group. Even the luckiest among them had few toys and games, they had but a tiny ration of candy, they had completely missed the joys of oranges, bananas, ice cream, of holidays and circuses. A great number of these children were displaced; they were living with strange families or they had not seen their fathers for years. Many were less fortunate than that – they had been bombed; they had lived though the hell of the Blitz; they were war orphans; they were wearing handed-down clothes from the "Bundles for Britain" and some were huddled each night on the dusty, dank floors of the Underground – a sight that tore our hearts and made us shake our heads in pity and in shame.

Above it all, these children were charming. They were well behaved and modest, they were friendly and yet respectful. They were being robbed of their childhood, so little kindness meant so much to them and yet they were good fun and good company.

So we saved our candy and chewing gum from the weekly canteen ration and when we visited town there were always cries of "Any gum, chum?" and "Candy, mister?" The response was so thorough and immediate that there were anxious questions in the Press: will not this new American habit be harmful to the jaws and teeth of young England? As the gum craze grew the demand exceeded the supply and Americans often ran a squealing gamut, shouting, "No gum, chum! No candy, no coppers, no cigarette packets, no American coins!" Since for every problem there is usually a solution, one enterprising youngster of my acquaintance, seeking what he thought to be the American approach, dressed himself in gangster togs and waylaid soldiers with a wooden pistol, holding them up with fierce ruthlessness and the terrifying demand, "Your gum or your life!"

The Children of Britain, Robert S. Arbib Jr

I commenced school in Coney Weston in 1941. The building still stands, but was closed as a school in the 1960s and converted into a house. Around this time, 1942, an aircraft crash-landed in a field on the outskirts of the village and, as they do, the local boys went to look. It didn't seem too badly damaged, but what intrigued us was the pile of bombs stacked nearby. With hindsight I think they were probably incendiaries. A day or two later the aircraft was dismantled and taken away on two or three large trucks. As it went through Coney Weston Street it touched the trees on both sides of the road. Shortly after this my father started working for a company building an airfield locally. At holiday times I would go with him to collect materials or arrange for delivery, such things as sections of buildings from Thetford Rail Station, or truck loads of wood chippings, which were rolled into the surface of runways to create grip for the aircraft that would use them very shortly.

When the Yanks and their aircraft and vehicles arrived, it changed the area beyond recognition.

All the country lanes had been widened to make room for the numerous Jeeps, command cars, large trucks and ambulances that proliferated, it seemed, overnight. By this time we had moved two miles down the road to Hopton, to a small cottage right on the road, which meant the road was slightly wider at that point, an opportune place for two six-wheeled Studebakers or GMCs to pass. On one occasion two of these trucks tried to pass a few yards down the lane and became locked together. I can see now one of the drivers standing on the load in one truck with a crowbar, levering the sides apart, while the other drove slowly along. And the load in the truck? Bombs! They were from the main storage depot near Thetford, heading for the bomb store at Station 136, Knettishall.

From where we lived it was only a few hundred yards to the airfield and, I learned much later, the dispersal area of the 562nd Squadron of the 388th Bombardment Group. Many other local boys and I would visit the airfield often, at weekends and holidays, to get close to the Flying Fortresses parked there. The favourite cry was, "Got any gum, Chum?" whenever we met a GI.

As well as gum, we were well looked after. When it came time for the ground crew to go to chow they would hoist us kids up on the truck and off to the mess hall, there to feast on a large plate of meat and vegetables consumed with a borrowed spoon, probably with tinned peaches on the same plate for dessert.

If I were on the airfield when the planes returned from a mission I would get a job clearing up empty shell casings from the floor of the plane. I have regretted many times not making note of aircraft names or serial numbers that I could refer to in years to come; but, when you are only eight or nine years old, you cannot see forty years ahead when these memories might be important. Maybe I have met crewmembers of these aircraft in England or the USA since, but have no means of knowing.

I remember on one occasion some pals and I were making our way home past an aircraft with one of the tail-planes removed. The ground crew wanted someone to crawl inside it for some reason and a nine-year-old boy was about the right size. We were asked to help but, to a nine-year-old, nothing gets in the way of mealtime, so we carried on. The next day I returned and asked if they had found someone to do the job. They had.

The nearest I got to actually flying in a B-17 was being on board while the engines were being run-up. That in itself was quite a thrill. Also a bit frightening.

On another day, while in school at Hopton we had a message that a B-17 had crashed on take-off and was likely to explode at any time. We all had to get on the floor under our desks. Before long, there were loud explosions and, when we eventually emerged, the desktops were covered in paint and plaster from the ceiling. I learned many years later that the name of the aircraft was *Hard Luck*. The navigator was Lieutenant Paul Arbon.

The base cinema was visited by us local kids, where we got in for free. We sat in the front row, or, if the cinema was full, on the floor. If our clothes got dusty we told our parents it was a cowboy film and it was dust kicked up by the horses. I don't think they believed us.

Other highlights were the Christmas parties given by the base for all the local schools. We were picked up from school in American trucks and taken to the base where we had film shows, a meal with more food than we had ever seen and a present off the tree from Santa Claus. I still have a book received at one of these parties, *Meetoo and the Little Creatures*.

As I mentioned earlier, my Dad worked on the building of Knettishall base and then worked on the base for the rest of the war. As part of his wages he received 200 cigarettes a week and a small cupboard in our kitchen was full of packs of Lucky Strike, Pall Mall, Chesterfield, etc. As boys do, an occasional pack was spirited away and my pals and I would enjoy a smoke among the bushes in the fens that were nearby, probably making ourselves sick in the process.

I would watch the planes take off in the early morning, then when we heard them returning in the late afternoon or evening I would call Mum and we would rush across the fields to the end of the runway and watch them land. Occasionally, there would be a red flare from one of the planes signaling wounded on board. We didn't like to see that. If they landed in daylight they came so low over our house we could read the names on the nose. A friend who lived along the road mentioned one day that she hadn't seen *Old 66* flying over lately. A while after this I saw the fuselage of the aircraft lying near one of the hangars. It wasn't until many years later, in 1993, that I learned from a book written by Richard Bing that *Old 66* blew a tyre on take-off on 13 August 1944 and ground looped off the runway, virtually destroying herself.

Although living so close to the airfield we – the kids anyway – didn't feel in any danger. One evening, at about the time the planes returned from a mission, we heard this noise and my father said, "That plane is making a funny noise," and went outside to look. He then rushed back inside and shouted,

"Get under the table, it's a Doodlebug!" This was the nickname of the V-1 flying bombs that the Germans were sending over. We crouched under the table and listened until the sound died away; we knew that as long as we could hear the engine we were okay. When the engine stopped, the Doodlebug crashed.

One of Mum's sisters, Auntie Elsie, met a GI from the Medical Center, Reg Brown, who, among other things, drove an ambulance. Whenever an ambulance was seen the cry would go up, "Ambulance, Elsie!" in case it was Reg driving. At the end of the war Elsie went to the States and married Reg. They lived in New York State, at a place called, if my memory serves me right, Napanoch. Reg worked in the Prison Service after the war. They had no children and both passed away some years ago.

Came the end of the war and all of a sudden peace descended on our corner of Suffolk, as it did around all the airbases in East Anglia. At the height of the war, it was said you couldn't go more than five miles without coming across an airfield. We settled into peacetime, although we still had rationing – food and clothes mainly.

The 388th and Me, David Calcutt

In America Christmas is the most festive holiday of the year and it is a family affair at which children are always in evidence. You just can't properly celebrate Christmas without children around – without Christmas trees and Santa Claus and presents and ice cream, cake and candy! ... I went around East Anglia that Christmas, visiting a few of the many celebrations that were being held all that week. At Newmarket our district headquarters was host to a group of thirty orphans from a nearby Dr Barnardo's home. The children in their grey uniforms were almost overwhelmed with the afternoon's programme – the Christmas dinner with real turkey and ice cream – the present-laden Christmas tree, the Mickey Mouse films. They were joyous and yet shy, these orphans, and I noticed a touch of sadness and restraint, of almost unbelief in the good things that had suddenly come their way.

In Huntington the engineer depot was giving a party for twelve children and a roving Santa Claus and other entertainers visited a local hospital where they had distributed gifts and played for the crippled children there.

Up at Honington, on the estate of the Duke of Grafton, all the children from the orphans' home housed on the Duke's estate were invited to the party. Here in a big Nissen hut that was decked with pine boughs, a hundred children watched a show, sang Christmas carols, played games and were carried around on the shoulders of their hosts, clutching toys in their hands.

At the hospital at Botesdale there was an even larger party, for here all the children of the neighbouring villages had been invited. Hundreds appeared, from tiny ones in their mothers' arms to boys and girls of twelve. They swarmed the jovial colonel who was in competition for popularity with the pillow-stuffed corporal Santa Claus. They, too, gobbled ice cream and cakes and late that afternoon all along the country roads and lanes were little groups of children walking home, their arms laden with boxes and parcels of toys and sweets to eat.

There were other, even larger celebrations. At Bury St Edmunds 1,500 children swarmed the largest hall in town for an afternoon of riotous entertainment and at Ipswich there was a similar party for 1,100 more.

At some airfields Santa Claus arrived from the sky in a Flying Fortress and at other camps they appeared in the inevitable Jeep. At Kettering there was a special party for six children who had somehow been left out of the first party for seven hundred. At Hull there were plays and pantomimes at parties where each child was adopted by an American "pal," while at Bedford the American soldiers were "buddies," and at Colchester the military police entertained ninety children – all of them with fathers who were prisoners of war.

There were stories in all the provincial newspapers that week, with headlines that read, "US Hosts to Northants Children", and "American Visitors Entertain More English Children", and "US Santa Claus Revisits Kettering", and "Yanks Play Santa Claus at Wellingborough", and "Thanks to the Yanks". But the truest one of all, I think, appeared in the *Rushden Echo and Argus* and it said "Americans Revel in Children's Visit". For that, in the end, was just about the way it was.

The Children Of Britain, Robert S. Arbib Jr

One wartime memory for me is of a Sunday morning picking food for my rabbit. Aircraft were always flying around, mostly from Mendlesham airbase, dogfighting, as it was known. Certainly three, maybe four aircraft hit in mid-air. I heard a tremendous bang, looked up and saw two aircraft coming down. I threw my rabbit food and ran like hell for home. I had just reached the door when another almighty bang as one hit the ground, just missing the council houses at Thwaite, beside the Wickham Skeith road. They were P-38 Lockheed Lightnings. My elder brothers and I went to have a look; looking from the allotments at the Firemen. When they moved part of a wing, it started a machine gun off. I reckon I hold the record for running down Church Lane! On reaching home, I needed a clean pair of trousers into the bargain. The tail of the plane laid on the allotments for weeks afterwards. I was too scared to go anywhere near it. As to the pilots of the planes, one parachuted to safety (Thwaite) and the one at High Lane was killed.

On another occasion I was blackberry-picking with my father on the footpath from Thwaite to Mendlesham. We were near Brockford Hall wood when a lone German fighter came over and decided to have a go at Brockford garage with his machine guns. We dived into the ditch for shelter. I could hear the bullets coming off the road. Quite some time later I saw the road surface had been torn out where the bullets hit. One, I am told, went through the toilet roof and bucket beneath the seat. Fortunately it wasn't occupied at the time!

I remember the American airmen marching along the A140 road in uniform, all in step, until they reached the "Buck's Head" where they would stop for two hours or so then all go marching back again in anything but order.

A schoolboy from Stoke Ash, Suffolk

Our village school owned a small plot of land a small distance away where youngsters could be taught the rudiments of gardening, aptly named, of course, the school garden. I was quite surprised to find early in the war that our headmaster brought a substantial box containing various seeds, explaining that these seeds had been shipped over to us from unknown American citizens. These seeds were to be used to help toward our own efforts to provide produce for the use of the British people. At that time we were severely rationed and foodstuffs of any sort were in short supply. I tried to conjure up some sort of image of who these caring people were and understand their kindness, as America at that time was not involved in the conflict. In my eyes the USA was a million miles away.

Later, I realized that those seeds had been sent over by the very parents of the servicemen and women who would later arrive in our midst. Even so, I was still wondering why America could not come to our aid in those dark days, as it had in the Great War of 1914-18.

How could I ever begin to dream or later to comprehend that as we fulfilled yet another dream to build our own home – which was to be sited on that self-same very spot, the old school garden – that shortly after its completion we would have as our guests, post-war, numerous sons and daughters of the self-same parents who had made the initial donations of those seeds, seated on the very spot within our home where they had been sown. Those seeds of friendship had well and truly been planted way back in 1940.

It's true to state that my involvement with the 388th at Knettishall has had a lasting effect on my life. Here I will report on my first official visit to Knettishall with the Air Training Corps cadet squadrons, of which I was a member – illegally and underage. We had received an invitation to visit Knettishall, a first for all of us. Our involvement with the 388th was due to a directive issued by the base commander, Colonel William David, that British Air Cadets could gain air experience where possible with aircraft of the 388th Bomb Group. The arrangements for our visit where made possible by our squadron commanding officer and full-time school teacher Major D.C. Reed, the original 562nd Bomb Squadron commander

The invitation began with a luncheon in the officers' mess on a Sunday afternoon. With our party of twenty or more, it was quite obvious that very few, if any, had ever experienced such an occasion, bearing in mind that it was wartime and that we had been accustomed to quite stringent rationing. It revealed a whole new world to all of us. I must add that our manners on that day were actually impeccable.

From the officers' mess, we were next introduced to the station gymnasium. We were shown various methods of self-defence, unarmed combat, along with techniques to attack a potential enemy. Following this we went to the parachute school and learned the art of folding and packing a parachute. I, for one, took great heed of these instructions, as I'm sure, in the back of my mind was, "Well, just supposing." The thought of putting your trust in a parachute and the particular person who packed it is sobering, indeed. But at fourteen-years-old, I suppose I didn't question anything, especially those whom we'd now have to trust with our lives. After all, these guys were so confident and highly skilled at their jobs.

Next, we made our way to the Military Police Station where we were introduced to a variety of small arms, then to the 1751st Armory Section where we were instructed to take apart a .50-caliber Browning machine gun, after having previously watched a demonstration on how this was to be carried out, step by step, by the real experts. And it amazed us that every gunner had to carry this out blindfolded. I understood, but again thought, "Supposing someone were blinded. He'd have no need of a machine gun."

That visit to the armory paid great dividends as our newfound friends informed us that we could visit their living quarters at any time and, if cycling, could leave our bikes there in complete safety. On our next visit we made use of our invitation. But further than this, these men of that particular section became great friends. Time after time we left our cycles there and we were always made welcome. This is probably where I discovered how the average GI thought and behaved, insofar as their presence over here was concerned – their thoughts of home, their own part in the conflict, the top brass, their thoughts on the survival of the air crew, their comparisons with the American infantrymen – this after D-Day: "There were no fox holes at 25,000 feet," my favorite saying.

We also became involved in a friendly banter as to the role of the Royal Air Force, being told that only the Americans dared to fly in combat during the day and that the British only operated under the cover of darkness. We retaliated by saying that the B-17s and B-24s couldn't even fly at night – that they could get lost over Britain even in daylight. Also that our Lancasters carried 15,000 pounds of bombs in comparison to the 5,000 pounds of the B-17 and B-24. These friendly arguments were usually replaced with references to pub-crawls, drinking, gambling and English girls, but not necessarily in that order. If, as a very young teenager, I was not aware of the facts of life, I became very much aware by mixing with guys who gave the impression they were all Romeos and Clark Gables, or so at least they thought. This is all part of how we saw the average American GI.

But, after all, they loaned us, without question, their eating knives, drinking utensils, etc. They gave us the latest copies of *Yank* Magazine. We in return brought them fresh eggs, a priceless commodity to anyone within the confines of the 388th. So, actually, we thought, "All's square."

Here I must return to that very first visit. From the confines of the armory, we made our way to a radio signals building, just short of the group headquarters building, but immediately opposite. We were given a demonstration lecture on the various methods used to contact and, if desired, control aircraft in the vicinity of the airfield.

Next, we went to the all-important group headquarters building itself, probably for us the most interesting of all. Here, we were informed that within these walls the whole of the group operations were controlled, each and every day, in relation to tasks carried out by the group's B-17s on Hitler's Europe. I noted a large wall map of Europe with targets near and far, but mainly the long-haul targets deep into Germany. I also noted the board referring to the group's B-17s and pilots, with reference to the four squadrons comprising the 388th. Much of this was of a highly secret nature, which we were warned of, so I was most surprised to be shown the various methods used to identify the various targets – the system of maps leading up to whatever target had been chosen. In fact, it appeared that almost every major town or city was a potential target and that the 388th, along with the rest of the 8th Air Force, could launch an attack on almost anywhere. We were given a great insight into how the 388th would and could operate. I, for one, was rather over-awed being a guest of the top brass, but more than a little intrigued as to their apparent friendliness and tendency to drop everything in their efforts to make us welcome. And here we were in the middle of a war, fighting for our very survival. They must have wanted us to think we were, after all, partners and to be treated as equals, as well as guests, by these strangers in our own country – a kind of situation I still recall with great pleasure to this day.

Our final port-of-call was to the nearby No.1 Hangar. Here was the real reason for our being there, because here stood the first of the group's B-17s I would ever go into. And, after we were shown around the now-familiar Boeing Flying Fortress from the outside, we were then invited inside where a mechanic pointed out or described the various crew positions, the .50-calibre arms, the bomb bay, the radio operator's compartment, plus the various escape hatches if need be. Since I had already experienced my first B-17 with the 385th Bomb Group, which carried the Square D symbol. I found myself immediately at home in a strange kind of way. And, with the eagerness and sharp mind of a typical teenager of that time, everything I had noticed in my previous flight in reference to the B-17 had been stored and memorized and I retain much of this, even to this day.

So to my next visit, which meant cycling four-and-a-half miles or so.

We had been invited by Major Reed back to Knettishall for a fast flight in one of the Group's B-17s. I can't recall how many of my ATC friends were on board, but I was astonished to discover we were to land at a nearby RAF station, which, at that time, was using a four-engine Short Sterling bomber. This airport was less than two-and-a-half miles due south of Knettishall. In fact, their circuit was dangerously close and by some kind of miracle there were never any collisions.

To resume my story, after a very brief meeting between the Royal Air force and a United States Army Air force Major, we then proceeded. This was to be the first of many such flights from Knettishall, as we had been informed that if we presented ourselves at the Group Headquarters building there was the possibility of taking further flights and we had been also advised that our squadron had been officially adopted by the 388th.

The technique used to hopefully obtain a flight was to approach a pilot or pilots just short of entering the headquarters building. It follows that even if the answer was a negative one, we only required the one affirmative. So we were on our way. But there was still one other stumbling block.

That was to present to whosoever was in charge a warrant, signed by our parents, which consented to any such flight. I always felt about six inches too short in the presence of the others, simply because I knew I was the youngest there and had joined these cadets somewhat illegally. I was just fourteen years old at that time, the legal age being sixteen

Luckily, the signed warrant didn't state my age, so that aspect was never queried.

I have referred to our official adoption by the 388th, which in fact gave us permission to eat at the airmen's mess, among many other things. I soon discovered the difference between dining at the officers' mess and the lower ranks', mainly the enlisted men's. Many stories abound, even to this day, of the fabulous food to be had at any American mess hall, so I will add at times the food offered was not of the best, but hasten also to add that after four years of wartime rationing, just anything was more than welcome.

I also recall those were the days of various "leg-pulling", asking us who would be paying for the meal, then someone saying Uncle Sam had to foot the bill for us "Limeys" – which again reminds me that prior to our presence at Knettishall, we had never heard the term Limey; but I was extremely careful in not referring to our hosts as Yanks.

Taking this one step further, I felt intrigued and fascinated by the unfamiliar, foreign-sounding names, discovering that although many had well-known English names, a great number had German, Italian, Polish, Czech or Scandinavian surnames. And so it dawned on me that these American crews could well be dropping high explosives on various relatives down below. We of course, although perhaps of Saxon origin, had no such worries; our connections long since severed with our European forebears. – Sundays were taken up by these visits and flights. We were instructed to sit down, usually in the waist; or, if on my own, maybe this was in the radio room area. It occurred to me that whichever crew we went with there was always a kind and clear consideration shown for our safety and well being on board.

Each time we went up we presented ourselves at the parachute room. Normal issue was a chest-type pack with the ever-familiar words ringing in our ears, "Remember, if it doesn't work, just bring it back. And don't take that home for your big sister to make a silk dress." Familiar words to us for sure. And if we went in an RAF aircraft about that time, those same comments were always part of the parachute ritual.

Once airborne, we would listen in on the chat over the intercom, as there were normally spare sets of headphones and throat mikes, which had been handed to us. Depending on the length of the flight, we were able to move around much as we desired, although we were normally told not to go back in the tail gunner position which was rather remote, because if we removed our headphones to go back there and an emergency arose, we would be none the wiser. My two favorite positions were either lying down in the nose compartment, which offered a fantastic view, or standing behind the two pilots observing every movement made, as well as keeping a keen eye on the instrument panel. I cannot remember anything instructive as to where to be on landing, although usually we'd be asked out of the nose position, again for obvious reasons. Just supposing the landing went badly wrong, which happily never occurred.

Our Air Cadet squadron issued us flying logs. So it became a part of the ritual to obtain the pilot's signature. The duration of the flight was also recorded, type of aircraft and number, if Royal Air Force, or serial number if US Army Air Corps. A column for remarks gave the reason for the flight. This log, which I retain to this day, has become one of my most treasured possessions.

I was fortunate enough to go on practice mission flights, practice formation flying, practice bombing, etc. Probably – or better still, most definitely – the best experience for me, ever, was on one particular flight to be called on the intercom to go forward to the cockpit, where, to my astonishment, I was then informed that, as I was there, I might as well get some stick time in. The co-pilot retired his seat and motioned me to occupy his position. The pilot then advised me as to the basic acts necessary for straight and level flight, rudder movement, how to rely on the artificial horizon indicator and to follow any instructions from the navigator as to our position. The next twenty minutes or so, yours truly was in control, even making a necessary turn successfully.

The pilot was Lieutenant Eugene Yarger who had helped me, possibly, become the youngest ever person to take control of a B-17 at the age of fourteen years.

Maybe a world record; maybe not.

But it was the kind of experience that no person of my age could ever forget.

Seeds of Friendship, George Stebbings

I smuggled Herbie Bart onto my B-24 for a check-out flight. Our crew chief looked kind of funny but said nothing. [Herbie had never even ridden in a car, or been as much as fifteen miles away from his home]. We flew him down for a look at London, up to the Wash where I took him up front to watch me drop a practice bomb, put him in the nose turret, up to the Irish Sea where I let him shoot a waist machine gun into the water, then home to buzz the farm where his parents and sisters waved madly.

Married 23-year old Albert E. Jones, bombardier, 44th Bomb Group, who struck up a friendship with the Bart family in Hingham, Norfolk

March 29th started like any other day did in 1944, for the young lad cycling to work with his mate the three miles to the Hall gardens, where they both worked as gardeners to the Lord Lieutenant of the County. Given their day's work by the head gardener, both lads then got on with their duties, while above them in the clear morning sky, B-24s of the USAAF, heavily laden with bombs and fuel, were climbing to get in formation before making their way to their target deep into Germany (Watten). The roar of the bombers overhead was an everyday occurrence in the skies over East Anglia and to the lads, the "Yanks" were out again today, when suddenly, above the usual roar of the engines, a ghastly high pitched noise of engines in trouble broke the air.

Looking skyward the lad saw to his horror, two B-24s locked together for a moment and then one of them breaking in half. With that still ghastly noise, both stricken B-24s plunged earthwards, leaving a trail of wreckage in the sky. To the lad it seemed that both would end up on top of him.

Now above him he heard a new noise. It was of falling bombs, whistling down. He then prayed – he had to, as he was sure his young life would soon be over.

The two bombs (each 2,000lb) exploded on the parkland near the earl's Hall. Not a pane of glass remained in any window, thick plate glass littered the lawns and not a leaf remained on the trees that grew in the park. Cattle were charging about the park terrified of all the noise (it was many a day before the milk yield got back to normal). Earth and bomb fragments were still flying through the air, as the two stricken B-24s crashed into the ground not more than a quarter of a mile apart. The nearest to the lads was no more than a stone's throw away and in one moment both thoughts were for the crew trapped in the wreckage.

Running across the parkland to the crash, the lads suddenly saw the earth and wreckage rise into the air (one 2,000lb bomb had exploded). They dived into the soft earth as once again earth and steel flew through the air. One fragment of a bomb embedded itself into the earth close to the lad – he still has this piece of metal. The blast and fumes took the breath away from the lads for a while and when they recovered, a sight laid before them never to be forgotten. A burning mass of metal and flesh were strewn about them. Nothing could be done and with heavy hearts they returned to their work while airmen from the nearby airbase arrived to put out the flames. This was not to be the end of the boys' ordeal, as shortly after returning to their work; there was another terrific explosion as the second 2,000lb bomb went off in the already wrecked plane. Blast and metal again tore through the air to tear into the ground inches away from the lads, who by this time were just about shattered and the head gardener who also was at his wits' end (all his glass houses were wrecked), saw the state of the lads and sent them home.

Of the two B-24s that crashed that fateful morning, both were from the 93rd Bomb Group based at Hardwick. Only two crewmen survived; they were the side gunners in the aircraft that was sliced in two. Eighteen other crewmen were killed and when the second bomb went off while rescue attempts were being made, another nineteen were killed and over thirty-eight injured. Nothing now remains to show what happened that morning except to those who were there, a top of a tree missing, a burn mark where bark should be, but most of all quietness now reigns over the spot where so long ago many young American lives were lost and left a scar in the memory of a young lad.

I know, I was that lad!

A Lasting Scar, Gordon K. Reynolds (a British friend)

Instead of doing our homework, we would sit at the runway threshold in the evenings and at weekends and watch the bombers land. We were called "little limeys". I got to know three crews in the 730th very well. They were billeted in the field across from my parents' house. One hut had paintings of a B-17 and half-naked women on the walls behind their beds. My friend, Pfc Dave Roberts, an armourer in the 730th Squadron, was a great artist. He painted names on the B-17s and drew my portrait, complete with lieutenant's forage cap. I virtually lived on the base. I sat on the edge of their bunks and listened speechless to tales of exciting combat. One crew I visited were there one day. Next day they weren't. I was a twelve-year-old kid. I was bewildered. "Are they shot down? Are they dead?" I asked. Men were stripping the hut of their belongings and moving them out.

I collected washing and cycled home to my mother with it in bags perched on the handlebars and front basket of my bike. My Mother would discover bars of soap and chocolate and cigarettes for my Dad, who mended their shoes, among the washing. I would check the crew status board for them to see if they were flying next day. I crawled under barbed wire to steal coke for their fires, which I would light before they returned from a raid and stood in line for meals at the EM Mess in my lieutenant's forage cap, coat with sergeant's stripes and "my" mess kit. Dave even painted a Fortress on my cup. The meals were better than at home – steak, spuds and sprouts, rice pudding, fruit juice – all on one big plate! The orange juice mingled with the meat and gravy but I didn't care!

At the base cinema one evening the air raid sirens sounded. We had been used to air raids since 1940 and just stood in amazement, wondering what all the panic was about as the Americans ran to the shelters! One pilot, who wore his pistol on the base, fired into the moonlit sky at the Ju 88 as he ran!

My best American pal was a nineteen-year-old ball turret gunner from Utah called "Junior". One day, my friends and me watched the B-17s return when a badly damaged Fort' flew over, landed and taxied quickly to one side. Being "blood-thirsty", curious kids, we wanted to see who was injured. I wondered if it was one of the crews I knew. "Was it Junior?"

The ball turret had not been retracted. The guns were still in, pointing forward. The glass was cracked and shattered. It had taken a direct hit. Trapped inside, the ball gunner was giving blood-curdling screams. I can hear them to this day. "Christ, how could anyone survive in a position like that?" They levered the jammed ball turret door open. His arm was just hanging off. Still screaming, they put him on a stretcher. His oxygen mask dangled over the side. They took him away to hospital. The inside of the turret was soaked in his blood. It was as if four or five bottles of milk had been poured into the turret.

I was friendly with Netzley, a cook at the base hospital and went around the wards with him and his fat spaniel next day, but the gunner was not there. Overnight he had been taken to hospital at Ely.

Twelve-year-old Jim Matsell

From my brother's sleep, I fell into the state,
And I hunched in its belly till my wet fur froze.

Six miles from earth, loosed from its dream of life,
I woke to black flak and the nightmare fighters.
When I died they washed me out of the turret with a hose.

The Death of the Ball Turret Gunner', Randall Jarrell

On the return from the mission to a rail station at Leipzig, Lieutenant Walter
A. Wesley landed his Fortress on the Podington runway and taxied away
to dispersal. While removing guns, the top turret turned and caught the
engineer between the turret and the side of the aircraft, crushing his head
and neck and causing death by asphyxiation.

92nd Bomb Group history 27 February 1945

During the school holidays in the winter of 1943/44 I had just turned
12 and was living in Carleton Rode, a Norfolk village sandwiched
between Tibenham and Old Buckenham. Our house in Norwich had
been damaged in a German air raid. The news that the Yanks in huge
four-engined bombers had arrived at Old Buckenham spread like wild fire
through the village. Our toy rifles and homemade uniforms, with which
we played soldiers, were quickly discarded. We jumped onto our bicycles
and peddled furiously up to the airfield. *They were there*! Some already
parked at their dispersal points and others circling the base for landing.
We watched in wonder as one came to a halt only a few feet from the
hedge by the roadside. The roar ceased as the engines were switched off
and the crew emerged, carrying boxes. They threw oranges over the hedge
for us to catch. We had almost forgotten that the fruit existed. I shall never
my mother's expression of surprise on seeing my orange and being told
that an American had given it to me.

In the ensuing months, Old Buckenham airbase was the centre of
attraction. Many hours were spent watching the Liberators return from
their missions and waiting for a hand wave from the crew as they parked
their aircraft. We each had favourite Liberators. Mine were *El Flako* and
Ohio Silver. When *El Flako* failed to return in November 1944 I was
terribly sad as I cycled home. The aircrews and groundcrews who serviced
the aircraft became our friends and it was thrilling to be allowed to go
inside a Liberator. A year after the distribution of the oranges, we boys
were invited to a Christmas party at the base. More excitement, as we
boarded the trucks and were driven up to and across the airfield to partake
of a *super* meal.

We Each Had Our Favorite "Johnny", Tom Brittan

We had a young boy in the armament shop on the base who had never had
a woman before. It was decided that he wasn't going back to the States
a virgin. We plied him with quite a few drinks and then took him to the
village to see "B— Lil'. He didn't come back for two days.

We had an armourer who never washed because he said the showers were always cold. It got so bad we called him "Stinky"; then we could stand it no more and scrubbed him down, clothes and all.

8th Air Force groundcrewman

When Les and I were in England together, it was in the wintertime. Coal was rationed and the huts weren't always warm. Les came up with the idea of going to the quartermaster and signing out a truck. "That way," Les said, "we can buy a cord of wood for the hut." If we could solve the heating problem ourselves, the Army would let us do it. So Les and I took off.

We had heard about a small town by the name of Wisbitch [sic] and we wanted to know what a town with such a name looked like. So on our way to buy the wood, we headed for Wisbitch. We didn't realize how far away the town was. We arrived there at about twenty minutes after two. The pubs closed from three to five. That didn't give us much time. Wisbitch actually turned out to be a pretty little town, with a river running alongside it. I saw kids getting out of school and walking home. I hadn't seen that in a long time. There were no American soldiers around and no MPs either – just bobbies.

We decided to visit the closest pub, even though it closed at three. Les remarked, "I've got forty minutes to drink beer." And Les made the most of his time. He put them down one after another. I couldn't stand the beer, but this pub also had gin. Talking to the lady at the pub, we told her, "We are looking to buy some wood."

"It's a little late to look for wood. I'm closing now, she said, "but I'll open again at five and there'll be a few girls coming in after work. There's a hotel and restaurant here, too."

Les said he needed to eat some food to settle his stomach. After eating and talking with the local people, we saw that it was already five o'clock. Les suggested we head back to the pub to see what was going on there. We hadn't done a very good job of finding any wood yet.

We enjoyed the girls of Wisbitch a great deal, but by the time we had begun partying with them, it was already dark and we knew we couldn't find our base from there because of the blackout in effect during the war. We knew we were in trouble. We asked the girls if we could spend the night at their place, but they told us that Wisbitch was a small town and everyone knew what went on there. They told us to stay at the hotel and that's exactly what we did.

We showed up back at the base twelve hours late with no wood and no gas ...

Eddie S. Picardo

Just Another Replacement

The radioman from West Texas is returning to his bomber group from a pleasant but dangerous weekend in London. His mind teeters between thoughts of the previous night and impressions from what passes outside the train window. The countryside is crowded – so much unlike the wide-open, sparsely settled land of his birth. He muses about the events of the night before – how he waded past the hustling Commandos at the Circus to a slim, petite girl standing against a wall, put his arms around her waist and said,

"Listen, you're just my size."

And she had hugged him back and replied, "Yes, I am."

The train slows down for the stop at Bishops Stortford. They had shared the night in a hotel that had been hit by a flying bomb the preceding day – everybody knows lightning does not strike the same place twice. The V bombs came over all night long – how he hated that god-awful sputtering noise they made! The buildings in the town are covered with soot from the coal burning locomotives. This morning he'd finally gotten a good look at the girl. A thin girl as he knew, but plain, pale and at least a dozen years his senior – never mind, there wasn't a mercenary bone in her body – a factory worker who had not seen her husband in three years – a soldier in the King's Own. He smiles as he realizes just how he fits into the scheme of things – lousy war – just another replacement – in and out of bed.

Abe Dolim

I had finished my last combat mission and was given a seven-day pass. I hitched a ride on a weapons carrier to Halesworth railway station to catch the London train. I bought my ticket and was going toward the train on the wrong side for proper boarding as it started to move out of the station. There was a track between me and the London train with another train approaching on it. I was 20 and had seen several movies of people catching moving trains. I quickly crossed the track, tossed my bag in an open window, jumped up and started thru after it. I had my head, shoulders and one leg inside with both hands on the window ledge. A young limey in civvies put his hands on my shoulders, pushed me backward and said, "You can't come in here!"

"Why not?" I demanded.

He said, "Because there are women and children in here."

I noticed it was a larger compartment than usual, there were several people therein including a lady with a baby in a stroller.

He repeated, "You can't come in!"

I looked out the window at the oncoming train and wondered if there would be clearance between it and me.

I said, "OK! Throw my bag off."

I jumped down bounded over the tracks just ahead of the train. It must have missed by inches! That Englishman nearly did what the Germans couldn't do in thirty-two missions: kill me!

Ivan Brown

The Bronx gigolo next door has conned the two officers who share a two-man cubicle portion of a Nissen down the line into letting him use their digs while they are in London for the weekend because Maria the Gypsy is coming to spend the weekend with him. Only one or two of the gigolo's close buddies know Maria is a Piccadilly Commando who has such a case on the gigolo she does freebies for him. Sunday morning he bangs into Hut 28 with, "Hey guys, I want you to meet Maria."

The Gypsy surveys the troops still in the sack – spots the nineteen-year-old co-pilot – makes a lunge for his body and the gang all cheer her effort as the virgin tries to climb the walls of the Nissen.

The Gypsy & The Virgin, Abe Dolim

There was one piece of the anatomy much beloved by the flight crews. This was shown by the extreme lengths they went to protect it – the groin. All who had sitting jobs in the aircraft sat on a piece of armour, as most shrapnel travelled upward. All sorts of ingenious methods were devised to protect the "family jewels". The fact that this fragile piece of equipment would avail them little if their head was blown off seemed not to matter; they surrounded it with armour plate. The married men were particularly solicitous in this behalf, although I am afraid we all overdid this piece of business. I think that all these elaborate safeguards were more symbolic than protective. It was just one of the many things we did to foster the myth of our continuity.

Ben Smith

As with all boys during the war, it was the practice to collect pieces of crashed aircraft, ammunition and any souvenirs that could be had. Len Bartram stored all his bits and pieces in the garden shed at the family home at Hunsworth near Melton Constable. His mother, afraid that something was liable to "blow up", threw quantities of his collection away. As his collection of ammunition was diminishing, Len suspected that his mother was throwing the ammo down the well in their garden. She later confessed to doing just this. His biggest worry was that it had contaminated the water. Len added incendiary bombs to his collection after German aircraft had dropped them one night on a local farm. He says, "We spent the next day digging the unexploded ones up with spades, not really considering the danger had one of these exploded."

Visiting the many airfields that were being built near Len's hometown presented a problem for him and his friends. Their only means of transport were their trusty bicycles. There were no signposts during the war and, as he says, "Apart for visit to these airfields I had never really left the village before."

Len and his friends also bicycled to Briston on Friday evenings to watch films in the small village hall. It was a hazardous three-mile journey owing to the black-out and the shield on the cycle lamp, which only cast the light onto the front wheel. Also, there were no rear lights on the bicycle. Len recalls that some of these were carbide lamps. Carbide is a substance which when mixed with water produces a gas and when lit with a match gives off light. It is also volatile and was prone to explode at times!

The projector for showing the films in the hall was powered by a generator, which Len says, "Had a habit of sometimes running slowly and then speeding up again. This made the audience somewhat restless and resulted in the stamping of feet and catcalls. One night the generator broke down completely. A lady in the audience saved the situation by playing the piano for an hour until the generator got going again."

Finding an old bowler hat in a friend's garden shed it was taken to Melton Constable and left in the middle of the road by Len and his mates. They then proceeded to chalk in large letters on the road, "DANGER LAND MINE". Hiding in a large drain, which passed under the road, they watched the traffic and people stop and treat this hat with great suspicion. They dared not stop to see the outcome and ran off, afraid of the consequences.

Len and his friends read all the aircraft books they could get their hands on. All this time the number of aircraft in the area was increasing with the completion of the airfields. Also, the American aircraft were arriving in Britain. Logging these aircraft Len says the number of aircraft seen from January to July 1942 increased from 500 a month to over 1,000. On 16 August 1944 he logged 1,400 in one day. All this spotting got him into trouble at school. He was moved from a position near the windows into the centre of the class because he would always get up and go to the window whenever he heard an aircraft.

Whilst spotting on an Easter morning in 1944 Len witnessed two B-24 Liberators collide and explode in mid-air over Bintree. He says, "I watched the debris fall to the ground. Ten minutes after the collision hundreds of small pieces of burnt paper were falling to the ground. I caught a large piece. This turned out to be a piece of a target map of northern Germany. Danger was never far away in those wartime days.

Dick Wickham

The young fair-haired armourer gunner has just returned from Paris – liberated from the French underground, which has kept him out of the clutches of the Gestapo. He has been assigned further combat duty to complete his tour. His sympathetic buddies crowd around – some of them remember the day he was shot down. One of them says, "Looks like you lost some weight old buddy – guess food was pretty scarce, huh?"

The evader replies, "No, it wasn't that – we ate real good but you know all the young Frenchmen are in Germany working for the Nazis now." He giggles.

His outraged buddies playfully cuff him about the ears.

The Evader, Abe Dolim

Tom Dungar lived at Stone Hill close to Rackheath airfield near Norwich with his grandmother during the war. The short runway was only about 150 yards from the end of their garden. A damaged B-17 Fortress bomber was trying to land on this runway when it touched down short of the runway in the field at the bottom of their garden. It then bounced into the air again, hitting a telegraph pole at the bottom of the garden and snapping it in half. The pilot, realizing that he was heading towards a school, pulled the aircraft round and crash-landed in a sugar beet field, breaking off one of the wheels and stopping just short of the main Norwich road. "Had it kept going," Tom says, "it would have run into a small lodge house where Mrs Kemp lived. She was looking out of the window and saw the plane heading straight for her. At the time she was bathing her small daughter in a tin bath on the table. Thinking that the plane was going to hit the house she lifted the bath with her daughter in it off the table and got under the table with them and 'just waited to die'." Once the aircraft had come to a stop Mrs Kemp and Tom's grandmother ran over to the plane. Seeing that some of the airmen were injured, they tore up their best bed linen sheets and used them as bandages. They also gave them the usual cups of tea. Later the crews' commander at Deopham Green gave the ladies a 'Commendation'. The aircraft was repaired, complete with new engines and a pressed steel track was laid so that it could be towed the short distance to Rackheath airfield. The engines were given a run, but the Fortress had suffered a cracked wing spar and it was consequently scrapped

Rackheath was the home of the 467th Bomb Group, it was known as the "Rackheath Aggies". This came about, Tom thinks, from an incident involving a Liberator that was very badly shot up. Close to the dispersal where the bomber stood were two prefabs. Mrs Aggie Curtis lived in one of them. The pilot was suffering from severe frostbite. After he had been removed from his aircraft to save him he had to have immediate attention and he was taken to Aggie's house where he was placed in a bath of ice-cold water. The Red Cross nursed him in this house for a week until he was well enough to be moved to the base hospital where the pilot fully recovered. Luckily, Aggie's house was in the right place at the right time.

Tom's best friend was Ken who, with his parents, lived in two old railway carriages on a farm near the airfield in line with the main runway. Tom says, "They were only allowed to stay there because the carriages were not very tall. When the aircraft took off they skimmed over the top of these with very little room to spare. The whole place shook. Everything rattled on the table and the pictures fell off the wall. If they were landing they must have been only about 10-15ft above the roof. Luckily for Ken there were no accidents."

Tom and Ken would go onto the airfield and collect the waste from the mess halls using a flat two-wheeled cart pulled by a horse. The "Yanks" ribbed them with such sayings as, "You British will get there yet!" The cart had iron-rimmed wheels, which made a clatter as they drove along the concrete roads. To get onto the base they were issued with a pass, which had a number of stars, stamped on it enabling the bearer to gain access to different parts of the base. In the waste bins Tom and Ken would find large unopened tins of jam and various foods which the Americans had put there for them. They knew that ordinary civilians could not get these. Tom and Ken also bought cigarettes from the GIs at twelve shillings (60p) a carton. Each carton contained ten packets of cigarettes. At times they left with as many as twenty cartons. These were hidden under an old cover, which they sat on at the front of the cart. Tom says, "Had we been caught we would have been shot". One particular day Tom recalls that he and Ken were caught on base without their passes. Being a warm summer's day they had left behind their jackets with their passes in them. They were taken in front of the American commander [Colonel Albert J. Shower, a strict disciplinarian known by the men as 'Black Al']. Tom says he must have been having a bad day because far from being his usual good humored self he tore them off a strip, saying that if he caught them on his base again without a pass, "The sergeant will kick your butts so hard your arse will end up around your necks!" Needless to say, their passes were not left behind again.

Tom and Ken got to know the ground crews quite well. The crews had built themselves a varied assortment of huts out of engine and ammunition cases. When the cows were taken in for milking one of the cows was not milked completely. The purpose behind this was so that Ken and Tom would return in the evening and milk the cow, taking the milk to the Americans in these huts, who had made a cooking utensil out of empty drums which once contained hydraulic oil. The milk was then made into drinking chocolate. "We had a good old fry up of eggs etc. with plenty of cocoa," says Tom. Also they were given a good quantity of American gin which sent them home very merry. They were still only fourteen to fifteen years old.

A party was thrown to celebrate the 100th mission. Beer flowed freely. Tom recalls that he and Ken each consumed two rums, nine bitters and two "Black and Tans". "We could still walk home in a straight line", he says, "It must have been because we had been used to all that gin, which was terrible stuff". One American airman whom Tom says came from Ohio liked to get on the farm. He liked to chew tobacco. Ken's father also liked to have a chew as well. Tom and Ken were persuaded to have a chew. Ken's father said, "Go on boys. It will do you good. It will keep the worms away". Not only did it upset the worms but also it certainly upset the two boys and made them quite ill. As Tom says, "You are supposed to chew and spit but we chewed and swallowed. No wonder we were ill.

Visiting the American Red Cross canteen on the base one evening Tom remembers some Polish airmen that had landed at Rackheath due to bad weather and were staying overnight. In the canteen one was persuaded to play the piano. He says, "I had never heard a man play like it. He played the "Warsaw Concerto" which brought the house down". Next day they left Rackheath with their torpedo carrying Beaufighters to attack some U Boat Pens at Brest. Out of the nine aircraft that left Rackheath, six were shot down and he wonders what happened to the piano player.

Tom had a dog, which used to watch all the aircraft. He says, "my dog was the first to reach the aircraft and would jump on to the wing and treat the crew as if they were old friends".

One morning the Americans were trying to take off on a mission when the fog came down very quickly. Tom recalls that the fog was so dense the Liberator crews could not see the sides of the runway, let alone the end. "The first one away did manage to get airborne", says Tom, "But it whacked the trees at the end of the runway. It staggered into the air and climbed away. A second one hit the same trees but crashed in a small field near to the railway bridge at Wroxham. A third Liberator also hit the trees but got into the air. As it passed over the aircraft that had crashed, the bombs from this aircraft exploded, bringing down the Liberator which crashed right on top of it". A fourth Liberator did get airborne but, Tom says, "It had to be diverted to Manston in Kent. One man from the other two Liberators survived the crash. He managed to walk back to base along the railway line to Salhouse station. Seventeen others though, perished." Having to cycle to work past the field where the Liberators had crashed Tom recalls the terrible smell of the crashed aircraft, which lasted for about a fortnight. "I hated going past the place," he said.

Tom recalls the very strong smell of petrol when aircraft refuelling was taking place. "The air was heavy with fumes and if anyone had struck a match the whole village would have disappeared in the explosion." Working in the small field which separated Ken's farm from the runway, Tom was on the base the night when the Liberators returned from a raid in darkness. He was a messenger for the "Home Guard" and an exercise was being held by the Rackheath and Horsford Home Guard units who were supposed to attack the base, which was being defended by the Americans. As the aircraft were landing "All hell was let loose", says Tom. German aircraft had got into the bomber formations and as they were landing, were shooting them down. One German aircraft tried to bomb the airfield. Tom remembers that one bomb hit the perimeter track. Another came down near the fuel dump and another hit a house near the Sole & Heel pub at Rackheath killing a woman and her daughter. Tom describes the whole incident as "Chaos and Panic". He goes on, "The bombers were trying to land. The airfield was all lit up and as soon as the attack began all the lights were switched off leaving the airfield in darkness. Some aircraft were approaching the runway and had to turn away again. All the ground defences started to open fire. An American airman was killed cycling across the airfield when a German fighter machine-gunned a Liberator, which was being serviced under floodlights. Two Rackheath aircraft were lost in this incident one crashed at Mendham in Suffolk and one at Barsham near Beccles". In all the confusion these aircraft had strayed a long way from their base.

Tom and Ken had a narrow escape one foggy day. They were lifting sugar beet and loading them onto a horse-drawn tumbril; the lights at the end of the runway were showing 'Red', which meant that aircraft were not supposed to take off. Hearing aircraft engines approaching Ken suddenly yelled, "Look out!" A Liberator roared off the runway right over the top of them. Tom recollects, "We dived onto the ground which was a sea of mud. The 'thing' must have cleared us by not more than about ten feet. I remember the huge undercarriage wheels still turning just above our heads and the blue flames from the exhausts. The poor old horse bolted. It smashed the tumbril against the gatepost and broke it off. The side of the tumbril was also broken off. We trudged back to the farm covered in mud and there stood the horse, calmly drinking water at the trough". Tom recalls Ken's father was not very happy about the broken tumbril. He was even less happy about the horse being frightened. He swore at Ken and whacked him across his behind with his belt. "I will never forget that day," says Tom.

Tom remembers the V-2 rocket, from close quarters. He was cycling home from work on day along Mud Lane at Rackheath when he heard what he thought was a flock of pigeon's rush over the top of him. It was in fact a V-2, which landed not far from him and the blast from the explosion knocked him from his bicycle. "A bit too close for comfort," he says.

Dick Wickham

Seething airfield was the nearest airfield to David Walpole's home and was visited by him quite frequently. David had joined the Air Training Corps and, later, the Royal Observer Corps. Seething became his home from home although he should not have been there at all. A "Snowdrop" (Military policeman) that he got to know very well had a liking for fresh eggs. Having some hens at home David could always get a few of these and they became his passport onto the base. He says, "Half-a-dozen eggs worked wonders". He also became very friendly with one of the aircrews and had a bed in their billet. One time when he injured his arm and was off work, he spent the best part of three weeks on the base. David was also taken up on air tests and some training flights. A couple of aircraft that he flew in he remembers were named *Fat Stuff* and *Hello Natural*. One aircraft that his aircrew friends were flying on a mission on a couple of occasions for no apparent reason almost "fell out of the sky". It was decided to try to simulate the same conditions on a training flight. Offered a flight David had no hesitation in excepting a ride. These tests were carried out in the Fens over two canals, which ran parallel to one another. At one time they towed a "Static bomb" to calculate the air speed of the aircraft. It turned out that this aircraft had a faulty air speed indicator, giving the pilot a false reading, which in this case was too high. In fact the aeroplane was flying too slowly and its heavy load and turbulence from other aircraft in formation was causing it to stall and almost fall out of the sky. Although this test could have been very dangerous David could see no danger and in no way did he expect the Liberator to crash.

The night of Saturday 22 April 1944 sticks out vividly in David's memory. He was walking on Seething airbase with a friend. "Being dark the aircraft were coming in with their lights on. I thought it strange that one was coming from a different direction to the others and commented on this to my friend. We soon found out this was a German fighter, which had followed the bombers home and was shooting at them as they landed. One B-24 was set on fire and it crashed in the middle of the airfield. All the crew managed to scramble clear without injury. There was a lot of confusion. Paratroopers had reportedly landed in woods near the airfield. The bombers were still trying to land and were running into one another on the airfield".

In the morning David went to have a look at the damage. He says, "It looked a sorry sight, the burned out bomber which crashed on the airfield had one wing pointing forlornly at the sky. There were three that had crashed in a heap at the end of the runway. One called *Ice Cold Katie* was sitting quite happily on top of another one". As David said, "*Quite an exciting evening*".

More of David's memories were connected with the Observer Corps. He saw V-2 trails and before most people knew much about these, they had been reporting the explosions to the plotting centre. After reporting a fair few of these the plotters decided to ask what they might be. The answer they were given was that the explosions were Mosquito aircraft crashes. When one of the V-2s came down close to the ROC post they decided to go and have a look at the hole. The Mosquito was made mostly of wood but, "As there was a lack of wood to be seen we knew this was no Mosquito crash", says David.

Dick Wickham

Eddie Clarke lived at Toftwood during the war. Driving a lorry around the perimeter track on Wendling airfield one October day in 1943 when B-24 Liberators of the 392nd Bomb Group were taxiing out for a practice mission. And unbeknown to Eddie, they were coming up behind him. Glancing in his rear-view mirror he suddenly saw these Liberators and they were catching him up. He decided that he must get out of their way in a hurry. He turned off the peri track and onto the grass. The pilot of the leading bomber thought Eddie was about to turn around so he immediately braked and slipped the aircraft off the peri track into the soft ground. The Liberator's nose wheel became stuck in the mud and the rear end of the bomber obstructed the peri track holding up twenty other B-24s. A hold was put on the mission. Eddie was brought in front of the group commander, was severely reprimanded and fined £1. He says that he never drove in front of the B-24s again.

Eddie became friendly with an American top turret gunner/flight engineer and used to watch him and the rest of the crew get ready for a mission. The top turret gunner was twenty-nine to thirty years old and quite a bit older than the rest of the crew so he was always known as "Pappy". His aircraft was on a hardstand near to what was known as "Honeypot Wood". Unfortunately for Pappy, just before he was getting kitted out to board the aircraft, he suffered from what was known as the "trots". As there was a small copse near to the wood Pappy and Eddie decided to dig a hole in the ground and place a bucket in it. This became known as the "Honeypot". Before setting out on a mission Pappy was able to spend a few minutes on the bucket. As his aircraft at that time had no name on it, it was decided to paint a toilet on the nose and it was christened *Trips Daily*.

Dick Wickham

Sixteen-year-old George Foster lived at Holton and was employed as a handyman in the American Red Cross canteen on the base, keeping the canteen clean, looking after the fires and keeping them lit, cleaning the toilets and doing any jobs that needed doing. He worked two shifts: 7.00am to 2.00pm and 2.00pm to 10.00pm. At one time he was working a double shift from 7.00am until 10.00pm. This was mostly on Sundays when the older married employees wanted time off with their families. The canteen was open to all the personnel on the base as a recreational center where they were able to obtain such items as coffee, doughnuts etc., there was a games room where they could play billiards, table tennis and the like.

Another room was set aside for reading and writing letters and just generally relaxing.

George remembers that some of their favourite food was fried young rabbit and corned beef fried in batter, which they called "Westons". He also recalls that they were very fond of fried jam sandwiches. The dining room was utilized as a dance hall, especially on Saturday nights when young ladies from the local area were brought onto the base. It was also used by entertainers to entertain the personnel. The stage was made up of beer crates.

At this time the 489th Bomb Group were the residents at Holton. On Saturday, 29 October 1944, their 100th mission party was thrown on the base and George and another handyman were invited. He recalls how interested he was listening to the crews returning from this mission. A fair had been brought onto the base. The cooks from the canteen had made a huge cake with 100 candles on it. One of the hangars was turned into a makeshift theatre with all sorts of entertainments going on. The famous Glenn Miller band had just played in the same hangar. Unbeknown to George, one of the rooms in the canteen had been made into a makeshift dormitory for some young ladies that had attended the party. Early next morning George went into this room. Suddenly, young ladies in various states of undress confronted him. They let fly at him and he had to run for his life. He says, "I had to seek the protection of a 'Snowdrop' (Military Policeman) who suggested that we went round the building instead of through it."

Whilst on night-duty in the canteen George heard a Doodlebug fly over. He says, "It was making the devil of a noise and when it seemed right over the top of us its engine stopped. There was nothing we could do but wait for the explosion. Funnily enough I can't remember hearing the bang but it must have come down locally."

Dick Wickham

David Bacon … lived at Clay Common at Frostenden … Being a farm worker he was classed as being in a reserved occupation. This meant that he was exempt military service but it did not, however, prevent him being sent to work at other farms, like Brook Farm, Sotherton, where he worked for the owner, an old lady and sometimes a couple of Land Army girls. Some of the land bordered Holton airfield where David would watch the American Thunderbolt fighters taking off and landing. "They looked very big and heavy to me, not at all like our Spitfires and Hurricanes," he says. Liberator bombers replaced the Thunderbolts. Gunners in the waist position would wave to him as they took off. "I would try to count the bombers as they went out and count them as they returned, to see how many had been lost. I saw many with their undercarriage shot away crash-land in a shower of sparks, then watch as the ambulances took away the dead and injured. Some poor old boys were in a bad way". One particular winter's afternoon he recalls it was snowing hard and was getting dark. The returning bombers were having difficulty in finding the airfield. Flares were being fired to try to help them. They kept circling around and around. "I thought they would run out of fuel and crash. I will never know how they all got down".

Taking off one morning and forming up into their formations, David witnessed two Liberators touch wings. Both crashed in Henham woods, one each side of the Beccles to Blythburgh road. One crashed into the tops of some pine trees, levelling them all off. The other one crashed into a pit and caught fire. The Halesworth fire brigade was called out to deal with this. As they were fighting the fire the bomb load on the bomber blew up, killing seventeen firemen as well as the aircrew. The crew from the other aircraft was also killed. "I went to the crash site to have a look. It was terrible. There were parachutes and bits and pieces all hanging up in the trees. It was terrible."

Ploughing a field one morning David saw three American officers walking towards him, each carrying a twelve-bore shot gun. They asked if they could shoot a few rabbits. Not really being able to give them permission, he told them it would be all right but to do a bunk if they saw an old lady in the fields. This they promised and off they went. Next day the three officers returned. They thanked David very much. "Much to my surprise they gave me a carton of 'Camel' cigarettes and the biggest cigar that I had ever seen." He cannot recall ever smoking the cigar but his wife had a good laugh when he walked in with it stuck in his mouth. The officers commented that they had a good day and had shot a few rabbits. They had not come across the old lady that owned the land.

The Angel and Lion pubs at Wangford were favourite drinking places for a lot of the Americans and David recalls a couple of amusing incidents involving them. A group of about five or six of them came out of the pub and set out for base. On the roadside a roadman had left his two-wheeled barrow turned upside down. The Americans decided that this would make a good method of transport. The wheelbarrow was turned right way up. With one man at the shafts and the rest on the barrow they set off. Unfortunately, it was downhill. With the weight of the men in the barrow the man pushing it lost control and let go. The barrow shot off down the hill out of control and turned over, throwing its passengers all over the road. Fortunately none of then were injured. "They all had a real good laugh about it and it was something to see."

Gathering wood for the fire one day in Reydon woods to supplement the coal, which was in very short supply, David was showing his small son a Fortress bomber flying over when quite suddenly the whole tail plane fell off. The bomber then dived straight into the ground killing all the aircrew. He thinks it came down near to Reydon church. "It was really amazing to see the tail come off just like that," he says. Long hours were worked on the farm during the war years, the day starting very early in the morning and finishing late into the night.

"Then", says David, "I would have to put some time in during the night with the local Home Guard – very hard days".

Dick Wickham

5

The Four Overs

From all we can hear, the English said we were "overpaid, oversexed and over here", but when you go back they treat you like royalty.

1st Lieutenant James 'Jim' H. Royer Jr, pilot, 446th Bomb Group

Over Here

We were certainly guilty of overdoing a lot of things but it wasn't all our fault. The British complained that we were "overpaid, oversexed and over here." It wasn't our fault the Empire was going broke and perhaps unable to pay their troops more money. As for being oversexed, we had a lot of help from lonely British women looking for some comfort in a battered island of blood, sweat and tears. And I do believe the British were glad to see us "here".

Abe Dolim

Women on Base

Behind our squadron quarters on the base was a vacant lot. In the summertime, English girls would put up pup tents that slept two. And these tents were open for business, if you know what I mean. The authorities didn't seem to care about their presence on base in the middle of a war. I suppose they thought they were good for GI morale or something. Who knows? No one ever really talked about it. They were a wartime reality and that was all.

Personally, I never fooled with them. Not that I didn't want to, but I was too afraid of VD. But some of the other guys did. Every now and then, we would get these girls some food from the mess hall. Whenever we lost a crew, we would have empty bunks in our hut. One morning when we did have some empty bunks, a girl with long red hair let herself into the hut. She asked me if she could sleep in one of the empty bunks. I told her, "Take any one you want." In no time, she was sound asleep. Business must have been good that night and she was looking to find forty undisturbed winks. Funny that to do this she needed to come into a hut with a bunch of GIs!

About an hour after she arrived, someone came into the hut and informed us that the captain was on his way to inspect the place. This only happened about every three weeks. Fortunately, they were never very tough on us, because in three weeks we could lose more than a few crews and some of the guys just wouldn't be around anymore. In that kind of environment they took it easy on us.

In response to the captain's imminent arrival I grabbed an overcoat and threw it over the sleeping woman's head and back, doing my best to cover up her lovely red hair. The captain walked in and someone yelled, "Attention!"

The captain responded with the standard. "At ease." He walked around and, within a matter of seconds, pointed at the bunk where the girl was sleeping peacefully.

I said, "He was on guard duty last night, sir.

He nodded and looked around some more, spotting an empty bottle of Scotch on the floor. He said, "I'll be back in about a month. Do you think you can get rid of that empty bottle by then?"

We answered in unison, "Yes sir!"

Without further ado, he walked out. I always wondered afterwards what the captain would have done, had he pulled the overcoat off our guest. I'm glad I never found out.

Eddie S. Picardo

Dances were the big events in our lives in Hethersett as it must have been for most village girls. There were lots of American servicemen at these dances and it was noticeable that they paid a lot of attention to particular girls. I was very young and innocent and, as a dare with some other girls, I got one of the Americans to dance with me whom I knew was going with one popular girl. That was nearly my downfall; he must have thought I was leading him on. He asked if he could take me home. It was a bit early and I didn't want to go yet but, for some silly reason, I agreed. We didn't get too far down the road before he wanted to take me into a place we called "Kissing Alley". There I almost got more than kissing. He got hold of my wrists and held them so tight I couldn't move. I was frightened and told him that if he didn't let go I'd scream. He didn't, so I screamed and then he let go. The incident really scared me and I was a lot more careful after that.

Nancy Ruska

By and large the people of England had very good reason to feel that we were "Overpaid, overfed, oversexed – and over here." We were well fed, well paid, and the well paid part probably accounted for the oversexed portion of the saying because the men didn't know how long they would be there or, if flying personnel, how long they would live. So they flaunted their money and got any favour they could.

22-year-old Arthur L. Prichard, co-pilot, 467th Bomb Group

I believe the "Four Overs" were justified in many cases. Many of us Americans had come into the service just out of school or college. We never had a paying job before. Suddenly we became better fed and better paid than we had ever been before. Moral restraints from the American family, church and friends disappeared and "everything" seemed to be available for the buying, asking or taking. Boasting seemed to be a popular pastime. We *believed* that America really was what was depicted in movies and the magazines, although down deep we knew that this wasn't so, I guess. It was a bit of bravado that we had to put on to cover some of our insecurities. I can understand the British Tommy's "Four Overs" attitude. I can understand how an occupying military force, loaded with money, eating the best food, dating their women would draw resentment from an army that had been at war for years, received low pay and only adequate rations.

26-year-old William 'Bill' Head, navigator/staff officer, 445th Bomb
Group

The only portion of this saying that can he considered as accurate is "over here". That we were. By our standards we were neither overfed or overpaid. If anything the British soldier was woefully under-paid. Oversexed? It takes two to tango! One thing that I'm sure contributed to this feeling was, the British civilian could have sex in the privacy of his home. The American soldier in England of course did not have this luxury. So it occurred in locations where at times it was observed. Sex is a private matter but the American soldier and his girl unfortunately could rarely arrange it that way.

Twenty-year-old John Rex, 987th Military Police Company

The "Four Overs" arose from jealousy. People who were "hungry" saw the Americans as overfed, people who were "poorer" saw them as overpaid, people who were "reserved" saw them as oversexed and none of this would have happened if they had not been over here, the British thought.

Twelve-year-old schoolgirl Helen Chipperfield

I can't mention Shipdham and Norwich without telling about experiences in both places, though they happened after I'd been there for some time. What I remember about the cities themselves would only take up about a half-page, because my only passes to either place were at night and it was so dark from the blackout that about all I ever saw was the inside of several pubs. I recall several night passes and taking the shuttle trucks into each community during training and later after several combat missions.

One pass into Shipdham was made with our newly assigned replacement ball-turret gunner, having lost our troubled one from an accident. He wanted to make an impression on me and since he had been at the base for some time, already had a steady girl friend. And she had a friend that wanted to meet a Yank, so naturally he thought of me.

It was pitch dark that night, but he knew his way around the small village, so we met both girls just outside their home. I was introduced and a handshake was all the communications we had, as we made our way towards the local pub. (I was bashful and not too great at conversation with the opposite sex. She must have been the same, although we did hold hands on the way there, mostly so we wouldn't get separated in the dark.)

I felt a bit uneasy, unable to see the young lady I was about to enter the pub with, but I was sure my ball-turret gunner wouldn't steer me wrong. I had already convinced myself she would be one of those beautiful blond English girls I had seen so many pictures of.

During total blackouts, it was commonplace for all entrances to have a curtain, to prevent any light leaking out. We were told, "The tiniest of lights could be seen for miles from the sky." When the curtain of the pub was pulled back, I got the shock of my life and I wanted to kill my friend on the spot. My date was at least thirty years my senior and (forgive me) one of the ugliest women I had ever seen. The ugly witches I had seen in pictures and in the movies couldn't hold a candle to this woman. One look at my-used-to-be friend (who had the beautiful English girl I had seen in pictures) told me he wanted to crawl in a hole. And at that point I would have been more than willing to dig for him and cover him up after he crawled in.

Although the pub was crowded, it seemed to me every eye was on my blind date and me. One Englishman nudged me as we passed by and said, "Blind date, eh Yank?"

Even though I wanted to disappear, my upbringing told me this was something I would have to endure, so I ignored all the stares and remarks and tried to make the best of a bad situation. My partner turned out to be a very nice lady, despite her looks. Before the night was over my heart went out to her and soon her looks didn't bother me quite so much. On our way to her house, in total darkness, I actually enjoyed her companionship. What the good Lord took from her in looks, he gave back in a wonderful personality. I couldn't bring myself to kiss her (I often wondered if it was because of her looks, or older sister image) but we enjoyed a warm embrace before parting.

The walk back to the shuttle bus was spent with my ball-turret gunner making excuses and apologies to me, which I accepted. But I told him from then on I'd meet and pick out, my own dates. When we returned to base and everyone asked, "How was your blind date?" We both lied and said, "She was a beauty!"

Lieutenant Dan Culler

The visit of two British ladies to the airbase. They were mother and daughter and both were obviously pregnant. The other parent in each case was, they alleged, a sergeant named "Billy" – no last name specified. But they were not unhappy about Billy's expertise in bed – their complaint was that he had stolen their bicycles and they had not seen him since …

Jackson Granholm

... In the 96th Bomb Wing was one officer who cared nothing for sanity, his own or the world's. He marched to his own drummer and piped his own tune. That officer was the remarkable paddle-foot, First Lieutenant Max Sokarl. Sokarl often told us of his amorous adventures and usually we considered these far-out tales to be pure fables but occasionally Sokarl would stage a demonstration ...

Sokarl invited Irving Goldman and me to meet him at the Bell Hotel in downtown Norwich one evening, saying that we were to meet some noted English philosophers. Like idiots, we went. I had never been in a Norwich hotel before and after seeing inside this one I was happy that I had no need to stay there. Not that it was an unpleasant place but one would surely not confuse it with the Hilton, nor even with the London Regent Palace.

It transpired that the true reason for the evening's invitation was so that Goldman and I could meet Sokarl's paramours in person – not one, but two. Max introduced them to us with considerable amusement. These two, neither a candidate for a beauty contest, seemed to hold the view that there was nothing at all unusual in both of them sharing a room with the "American Lieutenant". To go one better, they issued a thinly veiled invitation for Goldman and me to join them.

Irving and I were both a bit embarrassed by this session. We thought up a good excuse to leave as early as possible and took the bus back to the airbase. I'm sure that as we drifted off to sleep that evening, *sans* the dual companionship that Sokarl was doubtless enjoying, we each prayed in our own fashion that God would help us keep our sanity and that we would not wander away into a flak-happy state, likely candidates for a Section 8 release and a free room at the funny farm.

... Sokarl told stories of fascinating content. He was, by his own modest admission, the greatest seducer of women of all shapes and sizes in the world and now that he was stationed in England he had a contest going with himself. He tried to set a record for getting into some friendly girl's knickers for the least expenditure of money. The Bell Hotel of Norwich was, according to Sokarl, the obvious spot to arrange a tryst, but it also required funding to schedule a room and it required the application of some sneaky tactics to thwart the nosy interference of the proprietors, who were self-appointed guardians of British Victorian morals. So Sokarl, taking advantage of the long, high-latitude, warm evenings of Double British Summertime, would arrange to buy one portion of fish and chips to share with his paramour of the moment, then attempt to bed her down in a convenient countryside haystack. He had, so he claimed, found a particularly eager local nymphomaniac who took to haystacking like a duck to water. In fact, she often could not bother to wait for the fish and chips but would run down the road to the nearest pile of hay in order to get with it faster and with considerable energy. Though this girl was hardly a beauty queen, what with a few missing teeth and all, her performance in the hay left little to be desired. However there was a hitch in Sokarl's love action. Miss nympho had another boyfriend who took exception to her bedding down with Sokarl. This boyfriend was manifestly either a physical or mental cripple or both since it seemed every Englishman who could see lightning or hear thunder was in some phase of military service at the time. But nonetheless, he apparently resented sharing the favours of his darling with some dastardly American officer. So while Sokarl was in the hay, hard at work with his lady partner and doubtless concentrating fully, the spurned boyfriend sneaked up on the opposite side of the great stack and set fire to the hay. By the time Sokarl noticed the towering flames both he and his girlfriend were about to become burnt sacrifices ...

Jackson Granholm

I started dating a girl who lived around twenty miles south-west from our base at Deenethorpe, a good distance when the transportation available was a bike. As Group Bombardier and a Captain I was able to pull a little rank and get pilots on local flights to land at Harrington, a base near her home. I'd jump out with my overnight bag and Jean would meet me outside the airfield with two bicycles. I discovered that her father was a local squire, a gentleman farmer who owned land in the area. The family had five satellite farms and Jean and I would ride out on horses with bread and newspapers in our saddlebags for these places. She was a great girl but I came to realize that she and her family were my intellectual and social superiors. Although they always made me welcome and treated me fine I was conscious of my background, lack of education and different lifestyle. I was a first-generation American, my folk having come from north-east England where my relations still worked as miners and on other manual jobs. This wouldn't worry most Americans but I guess I was too close to my roots not to be class conscious. Jean and her people didn't worry about my background; it was just me. I planned to go to college after the war and come back to England. But with separation we both went different ways and married other people. Even so, we have always kept in touch and remain the very best of friends.

Roy Winn

This incident occurred on a train trip on the way back from Wrexham, Wales, where I had gone visit my brother, Elmer, in the hospital at Penley Hall. (Unbeknown to me, on 24 December Elmer, who was in General Patton's relief force, watched us go over. He was wounded a few days later sitting in his foxhole on the front line when a mortar round went off right behind him. It shredded his helmet and filled his skull bones with bits of steel and rock. Elmer was two to three weeks past his injury and well on the road to recovery with only a little memory loss. He went back to his unit before the end of the war. Forty years later that I learned that Valley and Wrexham had to be within 25 miles of the Hughes ancestral home). At a resort two girls got into the compartment. It was a car with no aisle – only entry was through outside doors at the station. The girls were returning home from holiday. One had very recently been operated on for appendicitis. She was subdued and apparently not fully recovered. The other was vivacious and talkative. Apparently, they had been vacationing at a resort to encourage recovery from the surgery. They were in their final year of school, I guessed sixteen or seventeen and pretty, except the subdued one was pale.

The opportunity of a liaison immediately sprang to mind and I judged the pert one might be amenable, but I didn't know even know how to begin so we talked and talked. The ill girl soon had to wee wee. There was no place and the only waterproof thing that I had was a condom, which I carried in case my crewmen might have use for it. I had never used one. I offered my cap, but was too embarrassed to offer the other until things got almost desperate. Then it was declined. I suggested hanging out the window while I hung onto her, but that too was declined. That need distracted me from any thought of conquest until it was too late. At Manchester, I escorted them from the train and met the mother and father of the recuperatee. They were very nice people. They thanked me for escorting their daughter safely home. They invited me to visit them but they were too far away from the base and I never made it ... I still had more than ten missions to go. I'll never know whether it was the silver dollar from my Dad's birth year which I carried on every mission, not having sex, or learning that I must hate no man which got me safely through the war and home again. I am certain that it was some force far beyond my control. Prayer did not seem to have any effect but listening inside seemed to be my communication medium for survival.

The Girls, 1st Lieutenant Walter F. Hughes, 93rd Bomb Group

Over Paid?

If the weather was bad or our group was stood down, a lot of cards were played in the officers' club: bridge, poker and a game I never learned, called "Red Dog". The stakes must have been high, for both our bombardier, Jerry, and navigator, John, approached me for loans about the middle of each month because they had lost all their money playing "Red Dog". I saw crap games being played in a barracks when there were literally hundreds of pounds awaiting the outcome of the roll of the dice.

On a few occasions we visited Cambridge and ... found a music store, since I wanted to buy a clarinet for myself, having left mine at home in the States. I was studying music in college and clarinet was my instrument. I didn't want to bring my valuable instrument with me overseas and I bought this terrible metal clarinet for £100 – at the time a pound was $4.04 – which was extremely extravagant.

Shortly after we began to fly missions, I was approached by a sergeant who asked if I would like to join the jazz band on the base. Having had a lot of experience in such groups in high school and college, I said, "You bet!"

I was assigned a saxophone part and after a few rehearsals our group played for a dance at another field. Then the sergeant leader announced we were to play at a time I couldn't be there. He looked at me and said: "Are you flying *combat*?"

I said, "Sure."

He said, "I wish I had known that. You're replacing a guy who was shot down."

They found someone who was less likely to need replacing.

Robert L. Miller, pilot, *Son Of A Blitz*, 863rd Bomb Squadron, 493rd Bomb Group. This B-17 was named by pilot, 1st Lieutenant Donald J. Schmitt on hearing of his son David's birth, on 27 March 1945!

At night we usually played cards or shot "craps" in the hut. We didn't have much money and were paid only once a month so we tried to spread our gains over a long period and so usually bet small amounts in our games. On our first combat mission our crew was not bothered by fighters, but a long distance off to our left we did see a group of eleven planes being hit by enemy fighters and seven of the eleven went down, picked off one at a time.

That night, when we got back to the hut, one guy threw his total wad on the floor and said: "Damn, if they're all going to be like this one, *shoot it all*!"

Technical Sergeant Jack Kings, waist gunner

It seemed to me that our enlisted men could not hold onto money from one pay-day to the next. I gathered from what I heard that within a few days of being paid, all their money was lost in crap games or gambling of some sort. I often would loan them just enough money to get the necessities they needed from the PX; anything more would soon be gone …

Shortly before being assigned to the 44th Bomb Group, I happened to meet a very nice girl at a local ballroom in Norwich; her name was Margaret Colman. For some reason, the chemistry was right so we hit it off well from the very first encounter. She worked in a tearoom downtown. She told me she was eighteen years old but I later learned it was sixteen. She was a mature-looking young lady and I was anything but a mature-looking 21-year-old; this helped our relationship. After we had dated a time or two, Margaret asked me to cycle with her to her home to meet her family. Mr Colman's name was William, his wife was reared as a cockney in the East End of London and still, after many years, had a distinct cockney dialect. A lovelier couple has never been born. It was obvious from the first that they approved of me. They welcomed me into their home as if I was their own son. There is no way I can explain what this meant to me during my tour of combat. To have a place where I was welcome as if I were in my own home was a benefit to which no value can be assigned.

There was nothing extraordinary about the relationship between Margaret and myself. We were both young, it was wartime and we filled each other's need for companionship. Our friendship, which could be characterized as young first love, was beyond reproach. We enjoyed walking and cycling together. Before dusk, after the evening meal, we would often take a long walk in a wooded park nearby. Sometimes, on my day off, we would bicycle to the foot of Ringland Hills, taking along my portable radio. After parking our bikes, we would ascend the top of one of the slopes. There we would lie in the grass, listening to the American Armed Forces Radio music programmes. Overhead, the 8th Air Force would be assembling, squadron after squadron, group after group, hundreds and hundreds of four-motor bombers creating a steady rumbling drone. From seeming confusion would come order. This was especially interesting to me as often I was the navigator who directed the assembly when it was my time to lead and other times when I monitored the formation in our black and yellow assembly ship, *Lemon Drop*.

During the Blitz, Mr Colman had bought a small piece of property approximately five miles NE of Norwich. A narrow river flowed on the southern boundary; this was one of the many tributaries of the vast waterways of Norfolk County known as the Broads. Up the slope, away from the river and close to the road, stood a small cabin. When the Luftwaffe was bombing the city of Norwich, the Colman family would bicycle to this retreat. There they were safe but with concern that when they returned home at daylight, their home would be burned or destroyed by bombs. They could see the fires and hear the explosions. Searchlights, anti-aircraft shells and the burning buildings lit the sky.

Many an afternoon, the whole family and I would cycle out to the camp. Mr and Mrs Colman had a tandem bicycle. Mr Colman, wearing his billed cap, occupied the front seat while Mrs Colman, pedalling with all her might, sat on the rear seat. Between them they made a picturesque sight. The older daughter and husband, Fred, often came along. Margaret's bicycle had a wicker basket attached to the handlebars. In it she invariably carried her dog, a small shorthaired terrier. I rode the bike that I kept at the Red Cross in Norwich. Mr Colman almost had a fit when I told him I bought it for £50 ($250) from an airman who had completed his tour of duty. In today's coin, it would be like giving over $1,000. I did have at least two of the three attributes the English credited to all Americans: I was overpaid and I was over there. Money meant nothing to me.

1st Lieutenant John W McClane Jr, navigator.

Over Sexed?

If they got in with a married woman, that was the woman's fault. A lot of these women went after the Yanks for what they could get.

Gladys Lasky, a young married woman who found Americans respectful of her position.

I never met anyone in England who, sooner or later, didn't have a tragic story to share. Becky was no exception. She told me that she had married someone to whom her brother had introduced her when she was eighteen. He was in the RAF, a pilot of a Hurricane fighter. He was stationed in North Africa, flying in direct support of Montgomery's 8th Army, which somehow was driving back Rommel's desert divisions. One day Becky's Hurricane husband was flying low, strafing German troops, when his plane was hit. It crashed into the ground and exploded. There was no reason to ask if anyone had lived through the crash. I knew the answer only too well from so many of my buddies meeting the same end. I didn't know what to say.

He had probably carried a picture of her around with him everywhere. Boy, I know I would have carried her picture if I had been lucky enough to be her husband. I hope he looked at her photo one last time before he got in the fighter the day he died. There was nothing to say to Becky except that I was sorry. I thought to myself, "Who knows, I could be next?" And I could have been.

To follow the rules of my pass to the letter, I should have taken that 5:00pm train back to Norwich. But I was just having too good a time with Becky to leave so early. I said, "What the hell? They can't do anything worse than put me up in the tail of a B-24 and fly over an oil refinery. I'll take my chances with the punishment, but I just can't say good-bye yet to Becky." I had decided to spend three evenings with Becky rather than two. That still wouldn't be enough, but it would be better than cutting short our time together.

That evening we went out to a Jewish restaurant, down some steep stairs to a very small dining room. I can still remember what we had for dinner because there was only one item on the menu. We had chicken soup; a piece of boiled chicken with potatoes and Brussels sprouts. I noticed a beautiful display of Danish pastries and couldn't pass it up. We ordered some, but when we bit into them, it was like eating sand. They were sugarless, because sugar was a valuable commodity for the war effort and people still couldn't get it on the streets of London. We were both terribly disappointed, but Becky blamed herself for not remembering that sugar was impossible to obtain.

We went back to the hotel. Eleven o'clock rolled around and I really had to catch my train back to Norwich. There was a perpetual blackout in London to protect everyone from the German bombing raids, even though German offensive air power had become confined to rocket warfare. All we could hear on the streets of London was the clicking of shoes against the pavements. The last thing Becky said was, "I'll write to you as soon I can."

We smiled at one another, hugged and said goodbye. She left the hotel before me and turned down the street to the right. I left about half a minute after her and turned down the street in the opposite direction. All a sudden, with no warning, a V-2 rocket exploded nearby. V-2 rockets were faster than sound, so there was never any warning that they were coming in, as there was with the V-1 buzz bombs. The explosion lit up the entire sky – it seemed like daylight for more than a few seconds. I fell flat on my back and looked up to see one side of the Piccadilly Hotel weaving back and forth. I got up and ran as fast as I could away from the building. It gradually turned dark again and I ran right smack into a wooden bike rack, tearing my pants and bruising my knees. Those were the only injuries I suffered from the V-2 rocket.

Amid all the confusion, I somehow managed to get to Victoria Station and catch the midnight train back to my base. I arrived once again around 7:00am and sure enough, almost like clockwork, there was the first sergeant waiting to greet me. "Picardo, you are a complete mess! I warned you already about coming back late on passes. You are busted. As of now, you are Private

Picardo." In the wink of an eye I had been demoted from staff sergeant to buck private.

... I never heard from Becky again. There was no way for me to contact her because I had never seen her flat. I knew she worked in an office, but I never really found out where and I could hardly start looking for her without a clue about where to start in mammoth London. She had put her return address on the mail she sent me early on in our relationship, but I never kept the envelopes after I wrote back. I waited and waited, keeping my eye on the mail delivery every day, but she disappeared altogether from my life. I often wondered if the V-2 that had just missed me had gotten her instead? How tragic it would have been if she died just because I wanted to spend one more evening with her instead of returning to base when I should have. The thirty seconds she left before me might have made all the difference. Who knows? I heard later that the V-2 had exploded two blocks away from the Piccadilly Hotel. I wonder if Becky still had a smile on her face?

Life (and Death) in England, Eddie S. Picardo

The Washington Club was smaller, cosier, more intimate than Rainbow Corner, where homesick Yanks could sit on a couch in a fairly quiet lobby and write letters home, get a room for about the equivalent of two dollars, eat in the cafeteria, dance up a storm to a good band and maybe meet a nice girl who wouldn't steal their wallet. The girls were screened. I was one of them for about two years. As a volunteer hostess I learned a lot about the young American male, far from home, 1940s-type. They weren't the kind that we English girls had become familiar with through American movies. Sure, they were from big cities, some were sophisticated, but they were also from every small town and hamlet in the USA. Their average age was 19–23. I met a few who were even younger than 19 – they'd lied about their age. And there were many who had never tasted hard liquor or smoked and had little or no adult sexual experience. At the most vulnerable time of their lives, with adrenaline pumping, raging hormones and all, they were let loose in London, at that period the largest city in the world, with just about every temptation known to man available to them. London was renowned for its wide variety of entertainment as many an unsuspecting GI found out, not always to his advantage. But they learned fast and these were the men who frequented the Red Cross clubs, the "safe havens" from the blackout!

Lalli Coppinger

This particular Red Cross girl wasn't really pretty but there were compensations. Swimming and tennis had made her brown, firm, smooth. She was nearing thirty but bobby socks and a shrill gaiety helped her appear young enough for the 22-year-old pilot. Too, she was one girl among 1,500 men – a circumstantial belle.

They were jitterbugging to a waltz. He said, "Gee, you're smooth." And she answered, "You're kinda cute yourself."

So he was. When he wasn't flying, he was playing cowboy and Indian over the station on a motorcycle. He didn't hang his .45 automatic up in the locker after a mission as the others did, but dashed about the officers' mess with the weapon thumping his leg.

They walked outside by the roses growing on the clubhouse and kissed. He had the kind of skin that grows lobster-red in the course of such interludes. The eyes of both glistened and it would be hard to say whether it was the stimulation of the mating gestures or anticipation.

"Tonight's the night," he said.

"Is everything," she asked, "all fixed up?"

"Yeah, let's get started."

"But not dressed like this," she objected. "I'll go to my room and get into something else and meet you at the place."

She preceded him to the rendezvous out in the green darkness where 334th Squadron parked its planes. She nimbly climbed into the cockpit of a fighter plane. Soon he appeared and she raised up so he could get beneath her in the seat. She thus sat in his lap and he lashed her to him and both of them to the seat with the safety belt. The motor roared and the throttle grazed her brown knee as he gunned the craft down the runway. The fighter pilot and the Red Cross girl were airborne in the moonlight.

Over Cambridge and out to the Wash the couple flew, close-packed in the metal-smelling little cockpit. He pushed the stick forward and they dived on a barge. The girl pressed the red tit on the stick and the wings of the silver craft flashed orange. She felt the craft bucking to the recoil of the six half-inch machine guns. The pilot might not be Gable, but she was certain that few American girls had ever been courted in this fashion.

She gaily turned her blond head to his and kissed him. To express reaction, the pilot stood the plane on its prop. It was not a circumstance which led the pilot to consider such abstractions as the number of court-martial offenses he was committing.

As they taxied up the runway on their return, the pilot's crew chief halted the plane to warn that the squadron commander was waiting. The girl, dressed in GI clothes for disguise, jumped into a truck and sped back to the mess, while the pilot taxied on around to where the major was waiting. The major jumped up on the wing and poked his head into the cockpit without pausing to speak.

"What's up, sir?" asked the pilot sweetly.

"Where've you been and how come these guns have been fired?"

"Well, major, this is my new kite and I just took it out to test-fire the guns."

The major looked into the cockpit again. Then he growled and stalked off to find the joker who had lied that the pilot was flying about with a girl in his lap.

Grover C. Hall Jr

After we landed we would head for de-briefing. Before de-briefing we were served coffee and donuts by the Red Cross girls. At de-briefing the navigators went to one place, the bombardiers another and so forth and we would be asked questions. As navigator, I kept the mission log. I had to record as much of the mission as I could. Which planes went down, how many parachutes, what did I see, any fighters, any fighters destroyed? The questions at de-briefing were meant to elicit responses about these very crucial questions. Particularly how many 'chutes. I tried to count them, unless of course I was being shot at and then I abandoned my pencil for my two guns.

I mentioned the Red Cross girls. There's a lot of good and bad feelings about them. They were very helpful at times but some people resented the fact that they were selling their "wares" and some were getting quite wealthy. One woman went home with thousands of dollars which she had "earned" as a Red Cross girl. There were bad feelings about this. Perhaps some guys felt they should get it for free, rather than pay. No comment.

August Bolino, navigator, 388th Bomb Group, Knettishall

I remember the Liberty Runs and the occasional girl that was smuggled onto the base on the return trip.

Jim Brock

We were on pass for a couple of days and returned in time to meet the Luftwaffe attacking Norwich. We were getting into the Liberty Run trucks to get back to camp when the sirens began to wail. Having heard these before with no attack we just sat in the trucks gabbing. With that there was a new sound a high-pitched loud signal. We quickly learned that this signal meant the city was under attack. Scrambling off those trucks to check out a nearby shelter, we heard out of the darkness, "All right Yanks, run for the bloody shelters." This teed us off and we stubbornly remained outside the shelter.

A grey-haired English colonel advised us to at least take overhead cover, as the ack-ack going up from the guns would return to Earth as a hail of steel. He advised on other things when from overhead we could hear the mournful wail of a diving bomber.

The colonel yelled, "Down on your knees, Chaps, plug your ears with your fingers and open your mouths!" Some did and others just stood fascinated. The bomber pulled out and we grimaced waiting for the explosion. It never came. I said he probably didn't release anything. "On the contrary," said the colonel, "he did ... it was either a dud or a delayed-action fuse." Somebody shouted, "Some incendiaries hit a big building down the block." We ran down to see what happened. There was a large factory blazing fiercely.

Several Yanks were manning fire hoses. A Bobby standing nearby complimented them for helping out. Captain Packer said, "Hell, they're all drunk and having the time of their lives." I looked around and, shoot, all the hoses were taken.

Back at the base we learned that the field had also been hit and it was believed the raid was in retaliation for the successful strike against Vegesack the day before ... a "vergeatung raid" [*sic*] (revenge raid). The fighter opposition at Vegesack was by the kids from Abbeville and a host of others. The attack lasted one hour and forty-five minutes. The target was salvoed dead center. The Jerries lost seven destroyed, one probable and eight damaged. One ship from the 330th was shot down and I was shocked to hear it was *Hot Freight*; a close buddy from Jefferson Barracks, Jack Skall, was the tail gunner. Jack Skall was a great guy. I remember once in JB while standing on a chow line I suddenly heard singing. I thought somebody turned on a radio and it turned out to be Jack Skall softly warbling a pop tune.

Jack saw action in Europe, Oran and Libya. Jack's #1 mission was the 93rd's first ... Lille, France. Jack held the DFC, Air Medal and now would be awarded the Purple Heart posthumously. Our luck was holding but we were hurting with wounded ... Staff Sergeant Dauber was added to the growing list getting hit by flak at Vegesack.

The dazzle of war was rapidly turning to a drizzle of gloom.

March 19 1943, W.J. 'Red' Komarek

Each crewman had his favourite pin-ups on the wall behind his bunk. These were highly prized and usually came from *Yank* magazine. The favourites were Betty Grable, Chilli Williams in the two-piece polka dot bathing suit and Rita Hayworth in a silk negligée, the picture that was in *LIFE* magazine. Sometimes the movie stars sent autographed photos in response to requests. I had one of Ginger Rogers, which she had signed. A friend gave it to me. I still have it. I never saw a lewd picture as this was before pornography killed off the pin-up.

Chick's Crew, Ben Smith

Dear Yank:

I don't know who started this idea of pin-ups, but they say that it is supposed to help keep up the morale of the servicemen, or something like that. Here is my idea of the help it is. In the first place, I would say that 24 out of 25 of the men in the service are either married or have a girl at home whom they respect and intend to marry as soon as this war is over. How many of you GIs would like to go home and find the room of your wife or girlfriend covered with pictures of a guy stepping out of a bathtub, draped only in a skimpy little towel, or see the walls covered with the pictures of a shorts advertisement or such pictures? None of you would. Then why keep a lot of junk hanging around and kid yourself about keeping up morale ...?

I would much rather wake up in the morning and see a picture of a P-51 or '39 hanging above my bed or over the picture of my wife, whom I think is the best-looking girl in the world, than of some dame who has been kidded into, or highly paid for, posing for these pictures.

Pfc Joseph H. Saling, Myrtle Beach AAF South Carolina, *Yank* magazine, 1943

MOST ADMIRED AMERICAN FEMALE (the Whole Package):
Rosie the Riveter. (1943)
The girls who'd dance with you at the USO and make you believe they
meant it. (1944)
The one you were married to – or would be as soon as this damned thing
was over (1945)

Yank magazine

MOST ADMIRED AMERICAN FEMALE
(Limbs only):
Rita Hayworth. (1943)
Rita Hayworth. (1944)
Rita Hayworth, for Christ's sake! ... (1945)

Yank magazine

Now that we soldiers overseas are allowed to select the contents of our
packages from home, here are four types of gift boxes that we would like
to receive:
A – One Lana Turner and one case of Scotch.
B – One Diana Shore and one case of Scotch.
C – One Rita Hayworth and one case of Scotch.
D – One Scotch and one case of Jane Russells.

Cpl James O'Neill, *Yank* magazine, 2 July 1943

Dear Yank:
    We boys do not approve of your very indecent portrayal of the spicy-
looking female in a recent edition of our much-loved and eagerly read
Yank. It seems the intelligent-looking Irene Manning would never pose
for such a suggestive-looking picture ... Is this the much publicized
"Pinup Girl" that the Yankee soldiers so crave? We have our doubts!
Miss Manning is well dressed, but the pose – phew! (Hays office, please
take note.)

Sergeant E.W. O'Hara, Britain: *Yank* magazine, 1943

Dear Yank:
    I do not like your magazine! It is a trade paper for professional soldiers.
I am not a professional soldier. There are comparatively few professional
soldiers. I like civilian life. I like civilian life pictures. So I can see what I'm
missing and fight a bit harder to get back to it. Sad-Sack is OK. I am OK.
We're all OK. But *Yank* isn't.

Cpl W.H. Dundas, Britain. Mail call, *Yank* magazine 1945

The young lady wants to see her boyfriend's bomber. She is curious about the name *Frenesi*. She asks the young sergeant what the name means.

He replies,

"Oh you know, it's from the title of the song, 'Frenesi.'"

She hesitates and says,

"Oh, you Yanks can't fool me. 'Frenesi' means free and easy – and that's the way you like your girls."

Free and Easy? Abe Dolim

There was a particularly shy young air gunner on our crew who seldom accompanied the rest on the wild and erotic forays into London on three-day passes. One night, as he climbed into his bunk, lo and behold, there popped out of a GI blanket one of the ravishing local beauties, ready for fun and games. With a mission in the offing for early the next morning there was little the startled crewmember could do to handle the situation. As a matter of fact, he was in no position to handle anything. He held his fire like a gunner would do when confronted by so unexpected a target. She had come back from town in the back of one of the convoy trucks returning to the base that night. Several of the most daring of the town damsels did manage to smuggle into the base and stowaway in barracks for a wild night making the rounds of the beds. The girl was reportedly last seen dashing off into the adjoining farm fields before dawn and was never seen again.

8th Air Force gunner

According to one rumour, there would be 300 girls from Norwich and another 500 from London and Cambridge. One officer had said, "Confidentially, they have to find their own quarters and absolutely be off the base in *three* days!"

Richard Bing, radio operator

Two stalwart men of the — went down to London on a three-day pass. After a meager meal in the Mostyn Club, they were given tickets to a stage show on Shaftesbury Avenue. They were charmed by the pretty chorus girls, so after the show they went back to the stage door and bravely approached two lovelies as they emerged. The girls were friendly and accepted our two heroes' invitation to go to a pub. There they drank, got acquainted and before the "Time, gentlemen, please" call came, were very chummy. They paired off and one of our American representatives in Britain walked his girl home.

After some kissing and cuddling, our hero asked to come in and stay the night. The young lady said "Yes, I can put you up for the night but you will have to sleep on the floor." Not knowing why, but very excited by the prospect of holding this lovely in his arms, he willingly agreed.

The young lady took him inside. Her mother was waiting up for her and served the pair a cup of tea. Our hero was surprised at how young the mother looked. Then he learned that the father had been killed in an air raid. Finally came time to retire. The young lady took him to a small, empty room upstairs, made a bed for him on the floor and left closing the door behind her. Our hero was puzzled, but he undressed, got into the bed and waited, hoping.

The young lady knocked at the door and entered when he said, "Come in.' His heart beat rapidly to see her dressed in a filmy negligee.

"Are you comfortable, laddie?"

"Not quite," he answered, rising and pulling her warm body to his throbbing heart.

"No, no," she objected.

He kissed her, fondled her and held her tightly, excited at what lay in store for him.

She struggled, pushed him away. "I cawn't," she said, "I simply cawn't. I like my job too much and if I get pregnant I'll lose it."

He tried grabbing her again, but she eluded him and hurried out to her room and she locked her door behind her.

Our hero, very excited, cursed his luck. Then he remembered the young mother. Tiptoeing along the hall, he found the other bedroom, tried the door and found it opening at his touch. Silently, he walked to the bed, slid under the covers and gingerly reached out for the mother. She was reaching out for him. The night went swiftly, full of stars and fireworks. Finally they slept the sleep of contentment.

Came morning and the loving daughter brought in a cup of tea for her mother. Was she surprised to find her mother in the arms of an intrepid Yank! She put down the tea, cursing loudly. She ran out of the room, went to the room where our hero should have been sleeping. Our hero, wakened by her curses, followed despite his nakedness. He found her flinging his clothes out the open window.

Rushing to her he tried snatching the last bit of his clothes from her hand, but was too late. She gave him a dirty look and left. He looked out the window, saw his clothes scattered on the front lawn.

What was he to do? It was getting very bright outside and already there were people on the street, going to work. Forlornly, he walked down the stairs, opened the front door a crack, thought and thought. There was no way but to dash out and put on some of his clothes. He waited for the street to have the least amount of people on it, dashed out and pulled on his pants. An elderly lady gave him a sour look as she walked by, watching him quickly pull on his shirt and stuff it into his pants.

It was a sheepish hero who left that house, never to return, despite the charms of his lady's mother.

Anonymous

Americans made love to English girls in many bizarre places and situations. I had a crewmate who made love to his girlfriend in Hyde Park in the centre of London after the "All clear". Another made love in a shelter; another in the Underground, in the back of taxis, on the ground under the barrage balloons, in the booths of pubs, in London buses, in trains, in haystacks, in farm fields, in hay wagons, in boats on the Thames and in the blackout, without knowing who the girl was.

Forrest S. Clark, gunner

It was his first trip to London and he went with a buddy. On the Tube from Liverpool Street station to the Columbia Red Cross, where they had been advised to book a bed for the night, they sat beside a pretty girl. Being Yanks from a big city, they were not bashful and struck up a conversation with her. She was friendly, smiling and laughing at their jokes and they thought, "Hey, London is pretty good. It is easy to make a hit."

She got off at the same stop as they, Marble Arch and they stepped out into Oxford Street.

"What about a drink, Miss?" one of our heroes suggested.

She smiled and agreed, so they walked up to Edgware Road to a pub. Inside the rooms were full, the talk was noisy, the air full of smoke. But they managed to get three pints of mild and found a seat. Names were exchanged; the Yanks admired their newfound friend's figure while they got acquainted. More drinks, more talk, more cigarettes were smoked. But it was late and the time came for "Time, gentlemen, please". Reluctantly, they drank up and left the pub.

At the corner of the street, our heroes stopped. They couldn't split the girl. What to do? Yanks are never at a loss for answers?

"Don't you have a friend who'd like a good time, Helen?"

"Depends on what you mean by a good time" she answered.

"Well, you know, kinda like, sort of ..." stuttered one of the two.

"Do you mean a party?"

"Yea, a party. That would be fun," chimed in the other Yank.

"What kind of party do you want? An ordinary one, a good one, or a super?" she asked.

"Oh, super, of course," one of our heroes said bravely. After all, they had just been paid and their pockets had plenty of money.

"I'll need money for food and drinks and all that goes with them."

"Name it, baby. What do you need?"

"Twenty-five pounds each should pay for a roaring good party," she replied. "That should do it."

Our friends dug into their pockets and brought out £25 each, handed it over to the young lady. She stuffed the money into her bosom, told them to sit down on the steps nearby and wait for her to go for her friend.

"Don't leave this spot or I'll never find you," she warned. "I'll be back in two secs," she said as she hurried away.

Our heroes sat down on the steps she pointed to and blissfully awaited the return of two young chicks, licking their chops at the thought of a "super" party. They sat there for about ten minutes before a red light came on in their brains. Jumping up, they looked at each other woefully, then dashed in the direction the young maiden had gone. But it was too late. £50 had vanished into the night.

Two sad Yanks went to bed in the Columbia Red Cross that night, each £25 wiser.

                                                                    Anonymous

Looker walked with a slouch and shambled along. He was standing in the barracks as I checked in and fingering a .50 calibre shell in one hand and telling stories of Ploesti to scare the hell out of the new men. But it was the stories he told of Marrakech and Casablanca, on leave with Arab women and prostitutes, that shook up the recruits. He said whole crews had to be grounded because they got VD and others got so drunk they ended up in native jails infested with lice.

                                                                Forrest S. Clark

Word has got around, unofficially as yet, that the group dances may cancelled due to abuse of privileges by certain unprincipled individuals. For instance, a certain squadron has been quarantined because of an unusually high increase in the VD rate suspiciously following the last group dance party. Rumor has it a small group of renegades had stashed a blonde and a redhead in one of the Nissens for nearly a week and that the girls were responsible for all the trouble. This is clearly a violation of military custom and procedures. However, it is true that some of the girls are of questionable background and that it is difficult to arrange transportation for others who live at great distances. Then too, certainly, bad weather does occasion delays of a day or two – at times – and of course accommodations are scarce ...

                                                        Party Poopers, Abe Dolim

Continuous perfect health is an ever-present concern of every member of the crew. Should any one become ill, a substitute would be assigned to fly and function in his capacity. Hangovers and the common cold could ground you and the flight surgeons were ever vigilant. Mental fatigue, VD and other maladies were more easily detected. A sick man does not belong on a team in the sky. I didn't know it until we finished our tour of missions that one of my crew was a dormant syphilitic and experienced airsickness each time we were airborne. The rest of the crew liked this man so well they kept it a secret knowing full well that if I were aware of this condition, I would have had him taken off the crew and found a replacement. My crew was truly a family taking care of each other in the air and on the ground.

                                                                Robert H. Tays

6

The Things A Young Girl Should Know

Her mother never told her
The things a young girl should know.
About the ways of Air Force men.
And how they come and go.
Now age has taken her beauty.
And sin has left its sad scar,
So remember your mothers and sisters,
Boys
And let her sleep under the bar.

How were we to feel about being invaded by thousands of brash, flashy young men [with] too much money to spend? ... They wanted to take over everything and everybody ... too friendly, too quick ...

Barbara Braund, publican's daughter

I think the officers were the worst; they expected payment if they gave you a good time. When you met them at dances they'd often ask you if you would like a day out in London when they next went there on pass. If you accepted they would wine and dine you like you'd never known before and then they would somehow miss the last train home. Next thing they'd be offering to get a room for the night in a hotel. The girl had either to accept or stick it out on a cold station till the morning. It depended on the girl; some gave in to temptation. My mother always cautioned me not to accept gifts from Americans because eventually I'd be presented with the bill.

Rose Searah, who lived at Chatham, Kent

I didn't know that my fourth visit to London was going to be my last. While walking down Piccadilly I spotted a tailor shop. I needed to have some tailoring done, so I stopped in. When I walked in, a bell rang. I was in a comfortable waiting room with a sofa, chairs and a lamp next to one of the chairs. An elderly man walked in and asked me what he could do for me. I showed him my sergeant stripes and told him I wanted them sewn on to my new flight jacket. He said, "Come with me." We walked through a room where a gentleman was being fitted for a new sport jacket.

The elderly man pointed to a small room and said, "Go in there, Yank. There's a young lady who can help you." I took one look at her and right away I was aroused. She was a doll, petite with a slim waist, olive-colored skin, black hair and beautiful features. I showed her what I wanted done. She smiled and said, "That won't take long."

I told her I was from North Hollywood. She wasn't impressed. She said her name was Angela and she was from Portugal. She spoke perfect English with no accent. It was hard for me to believe that she was from Portugal. I was very much attracted to her. I lied and told her it was my first time in London and I hadn't seen any of the sights and really didn't know my way around. She said, "Everyone should visit London at least once." I kept talking, trying to impress her. Finally, when she finished sewing, she picked up the conversation, wondering what it was like flying in a plane and being shot at.

Finally I just came out and asked her, "What do you like to do?" Without blinking an eye she said, "I like to f——." I was shocked; my knees actually buckled. That was one word we didn't use much in those days. I know I didn't. I said to myself, "This girl is not from Portugal." It was early in the afternoon and I told her I was free for the evening and I would like to take her out when she was off work.

Angela agreed, on conditions, which included: first dinner, then a show and I had to pay her one English pound if we went to bed. I figured what better way to get your mind off the war. One English pound was about four American dollars at that time.

To hell with the VD film, I had my condoms. I was to pick her up later when she got off work. I was staying with the guys at a hotel nearby. I tried to get a room at the same hotel, but none was available. I got myself a cab and told the driver to find me a hotel room. He said, "I'll take you to Russell Square. There are always some available there." We found a nice hotel and I got a small room on the second floor. I was all set.

Later I picked her up. She was standing by the shop and looked like she had put on fresh make-up. I told her she looked great. Make-up was hard to come by during the war. She wanted to go to a restaurant called "The American." She said they had good food there. The name "American" was a come-on though. Dinner was the usual piece of meat with boiled Brussels sprouts, potato and unsweetened desserts. But they did serve Scotch.

From there, she wanted to go to a service club where Vera Lynn was appearing. She was Angela's favorite. Vera put on a two-hour variety show with singers, dancers and a comedian. Angela seemed to enjoy it very much. Leaving the club it was foggy and with the blackout we couldn't see much of the city. We got ourselves a cab and headed for Russell Square. When reaching the hotel I was hoping she wouldn't mind the smallness of our room. The air-raid siren started sounding, which wasn't unusual in London.

I don't think she noticed the room. We started playing around and ended up in bed.

When going for our second climax, I heard that sputtering sound that I heard so many times at the base. It was the V-1 Buzz Bomb. All I could think was, "Oh no, not tonight!" Looking up, I heard the sputtering stop. That meant it had run out of gas and was falling. My thing, like a rocket hurrying to be launched from its pad, melted like a candle. Then there was a big explosion, the building shaking, plaster falling down from the walls of our room, plaster dust all over the place. Angela was screaming. I jumped up, put my pants on and opened our door.

Running down the hall, I saw a couple trying to cover their private parts with their clothes. The woman was crying and the guy was white as a sheet. I shut the door. Angela and I dressed. She was shaking like a leaf, wanting to get out of there and away from the building. Once outside, fire trucks and aid cars showed up. Angela held on to me and we started walking. We must have walked about ten blocks before we were able to get a cab. When we got in the cab, she wanted to go to her flat.

We drove across town to her place. She jumped out and barely waved good-bye. How could I blame her? I think you've almost got to lose your life to know how to live it. The cab driver said to me, "She's in bad shape but she'll get over it. We always do. During the London Blitz, I took some of the wounded to the hospital in my cab and even some dead to the morgues."

I said to myself. "This guy has seen a lot."

When I got back to my hotel, the guys were up nursing a bottle of Scotch. They asked, "Where have you been? How did your clothes get so dirty?" They heard there were a few buzz bombs dropping in the area.

"Those Germans," one said, "they always send them over when it is foggy, so the Spitfires can't see them." I told them what had happened. Wide-eyed, they all listened. When I finished they all started laughing.

One said, "I bet at least seven guardian angels have quit trying to protect you!" I told them, "No more passes to London!" If the enemy was going to get me, I wanted to be after we dropped our bomb load.

All of a sudden, it dawned on me, "My God, I forgot to give her that one English pound." I guess I will always owe her those four bucks.

Angela, Eddie S. Picardo

We were on a bomb run, 24 September 1944 and I was discharging "Chaff", the metallic foil strips that jammed radar beams. At the time I was pretty scared, I could hear the thump of flak bursting all around. When I opened one chaff box I found a slip of paper with a handwritten note. It read:

If you've no girl friend to care
Where you roam
And if you've no wife sitting
waiting at home
If you'd care for a pen friend,
Then now is the time

To sit down and write Joy or
Winnie a line.

This was such a surprise I forgot all about the flak while looking at this note and wondering what the girls were like. Back at base I sent them a letter which must have been heavily censored because their reply indicated they thought I was writing from Italy. We were never able to arrange a meeting but I still have the note and the memory of the time two English girls made the air war momentarily stop for me high in the sky over Germany.

Daniel Freitas

I used to date the sister of one of the Red Cross girls. She worked as a secretary for an insurance broker in Norwich. I would usually come by about noon when I was in Norwich and find out if we had a date for the current production at the Theatre Royal. On this particular occasion her boss came out of his office and asked if I would like to go with him to his club for lunch. I accepted with pleasure realizing that this was a real honour. At noon he got his umbrella and bowler hat and we were off to his club located on the top floor of a three-storey building. He escorted me into the club and all of a sudden all eyes were on me and all activity ceased. He made a blanket introduction and the activities returned to normal. There was a pool game going on and I was invited to participate. I explained I was not much of a pool player but they eagerly persisted. I was assigned a partner who I'm sure was the best player in their club and, of course, we won. I could tell that they wanted to talk about the war and how it was going from our view but they were too polite to approach the subject directly. I tried tactfully to give them as much information as I could and they seemed very pleased with what I said. We had a nice lunch and after about two hours returned to the insurance office. Marjorie told me afterwards that I had made a good impression and that I had been accorded quite an honour by her boss. With the class system being what it was in those days I'm sure that had I not been an officer I probably would never have received that invitation.

Lieutenant Al Jones

Eleven-year-old Jean Gauld lived at Ilkesthall St Margarets, a stone's throw from Flixton airfield and has fond memories of the 446th Bomb Group. Her father was the village blacksmith and at times was employed by the Americans to carry out work on the airfield. He had been issued with a pass to get on and off the airfield. Her father took her at times onto the base. To enable her to get on she was disguised and dressed as a boy, her father telling the guards he had brought his son to help him out. She knows that the base personnel were not really fooled by this disguise and her cover was blown many times, but she says, "Never once did they say anything. Many times we were taken to get something to eat and drink at the mess hall." Her father made many American friends, so much so that they were invited to his home. Many of them almost became members of the family. Sunday lunchtime there would be quite a gathering at the table. Jean's mother made them fried chicken. The chickens were raised by Jean's father. She recalls, "The Americans, as is their custom, hardly used their knives whilst eating their meals. This used to upset mother. Treating then just as if they were her own sons, she would crack them on the knuckles and tell them to use a knife." One airman used to like to read whilst eating. This earned him a severe reprimand and he was told that it was rude to read at the dinner table and to stop it.

Captain Olsen used to send Jean his sweet ration. "I had never met him until a Christmas party was held on the airfield for the local children. We were all assembled in a hall. My name was called out and I was told that a surprise awaited me. I was taken outside where Captain Olsen was waiting. There were plenty of hugs and kisses. Father Christmas in his costume passed me and entered the hall to give the children presents. I was a bit perturbed by this and was anxious to be getting back into the hall."

After working on the base her father would be given big tubs of ice cream to take home to the family. Her mother would then take her and the ice cream around the village and give all the children a portion. Ice cream was very hard to get.

Jean's father, naturally, was fond of horses. He was also a cycling enthusiast. He struck up a friendship with an officer from the base with the same interests. And they both cycled on two consecutive days to Newmarket and back just to attend the races. "Being a young girl I cannot remember all the names or the family's friends, just their faces. Most of them were fliers. What I do remember is that the familiar faces would suddenly be missing." One of their friends, a pilot, survived the whole war, only to be lost over the Atlantic Ocean flying home.

"At school in Bungay we were assembled in the hall and the headmaster told us that an aircraft had crashed on our village. My friend who also lived in the village and myself did not wait for permission, but ran out of school and all the way home, a distance of about three miles. The run home I remember very well. If I wasn't crying then my friend was. Nearing home we realised that the bomber had not crashed on the village as the smoke was coming from outside it. When I realised that there was no danger to my family I was relieved of course, but disappointed that there had not been more damage. Reconcile these two thoughts if you can! We were told off by our parents for leaving school. Although there was still a lot of smoke and ammunition exploding, we could not see enough so while all the adults and American MPs were keeping their heads down, we dived into a ditch and crawled I don't know how far. We got very close to the wreck. Cautiously, we peered over the edge of the ditch at the wreckage strewn all over the field. Just then another lot of ammunition went up and down into the bottom of the ditch we went. I thought bullets really do whine just like in the cowboy pictures. That was enough heroics for us. We slid down that ditch faster than we went up it and home for another telling off for getting our dresses dirty. My mother never knew how I got into such a mess."

Dick Wickham

They would almost go into hysterics watching me pick up the fork with my left hand, the knife my right, then switch the knife to the right hand, fork to the left hand to "jab at my meat" while I cut with my knife, then lay the knife down, switch the fork to my right hand and once more jab at my food.

Lieutenant John McClane Jr, navigator

There was not much to do in Sudbury, but we managed to have pleasant evenings. Perhaps it was a movie at the "County" or the "Gainsborough" or a few beers at "The Christopher" or we would play the pinball machine and drink our ales at "The Bear". And sometimes it was a walk along the riverbank and out across the meadows. Often, when I came to town in the morning, Daphne [Cook] was out in the [family butcher's] van and I would leave a letter for her ... and pick up a letter from her, in her sweeping, round, bold hand. "See you Saturday night" – it said. Signed "Dee."

And sometimes, as we were walking across the market, or driving through town, we would hear the sudden din of a car horn and there would be the little white van, a pert smile and a bright blonde good morning. Then again, we were grateful for England, for Suffolk and for Sudbury.

Daphne was not properly a Sudbury girl, for she had been born in London. But she had moved to Sudbury with her mother when she was fourteen and lived in a tiny cottage on the meanest street in town, supporting, with her slim wages, both of them.

I went to dinner on Sundays now and then at Daphne's house. I resisted the first invitation and evaded the second because we had been told how scarce food was in England and how it was rationed and that we should not eat food the civilians needed for themselves. But I could not resist the third, for Daphne wanted me to test her cooking and she assured me that she and her mother had more than enough to eat. "See! I'm getting fat!" she said – hands on hips, slowly turning her slim figure for me to admire.

So in the end I gave in. I knocked at the little cottage door just before noon one Sunday and Daphne called from upstairs for me to come in and make myself at home. I stepped though into the tiny room where Daphne lived and entertained. It was a small room, there were no deep carpets on the floor, or tapestries on the walls – or carved oak furniture. But it was a friendly, lived-in, comfortable room and you felt it was a home. So this was where the beauty hid!

I lounged in an easy chair before the fire and stroked Daphne's huge silky black cat, as Daphne busied herself in the kitchen. Soon the table was set before the fire and heaping plates of food were set down. A run next door to "The Half Moon" resulted in two bottles of ale – and we sat down to a dinner that would have made the chef at the Savoy smile with pride. Daphne was pretty in a blue dress – sitting by the fire on a little stool. We ate and talked and drank and listened to the Sunday favourites on the radio by the window. Up on the hill the bells of St Peter's chimed the hours and half-hours and here in this little room in this little cottage – here, too, was a corner of England.

Only much later did I learn that the meat that had heaped our plates was the family ration for the week and the butter had been most of it and the delicious tarts had consumed the better part of the jam ration. And that too was something to remember.

In England The Girls Are Delightfully Pretty – Erasmus, Robert S. Arbib Jr

When you see a girl in khaki or air force blue with a bit of ribbon on her tunic – remember she didn't get it for knitting more socks than anyone else in Ipswich.

A Short Guide to Great Britain (which was issued to every GI)

The Express, while extremely crowded, was a bit larger, faster, had a passageway, not down the center like American trains, but along one side throughout and from car to car and a lavatory at the end of each car, even though they were perpetually occupied from the overcrowding.

One thing about the war was that it seemed that everyone was involved with something that was somewhere else, because public transportation was overburdened with everyone trying to get from where they were to some other place. But then, everything was in short supply. Even the traditional British reserve.

In search of a bit more personal space I pushed slowly through the tightly crowded corridor, struggling to make my way to someplace that was not so claustrophobic when I was physically trapped in a scene of khaki. I was attacked.

Yes, I was actually hooked by a firm grip onto my left buttock. It was a commanding grasp of a heavyset middle-aged woman in uniform who wore sergeant stripes and the emblem on her cap had the letters ATS, which stood for Auxiliary Territorial Service, the British equivalent of the American WACs or Women Army Corps.

I was shocked by this new experience of being put upon by the aggression of a female. It was scandalous. I was actually more frightened than shocked, since fear is based on the unknown and I certainly didn't know what was going on. I was more familiar with aerial combat, but being groped on the butt by a hefty female British sergeant who had more hair on her upper lip than I; well, it scared me. I was frightened because I was not in control of the situation.

Was I going to be raped?

Was that even possible?

Should I call out for help?

No. She was not alone. She had a dozen other uniformed women under her command, all giggling, shouting – gone crazy like the bobbysoxers at a Frank Sinatra concert that I'd heard about.

The situation was not only scary but humiliating, a commissioned officer of the United States Army Air Force being attacked by loopy and turned-on females in khaki who had captured themselves a naïve twenty-year-old American Lieutenant, spit-n-polished in his Class "A" dress uniform with silver "leg-spreader" wings.

"Roll me over Yankee soldier," the sergeant sang and was joined by the others, "roll me over, lay me down and do it again."

I was bagged!

It was a primitive frenzy of bawdy behavior. I was completely surrounded by a superior number of flighty females, singing their loudest and noticeably enjoying my discomfort.

There was no choice but to abide their merriment and to sweat out the lengthy lyrics from, "This is Number One, the party's just begun ..." through, "This is Number Two, shoe ..." to "Three, his hand is on my knee ..." then "Five, the bee is in the hive ..." until the whole bloody thing should have ended with, "Ten ..." But it rhymed with "again" and the entire thing was repeated with the chorus, "Roll me over Yankee soldier. Roll me over, lay me down and do it again!"

I was happy to see, therefore, another "Yank" enter the melee from the opposite end of the corridor.

Dressed the same as I, his over-six-feet-tall stature and toothy grin made him more attractive than me and he welcomed the attention turned his way. He grabbed almost six women into his arms in a giant bear hug and joined in the chorus of "Roll me over Yankee soldier. Roll me I over, lay me down and do it again."

Lieutenant Truman J. 'Smitty' Smith, co-pilot, 385th Bomb Group,
Great Ashfield, Suffolk, May 1944

Like most young Americans of my time I went looking for adventure and was certainly not afraid of strange places or customs. Naturally the main focus for adventures was the opposite sex. On my first evening pass after arriving at Raydon I went to Colchester. There I got into conversation with a girl I met in the main street and we got along famously. She was married to a British soldier who was serving overseas but this didn't appear to inhibit her. On the next date she brought along her sister who appeared most anxious to meet a Yank. Here I was with two girls and one was all I could handle. So I had to do some fast thinking. We were outside the Red Cross club in Colchester and just then I happened to see a GI come out the door. I told the girls to wait where they were while I walked over to this guy and said "Are you interested in a real nice date?" My luck was in: "Hell, yes!" he said. So I took him over and introduced him to the girls; "This is a good buddy of mine." The truth was I'd never before seen him in my life. Could hardly see him anyway because of the blackout – couldn't see the sister for that matter. Anyhow, these two paired up and solved my problem.

A very nice friendship developed with the Colchester girl but our stay at Raydon was short and the group moved to another base twenty-five miles northeast. Around this time I was sent up to a base near Grimsby on detached service. To get there I had to first catch a train to London. Being a city boy I took the opportunity to look around and decided this was the place for me. So from then on whenever I got my monthly three-day pass I was off to London. Found a nice little pub in Kensington High Street. The blonde at the back of the bar took my fancy and I thought maybe I can do something here. I started by buying her drinks and it was soon obvious the interest was mutual. She was another married girl and her husband was a Jap prisoner, having been picked up at Singapore. We dated regularly and she brightened life considerably for this 22-year-old. Thousands of miles from home and without the inhibiting influence of family and the local community, there was no check on the randy tendencies of a young man at that time of life.

I could usually only get to London once a month and there were attractions nearer to hand. When Jerry started launching buzz bombs from out over the North Sea, the British moved in AA guns around our base, which was close to the coast. Several of these batteries were partly crewed by ATS girls. For we GIs it was like shooting fish in a barrel, there were so many of these girls at the social events. We also discovered the Palais de Dance at Lowestoft, a small port with a heavy Royal Navy presence. Fourteen of us went there to give a buddy who had volunteered for the infantry a good send-off. Whether it was the glasses of gin and orange or the GIs that attracted them I don't know, but we soon found we had a host of the navy girls, Wrens, round our table. However, my local attraction was an air force girl, a WAAF who was based at the radar directional station near Dunwich. She was single, a nice girl and good fun. Yes, I enjoyed my adventures in England.

Art Swanson

Why We Fought

On a chilly, blustery, grey day in May 1939, a young, dark-haired Austrian girl crossed the choppy English Channel and walked shivering down a gangplank to plant her feet finally on "safe" British soil. She was shivering as much from uncertainty and anticipation as from the cold, because she had escaped from Nazi Austria just in time, three months before the start of World War II. Her parents had sent her alone the best way they could, hoping that at least she could escape the persecutions that were then sweeping through Austria and all the occupied countries.

Fortunately, I had studied English as a second language in school and although I had no family or friends in England there were refugee agencies that took me in. As soon as I became old enough I joined the British Auxiliary Territorial Service, or ATS, which was the British Women's Army Corps. In January 1942, the same month the Eighth was formed, I was posted to Bury St Edmunds at Gibraltar Barracks, which was then the headquarters of the Suffolk Regiment.

Life in the ATS was not a glamorous affair. We slept in unheated barracks rooms even when snow covered the parade ground just outside the windows. We piled sweaters, greatcoats and anything else we could get hold of on top of our Army issue blankets at night. Coal was scarce and a small fire in a communal sitting room was the only source of heat during our off-duty hours.

Our main function was to relieve men from behind-the-front duties and free them for combat and other front-line activities. The ATS was run totally by women. Our basic training was administered by women sergeants and women officers ran the whole show. ATS members worked in the mess halls and cookhouses, feeding thousands of troops every day. They were active in offices, warehouses and even on anti-aircraft guns, as long as the guns were located on British soil.

Soon after Pearl Harbor was bombed American airfields sprang up all around us in East Anglia like mushrooms after a rain. The Yanks had arrived! It seemed as if the entire US Air Force was filling the streets, the pubs and the countryside. Each morning at dawn we awoke to the roar of American bombers taking off on missions across the English Channel to the European continent. Sometimes the sky was darkened by formations of Fortresses, Liberators and fighters.

I remember well the airfields, the busy streets, the dances, the bomber jackets and especially the indescribable treats often bestowed on us by the Yanks: chocolate, which in luxury-starved Britain was but a faint memory; oranges; Ipana toothpaste; and scented soaps. But having escaped from our homes on the continent, my friends and I had few illusions about what would happen if the Germans succeeded in invading England; and we instinctively knew that the presence of the 8th Air Force meant more to us than having dancing partners and chocolate treats.

At night the 8th Air Force boys would drift into Bury St Edmunds where weekly dances were held at the Corn Exchange building. This venerable building had, no doubt, never seen such an outpouring of energy. How those Yanks could dance! The walls shook as couples jitterbugged wildly to the popular tunes of the time: "Don't sit under the Apple Tree", "In The Mood", "Give Me One Minute More", "Chattanooga Choo-Choo" and many others. They did this at night, while during the day they were making history, fighting and dying in the greatest war of all time.

At Bury St Edmunds we encountered very few American servicewomen – WACs, nurses, etc. But on visits to London or Edinburgh we met them on the subway, in the streets, or while staying at the service clubs. To us, they were the epitome of smartness and glamour. Their uniforms were cut of fine, dark cloth, compared to our own thick and rough khakis. The names of the towns they came from reminded us of our geography lessons in secondary school in Vienna – Tuscaloosa, Phoenix and San Francisco. And, like their male counterparts, they spoke with accents right out of the John Wayne movies we loved. We also liked Dick Haymes, Betty Grable and *Gone With The Wind*; in fact, almost any movie or movie star.

Frances Nunnally

Uniforms

The term uniform used to identify the attire of the military obviously implies a degree of uniformity on the part of the wearers. While the term was reasonably accurate in describing the attire of infantrymen or sailors, it became a complete misnomer in describing that which was worn by Air Force personnel, particularly the officers.

Unfortunately, the Air Force permitted a wide variety of legal uniforms. It was the "mix and match" philosophy that resulted in the non-uniformity. The basic Class A dress uniform consisted of a dark green belted blouse, a rather decent looking garment, which could be worn with either matching green slacks or contrasting pink slacks. The blouse was usually worn with a cotton khaki shirt and tie. Unfortunately a number favored the monochromatic look featuring green blouse; green slacks green shirt and tie. This outfit gave the wearer a somewhat sinister look which is I guess what turned some of them on. Pink shirts, usually form fitting, worn with a pink, green or khaki tie were also favored by some. Really awful! When not wearing the blouse, the shirt, tie and slacks could be any combination desired. Olive drab slacks were also permitted which further increased the diverse attire of the troops. I typically opted for the green or OD shirt with khaki tie and pink slacks. I felt that these combinations were the most tasteful of the various options.

Then there were the battle jackets, which were originally copied from the British. The battle jacket was typically worn in lieu of the blouse. The US version became known as the Eisenhower jacket since Ike seemed to favor it for everyday wear. His was usually OD worn with OD slacks. The battle jackets were not government issue and were purchased by the officers that desired them.

Unfortunately, I didn't care for the Eisenhower- type jacket since it was not bloused, as were the British models. If you were fashion-minded, you opted for a beautiful bloused type of dark green whipcord material with a red satin lining. With embroidered wings and patches, it went for the princely sum of £130, about $600 in current dollars. It was my only extravagance, but worth every cent in my estimation. The jacket was always worn with pink pants.

For outerwear, officers had three options. An OD overcoat (long), an OD overcoat (short) referred to as a shortcoat and a grayish trenchcoat. I opted for the shortcoat with shawl collar and belt. The shortcoat also came in a form-fitting version with peaked lapels and no belt. I hated it!

Brown leather flying jackets, referred to as the A-2, were issued and were worn extensively when the weather wasn't too cold. Interestingly, the A-2 jacket is again being issued to Air Force flying personnel after a break of many years. The leather jacket could not be worn in the officer's club as I recall. Too cold in the winter, most wore dark green lined flying jackets or an outercoat in those conditions. I wore the shortcoat most times. We also had light green unlined jackets, which were OK in warmer weather, but no good in the typical cold and damp English weather.

Not permitted in England was the khaki summer uniform with khaki overseas or visored cap. Some even did a little mix and match with the summer visored cap worn with the winter uniform. I did on occasion after returning to the States. For that matter, I recall a period where I affected red argyle socks!

Shoes were either brown dress oxfords or reverse calf high GI shoes, which were often worn around the base because of the ever-present mud. At one point I even favored dark brown Indian moccasins, great with the argyle socks.

Headgear for the officers was usually the famous fifty-mission visored cap. The most popular was the Bancroft flighter as worn by Terry in the comic strip *Terry and the Pirates*. Very racy. The grommet was always discarded when the hat was removed from the box. The top was then pulled back into the desired shape. In theory, it reached this shape through the wearing of earphones, but most achieved the shape by immersing in hot water, then molding the hat to the desired shape by hand. The hats soon became rather grungy and most soon looked as if they might well have survived fifty missions. I wouldn't have dreamed of flying without mine, packing it on top of the Gee Box in the navigation compartment when it came time to don the helmet and goggles. I expect some guys had theirs bronzed after the war. Mine went in the trash barrel somewhere along the way.

Flying clothes again varied widely. We were issued long dark green lined jackets and matching lined pants. These were reasonably warm but no match for forty or fifty-degree temperatures usually found at altitude. Before each mission, you could check out an electrically heated suit, shoes and gloves. I always wore the heated suit under the green jacket and pants. You could also have a heated suit cut to look like a uniform. These started to appear when they learned that the Germans were executing downed airmen since they were considered not to be wearing a uniform. I guess they felt that they could do it legally since they looked more like civilians. The early heated suits were in one piece and light blue in color. For obvious reasons they were referred to as Bunny Suits and sure as hell didn't look at all like a uniform.

When flying, I typically wore a rather dirty khaki shirt, rumpled pink pants, the heated suit, gloves and slippers, the green jacket and pants, big leather flying boots, life vest, back parachute, leather helmet and goggles. When encountering flak, I put on or more to the point draped a 35-pound flak suit over me, plus a large steel helmet with big steel earflaps that went over your earphones. You were tied to the airplane by the radio and intercom cords along with the heated suit cord. Since I stood most of the time, I felt extremely ponderous; thus I only grabbed the flak suit and helmet when I thought it absolutely necessary.

Since most crewmen wore the big flying boots which could be expected to come off if you had to bail out, you were supposed to wire a pair of GI shoes to your parachute harness. Thus after you landed you'd at least be wearing a pair of shoes. I put up with the shoes getting in the way for a few missions, then said the hell with it and took them off. The stupidity of this came home to me years later when driving around Germany in the wintertime. I'd look out in a field near the autobahn and picture me floating down in my stocking feet. Ah youth!

I used to envy the RAF pilots for what I felt was a really nifty everyday uniform, consisting of blue pants stuffed into black rubber boots (Wellies), a white turtleneck sweater and bloused battle-jacket. They looked really neat, particularly the boots, which were easily cleaned of the ever-present mud by sticking them under any water tap.

In sum, the Air Force in England presented a rather motley appearance in stark contrast to today's immaculately turned out Air Force personnel. In recent times I had the opportunity to speak to a group of student pilots at Randolph Field in Texas and complimented them on their appearance. I spent a few minutes describing some of the 8th Air Force outfits. I don't think they believed me.

Ronald D. Spencer

My mother drove a "tea-wagon" for the Church Army to Hethel and Seething airfields and we acquired a weekend American "family" of homesick armourers. They joined in everything we did, always bringing a bag full of canned fruit, ham and oranges, as their contribution to our inadequate larder ... In 1944–45, I was working at the hospital in Bury St Edmunds and in the evening, as a volunteer for the American Red Cross officers' club. I learned how to drive (illicitly and at night) on a command car, played endless table-tennis and darts and served up "creamed chicken on toast" almost every night, which was blanched minced rabbit – none of those extremely well-fed Yanks would have knowingly eaten rabbit, so it was a deadly secret! The rabbits came un-skinned from some countryman and those skins eventually altered my life for good. Cured and softened, I made fur gloves, which the Yanks bought for their girlfriends and that money paid for my sea fare to the US in early 1946.

22-year-old Sheila Peal

We gave parties in the Red Cross club kitchen when a crew finished thirty missions – fried eggs ... For the group's 200th mission they sent me out to recruit *girls*. The first place I went a stern WREN officer said, "No." "Didn't the girls have a good time at the 100th mission party?" I asked. I guess they did. She said it was several days before she got them back!

Mary Carroll Leeds, American Red Cross

... The party was a Lulu, a super-duper, a lahlapaloozer. Everyone let his hair down, and some had such long hair that they were blinded for hours ... The excitement began with the arrival in nearby Thetford of a specially chartered train from London. With laughter and giggles 400 girls poured out of the train cars and then had an hilarious time scrambling into the twenty GI trucks from this station which had met the train. It was one o'clock in the afternoon. Throughout the afternoon and evening girls continued to arrive at the airdrome. All told, the enlisted men had a thousand guests. Officers' guests totaled 400.

The large athletic field was alive with color and movement, looking very much like the county fair grounds on the busiest and gayest of afternoons. When the baseball game was over, came the announcement that refreshments – another word for free beer – were now at the disposal of all, and the crowd surged to the long, long row of beer kegs ... Beer in the afternoon was followed by a barbecue supper, which would please a gourmet or a gourmand. The menu consisted of potato salad, tomatoes, pork, chicken, pickles, ice cream and cake. A dance was scheduled in the evening for the EM in Hangar No.1, and a dance for the officers at their club. A floor show was engaged to be staged at each of the dances.

That was not all! Famous speakers and entertainers were asked to highlight the party at the close of the afternoon when they would appear on the outdoor platform ... The afternoon sun was reaching the horizon.

Attention had shifted entirely away from sports and refreshments, was centered upon that platform. Suddenly the sirens of two MP motorcycles were heard approaching the athletic field. In a fit of excitement the Master of Ceremonies implored the crowd to move back, to make way for a motorcar that was bearing the great Field Marshal, Sir Bernard Montgomery, to the platform.

At this announcement the spectators stared with speechless amazement at one another and the crowd, giving way to murmurs and chattering, fell back. As the field marshal mounted the platform his walk and his manner suggested that he was the cockiest man in England, and second, that he was a tough guy. In a moment he had quieted the applauding crowd. His speech was blunt, though kindly at first. Then he had his listeners hanging on the ropes as he told them: "I congratulate you upon the completion of 200 combat operations! But – I understand that actually you have completed only 196 operations. How like Americans.

"I think it is shocking and outrageous to find here British women as guests of Americans, women who have brave husbands and sweethearts fighting thousands and hundreds of miles from comfort and safety, fighting for these women who have deserted them!"

The crowd made a feeble attempt to laugh off these harsh rebukes and began to wish that the great (bah!) field marshal had never come to throw his wet blanket over the party.

It was then that the true identity of this speaker was revealed – he was Leslie Strange, famous British actor and impersonator. Given a little time, the spectators were able to laugh heartily at the hoax.

200th Mission Party at Knettishall, 10 September 1944

By early evening, the field and its surroundings had "took on a festive air." The cooks and bakers had "labored hard and long," while "out on the perimeter, strange shapes were rising, and pits were being dug. Contacts had been made for visitors." The invitation cards read:

THE CENTURY BOMBERS
Cordially invite you to attend a
200 Mission Fiesta Party
AT THEIR BASE
on 30th September 1944
from 8pm to?

The question mark anticipated the fact that days later, visitors were still being combed from the buildings. The carnival was open until 1830 hours and was quite the affair, with different rides, gambling games, a fortune teller, etc. The hot dog, coca cola and ice cream stands were set up around there, free of charge. At 1700 hours the big barbecue was in progress. The meat would have been delicious if it had been cooked better. It was really something to see the girls dig into the steaks, buns, ice cream and hot dogs.

The dancing started in Hangar No.2 at 1900 hours for the enlisted men, with the "Century Bombers" and "Flying Yanks" furnishing the music. They had around 1,500 women on the base – WACs, ATS, WAAFs, WRENs and civilian girls from London, Newmarket, Norwich, Lowestoft, Yarmouth, Cambridge, Ipswich, Bungay, Harleston and Diss. The dance lasted until 0130 hours Sunday morning ...

The officer's dance was in the ground officer's club and part of the enlisted men's combat mess. They had two orchestras playing, but no one seems to know what time their affair ended.

****

October 1st and the party is still in progress ... Of course most everyone slept until it was time to go to Protestant services at 1000 hours or Mass at 1100. Quite a few of the boys after getting up just started right out celebrating again. Had a real dinner of steak, which went over okay with the GIs and women ... The party was a fairly good success from what everybody says. It was supplied with 40,000 cookies, 21,000 rolls, a cake weighing over 200 pounds, 33 gallons of ice cream, 5,500 pounds of steak, 3,405 pounds of pork loin, 935 pounds of hot dogs and cost between $12,000 and $15,000 ...

Vernon Sheedy

Next to the Nissen hut on the Bury–Norwich high road, several hutmates are lying about on the grass trying to get a suntan. A lovely English miss pedals up and stops at the side of the road facing the men at rest. A lieutenant, a co-pilot, goes over to talk with her. Later his buddies ask him what she wanted. He replies that she was looking for Lieutenant— who was shot down last week. Three days later, the men are still trying to get suntanned and the same girl pedals up only this time she has a blanket in her basket. The co-pilot gets on his bicycle and together they pedal down the road along Sir John's woods. This happens several times on succeeding days. Two weeks go by. Then one night his buddies take the wandering lieutenant to the officer's club, get him smashed and then give him the business about the girl. The lieutenant breaks down and blubbers about how much he misses his wife. His buddies all feel like first class heels.

The Lonely Co-Pilot, Abe Dolim

In Belfast, we had our first experience at a British dance hall. The dance floor was very large with several hundreds of couples dancing. Whereas Americans dance in a small area of the floor, maybe getting around the whole floor once to a dance number, the British move fast, almost run, with the whole floor of couples moving like a wheel. Also, they did not like to talk much or carry out a conversation like American couples do. However, they will all burst out in song if a catchy tune gets their attention. This was our first experience of a mixed group singing a song that to us seemed a little off-colour for mixed company. The title was, "Roll Me Over in The Clover".

1st Lieutenant John W McClane Jr, navigator

"The Warrant Officers and Sergeants of the 7th Battalion Highland Light Infantry request the honour of your presence at a Dance, Crown Hotel, Woodbridge, Saturday evening at 8pm."

Thus was worded the invitation to the first and probably best dance I attended in England ... Perhaps the crested invitation over-awed some; perhaps others could not get passes that evening, but when I arrived at the Crown Hotel for the dance, I found myself to be the only American present. The dance hadn't started yet and two sergeants, whose names were Paul and Arthur, welcomed me and escorted me to the bar.

We had whisky all round and the usual questions were asked. "How did I like England? What did I think of the weather? Had I ever been to Scotland?" I was diplomatic and they were friendly and after the second drink we were buddies. The privates behind the bar eyed these sergeants of theirs with respect. Most had been sergeants for a long time, they were old soldiers and they had been through campaigns and then Dunkirk. They were older, steadier, family men, tried and tested. There was nothing haphazard, you judged, about their selection as sergeants.

By ones and twos the young ladies arrived; few if any were escorted and soon the music sounded in the big hall downstairs and we went down to join the dance. Some officers had arrived as guests of their sergeants. They were immaculate in their jackets and kilts, or trousers of dark green tartan. Their brass sparkled and their leather shone; they were polished, correct, formal and yet they had a friendly, comradely word for everyone.

... The dance was fun. There were all kinds of dances new to me, dances which I later learned at the Ipswich dance halls – the "Chestnut Tree" and "Valeeta" and the "Boston Two-Step" and the "Barn Dance," and the rest. And later in the evening the battalion bagpiper came out, resplendent in his full attire, with kilts and white leggings and the big-buckled belt with the sporran dangling in front, the dirk in his stocking and the glengarry on his head. He blew the strains on the pipes and the band joined in, the dancers formed a ring and I saw a Highland Fling.

It was wonderful to watch. It matched any American jitterbug dancing I have seen for agility and excitement and it had the added fun of being a group dance. One diminutive major was a star performer and took the centre of the ring, performing amazing feats of spryness. I watched with mingled admiration and jealousy, for it was plain that I'd never be able to do a real Highland Fling and what's more, even if I could, I'd never look the part.

Dance At Woodbridge, Robert S. Arbib Jr

Dancing with English girls is like learning a new language. She is shy, very patient and tells you she is "thrilled to death".

A lieutenant in the 93rd Bomb Group

Dancing was big in England. Many older people danced, ballroom dancing, as they called it and they were good at it. Waltzes, fox trots and Latin dances were popular. Each city had its ballroom, the larger cities sporting large ballrooms like the Trianon and Aragon in Chicago. The typical English couple was vigorous, taking long dance steps but gliding with some grace rather quickly around the ballroom, all couples going in the same direction, as at a roller rink. Of course, after Americans arrived in England the English girls also took up jitterbugging.

Although one could go to movies or to plays and vaudeville shows, or join the family life of the pub, dances were where most of the entertainment action could be found. During my short Alconbury stay I attended two dances at Cambridge. Besides learning, through Tversky, such a valuable piece of information as how to ask an English girl if she wanted to make love, I became friends with an Iris someone, perhaps Canfield or Cummings. Nine of ten English girls of that vintage were named Iris, Joyce, Joan, Allison, or Jean. An occasional Jacqueline or Jocelyn would also slip in and Beryl was not uncommon. Iris was decently comely, rather quiet, but pleasant and nice. I did not even think, therefore, of asking her to "have a go", not even an "on".

When my assignment to my operational base at Hethel came, which was near Norwich and a county away, I asked if I could return to see her on my first two-day pass. She agreed and that pass came quickly, perhaps within two weeks. I was to stay overnight on Saturday at her parents' house, she said. I took the train from Norwich to Cambridge and Iris met me in the twilight at the station. We ate at a restaurant what would have to be a very modest meal in wartime Britain, perhaps spaghetti, or powdered eggs, beans, or sardines on toast and then proceeded to her house. It was a very small, modest laborer's cottage – her father worked for the railroad.

Of course, I was dressed at my prettiest, an American officer's green (jacket) and pink (trousers) uniform with gold bars, silver wings and perhaps two ribbons (already) being quite dashing and impressive. Quite soon, Iris' mother and father ushered the two of us into the small parlor and sat us on a loveseat opposite the fireplace. Soon a knock came at the door and in came an adult couple from next door. The four older people and Iris' little sister then sat in chairs, flanking Iris and me on either side. Beer was served while we made difficult conversation and while I was being both inspected and admired. The atmosphere became rather uncomfortable; hardly like the airy romantical mood that dancing with Iris had brought on.

I slept fitfully in a tiny bedroom, one that may have been Iris' sister's, without any thrill or fantasy with respect to Iris. The next day was Sunday and before my train left in the afternoon, Iris and I walked around the city and through Cambridge University. I thought about returning to that university some day, not because of Iris, but because I knew that Cambridge was a great university. There was no renewal of romance with Iris and I had noted besides that she had some teeth that needed fillings.

Iris and her parents were lovely, of course, to treat their American guest with all proprietary, but I was uncomfortable and perhaps a bit snobbish, about being taken so thoroughly into the family, as it seemed. But another factor loomed evermore conspicuously in my conscience that Sunday afternoon and as I rode the train back to Norwich: Iris was plain in all ways by comparison with an exciting girl named Beryl whom I had already met in Norwich.

Dancing with Iris, Bob Shaver

In 1944 I was ferrying aircraft out of Warton after completing thirty-three missions with the 93rd Bomb Group at Hardwick. After delivering a plane to a base on the south coast and finding no quarters available, two officers and I went into Brighton looking for a hotel. As we walked out of the train station a taxi pulled up and the girl passenger asked if we were looking for a place to stay. She explained that she had a large home and, as her contribution to the war effort, she offered free quarters to military people since the hotels in town were usually full.

We were quite sceptical but, since she was a conservatively dressed, average looking girl in her late twenties, we figured we had little to lose. The taxi took us to a large, gloomy house and we were ushered into a drawing room with one wall of tennis trophies. The girl introduced herself as Doris Dillon and mentioned that she had been a ranking tennis player before the war.

After giving each of us a room, she offered to call two girl friends so that we could all go out to dinner. We agreed, the girls arrived and we went to dinner with Doris as my date. Doris was pretty far out and seemed to have all sorts of hang-ups. She complained of a toothache and explained that she couldn't go to a dentist because of what happened to her mother. It seems that her mother had a great fear of dentists but was finally forced to visit one because of severe dental problems. She died of fright in the dentist's chair! It was an entertaining evening simply because Doris was so unusual.

We flew back to Warton the next day and about a week later a note arrived from Doris saying that she might come up to visit me. After I replied that I was constantly delivering planes around Europe and was never sure of my time at Warton, she phoned and said that she was coming up next weekend anyway. Just before the weekend, as I was frantically trying to get an over-the-weekend flight, a note arrived from Doris saying, "I can't make it this weekend since I am getting married but how about next weekend?"

I wrote back and said that I was too virtuous to go out with married women.

Tom Parry

7

GI Brides

When war was declared in 1939 I was fifteen years old and lived in a terraced house, 31 Belvoir Street. My aunt was responsible for my upbringing after I'd lost my mother when I was four years old. After passing the school examination in July 1940, I stayed on at Blyth Secondary School for Girls to take a business course in shorthand, typing and book keeping. As the course progressed we went out for job interviews because many of the men were being called up into services and were being replaced by girls. I was ready to leave for school one Monday morning in 1941 when a letter arrived informing me that I was to report for clerical work at the Goods Office, Thorpe Railway Station, Norwich, at 8:30 that same morning. There was no time to prepare: one minute I was a schoolgirl, the next a wage earner! At that time, both my elder sister and younger brother worked in a shoe factory in Norwich. I had worked at the railway station for about a year when the city was bombed very heavily by the Germans in a series of quite devastating raids. Being near the east coast we witnessed many low-level attacks by German fighters and bombers.

On the night of 14 April 1942 the air raid sirens began their mournful wailing at about 11pm. We stirred in our beds waiting for the distinctive sound of the hooter, which told us enemy bombers were getting closer. It went almost immediately as we scrambled from our beds, hurriedly dressed, grabbed our torches and had just began to race downstairs and out to the Anderson shelter in our backyard when the first of many bombs came whistling down. We cowered helplessly on the stairwell in the middle of our house hearing the frightening whine of falling bombs, the awful droning of the enemy planes and the house-shaking explosions. Then the windows suddenly shattered and were blown inwards, closed doors were blasted open, ceilings cracked, then collapsed in clouds of choking dust around us. We were absolutely terrified and were convinced we wouldn't live to see the morning. My sister, aunt and I clung closely together while wondering if my younger brother, who was at that time a messenger for the Air Training Corps, was in the immediate area. It later transpired that he was quite safe. Flares lit up the whole city like daylight as they floated down from the stream of bombers, dozens of swaying searchlight beams, streams of bright tracer bullets were flying, anti-aircraft guns booming defiance. I can't remember how long it all lasted, but it seemed forever.

When we could no longer hear the bombers overhead we ventured out into the street. Shocked, shaken and in tears, we saw an unbelievable scene of destruction. Most of the houses in Belvoir Street were damaged. A few had been reduced to scattered piles of fiercely burning matchwood and rubble. Many people had been killed, even more injured, some seriously. Other areas of the city had been hit much harder. By some miracle No.31 appeared to have been one of the least damaged houses in the street, but it would be some time before we got our windows replaced and all the repairs completed.

The sound of the anti-aircraft gunfire, the strict "black-out", the Air Raid Precaution warden, the food and clothing ration books issued to each family, gas-mask drills, steel helmets at work, sleepless nights in the shelters, shortages, and long queues for everything, and evacuation drills, were a part of every-day life.

Two nights later [on Wednesday 29/30 April] Norwich was again the target for German bombers. More high-explosive and incendiary bombs fell, causing more fires and more loss of life but we were in the comparative safety of our Anderson shelter that night. [In all 69 people died and 89 were injured as 112 HE and machine gun fire rained down on the city] Many people were so apprehensive that they left the city during the nights, sleeping in any kind of shelter available in the surrounding countryside and returned to their homes the following morning. During the next seven or eight days after those two air raids, our family would leave our home after tea, walk out of the city, carrying blankets, pillows, sandwiches, hot tea in flasks and our torches to the Mile Cross bridge and sleep under the bridge each night. We were up early the following morning, walked home and then went to our various places of work. About thirty barrage balloons were installed around Norwich shortly after the two raids and in early May 1942 they proved their worth because here was another, larger air raid, but the bombs fell on the outskirts of the city.

We'd become used to seeing strange-looking service men in Norwich from the early days of the war. When the "Yanks" first appeared in the city in 1942 they were also very noticeable in their different style uniforms, and different language, which was English and yet it wasn't! For example, we'd never heard of a drawing-pin described as a "thumb-tack", a torch as a "flashlight", nor petrol as "gasoline." Completely foreign!

I first met my husband-to-be, Sergeant Herman Canfield of the 392nd Bomb Group, in May 1944 at a friend's home near Wendling. He was a clerk in the Group Operations office. When we got engaged in August 1944, we immediately began the necessary procedures to obtain permission to marry. [Servicemen had to seek the approval of their commanding officers two months in advance of a proposed wedding] He had to write a letter to the chaplain at the base, giving my reasons for wanting to get married and that I was single, of good character, etc. My aunt, who was responsible for my upbringing after I'd lost my mother when I was four years old, also was required to write, confirming her approval and giving her permission. Herman had to go for a personal interview with the Base Chaplain: Why did he want to marry? Was he being coerced in any way? How long had he known me? etc., etc. Then began the waiting while Herman's record was investigated to see if he really was single or married or divorced, etc. We went ahead and planned our wedding for early December, as we knew it would take some time for official permission to filter through. Our banns were published in the local paper and we made all the necessary arrangements with the vicar and the sexton of my local church. In mid-November, permission was granted and we were married at St Phillip's Church in Heigham Road on 2 December 1944. [On Friday 24 November a Liberator bomber from Horsham St Faith, now Norwich Airport, had hit the top of the church tower during a practice flight and careered across the city at rooftop height before crashing, killing everyone on board. Michael Flood and his pals playing in the trees had lost sight of the Liberator but, a short while later; they heard a "bang." "We all thought the plane had come down in the cemetery so we went to have a look. Down Heigham Road, we noticed the wing tip against the church tower. Me being small, it seemed like the whole wing stood there."] The reception was held at "The Volunteer", which was owned by my uncle, Harry Brock. Herman and I went to Blackpool for our honeymoon and as I had a free rail pass and he was a serviceman it didn't cost much."

Herman left Norwich on 3 July 1945 and Nora followed the next February having spent three weeks being "processed" at Tidworth. Nora was given permission by the manager of her office to go out to the train platform and say goodbye to Herman. "It was a very emotional parting, as we really had no idea when we would see each other again. We began our lives together eight months later when after thirteen-and-a-half days of seasickness I arrived in New York to a reception of snow and the bands playing."

Nineteen-year-old Norwich teenager, Nora Norgate. Nora's friend Ivy Seabourne, who was also brought up in Belvoir Street, loaned her wedding dress to Nora to wear. Ivy had married Charles Holston, a cook in the 44th Bomb Group at Shipdham on 20 May 1944. By October 1945 60,000 G.I. brides were still waiting to he transported to the States. Ivy Seabourne sailed for America on the *Queen Mary,* in February 1946. "There were four of us in the cabin with babies. One of the girls was seasick all the time. She couldn't get to the dining room for meals so we would bring her crackers." After arriving in America Ivy and Charles travelled by train for two days to Elkhart, Indiana. Nora found it took some adjustment to become a farmer's wife in Indiana. Nora and Ivy Seabourn now live 180 miles apart, still keep in touch and visit each other two or three times a year

Riding my Raleigh bike on the way to lunch at Horsham St Faith mess I saw a very attractive blonde girl in civilian clothes come out of the Red Cross office. Having taken note, when I got to the mess I found one of the

American Red Cross girls to ask who this attractive blonde I had seen might be. When told she was Joyce, an English girl working for the Field Director, I said that I'm in love already. She asked what I meant and I told her that I came from New York and when young, as my family didn't own a car, I only dated girls who lived no more than ten blocks away from my home. But for this one I'd make an exception. She laughed and said she didn't know if she could get me a date but would try. So she told Joyce about this love-smitten fellow, who laughed and said that she couldn't be bothered. Cupid's lot is not easily cast off so I suggested to the Red Cross girl, Jean Marshall, that if she brought a date I could invite Joyce to make up a foursome for dinner. She agreed and I phoned Joyce at her office and she accepted my invitation. Jean Marshall's date happened to be a young captain who within a year became one of the top fighter aces in England. Joyce and I dated regularly after that and married seventeen months later. I'm glad I made an exception to the ten block rule; the smartest move I made in my whole life.

Jordan Utal, an officer with 2nd Air Division Headquarters near Norwich

I met my future wife at Christmas 1942. We had a few dates and then didn't have any dates, then had some more dates. We had to get permission to marry and I had to fight like hell, 'cause my commanding officer did not believe in marriage. He said, "Have as many common wives as you want, but don't sign no papers and get married." He did his best to talk guys out of it. I was persistent and I got a couple of other officers to talk for me and finally he consented. We finally got the job done, Tuesday, 15 August 1944 at 2.30pm at St Leonard's church in Bedford.

Technical Sergeant Walt Hagemeier Jr, radio operator, 306th Bomb Group

My first experience of Americans was that they were extremely cheeky, very forward, not at all like British boys; but they were extremely friendly. The way I met my husband was in a Peterborough restaurant.

My friend and I had gone in for afternoon tea before work. At the next table were three American servicemen and they started to eye us. We thought they were trying to pick us up so, being well brought up English girls, we would have nothing whatever to do with them. About a month later, when we were back at the same restaurant for tea, one of the American boys who had sat next to us on the previous occasion came in. He marched right over to our table and before we could say yes, no or maybe, he sat down and introduced himself. We were quite taken aback – a British boy would never have pushed in like that. His name was Joseph and my friend thought he was smashing, while I thought he was extremely rude. I didn't encourage him but he found out from my friend that we both worked at the Embassy Theatre. From then on he haunted the Embassy until I finally gave in and dated him. I don't think my Mother thought it would turn into anything serious. In fact she said on several occasions why not bring these American boys home to tea; they are away from their homes and families and must get quite lonely. So we had Joseph and some of his friends on numerous occasions and mother really took to him: thought him the best of the lot. I didn't think that way but eventually his courting won out and I married him.

Iris Falcone

I started to go to dances when I was sixteen years old, and one Saturday night I went with some friends to the Oddfellows Hall at Weldon. The music was Glenn Miller, who was playing live over the radio. There were large windows in the hall with big sills on which we girls put our handbags. While I was dancing a group of Americans came in and sat on the chairs below the window where we girls had been sitting. When I went to get my handbag I said, "Excuse me, can I get my bag." And this Yank says, "I'll think about it." Cheeky so-and-so. Anyway, he asked me to dance to "In The Mood" and later he wanted to take me home. Now we girls had heard lots of things about these Yanks and were not sure what we might be getting ourselves into. So if you let one you weren't sure about take you home then the thing was to take him to the wrong house so he didn't know where you lived. My mother had no time for Americans but a few nights later she came in and said, "There's a Yank walking up and down the road outside with a torch and asking for you." As she was worried what the neighbours would think she told me to go out and ask him to come in. It was the same fellow and it was the start of our courtship.

One night I lent him my brand new bicycle to go back to his base. The next I heard he'd got burned in an explosion and was detained in Lilford hospital. While he was there I borrowed a bike and cycled the thirty miles round trip to see him. When he came out he found my new bike had been stolen, but he promised that one day he'd buy me another one. We married in the summer of 1944 when I was 17 and went to London for our honeymoon. The flying bombs were coming over at that time and we heard one's engine stop, which meant it was about to drop and explode, at just the wrong moment, for it wasn't the only thing that got out of control. Our son was born the following year and we always said he was conceived with a bang. It took Bob a long while to keep his promise, but eventually, after eight grandchildren, he did buy me a new bike.

Stella Auger

I met Lilian Algar at the officers' club dance at Watton in June 1944. Later, I asked Colonel Gray for permission to marry her. He refused! He said: "You have the right to know it's because 90 per cent of overseas marriages in World War I failed. I might hurt 10 per cent, but I'm helping 90 per cent!" I was lamenting to one of my friends at mess when the Judge Advocate, who was sitting there, heard me. He said: "He can't do that. For an enlisted man, yes, but not for an officer – you have the right to petition a higher office." My petition went through channels to General Spaatz, but he was in America on R&R so it went up to Eisenhower at SHEAF. I received a reply, which said: "You have permission to marry Lilian Algar – no-one else."

1st Lieutenant Byron Pollitt B-17 pilot

For a time I went with an English girl called Doris and she took me to her home. Her parents had me to meals and I could see this was putting a strain on their rations. Her father cut the roast in slices that were not much thicker than paper. So I used to try and take something from the base every time I visited. I'd smuggle out gallon cans of pineapple or spam in my knapsack. As you can guess, this made me popular. After a few weeks, when we were alone, Doris's father asked me what my intentions were towards his daughter. "Honorable," I told him, but how could I tell him that you don't take a non-Catholic English bride home to a Polish mother.

Stanley Sajdak

I was dating someone from HQ who entrusted me to American serviceman Keith Vorhees for the dance at Metfield village hall. When I found Keith was a natural at the jitterbug things went from there.

Edith, who married Keith Vorhees

Not many people can bless the day they broke a foot, but I can. Some horseplay during cadet pilot training resulted in this injury, putting me two months behind the rest of my class. Most went to Italy but I eventually ended up at Grafton Underwood. Shortly after my arrival I attended a dance and noticed a pretty girl on her own who appeared to be somewhat uncomfortable. After asking her to dance and getting acquainted, it turned out she had been stood up by another Grafton airman. I then started bicycle missions to Kettering nearly every evening. Couple of weeks later she found out that the man who dated her for the dance hadn't shown up because he broke his foot that afternoon and was in the base hospital. So one broken foot sent me to Grafton Underwood and another broken foot started a partnership that resulted in four children, seven grandchildren and on.

Bill Barnett of 384th Bomb Group

I was one of the first men at Bassingbourn to have an English bride. I didn't drink and was having tea and sandwiches at some function in a church hall and got talking to a girl in British Army uniform, the ATS. When I asked for a date she backed off and said that I better write her a letter to ask! Never met such a shy girl. Well, eventually she accepted my proposal of marriage but the chaplain was told to try and talk me out of it. Don't think the US Army was too keen on its men marrying foreign girls at that time. To complicate matters I was Catholic and my future wife Protestant. In the end the chaplain was convinced I knew what I was doing and said go ahead. The chaplain on my wife's ATS base also had a long talk with her.

Robert Cayer

Got married in October 1944 and we had a room in my wife's sister's house in Sproughton Road, Ipswich. Providing I was in by 7 o'clock in the morning I was allowed to spend the night off base. It was about ten miles from the Hitcham depot to where my wife lived and for the rest of my time in England I cycled there after coming off duty and back each morning. The trip took about an hour and in the cold and the blackout it wasn't easy."

Marion Smith of the 4th Strategic Air Depot

Wartime and particularly the GIs of Chelveston are most fondly remembered by those, like myself, who lived through those times. During the war, I worked with many other local girls at the John Spencer Shoe Factory, in Station Road, midway between the Manor House and the turning to Crow Hill.

My best friend, Florence Goosey, and I would do most things together, including riding our bicycles around the village and along Station Road. It was on a journey along Station Road that, in early 1943, Florence and I met our "first" Americans. As we peddled our way down the hill, towards the A6 and Marsh Lane, we were suddenly confronted by literally "dozens of Yanks". They too were riding bicycles, but had no road sense whatsoever. They had spread themselves right across the road and seemed to at least the same in depth! Each man had his bicycle pointing in every which way, wobbling too and fro! Both Florence and I could not avoid this sea of GIs, our combined speed meant that avoiding action would be useless.

In a flash, Florence and I crashed through the crowd of Americans, both of us shouting, "Get over!" and "Watch out!" This was quickly followed by, "You daft so-in-so's!" Somehow, we managed to miss every single Yank and bicycle upon which he sat. We stopped, looked back and exchanged a few more words, which, I think, were less than complementary to these foreign visitors! I couldn't believe how stupid they had been in not following "our" Highway Code.

From the moment of that very first meeting, my friend Florence and I knew that life in the sleepy village of Irthlingborough was to change dramatically. Overnight the local pubs and clubs were filled with GIs from all parts of the United States. From New England types to deep southern drawls; we had them all. Indeed I well recall the northern Americans, or Yanks, would say he lived on a ranch, where as a southerner, or Reb, would say he lived on a plantation.

The local public houses and working men's clubs would be the meeting places for many of the American servicemen from Chelveston. A common sight was the rows and rows of bicycles, parked outside the Bull pub on the Cross. Later in the evening, around last orders, the GIs would be seen leaving – in some cases staggering – from the bar. They would leap upon the first available bicycle, not necessarily the same one on which they had arrived! Heaven knows how they managed to travel back to Chelveston, especially along strange country lanes in the Black Out!

The village of Irthlingborough, as small as it was, did seem to be a major meeting place for many Americans. For such a small place, we did have a large number of public houses and working men's clubs. Places now long forgotten such as The Drum and Monkey and The Vine along with others such as The Horseshoe, The Bull, The Brittania and White Horse and Sow and Pigs were all well visited. Indeed many GIs would make a point of visiting all of these in one night!

Weekly dances were held in the centre of the village, at the "Harmonic Hall'. The band was made up of local amateur musicians and was very good. Many of the local girls, including myself, would go along to these dances. At that time it was our only real entertainment, other than the local cinema. The Americans from Chelveston soon got to hear of this and so each week there would be large numbers of GIs all hoping to find a date for the night! Usually I would be with a group of girls that I knew well and we usually kept our distance from the Yanks! We all knew, however, we could not afford to be late home. It was certain that I'd be for it from my mother if I wasn't home before midnight!

Occasionally, scuffles would break out either outside the dance hall or a near by pub. Most often it would be between the Americans themselves and often over who would be walking home a particular girl. Having said this, it was good humoured and no real harm came about. In any case, there seemed to be plenty of the American military police about to sort any troublemakers.

They were exciting times. The whole area was overflowing with American uniforms and varying accents.

Not long after the arrival of these "strangers", a number of romances started up, many with girls from our village. All "us" girls at Spencers shoe factory had agreed between ourselves, that we would have nothing to do with them foreigners, or so we all thought. It was with great surprise that my best friend, Florence Goosey, made the announcement; "I'm going out with an American!" Neither I nor any of the other girls could believe it. Florence had given in! It was even more incredible because Florence was so quiet; the quietest girl in our group. Others I could have accepted, but Florence!

Once I'd got over the shock, I asked the questions. "Who?" "Where?" "When?" and "How?" It turned out that his name was Eddie Karczewski and he came from Perth-Amboy, New Jersey. His job, at the nearby airfield at Chelveston, was an MP or military policeman. I can tell you that it took a while for all this to sink in.

Once I had been introduced by Florence to Eddie, I realised all would be well. Very soon I became their unofficial chaperone, going along with the both of them a lot of the time. Often I would protest at this, but they both insisted I be with them when Eddie came visiting.

Bicycles were the preferred and only way to travel about! In those days it was either this or walk. The three of us would cycle about the countryside many times.

Once, Eddie forgot his overcoat and it was raining. As he went to leave Florence's parents' house, Florence's mother offered a raincoat for him to wear. I well remember the three of us peddling along towards Chelveston, fighting our way into the driving wind and rain. As we crossed the bridge, just by the railway station, I turned to see Eddie literally blown up just like a Michelin man! The wind had become trapped inside the front of the raincoat, the buttons straining with tension. We all laughed uncontrollably for the rest of our journey, trying our best not to fall off our bicycles!

As with most of the Americans, Eddie gave the impression of a friendly and likeable person. Being from the New Jersey State, he didn't have such a heavy American accent, as would perhaps be expected by us locals. Until the arrival of the GIs we all had expectations of how an American would be, from watching the Hollywood films of the day. How wrong they proved to be! Eddie seemed more English than American and perhaps this was because his parents were Polish, having moved to America before his birth.

The friendship between the three of us was strong, although there was one occasion when I thought it would be in jeopardy. The three of us had just cycled from Florence's house back to the airfield. Eddie had to return back to camp after a spell of leave. Upon arriving at the main gate, we stopped and began to exchange good-byes for the evening. In a second, somehow Florence lost her footing and slipped head first down a grass slope, into an adjoining ditch! Well, Eddie started to laugh and then I joined in. it soon became very clear that Florence didn't share the joke. It took quite a while to get her to see the funny side of what had happened. I still can see her face, like thunder and us two in stitches of laughter!

The weeks went by and the friendship between Florence Goosey and Eddie Karczeweski became closer. Finally at the end of the war, they became engaged and were married. To show the kindness of Eddie, I recall what he said on the day of the wedding to my best friend. He said "I am just a simple hard working guy, from a hard working family. I'm no millionaire from Hollywood and if Florence has second thoughts and wishes to change her mind then I'll understand". Of course, Florence didn't!

Florence Goosey became Mrs Karczeweski and soon after the war ended made the trip by ocean liner, to her new home in America. This was to be repeated by many others during those few years after 1945.

Eddie Was More English Than American! Joyce Reade

Daddy met him somewhere and invited him to call, but failed to advise Mummy of the fact. One evening this Yank comes knocking on our front door wanting to know if Mr Smith is home? No, but we expected Daddy shortly if he would care to come in and wait? He did and showed up the following eight evenings. It was quickly obvious that Daddy wasn't the attraction. The relationship developed steadily but when we decided to marry, Daddy wasn't very happy. I was the only child and he didn't like the thought of me going to America, which seemed so remote from England in those days of long sea journeys. But Daddy had no one to blame but himself; he was the one who had invited the Yank home!

Cecilia Tripp

I was born in London but at the height of the war my family moved to the coastal town of Ipswich in Suffolk. It was there that I gained my first impression of real live Americans. During the war years I left school at fourteen and went to work. We had long since learned to respect the air raid sirens that told us when enemy planes were approaching. We had learned to live in a world of darkness, as no light could be visible from a home, church, factory, car, or even our bicycles, because a light might lead the German bombers to us. I remember the first time I was fitted for my gas mask, how I galloped home to show my mother, dad and sister. I was twelve at the time, but it soon became second nature to pick up our gas masks and tin hats when we left home. War or no war, life went on. Everyone was doing their part. Our fathers who were too old for the army were recruited into the Home Guard. Women were recruited for Air Raid Wardens. Both men and women were fire fighters.

I was too young for any of these jobs, so I volunteered to work weekends at the YMCA canteen where we served what food we were allowed. All types of food were strictly rationed and there wasn't much variety. We managed to have tea, coffee, toast and sometimes some little plain cakes, which often became the brunt of the soldiers' jokes, as they would say, "If we ever run out of bullets, we can always use these cakes." There were three of these canteens in our town and we worked in whichever one needed us. At first it was only our English boys that used these canteens.

I grew to love my work at the canteen. In a small way we helped to pass time for some of the soldiers who were lonely. There wasn't any dancing or recreation, only a few tables and chairs, an old piano and a radio. It was just a place for the soldier to go to get in off the dark streets, especially if one didn't have much money. I have seen many a homesick soldier come in just to find someone to talk with. There was a friendly atmosphere in our canteens, so if someone could play the piano, it wasn't long before he would be surrounded by a crowd of fellows singing the songs that had literally become a part of England.

English people have always been said to be reserved and stuffy. I believe that it was the singing and laughter that brought us through the six years of war. Never let it be said that Englishmen haven't a sense of humor, because my friend, I know differently. We learned to laugh at Lord Haw Haw, who night after night broke in on the BBC broadcasts to inform the English people exactly where the German planes would be dropping their bombs that night. Invariably some soldier would mimic Lord Haw Haw and everyone would end up in fits of laughter. I always thought that little bit of German psychology backfired, for while these nightly messages were meant to frighten the people, it always ended up as the joke of the evening.

When the first Americans reached our town, it did not take most of them long to find our number one landmark, the English pub. I will never forget the first American soldiers I saw. There were about five of them who were very much under the influence of alcohol. Their hats were on the backs of their heads and their ties were every way but the right way. Two of them were sitting on the kerb and the others were holding up a lamp post. They were singing. My immediate thought was, "If this is a sample of the Americans who have come over to help us, heaven help us".

In the next few weeks the town literally became full of American soldiers. My first encounter with these GIs left the impression with me that they were loud showoffs. They would call, "Hey there Limey," after the girls as they walked down the streets. This used to embarrass us English girls to death.

As time passed, we had servicemen from several different countries coming to the canteen regularly. One Saturday in January 1945 I was working at the little canteen at the railway station. I was alone at the time, as my two girl friends hadn't shown up yet. I was trying to keep a supply of good hot coffee and tea, while washing and drying cups and saucers and waiting on the servicemen who came in. I was beginning to get a little panicky when through the door came an American soldier that I had never seen before.

I remember that at the time it was all I could do not to giggle. This soldier seemed so different from the other Americans I had seen. He was big built and of course his army overcoat made him look all the bigger. His face was round and covered with freckles. Under his cap was the brightest head of red hair that I had ever seen. His manner was very kind and friendly. By this time he had sized up the situation. Only he wasn't looking at me, it was I looking at him. He was looking at the stack of dirty cups and saucers that I was struggling with. I was quite unprepared for his next statement when he asked; "Can I help you wash dishes?"

Well, by the time I could bring my thoughts together he had his coat off, sleeves rolled up and his hands in the dishwater. At the same time he was saying, "I don't mind washing dishes, but I won't dry them." At those words I sprang toward a tea towel, after all what else could I do? We washed dishes side by side for quite a while, hardly saying a word to each other, until a British MP walked in the door and demanded of my dish washer, "What do you think you are doing behind the counter?" It was quite obvious, he was washing dishes. But the MP said, "Don't you know that servicemen are not allowed in back of the counter?" I tried to come to the defence of my dishwasher and the MP softened a little, saying to me, "It's nice that the boy should want to help you out, but orders are orders."

Both my American soldier and I were a little embarrassed by the incident and it wasn't long before the soldier put on his coat and left the canteen. I hadn't even found out anything about him, so I decided to call him "Red."

The next weekend I was on duty at the canteen that was about a block from the Railway Station. My two girl friends and I were kept pretty busy. I turned around from my job of filling up the cake tray to find myself looking into the face of my freckle-faced red head. He said, "Hi! How are you?" I replied with, "Hello, can I get you something?" He said that he would like a cup of coffee and cake. The English coffee is a bottled liquid and you put one teaspoon full in a cup and fill it with boiling water and milk. Milk was hard to get and it was really a luxury if one could have a cup of coffee made with milk. I remembered how nice "Red" had been to help me the week before, so I decided to give him a real treat, a cup of coffee made with milk. I thought Americans like sweet things so I put in two teaspoons of sugar.

I carried the coffee out to him with the same elegance that a waiter in tie and tails would carry in a roasted duck. I thought to myself, "He will be so pleased when he sees the trouble that I have gone to." I put the cup down in front of him and then he spoke the words that shattered me to pieces. "What on earth is this?" "Why it's the coffee you ordered," I said. "You call that coffee? What did you make it with?" he demanded. I told him, "I made it with boiling milk and used two spoons of sugar, which is a luxury these days. Believe me, any English boy would be glad to drink it."

I was unprepared for his next statement. He simply said, "Well, let some English boy drink it then, because I don't want it." Boy, was I hurt! I took my special cup of coffee back and gave him a cup of the regular coffee and cake. I took his money and walked away, thinking to myself that I might have known that he would turn out to be rude like most of his fellow Americans. I thought, "If he comes in again, I just won't speak to him."

The next time he came in, I had my girl friend, Vera, wait on him. He said, "Hi" to me. I felt like sticking my tongue out at him, but I remembered my manners. "Red" came in almost every week for several weeks. I finally decided that I could at least be civil to him. After a time, I was quite surprised when he asked me to go to the pictures with him. You will notice that he didn't say that he would take me.

After I got off at the canteen we walked to the show, where I ended up paying my own way. As if this wasn't bad enough, it seems that he didn't have quite enough money to pay for his own ticket. It was lucky for me that I had enough money. Needless to say, I was beginning to have some pretty mixed feelings about this Yank. He did pay me back and explained that he was just broke that night.

Weeks went by and he would walk me home from the canteen. Though sometimes he would complain that it was too far to walk. We would talk about his plans for the future. I realized that he was just walking home with me because he was lonely. This was all right with me because I was writing to a boy that I had known for years who was now in the Royal Marines.

In the weeks that followed, Red and I learned quite a lot about each other, as well as about the countries that we both came from. My mother invited Red, along with my two girl friends, to tea for my birthday. He said that he would try to make it. But when I came home on the day, he wasn't to be seen. It was then that I realized that I was disappointed because he wasn't there and that it mattered that he hadn't come. Then, as I entered the house, someone grabbed me and said, "Happy Birthday." He had come.

April was upon us. The war in Europe was rapidly coming to an end. Red's Group had been away while their runways were resurfaced. When he returned on April 1st he did not talk much, but did say he had missed me very much. Later that day he asked me to marry him. I thought it was an April Fool's joke. But he asked me again a few days later. I told him that he would have to ask my dad. To this he said, "Why? I don't want to marry your dad." But ask dad he did. Dad wasn't surprised, but my mother wanted to know if I had thought about leaving home, family, friends and customs to move to a new country.

It was a hard decision for a girl of 18 to make. I wondered, "Would love

American officers from Eye (Brome) playing bowls. (via Don & Peggy Garnham)

In a pub near Debach, Suffolk. (via Truett Woodall)

What a treat, a ride in a Jeep! (USAF)

Bemused children choosing presents. (TAMM)

Right: A young lad and his sister put on boxing gloves at the 100th Bomb Group 200th mission 'Fiesta Party' at Thorpe Abbotts on 30 September 1944. (TAMM)

Below: Local children at a base party at Framlingham, Suffolk on 23 December 1943. (TAMM)

Left: A B-17 in the 96th Bomb Group ablaze at Snetterton Heath following a landing accident on 28 December 1944. All of Lieutenant Len Kramer's crew got clear. (USAF)

Below: P-47D Thunderbolt *Damn Yank* in the 355th Fighter Group is craned off the grass at Steeple Morden after a landing accident in November 1943. (Crow)

Wreckage of a burned out Mustang at Steeple Morden. (Crow)

As 1st Lieutenant Lawrence M. deLancey's Flying Fortress was approaching Cologne on 15 October 1944, an 88mm shell penetrated the nose. The denotation killed Sergeant George Abbott, the bombardier and took away the whole upper nose section back to the cockpit windshield. Miraculously, the navigator, though momentarily stunned, was not seriously wounded and was able to make his way back to the flight deck. DeLancey and his co-pilot had to contend with an icy blast, failed instruments, no oxygen and no maps in bringing the bomber down to lower altitude and maintaining control all the way back to home base at Nuthampstead. (USAF)

On 19 July 1944 at Duxford B-17 *Ready Freddie* with two P-47 fighter pilots in the 78th Fighter Group among the eleven men on board clipped the mast on the control tower and the impact sheered off part of the left wing, which folded back and tore off the left horizontal stabilizer and part of the rudder. The B-17 rolled inverted and crashed into a main barrack block. All thirteen men on board were killed and one man in the barracks also died. Two others were badly burned. (78th FG)

On 13 February 1945 B-24J Liberator *A Dog's Life* in the 458th Bomb Group at Horsham St Faith crashed at the junction of Spixworth Road and Church Street, Old Catton, Norwich, during a training flight after two engines cut out at 800ft. All nine crew died and one woman civilian was injured. (USAF)

B-17 *Just A Snappin'* in the 100th Bomb Group, which crashed at Ludham, Norfolk on 8 October 1943. (TAMM)

A B-24 Liberator crash near the 100th Bomb Group B-17 Fortress base at Thorpe Abbotts. (TAMM)

A briefing in progress.
(USAF)

Colonel Irving Rendle,
Commanding Officer,
392nd Bomb Group
at Wendling, Norfolk,
gives bombardiers
a time 'hack' for
synchronisation of
watches at the end of
briefing, June 1944.
(USAF)

'Gentlemen, your
target for today is ...'
(USAF)

Ground crew in the 93rd Bomb Group pose for the camera in front of *Eager Beaver*. (USAF)

Ground crews working on the Twin Wasp engines of a B-24 Liberator. (USAF)

Ground crew carefully hoist a bomb into the bomb bay of a B-24 Liberator. (Charles Nigrelli)

and understanding be able to outweigh the loneliness for the folks you know and country you love when it came time to leave them?"

We were married on May 20, 1945 in St Clement's Episcopal Church in Ipswich.

A Fine Romance. The wedding of Clarence "Red" Burnett from Chillicot, Illinois and Lillian Lambert was witnessed by bridesmaids Betty Lambert, Lily Harbour, Vera Harbour and Gwen Pallant. Norman Protsman from Cincinnati, Ohio, Red's friend from the 860th Squadron, 493rd Bomb Group, was best man

... I shared a barracks room with five other officers, one of whom was Tommy Volkman, a navigator from Streator, Illinois. It was a small world. Tommy was the son of the hamburger proprietor at whose shop my family always stopped after a movie during the period between my fifth and tenth years of age and when we lived at Long Point. Tommy was killed very shortly after beginning his tour of duty in late September and five others of the total of fifteen of my roommates in that same room were also killed before seven months had lapsed. Tommy's death was not owed to the Germans; rather, his plane collided with another of our group as it was assembling into formation over a rendezvous point in England. I supposed that his parents were told that he was killed in action and technically he was, but dammit, where was justice in this world and where was there need for this kind of accident?

Only a few weeks earlier I had gone with Tommy on my first visit to Norwich, a city of 126,000 persons and the county seat of Norfolk. Norwich was the principal liberty city for much of the 8th Air Force. Personnel carriers left Hethel and dozens of other bases each evening after supper and discharged their cargo at Norwich, seven miles distant. They returned at 11pm.

Tommy and I went to the Samson and Hercules, a dance hall that had been the city indoor swimming pool but was floored over for the duration so as to serve as a more interesting diversion for the American guests and so as to make more money for the city. By custom, the S&H had become the entertainment haven for officers; the enlisted men mostly habituated another dance hall. Tommy had already been there and he would show me how to operate, he said. True to his word, he soon ushered me up to two girls and made wholly proper introductions to a blonde, Elaine Burt and a brunette, Beryl Burt. We talked and soon Tommy was off dancing with Elaine, probably without then knowing that she was a French-Canadian girl, née Toujenon, married to Beryl's Royal Air Force brother, Joseph Burt. Left with Beryl, I soon got the idea that it would be quite proper for me to ask her to dance whether or not she wanted to.

My god, could that girl dance! At 5ft 4in, 118lb and wearing a Sunday type of black dress, she was the smoothest thing with whom I had ever danced. Music and rhythm were in her soul and it mattered not whether the rhythm was set to waltz, tango, fox trot, rumba, polka, or Glen Miller's "Roll out the Barrel". Her rhythm moved from her soul and through her body, the two blending perfectly as one. There was magic in the feel of her waistline and small of her back – mad enchantment in the gentle pressure of her breasts against me.

I was charmed and from that evening I do not remember the exact sequence of events. I asked Beryl for a date and she accepted but I still had my prearranged Cambridge visit to carry out. Whichever came first, Beryl proved to be my only remaining interest. On our date we were to meet at the Red Cross club on Bethel Street. She lived a mile farther along, on Earlham Road. From there we would go to the Samson and Hercules. I stood outside the Red Cross entrance and kept watch along Bethel Street. She approached in a rust-colored tailored suit, her head held erect. She wore her hair in the then popular style, loose waves and rolls beginning atop the head and sweeping asymmetrically downward and backward to partially reveal one ear and to end above the shoulders.

Her face was not that of a Hedy Lamar and not even that of a Virginia Taylor. Rather, it had a distinct character, especially around her eyes, there exhibiting an extra crease. Her nose was straight and the whole appeared ever so slightly haughty, which yet was overlain with a wistfulness that said both she wondered if I would be there and was glad to see that I was. Years later, my father said her face was regal, like that of Queen Elizabeth.

To me Beryl was a vision approaching. She had class, she had sex, she had character and she had me. We walked on hand in hand to the Samson. We danced and we talked with no one but ourselves. We invented a silly but exhilarating "Around the World" game. It was we who were going around the world, perhaps dancing our way. Beryl had gone to the best of public-run English schools up to her age – then 18. The English system was a competitive one in which only the highest ranking students were passed on to the next school that was not terminal in itself; lower ranking students on reaching teenage were assigned to terminal schools that emphasized vocations.

Beryl could speak French ever so better than I could speak Spanish, she knew geography, she had culture, she was gentle and she was genteel without fuss. She had won the Queen Mother's Prize for needlework in a national competition for school children in her age group.

With Beryl I became an excellent dancer beginning with my first two evenings with her, but only with her, no matter how long and with whom I would dance for many years to come. By myself, I was poor at "hearing" the rhythm, but with Beryl I could do all but a few things, such as the polka. It was Beryl, of course, who made me look good. In new things for me, the Latin dances, for example, I only appeared to lead with the standard man-woman embrace. It was the ever-so-gentle pressure of her hand on my one shoulder or arm and of her torso against my enveloping arm that showed me in time the next transition from one rhythmic glide to another or from sway to asymmetric rest to sway.

Her rhythm and musical sense blended as one with the sensualism of her almost perfect 5ft 4in, 118lb body. With that, I had only a momentary setback: I noted that her lower legs were a bit thick. I thought of sturdy English oak saplings! But never mind, I was already in hog heaven! Actually, "hog heaven" was not high enough; my euphoria had a more lofty, refined and ethereal quality.

Intermission came. We ate currant cake and drank orange squash. The cake was not sweet except for the currants. The exigencies of war had made sugar scarce but evidently currants grew in Britain. Cake and squash were but momentary objectives of Intermission. Beryl and I walked to the outside and fresh air in an alley beside the Samson. There in the dim twilight I sat on a stone wall, my legs apart and Beryl stood facing me. She came close to me and we kissed searchingly. I unbuttoned my tunic, she put her arms around me on the inside and I enfolded her body to mine longingly and gently. We continued to kiss, giving our beings to one another. We trembled to think of what had come between us. We returned to the dance and "Tango of the Roses" became our song, just as Beryl had become *my* girl.

During this pre-Christmas period, Beryl and I saw each other frequently, perhaps two or three times a week and became more and more devoted to each other. We scarcely frequented the pubs but went to the Samson and Hercules, to other dances at Black Friars Hall, to movies and to stage productions, including Ed Sullivan kind of vaudeville. I had fallen into a regular kind of sweet and sour routine. The daytime missions were the sour part. One always came home fatigued from a mission. Tension from combat was one part, but the other was the many hours (sometimes as long as eight or ten hours) of sitting in cramped positions with heavy backpacks and flak suits (part of the time) and, often, having to go the rest room. The latter could be done on the plane, but the trial was so great that one suffered in hope of reaching base before being overcome.

The thought of seeing Beryl conquered fatigue, however and I sometimes got on the personnel truck after supper on a mission day, rode the seven miles to Norwich and saw Beryl, the sweet part. On days when I hadn't been awakened before dawn to prepare to fly, I remained in my bunk, sacking it out and skipping breakfast. At about 11am I headed for the officers' club, there to read the American Armed Forces newspaper, *The Stars and Stripes*, and two or three London newspapers. These newspapers always carried news of the 8th Air Force's raids over Europe on the days following the raids. They carried some detail, including how many planes, tonnages dropped and targets, but we crewmembers were not allowed to mention the raids in our letters home, not even that we or our group had been on a raid. My means to keep my parents informed, nevertheless, was to clip the articles from *The Stars and Stripes* and send them home without comment.

On non-flying days I repaired to the mess hall at noon and then returned to the Officers Club. I called Beryl to talk about anything and everything during her lunch break. Later in the afternoons, bridge was a popular diversion for me, or when the weather was nice, a softball game or bicycle riding. This sweet part of my days, therefore, was in great contrast to the flying days. The war was in my consciousness, but it just didn't fit well with the lazy days.

I originally called Beryl "Bebe," as did her friends, the name being in reference to the initials standing for 'Beryl Burt." Bebe (Bee-bee) asked her mother if she could bring me to their home at 140 Earlham Road to meet her. For a time her mother said no. She didn't want any bleedin' rich love-'em-and-leave-'em Yanks in her house! In time however, Beryl defied her mother, Eva Nellie, and brought me in unannounced, sometime in October or November. Her mother recovered nicely after being startled and it was not long before I gained her confidence. She liked me and I was different, she agreed, as Beryl had told her. "Being different" meant that I hadn't asked for the treatment that we Yanks often expressed, riding back to camp at night, a bit high in the personnel carriers, with these rollicking song words: "Roll me over in the clover, roll me over, lie me down and do it again!"

Eva and I did hit it off and she could josh with the best of them. She liked a good time – why not have one when one could, considering that Britain had then been at war for five years, had been bombed terribly, suffered great loss of life (especially in the military) and was slowly starving in the sense of national nutrition? Beryl and I accompanied her to the neighbourhood pub a few times and there I did assimilate a feeling for one the principal social outlets for the English people.

Eva, when I first met her, was separated from Beryl's father, Joseph Henry Burt, who then worked in the Bristol aircraft industry as an engineer and in the city by that name. Like all able-bodied Britons, Eva was employed in a war-critical capacity, just as was Beryl, in Britain's scheme of total mobilization. Beryl was an accountant in the Norwich telephone ministry but I have forgotten Eva's job.

Sometime in early 1945 it became evident to Eva that Beryl and I were very much in love, or should have been, considering the amount of time we spent together. One winter evening as the three of us sat watching a coal fire in the fireplace of their dining room, Eva said that she wanted to talk seriously with us; particularly me. It wasn't right, she said, for us to go on this way without Beryl or her knowing my Intentions. We probably ought to plan marriage – we had already discussed it – or stop seeing each other. Then, half-joking, she said, "I'm giving you a choice, you have to marry either Beryl or me."

The Sweet and the Sour – Beryl and the War, Bob Shaver, who married
Beryl Burt on 25 May 1945

Ken and I met at an amusement pier in Southwold, England, in May 1944. I stepped on a scale to weigh myself and before I could open my purse, a stranger put a penny in the coin slot. This stranger was later to become my husband. We were both in uniform. I was a Wren in the Women's Royal Navy. Ken was a Sergeant Flight Engineer in the 489th Bomb Group at Halesworth. When he offered to take me for a steak dinner, which was a rarity, I could hardly say, "No." On the following days, when Ken was off duty, he would cycle the eight miles from Halesworth to Southwold to see me.

Shortly after we met, I found out that I was to be transferred to the Royal Navy College at Greenwich, London. When I telephoned Ken and told him I was to be transferred, he said, "You are the girl that I'm going to marry." This was not a proposal, but a declaration. I don't recall agreeing to this, or saying yes.

After my transfer, we spent our available time together in London. My family found Ken acceptable and made him welcome at our home in Sutton, Surrey. It may have been my family that said "yes" for me, as I soon found myself preparing for my wedding. We might have been married sooner but the 8th Air Force required a ninety-day delay. It was during this delay, on 3 August 1944 that Ken had occasion to bail-out of his B-24 Liberator bomber over Caen, France. A few days later, he returned from France with the parachute that saved his life. That parachute enabled me to have a "White Wedding" which would have been impossible in those days with clothing rationed. My Aunt Winn, a dressmaker, made the parachute into a beautiful wedding dress, utilizing 65 yards of white nylon.

Ken and I were married on 28 October 1944 in St Nicholas Church in Sutton, Surrey. Ken's best man was Sergeant Warren Diffendall, just released from the hospital recovering from flak wounds. My Maid of Honour was my cousin Mavis and my bridesmaids were my sisters Beryl and Jean. My family gave us a wonderful reception at our home. Most of my cousins, who were in uniform at the time, were able to attend. It was an occasion we will long remember. We had a one-week honeymoon in Halesworth. One afternoon during that week, a friend of Ken's, a Sergeant Gladish, came to see me. On a mission to Munich, he had seen Ken's aircraft going down with an engine on fire. Gladish was trying to break the bad news to me, but he delayed so long that Ken returned before he got around to it.

Betty Koch

Buzz and I were married in 1945 after he got back from England. We were both from the same small town, but hadn't dated until he came home from overseas. I'd written to several service men during the war and was familiar with V mail and sometimes mail had been censored and blacked out. So when Buzz showed me his diary he'd kept during months in England and I saw some of the things inked out I thought they were military secrets. For years I thought that until one day it dawned on me they weren't military secrets, but his secrets. After all those years to his dismay he couldn't remember what he'd blacked out ... or so he said!

In 1972 we made a trip to England: our first since 1944. On a bus tour to Cambridge the tour guide told us we'd stop at "Dorothy's Tea Room" for lunch. Buzz said that was where he used to hang out when he was on liberty. My response was, "You can tell your Mother you hung out in a tea room, but I'm not that gullible." Well, when we went up the stairs and I saw the bar and the ballroom in the back, I had to eat my words.

Kay Fielding

As a country boy who spent his youth in Burlington, a small town in North Carolina, all of my time in England was one of enlightenment and pleasure. My father passed away in 1935 in the middle of the Depression when I was thirteen, leaving a family of ten plus my Mom. Brother Tom was two-and-a-half years older, very intelligent, self-starter and go-getter. He paid every penny of his way through college and saw to it that I followed him. This was where my interest in wartime England began. Tom and I were in college at North Carolina State in Raleigh and in ROTC (Reserve Officer Training Corps) so when war began in 1939 we had more interest than average people did. At the same time the Battle of the Atlantic was beginning and as a result, British ships were being repaired at Norfolk, Virginia. This was my first real opportunity to meet real "furriners" and they had to be British. Periodically, there would be noticeable groups of them visiting our campus.

I joined the Air Corps on 23 September 1942 and received my wings on 8 February 1944. After being trained as a fighter pilot, I arrived at Prestwick about 3 August 1944 and then went to Stone for a few days processing. Then it was to Goxhill near Hull for check out in a Mustang. I went to Wattisham about 1 September and was assigned to the 434th Fighter Squadron, 479th Fighter Group. It was a hell of an exciting time and learning just how war takes place was an eye opener. My first mission was Berlin on 28 September.

I appreciated being lucky enough to live in permanent quarters with steam heat, 60ft to the mess and a beautiful lounge. There were Liberty Runs to Ipswich in the black out – hair-raising! – to attend movies. The first and subsequent trips to London were out of this world for a little ol' country boy. I had always been a people watcher so you could imagine me in London. My first trip to London was with three others and only one had been there before. We arrived there in the dark at Liverpool Street station and took our first taxi to the West End, having our wits scared out of us as we dodged other blacked out taxis and buses. We were naïve enough to think that we might just get a room at the Savoy. After all, we were now one of those "overpaid", "overfed", "oversexed" and "over there" Yanks. We soon realised that we were slightly out of our class so we headed for the American Red Cross Jules officers' club in Jermyn Street near Piccadilly Circus. Nice polite English ladies welcomed us and soon we had consumed hot tea and coffee and donuts. Then off to a narrow cot with "biscuits" and clean sheets.

At the time London was the centre of the universe. Our first sightseeing was the Palace, Westminster, and the Parliament buildings. Our first dinner was at the Grosvenor House where food was delicious and cheap. Our first show was at the Palladium. At Peale's Bootery one of our group, Harold Jenkins, paid $50 for a hand-made knee-high pair of boots. I couldn't even entertain the thought of paying one week's pay for something to go on my feet but they were beautiful.

About February 1945 I visited Dan, a lieutenant friend of mine who was assigned to 8th Air Force HQ at High Wycombe. His girlfriend had made a picnic lunch and set up another girl and the four of us went on a hike and in a glade near a golf course we spread our "feast" of bread, butter and jam. On return to Jermyn Street Dan paired me up with Andy our flight engineering officer. We headed for Liverpool Street station and while waiting for them to open the platform gate I observed three WAAFs who were "in the same boat" as us. We agreed to watch which carriage they entered and then, by "coincidence", ended up opposite each other in the same for our trip back to Ipswich. Andy was quite nicely married and me not being a personality kid, we slowly commenced a conversation with three reserved English girls. The train huffed and puffed through the different stops and about the time I learned Margory's name she informed me that Colchester was her station and from there they would have a two hour walk to their huts. "Marge" was a telephone operator and she had spent twenty-eight months in Northern Ireland before being re-assigned to Earls Colne in Essex. I think my first attraction to Marge was her smile and general demeanour. And she didn't smoke.

We had a phone in the hall of our quarters and so our relationship grew. Soon we would meet each other at the bus station in Colchester, have a nice dinner at a quaint hotel on the High Street just above the Roman ruins, maybe see a movie and then back to Ipswich. We didn't date a great deal but when we had time off we would go to London and I would stay at Marge's home in North Finchley. Movies and sightseeing occupied most of our time. We expanded our sightseeing to Hampton Court, via the Thames, Crystal Palace and many others. We would frequent a small restaurant called "Athens" where we enjoyed "good" horse steak – it got better all the time. There was a famous stage comedian called Sid Field, who we saw a couple of times. He had this little country boy in stitches from laughing so much. Having grown up in such austere times and conditions, sometimes I thought I had died and gone to heaven. One of my biggest regrets was not having more knowledge of English history. Learning more and more about English sacrifices was interesting. Marge's dad was a volunteer warden and her brother Ken, who was of my age, had been killed on a bombing raid over Germany in 1942.

Because of the long days Andy let me take a Mustang down to Marks Hall and spend a short visit. My departures would usually be a little "Smart Alec" but the tower seemed to enjoy them. I also knew where Marge's hut was so I gave them an occasional "low pass".

The war ended. I had completed my tour prior and had started a second tour. We were notified that we would go to Japan so I volunteered – until the big blast in Japan. We were having a weekend party and Marge was visiting a second time. I went to my boss and suggested that as Marge was in the RAF there should be no restriction on her flying in our planes. We had a war-weary Mustang which by removing an eighty-gallon fuel tank behind the pilot plus a couple of electronic items, there was sufficient room for a passenger to squeeze in and sit on a makeshift seat. All agreed that Marge could fly and I fitted her into a flying suit and she climbed aboard, big dimples, rosy cheeks and all! Or plans were to fly over Earls Colne and maybe to North Finchley. Foolishly and rather stupidly, I revved the engine up, let go of the brakes roared down the runway, held it low to the ground long after reaching take-off speed and then proceeded to pull up sharply in a chandelle. That was the beginning, We levelled out and headed for Earls where I began to circle so that she could get a good view. I could talk to her but she could not talk to me. Soon she was tapping me on the shoulder and motioning a return to Wattisham. It required no great imagination to see that she wasn't doing well. I smartened up, flew gently back, made probably the smartest landing in my career but taxiing in, she could resist no longer but she did a magnificent job in not "exploding". When the crew chief climbed up to the cockpit he looked at her face and remarked that it "looks like you left your roses upstairs". Marge quickly remarked, "That's not all I left".

Our unit was headed for home and discharge but I wanted to fly and stay in. Luckily four of us were able to get assigned to the Continent and later to an airfield in a suburb of Munich.

I continued to correspond with Marge. Married couples were rapidly filling up the base and fraternization was taboo. So one thing led to another and before I knew it she had talked me into hitching. England was planning to celebrate Battle of Britain day on 15 September 1946 and a contingent of aircraft from our base was to participate. However, I was only a spare pilot so we decided it would be a pretty good time to tie the knot. We had four days to arrange a marriage. I left for Neubiberg about ten miles from Munich but Marge had to go through the usual red tape to procure a military pass, etc. and so started married life in a country we had just been at war with. It was an experience. However, we both survived!

Clarence 'Buck' G. Haynes

8

Rest & Recreation

Furlough

During the late afternoon of 25 November 1942, an orderly room clerk came through the barracks looking for persons from Boston, Massachusetts. He instructed us to get dressed in our Class A uniform and get on the truck in front of the orderly room pronto. We were to take a "special excursion" to Boston, England. Thomas "Joe" Kasberovich and myself from our barracks got in the back of a 6 x 4 GI truck with several other GI's and off we went to Boston, a town located in Lincolnshire, near the Wash. When we arrived we found a few other trucks from a couple of other airfields also there. I remember the following day's events because of a special "programme" given to us as we attended a reception given by the mayor, George H. Bird, at the council chambers. As we waited in the assembly room for the entrance of the mayor, I was impressed with the "pomp" of the master of ceremonies as he announced, "His Worship, the Mayor." In came a short middle-aged man bedecked with gold chains and medals around his neck. I couldn't help but think how ludicrous this must have seemed to most of the American GI's attending.

After a short ceremony, we were led on a tour of the Guildhall and cells. This was where Nottingham puritans, who sailed to Boston, Mass. (via Holland) in search of religious freedom, were caught before embarking and tried in the Guildhall courtroom. Some were placed in the adjoining cells. Following the short tour we assembled at the South Square from where we paraded to the parish church called the "Boston Stump." As our group of Americans, consisting of about thirty-five to forty men, marched down the street to the church, people were standing along the route cheering and waving American flags and giving the "V for Victory" sign as we passed by. Our appearance was not very military. I doubt whether any two wore exactly the same uniform. Some wore Class A with variations, some wore field jackets or raincoats and a few wore non-regulation scarves – even some with flying boots. A real motley crew if there ever was one. However, it did not dampen the spirits of the British civilians lining the route. This was November 1942 and few people in Lincolnshire had yet seen American personnel.

We reached the church and watched as Lieutenant Colonel A.L. Streeter (US Army Medical Corps) laid a wreath at the monument for the five men associated with Boston, England, who later became governors of Massachusetts. Then we attended a special Thanksgiving Day service conducted by Canon A.M. Cook. The bible lesson was read by Captain James Lawrence USA and a short address was delivered by Chaplain Herbert Hamburger USA. Following the playing of the anthems of both countries and a blessing by the Archdeacon of Lincoln, we proceeded to the mayor's procession to the Assembly Hall for the Thanksgiving luncheon. Food in England in 1942 was not sumptuous by any means, but they did their best with clear noodle soup, cold ham and beef, roast potatoes, vegetable salad, stewed apricots and cheese biscuits. Personally my memory of the meal is blurred and my recollection is primarily of the toasts to His Majesty the King and to the President of the United States. Water was used for the toasts, of course.

Following lunch, we had a conducted tour of St Botolph's, the parish church. St Botolph's is on the site of a seventh-century monastery, founded by St Botolph, a pious Benedictine monk for whom the town was named. The name Botolph evolved into Boston. The church's 290ft tower was called the Stump because it did not come to a point like most of the churches of the time. In 1620, the first journey of the Pilgrim Fathers to America was the vanguard of a great tide of migration in which the town of Boston was closely involved. A second and greater Puritan exodus began in 1628. In 1633 the Puritans under John Cotton sailed from Boston to the Massachusetts Bay capital, renamed Boston. These events tied the two Bostons historically and was the reason we Bostonian GIs were invited to celebrate our first Thanksgiving in Boston, England. These historical ties resulted in a gift (in 1931) of £11,000 to help in the restoration of the church. The money was used to "restore the tower, which now stands firm and secure in all its loveliness." The preceding quote is from the book, *Boston – Botolph's Town*, which was given to each of the Americans in remembrance of the day's events.

After the tour of the church, we went to the Scala Theatre for a variety show especially dedicated to American personnel. The acts included singers, dancers, musicians and comedians. Unfortunately, we hadn't been in England long enough to understand the British accent or their humor. By this time, Joe and I had enough of all the formalities, so we decided to rent a room at the Peacock and Royal Hotel. We had dinner at the hotel's Silver Grill. Can't remember what we ate, but it was an improvement over lunch and cost all of ten shillings.

The next morning, we took a train to Bedford and back to the base at Thurleigh. Luckily, no combat missions were scheduled during our absence. It was a memorable visit to an extremely historical and interesting place, one of many to be enjoyed during my three-year stay in England.

Paul G. Tardiff, 306th Bomb Group

Going to Boston! I was going to Boston! As the automobile sped across the level landscape on a road that was raised above the fields, now ploughed and waiting for winter, I tried to justify the excitement that filled me. For by now I was no newcomer to England ... The first reason for that longing was the picture in my mind of the tower of St Botolph's Church, known far and wide as the Boston Stump. For four years I had lived under the shadow of its replica in America, the lovely Harkness tower in New Haven. For four years I had admired that tower in sunlight through the tracery of spring-green leaves and in winter black against a sodden sky. I had known a pair of pale barn owls that had haunted that tower and I had listened to its carillon each evening, ringing out the slow melody of the fine old spiritual that we know as "Goin' Home." So this was a pilgrimage in one way, a pilgrimage to the Boston Stump, under whose alter-shadow I had studied and dreamed of long ago.

... It was almost evening this November day. It had been a sunny day; only now were clouds growing in the sky, which still held a wan winter glow, when we first glimpsed the "Aould Stoomp." Caught in a last shaft of sunlight that could not reach the earth beneath, it shone across the fens like a white beacon lighting our way. So it must have looked to those other older pilgrims who, not coming to Boston but leaving it, had seen it shining across the fens thee hundred and more years ago.

We were going to Boston this day because the town had invited the American army to celebrate the Thanksgiving holiday as their guests. A hundred soldiers were coming. They would attend a service in St Botolph's Church, where the Archbishop of Canterbury would preach the sermon. They would dine at the Assembly Halls, Boston homes would be open to them and there would be a dance in their honour.

We came into Boston that evening in the darkening twilight and it had been market day. Just as I bad dreamed it the old houses stood about the square – and there was the statue to the local hero, the windmills by the canal, the carts and stalls now departed but a flock of sheep still stumbling though the Little Bargate. And dominating all the grand old Stump floating up against a now-lowering, racing sky.

We found a café that was open and had a supper of Welsh rarebit and tea. We found a room in a small hotel. We left our baggage there and walked back to the market place as it started to rain. We ducked into a public house called "The Rum Puncheon" and sat drinking pints of bitter, talked to the men of the Lincolnshire Regiment who were playing darts and listened to a tipsy bearded sailor singing "White Christmas ". "Why don't you go across to the hall tonight, boys," said the buxom barmaid. "There's a good dance on. United Canners. You boys are the first Yanks to come to town. You'll have a fine welcome!"

... The next morning was Thanksgiving Day – and the ceremonies began at ten o'clock with a reception in the council chambers ... From the council chambers a procession marched though the streets of old Boston, through the crowded market-place to the church, witnessed by the entire population of the town and thousands more. It was a colourful parade: the Archbishop in his robes, the Bishop of Lincoln too, other Church officials in full attire, the mayor and his entourage in robes and chains of office, the band of the Lincolnshire Regiment, detachments of the Royal Navy, the Royal Air

Force, the air-raid wardens, ambulance corps, nurses, sea scouts, boy scouts, fire service, the women's volunteers. And the American guests. Children scrambled to the top of the air-raid shelter in the centre of the market-place and flags were flying from the buildings surrounding it.

Inside the church November sunlight filtered through the windows and fell in gauzy gold on the garden of colour that filled the floor. Not a seat was vacant and behind the seated congregation the people of Boston were standing. Here were blocks of olive drab, of navy blue, or brown, air force blue, of tan and here and there a spot of white, or black. The choir lifted its sweet chant, the organ rolled, the words of the prayers and the sermons echoed bell-like through the church. Here, I thought, is the pure essence. Here is the return of John Winthrop and his company – the pardon, the blessing, the warm welcome. Here we were united again, working and fighting and now praying side by side – celebrating here in England an American holiday. And when by some quirk of fate the organ pealed the strains of "Goin' Home," I was back in Connecticut again; there was no Atlantic Ocean and for that moment no difference at all between old England and the new.

Thanksgiving At Boston (1943), Robert S. Arbib Jr

God! I will pack and take a train
And get me to England once again!
For England's the one land I know.
Where men with Splendid Hearts may go;
And Cambridgeshire, of all England,
The shire for Men who understand;
And of that district I prefer
The lovely hamlet Grantchester.

Rupert Brooke, 1912

Someone once said that the River Cam along the Cambridge "backs" was the most beautiful half-mile in England. Standing now on the carpet of green lawn of King's College on that bright June afternoon, I was in no mood to disagree. Here, if anywhere in England, was a spot where tradition, architecture, history and landscape blended into a perfect, harmonious whole. Here was the past in the magnificent old chapel and the perfect classic proportion of the adjacent Clare; here was age and beauty. Here, too, overhead was the present, as British bombers wheeled and manoeuvred in the afternoon sunlight. Here, too, was the future, walking about the courtyard in the uniform of air cadets – talking from window to window across the court – lazing idly at the riverbank. Here all ages met.

Cambridge University, if you excepted the sky above it, which invades all sanctuaries, was an island of peace and contemplation set in the stormy sea of war that swirled around Eastern England. The streets of the town were crowded with British airmen, WAAFs; farmers come to market, Americans who flocked to their club in the Bull Hotel. But once inside those massive iron gates, you left the noise and hurly-burly of the world outside; you entered a cloistered, ordered and somehow a remote world where every stone and every blade of grass cried out, "I belong here ... just here!"

Only the aeroplanes in the sky above seemed out of place. Rooks, yes, wheeling and turning above the tall trees across the river. But not Lancasters, Halifaxes, Wellingtons and Ansons. Could a man seriously ponder his Horace or his Newton with this new-celestial roar in his ears?

As I stood and thought, a voice behind me asked politely, "And what do you think of our college?"

I turned to see a thin, rather bent man in a shabby jacket and baggy trousers, with a three-day growth of beard, who was also admiring our surroundings and puffing damply on a pipe. "I think it's a beautiful place," I said. "I thought of coming here to study once – seven years ago. And so now I thought I'd like to come and see what I missed."

"And does it meet with your approval?"

"Unqualified," I said. "I can't imagine more perfect surroundings for study and for education. Although I suppose it was a bit more conducive to thought when those things were not overhead all the time."

"You get quite used to them, you know," he said, belching loudly by way of emphasis. "Of course, there's still a lot to be desired in the way of improvements but in some ways our system does give a man a sort of polish and if he exposes himself to it enough – a fairish education?"

Our talk continued and led to American universities, which this disreputable looking character had once toured (and where, I thought, he probably had got his last haircut!) and to the various differences between American and English university life, to architecture and back to the Cambridge scene before us. "I suppose you'll want to go along the river to Grantchester," he said, belching again with great unconcern. "Most Americans do. Rather a nice walk – Rupert Brooke, who lived in this college, made it quite sought after."

"I hadn't thought of that," I admitted. "I'd like to see the rooms of some of the other Cambridge favourites though, Spenser and Herrick and Coleridge and even Milton."

"Quite. Yes, you'll doubtless enjoy seeing them, though there may be some young lads installed there now who have changed things around a bit. Well, getting late. Must be going. Glad to have seen you." And he was off.

Later that evening I asked Clement, my host, who this strange, unkempt, informal character could have been. I described him carefully, while Clement pondered a moment and then smiled ... "Oh, that must have been old — he's a brilliant scholar really. One of the country's leading authorities on his subject. A bit eccentric but a good fellow. Knighted quite recently, as a matter of fact."

The next day Clement took me on a tour of the university. Though it was between terms and most of the students were gone, I enjoyed that walk around the university grounds and through the quiet courtyards. Here was the ancient Elizabethan brick of Queen's, here was old Trinity with its host of famous names, here was the dark, crumbled stone of Magdalene. ... raftered dining halls with their carved oak tables black with age and their ancient nameless portraits on the walls. Here was a place for a young man to live and let history and knowledge and manners seep into his skin and run in his blood. Here while he studied he could see for himself the qualities that had slowly brought this gem to England and England its prominence in the world. He need not be taught English history here – it was all around him and if he listened he might still hear the whispered voices of Wordsworth and Newton, Darwin and Pitt, Cromwell and Milton and perhaps even Chaucer!

You couldn't help doing some thinking here at Cambridge – and that, I suppose, is just what it is for.

Thoughts At Cambridge, Robert S. Arbib Jr

I had gone to a party in Cambridge and had left late. I was scheduled to fly the next morning and didn't dare miss a combat mission. I got into a taxi and told the driver to take me to Honington. I went to sleep and when the driver woke me and said we had arrived I found we were in Huntingdon! He'd misheard my southern accent.

Lieutenant Curtis Smart

At the Red Cross in Cambridge, the lovely old university town, I got the name of an English family that entertained American fliers on weekends. Their name was Newman; and they lived in Royston, a town nearby. I was to spend many happy hours with them. Their home was a fine old Georgian mansion with lawn tennis courts, orchards, formal gardens and beautiful groves of trees. These people were very kind to me. Each night my bed would be turned down. A glass of milk and a bowl of fruit were on the nightstand by my bed. Sometimes there would be a book of poetry or a magazine, too. They treated me like a son and I shall never forget them.

It was near the end of my tour that I obtained a three-day pass and first visited Cambridge. It was only about twenty miles from Molesworth. I fell in love with the place. Its fine old Gothic buildings, many of them dating from the thirteenth and fourteenth centuries, were deeply satisfying to me. I could not get enough of roaming its medieval streets. Everyone walked or rode bicycles; the streets were almost too winding and narrow for automobiles. Here the timbered veneers of Tudor England were very much in evidence. Some of the houses and inns were many centuries old. The University owned all the land thereabouts and they did not countenance any of the tomfoolery called Progress. They wanted Cambridge left just as it was; a decision I would have to applaud wholeheartedly.

The University was made up of a number of colleges, thirty-five to be exact; each having its own identity, such as Queen's College, Trinity College, St John's College and the like.

I learned that in ancient times Cambridge had been a monastic establishment built in the fens of East Anglia. Eventually it began to be a center of learning. It was already a great university when it was visited by the great Erasmus, the foremost prophet of the Reformation. He came to Cambridge in 1500 and remained there at Queen's College for three years.

The finest of the medieval edifices was King's College Chapel, begun in 1446. With its inspired fan vaulting, it was the supreme example of the perpendicular Gothic. I had only a rather general understanding of the decorative vocabulary in those days, but there were many knowledgeable people about who were glad to explain these things to me.

The loveliest area of all was that part of the university called The Backs, where the tree-shaded lawns and gardens ran from the backs of the colleges down to the picturesque River Cam from which the town derived its name. I strolled along the grassy banks of the green river with its weeping willows and ancient stone bridges and thought to myself, "This is the loveliest spot in the world."

I happened upon a cricket match and was fascinated. The players were immaculate; it seemed a very antiseptic sport to me, but as I watched I could see that a lot of co-ordination and agility were being displayed. I never did fathom what was going on despite a friendly bystander's attempts to tell me.

The Backs had once been marshes but in the seventeenth century had been filled in by one of the distinguished alumni, Oliver Cromwell, the Great Protector [sic], to become the beautiful garden spot that one now sees. I was told that a great summer fair had been held annually on the Commons in olden times. The Commons was a great grassy expanse near the River. Here the stout English yeomen had come from every part of the Midlands and East Anglia to socialize, carouse, shoot their longbows in competition and vie with each other in feats of strength. Farmers, merchants and artisans hawked their wares on all sides, drinking and wenching betimes. It was said that the fair was the model for Vanity Fair in Bunyan's *Pilgrim's Progress*. It was a lusty, brawling time. Now a hearty new breed had invaded the Commons. The Yanks were to be seen everywhere, intruding a jarring note upon the timeless, pastoral scene.

I wandered again along the banks of the Cam and saw an apple-cheeked underclassman poling a punt down the meandering stream. His passenger, an upperclassman, was eating an apple and reading a book. Being an American, I did not understand why the boatman was not rebelling at the supine role he was forced to play. This custom, which to me seemed an anachronism, had wide acceptance, going unchallenged by the underclassmen. But who knows what noble concepts had germinated in these verdant surroundings. Here the young Tennyson might have dreamed dreams, which became *The Idylls of the King*, or the youthful Charles Darwin might have explored broad vistas of the intellect, which eventuated in the *Origin of Species*.

Since the Middle Ages Cambridge had been a market town. Farmers from the surrounding country brought their vegetables and produce to the great open market place behind St Mary's Church. A lively place, it held great fascination for me, as I had never seen an open air market before.

What a delight to rest in an ancient inn drinking the excellent light brown ale! While chatting convivially with the other customers, I exulted in a milieu of Jacobean tables and chairs, mullioned windows, exposed ceiling beams, rich dark oak wainscoting, an open-hearth stone fireplace and finally church warden pipes on the wall, not added as a decorator's touch but centuries old and once used by the patrons of the inn – a jewel of a setting for one who needed no such encouragement to drink. Had this genteel place once been the favourite haunt of Edmund Spenser or John Milton? Had the youthful Wordsworth and his friend Coleridge sat in these very chairs quenching their thirsts from the lovely old pewter tankards? I did not know, but I did not doubt it, for this was a place of poets.

The next morning I resumed my exploration of the old medieval town. In the narrow streets I saw the handsomest shops I had ever seen. I had a thing about bookstores and here was the oldest one in England, Bowes and Bowes founded in 1581. Bookbinding had been a major craft in Cambridge for centuries and the shop was a treasure-trove of handsome and rare volumes. Moving along, I was delighted to find a shop that had an amazing collection of jazz records. The proprietor told me that the college students and many of the professors not only loved jazz, but there were many connoisseurs of the idiom at the university. These were collector's items, some of which could not be found at home. I bought an album of a recording session by Louis Armstrong and Earl "Father" Hines, featuring the venerable "West End Blues" and "Tight Like That." This was really vintage jazz and I was amazed to find it in this place. It only increased my esteem for the kind of people to be found hereabouts.

I had seen the genius of Sir Christopher Wren at St Paul's and St Mary-le-Bow's in London. I hadn't realized he was here also. The outstanding examples of his art in Cambridge were the magnificent Wren Library at Trinity College and the Emmanuel College Chapel. There were many quaint churches in the city. I was fond of poking and prowling about the graveyards. I was no necrophile, but the epitaphs on the tombstones were an unending source of delight to me. I sought out these places. They did not depress me. On the contrary, I rather fancied the idea of resting in one of these lovely old churchyards one day, for they did not seem like places of death to me but rather fitting ambiences for departed spirits.

And now I began to understand why Cambridge held such fascination for me. I had been looking for a place like this all my life. I felt that I was part and parcel of this greatest outcropping of the human spirit. In those days I only dimly understood the great thirst of the spirit that was growing in me, but I sensed that somehow in this place was the repository of every value that I held near and dear. My very soul sped across the centuries to unite with the antique refrain of the old medieval town.

In desperation I began to think of ways that I could manage to stay here. It seemed logical that every human being should be in a place where he was contented and happy and safe. I was in such a place. Here in this green Eden was peace and sanctuary. Twenty miles away the apparatus of death and terror was in ceaseless operation, but now it seemed to have nothing to do with me. I did not want to be wasted just as I had begun to catch a vision. I knew that I belonged here. The other Americans did not care about this place, but I did. So my mind raced – was there a way? In the end I knew it was no good – I had to go back to Molesworth and finish the other business, one way or the other. It would have been better had I never come to Cambridge. Sadly I turned my back on the place and boarded the bus.

Chick's Crew, Ben Smith

I was initiated into the mysteries of cricket at Lord's, the famous arena in London ... In cricket, it seems, each team comes to bat once, with every man taking his turn at bat (his innings) before the other side gets in a lick. The batter (or "batsman"), as it was explained to me, stays up there and swings as long as he is not put out ("down"). If he hits the ball a good crack, he can run down a little path (the "pitch") to the other wicket and back to his own wicket. This counts for two runs. If he really wallops the ball out of the park, the equivalent of our "home run," he can run up and down the path six times, scoring six runs, or "hitting it for six," which will win for him a modest burst of handclapping from the crowd. Even if he hits the ball, he need not run if he'd rather not risk being thrown out by a fielder. His job is twofold – to protect his wicket and to score runs.

The batsman is out only if the pitcher ("bowler") succeeds in tossing the ball past him and hitting the wicket, which consists of three low stakes set in the ground behind him, across which are balanced two little horizontal sticks called "bails." It is of the utmost importance to know that these "sticks" are called bails. Every one of the many people who tried to explain cricket to me whispered the magic word "bails" with the air of letting me in on a real secret. The batsman is also finished if one of his batted balls is caught on the fly, if he is thrown out at the wicket ("stumped"), if he does something called lbw, which apparently is not quite cricket and under several other conditions. If the wicket is hit the bails go flying off; the batter has been "bowled" and this time the bowler receives the polite and scattered recognition of the audience.

The game is complicated and considerably delayed by the fact that there are two batsmen, one at each wicket and after the bowler has tossed the ball six times at one wicket (an "over") everyone on the field moves around to new positions and the bowler faces the batsman at the other end of the pitch. Thus it often happens that an expert batsman continues to play for hours, while less fortunate or less enthusiastic members of his team come up, score a few runs and retire. It is quite possible for two good batsmen to exercise all day, leaving the rest of their team to wonder why they didn't spend the afternoon at the beach or at home by the radio. However, even in high-quality play, a one-man score of one hundred runs (a "century") is an item worthy of the sporting columns in the newspapers the following day. Since the ball can be hit fairly in any direction, batting becomes a science of placement, of "hitting it where they ain't," and there are, it was averred, many fine points behind that peculiar batting stroke which looks like a combination mashie shot and a man chopping down a tree.

For the bowler, his object is to set those bails flying, or somehow induce the batsman to give up and walk slowly towards the pavilion (clubhouse). The bowler's delight, the "no-hit" game of cricket, is the hat trick, when he takes three successive wickets with three straight balls. I don't know what the record is for the least number of balls thrown during a game by a bowler (par would be ten) but it was undoubtedly set the day a British Army team played an American Air Force team, which amassed the modest total of twenty-nine runs, all out.

... To me, cricket is a game almost without climaxes, without tied scores, without seesaw changes of advantage or evenly balanced duels. In a more monotonous way, it produces the lack of suspense that would result in a baseball game if each team batted through nine innings uninterruptedly, or if in football or basket ball one team kept the ball for the offensive for an entire half. Here again, as at the invisible horse races at Newmarket, the only thrill comes in the last few moments and then only if the score is very close.

We departed after about three hours with the game still in progress and the next day I looked for an account of it in a newspaper, to find out who, if anyone, had been the winner of that sleepy session. I was amazed to read, "In one of the most exciting and well-played matches seen at Lord's during the war, a team representing the Civil Defence Services ..."

At a cricket match any less exciting, I am certain, the average American would be the Dormouse at the Tea Party and contribute to the spirit of the occasion with loud and cotupicuous [sic] snores. But then, it might be fun to play.

Brief Introduction To Cricket, Robert S. Arbib Jr

My first and only furlough in England began on an appropriate occasion, "Derby Day", and as an old improver of the breed with diplomas from Belmont Park, Jamaica and Aqueduct racetracks on Long Island, I was determined to add a war-time Derby to my sporting experiences.

I caught the bus from Wattisham to Ipswich, the train from Ipswich to Newmarket and walked the remaining three miles to the site of the debacle. It was a warm June day and the sun shone and I was in one of those expectant moods – the somewhat elated, "anything-might-happen" mood that accompanies one to race-courses and then silently steals away immediately after the last race. In spite of travel difficulties there was a crowd of about nine thousand at Newmarket that day, all obviously in the same mood. They had come by train from London to Cambridge and Newmarket; some had hitch-hiked, others had walked and some had come on bicycles, of which there were hundreds stacked in fields beside the grandstand ... I rode back to Cambridge that evening on the most crowded train I had ever seen. I rode standing up on the seat of the toilet in the lavatory. I couldn't even assume the dignity of a sitting position, for there was no room for my legs. We closed the door to make extra room for an additional passenger and that is how five racing enthusiasts journeyed from Newmarket to Cambridge. There were many, I think, less fortunate.

The Sporting Life (Derby Day 1943) Robert S. Arbib

... The first day I spent walking around Glasgow in the rain. It was a big, bustling, busy, dirty city – a city of industry, sprawling out over the valley and on both sides of the river Clyde. In appearance I found little to recommend it, although it reminded me strongly of the English-speaking parts of Montreal and not without reason. Here was the same predominance of red hair, the same Scottish names on the stores, the same Scottish faces, the same type of sturdy northern architecture, the busy narrow streets with their trains and buses, the same beautiful surrounding countryside ... I debated whether to spend a few brief hours in Edinburgh, which everyone had said was the pride of the North, or to take a trip out into the Scottish hills. The penny fell heads for the hills and I boarded a train which was to take us to Loch Lomond. One hour later I was aboard the little steamer in company with about a hundred other hardy tourists, standing on the deck in the rain and looking out over the magnificent Scottish scenery. It seemed incredible that this dark lake, set in the midst of this lonely, majestic wilderness, could be just an hour distant from the noise and commerce of Sauchiehall Street.

... Piper on the hillside, black waters of Loch Lomond, green barren hills rising into the clouds and a stuffed loon in a glass case at the inn at Ardlui, these are my pictures of the Scottish highlands. And above and about all are woven a pervading mood of great loneliness, of sadness, of a melancholy approaching despair that seemed to me to be the essence of Scottish atmosphere. I am glad that I did not see the Highlands in bright sunlight with birds singing and clouds floating in a blue sky. This, I thought, was a truer picture.

A Look At Scotland, Robert S. Arbib Jr

Travel around Britain by train was a confusing proposition to the foreign soldier. Not only were the stations unmarked but the station porters who called their names were almost unintelligible to us.

... And just then, our train, all two cars of it, chuffed in. A couple of hours later we were in Hull. We were five hours late, it was dark and raining and how we got a place to sleep in that crowded town that night is another story ... From across the water the town of Hull lies low, with scattered church spires above the red brick houses, reminding us of old *P* prints of New York in the eighteenth century looking across the bay from Brooklyn. But in place of spars and sail in the waterfront sky, there were the thin steel fingers of the cranes, reaching across the horizon, moving in a slow sign language that had but just one word.

The town of Hull itself was bruised and battered and scarred by war. German bombers had blitzed it and the worst raid had eaten out the heart of the city and left it as though some enraged giant had hacked it with a mighty rake. The business centre was a wide expanse of empty space where brick dust swirled in the wind and there was no street anywhere that did not have its patched roofs, its gaping, windowless shells of buildings, or its ugly gaps where a bomb ripped out one of a row of cottages, leaving a gap as conspicuous as a missing front tooth.

... I loved to ride on those trains, though they angered me and tried my patience every time. When I was riding the LNER I was certain that this, of all the railways I had ever seen, was the worst. When I was riding the

LMS I wasn't certain after all but this was even worse. And certainly the Great Western seemed no better. But when we thought about the incredible conditions under which railways were operating in those days, we forgave them. There was the time on the LNER when a lucky bomb had split the centre of an embankment between Chelmsford and Shenfield just ahead of a train. It took three days to fish that locomotive out of the hole with cranes. Everyone said, "Why don't they just blow the thing up and fill in the hole?" But every locomotive was needed and they worked on it night and day for three days and shuttled passengers around the obstacle by bus.

There were the trains that came into Peterborough North and the connecting train left from Peterborough East, a mile away through the town, just twenty minutes later and no way to get there but to run, dragging your baggage behind you like a mule hitched to a balky plough.

There was the time in the train going out to Watford when I closed my eyes and dozed off to be suddenly awakened by an ominous roar, to find everyone else crouched on the floor. Showing my usual lightning reaction to danger, I froze where I was and the buzz bomb passed overhead to crash a mile away. Brave, these Yanks. Don't know what fear is!

There was the train in Scotland that got completely bogged down somewhere between Loch Lomond and the Glasgow station, when I had just one hour to catch another train to Gourock to meet a third train that was taking an Air Force squadron to King's Cliffe, on which I was to be escorting officer. My flight to catch that last train will ever be a nightmare in my mind, involving a jump from a crawling train, a run for half a mile along the track, a slow tram-car into town, the last bus to Gourock and then another mile run to the pier … just in time to swing aboard the already-moving troop train to King's Cliffe.

Yes, train travel in England was fun those days. Is that a grey hair I see, just above my wrinkled brow?

Robert S. Arbib Jr

Sometimes as we went along the road down the hill from camp, we passed farm children on their way to school. Then we stopped and I jumped out and tossed them, squeaking with delight, into the back of the truck and let them ride with us. Down at Tuddenham every morning we ran into the same farmer leading his cows into the meadow. We stopped to let the slow-moving beasts pass. And often on the hill beyond Tuddenham we found the Ipswich bus stalled because it couldn't make the steep grade with a load. The passengers alighted, we stopped and we all pushed the bus up the hill.

In Ipswich, our first stop, we also had a routine. Our first stop was the YMCA where we could shave and wash in that greatest of luxuries (to us then) – hot water. Then we went upstairs and had breakfast for a few pennies. Coffee and hot buttered toast, with jam and a few pleasant words from the girl in slacks who worked behind the counter.

If we had errands in Ipswich, we would attend to them. The dry cleaners, usually, for we always had a load of filthy clothes. Vera, at the shop, was another friend, who could do the impossible and rush our most urgent orders through in not the usual ten days but in two – or if we spoke nicely – perhaps even one! And there was always the beautiful girl walking up the hill to work – who always smiled and waved to us.

Then off we went towards Sudbury. Up the hills and around the turns, through Hintlesham, where we might give lifts to the convalescent British soldiers in bright blue suits and red neckties who stayed at the manor there. And winding up past the big, immaculate farms with their fine cattle and horses and between the high thorn hedges and then down into the valley again at Hadleigh. Timeworn, mellowed buildings – empty streets – Hadleigh was old; it had seen its prime when it had been a great wool center, centuries ago. Now, all of all Suffolk villages, it seemed tired and old and almost deserted. There were a few young people in the streets – few people at all – in Hadleigh. We raced through it .... From the valley at Boxford the road wound up and over the hills to a broad plateau, with fewer old trees and larger fields and fine, wide vistas. It made more turns than ever in this countryside – it was doubtful whether there were fifty yards of straight road on the entire stretch. But here, too, were daily landmarks – the broad field that always had its flock of magnificent black and white lapwings, most beautiful of English plovers, some sailing across the ploughed land like big black-and-white butterflies, some standing erect and motionless, their cocky plumes blowing in the wind.

Down at the corner where the road turned left for Polstead, the scene of the famous Murder of the Red Barn, we turned right and every morning – there was the "Old Bearded Man." Ancient he must have been, nearly ninety but still stout and hale, big broad white beard, big broad black hat, taking his slow walk along the road, waving his cane in greeting to us as we passed.

Then to Newton Green, where there was a tiny golf course and an inn called "The Saracen's Head." And then straight along the road, past the farm where the beautiful girl with the blue eyes lived, past the farm where the tall, blonde girl worked and into Sudbury.

... how the Land Army girls waved to us from the apple orchard and from their ladders in the plum trees. The trees were ripe then in September and we were tempted to stop and talk and take an apple or two. But we never did. We saw that orchard ripen, we watched the girls slowly move across it each day and finally harvest it. We saw it lose its leaves and lie bare and open in winter and bowing under the winter rains. We saw it turn green again in spring and the beautiful white blossoms powder the road.

Suffolk Cross-Country, Robert S. Arbib Jr

Sudbury's river is the Stour, pronounced "Stoor" and it is a lovely river, made justly famous by the paintings of Suffolk's two native sons, Constable and Gainsborough. From Sudbury to the sea it winds its way through a verdant valley, with rolling slopes on both sides, dotted with red-roofed villages, squat, square grey churches and the neat Suffolk fields, enclosed in their modelled hedgerows, curving up to the sky.

From Sudbury it winds down through willow groves, where primroses make golden carpets in spring, down past big old mills, under arched stone bridges, evenly, smoothly, past old Bures and the Colnes to Bergholt and the marshy reaches of the sea at Manningtree.

By American standards it would not be a river at all, hardly more than a brook, a stream, or a creek – but in England it is a river indeed – with as much personality in its quiet way as the Hudson …

Evening On The River, Robert S. Arbib Jr

I took the Reading railroad west to Maidenhead. I walked the streets and up the hill to the walls of Windsor Castle, then down and east to Eton. One impression was how barren the famous playing fields of Eton seemed and another, the quaint, cobblestone appearance of Maidenhead. I rode further out on the Reading Line and enjoyed the quiet serenity of the countryside, a tonic for the war I had to return to the next day.

1st Lieutenant Walter F. Hughes, 93rd Bomb Group

I was sitting under the crossing of the cathedral, looking up into the cream-coloured stone tower, as the sun streamed through the windows high overhead. The massive nave was empty now and there was no echo in the high arching Norman vaults – but I was surrounded with a host of people who passed beside and around me without word or sound.

Some of us go to ancient cathedrals to worship, some go to admire and study the architecture, the sculpture and the glass and some go to meditate. But sitting here under these time-worn stones in this empty hall, I was dreaming – lost in fancy. I had forgotten my uniform, forgotten why I had come here, forgotten even my name; but the great columns, the vast silent aisles, the worn stones of the pavement, unchanged by centuries, had taken me out of the present and into an ageless dream transcending time and reality. Here around me was a silent concourse of the past – here visible to me in the original setting and just as visible as these stones before me, were the figures that peopled this place in the past, moving in a ghostly pageant …

… The reveries ended with the hum of an aeroplane overhead and the ancient cawing of rooks in the tower. I was in St Albans Cathedral and it was 1943 and the third button on my jacket needed polishing …

… After the excursion to St Albans I made several other one-day trips to other historic towns in England within reach of London. There was the day in January when I went down to Kent and walked through blitzed Canterbury. Here again was a town filled with the evidence of history – ancient weavers' houses along the river, the sign that said "Falstaff Hotel – 1403," the early Christian ruins of St Augustine's Monastery and the Roman arches in the cathedral yard.

Canterbury, unlike St Albans, was scarred and hollowed out by war – badly hit in a Baedeker raid and again at other times. Although the cathedral, except for the library, was spared, the business district was gutted – a barren waste land where weeds were growing and where there were little signs planted in the rubble – signs like "Walker, bootmaker, now at High Street ", "Jones, Established 1750, still on the Parade."

There were barrage balloons now over the Close but the cathedral itself was still a thing of beauty. I joined a group of British and Canadian soldiers touring the cathedral under the guidance of a lady verger. Together we gaped as she showed us the spot on the floor where Thomas à Becket had been murdered and the chapter house where the *Murder in the Cathedral* had been first performed. We stood and looked at the tomb of the Black Prince and the Fair Maid of Kent and then we stopped before the tomb of Simon of Sudbury.

"Here," said the lady verger, "is a strange tomb. Simon Theobald, or Simon de Sudbury, was the archbishop in the fourteenth century, who unfortunately sided with the aristocracy in Wat Tyler's rebellion and was beheaded by the irate peasants in 1381. His body is buried here but in place of his head there is a leaden cannonball. His head is now in a church in Sudbury, where he was born. I forget the name of the church ... St"

"St Gregory's," I said, from the back of the group.

"That's right," said the lady verger. "There's a soldier who must come from Sudbury. Why!" she said, looking up, "You're an American! How did you know that?"

"I've been in the church and seen the skull in a little niche in the chantry wall," I said.

"Trust a bloody Yank," murmured an English sergeant ...

I visited Lincoln on a foggy, rainy day and the cathedral, said to be one of the most perfect in England, was cold, damp and dark. Perfect it was, of a uniformity of design rarely found but of a style and a stone more ornate and less airy than the earlier Norman that I prefer, or the later, lacier Gothic that I like best of all.

... Colchester is another ancient town, like Lincoln and St Albans, full of Roman relics and narrow streets with venerable houses, old staging inns and a castle that dates back to Norman times. But to me the most fascinating aspect of Colchester was a contradiction. It was the Roman wall which runs along the north and east sides of the town below the hill down which the town flows like sauce on a pudding.

... One day in the autumn of 1943 I went to Colchester to watch the breaking out of the American flag – a gift of the town – at our district headquarters there. The Mayor of Colchester spoke of the warm feeling that the people of the town had for their American visitors, of the fine associations and friendships that had been made. The district commander replied by thanking the mayor and the town for its hospitality and help and fine spirit. These were no mere empty words – they brought spontaneous cheers from the townsfolk and the soldiers gathered round.

Of the other great cathedral cities of England, I visited Peterborough, Ely, Gloucester, Salisbury and Norwich and found in each beauty and inspiration. I saw the gaunt skeleton of the wrecked Coventry cathedral but I missed Winchester, Wells, York Minster and other famous ones. My favourite English church and perhaps one of the most spectacular sights in England, is Durham ... travel difficulties and lack of time prevented me from visiting the south and west of England. But then, this never was intended to be a tourist guide!

Tourist Days, Robert S. Arbib Jr

In 1938 I began to write to a pen friend, Miss Joan Green, in Leeds, Yorkshire. After a year or two we lost contact. However, Joan's address stayed somewhere in the back of my mind and after I arrived in the UK and became settled in at Debach in September 1944, I wrote Joan, knowing she probably wondered what had become of me as the war unfolded. She and her mother both wrote back urging me to come to Leeds at the first opportunity. There was much hesitation because I knew about rationing in England, besides which the rail connections were very vague. There were no regular advertised schedules, probably for security reasons. I finally decided to give it a try and, after the first time, made the trip frequently, but I never got to Leeds by the same route twice! When I boarded the train at Ipswich it was with the understanding that the conductor would tell me where to get off to make the first connection. Then in the next station I'd ask someone which train to get on and the next conductor would tell me where to get off again and so on to Leeds.

On one occasion in the bitter cold winter of 1944/45 I had an interesting encounter. It was so cold that at each stop I would buy a cup of tea and two or three of those hard little cookies or crackers. The tea wasn't just to drink, by holding the cup between my hands I could warm them, as there was no heating in the carriages. On one leg of the journey I found myself in a compartment with a young RAF sergeant. His insignia indicated he was an aircrew member and I immediately felt that I had a friend. However, I tried without success to strike up conversation. He would only answer my questions with a very curt "Yes" or "No". At the next station we both changed trains and I heard him mention that he was going to the Bradford area. I knew Bradford was near Leeds so I stuck to the young sergeant like wallpaper – you better believe I was having a hard time with the English accents trying to understand directions.

When we set off again there was an older man sitting opposite us in the compartment who noticed my attempts to engage the RAF sergeant in conversation. He explained that British enlisted personnel do not converse with officers except to answer questions and then as briefly as possible. This older man then pointed out to the young sergeant that the Yank was trying to be friendly and that he, the sergeant, was not being properly polite. The RAF man relaxed after that and was soon all smiles. He proved to be as curious about the 8th Air Force as I was about RAF Bomber Command. He was a Lancaster gunner and had completed a tour of duty but was hoping that his pilot could pull a few strings so that he could remain on operations. He felt that if he was grounded he might end up in "the pits" – the coal mines, which I assume was his peacetime job. He was fascinated by our going to targets in broad daylight while I couldn't imagine milling around in darkness in the midst of other aircraft. We talked about how interesting it would be to trade places for one mission.

As the journey wore on it became apparent that at the rate of progress we were making I was not going to arrive in Leeds until two or three o'clock in the morning. I asked if anyone in the compartment might recommend a hotel close to the rail station. Immediately a woman said that there should be no need to find a hotel as she was sure that any householder to whom I explained my predicament would be happy to find me a bed for the night, further suggesting that when I got to Leeds I should "knock someone up". I was momentarily taken aback by this statement as in American slang it means making someone pregnant. This was the first time I had heard this expression from a Britisher but quickly realised that the woman was telling me to go bang on a door. At the same time my newfound RAF friend invited me to go home with him if I didn't mind getting off at Bradford, taking a bus with him to a smaller place and a mile walk. He pressed me but I had to decline. I knew how few rations these people got. For example, my friends the Greens had nine people in their home and could only buy two eggs a week. I was also aware that the sergeant's family was not aware he was coming on leave and I could picture the scene when he arrived, unexpectedly in the wee hours with a Yank in tow. His offer was appreciated more than he probably realised but I begged off on the grounds that my leave time was too short, which was true. That night was spent at the Queens Hotel, an act for which Mrs Green scolded me soundly when I arrived next day. Felt badly about the RAF man's offer as I probably hurt his feelings in declining. Wish I had gotten his name and address and I often wonder if he survived the air war.

John Ramsey

The villagers near the air bases quickly adopted the American fliers as their own. The Yanks visited in their homes, shops and churches and became a part of village life. Each day the villagers anxiously awaited the return of the mission in the afternoons, counting the planes in the formation just as we did.

While we were recuperating I visited a lot in nearby towns and villages. Kimbolton was nearby and Thrapston, too. These picturesque villages with thatch-roofed cottages were a delight to me. I was fond of the dignified, sturdy villagers, who were friendly and hospitable once I learned a few "ice breakers".

Our base was in a lovely section of England on the perimeter of what is usually referred to as the Midlands. The countryside was unbelievably green and rolling. Many stately groves of trees ringed the base and I was fond of taking long walks and bicycle rides in the countryside. I loved this verdant country. Somehow, I had the feeling that I had been here in another life. I knew that my roots were here – that my people had all come from England in earlier times. Anyone with a passion for literature could not help being in love with this lovely pastoral land. Beginning with *Mother Goose*, this land had shaped my life from childhood on. I knew it intimately from my books. So I bicycled constantly over hill and down dale, rejoicing in the lush greenery of Huntingdonshire. The war seemed far away.

The English had been cultivating the same farms for thousands of years, but they were still fertile and productive. These people had a deep reverence for the land; they did not exploit it. The farmhouses were quaint and attractive with flower beds and rose gardens in profusion. One never saw a bad piece of landscaping. It had been going on for centuries, just getting better and better. A cottage would be set down in the perfect place, every tree and every shrub in proper place and scale. Yet it was not a studied effect at all but completely artless and charming.

I could almost believe someone was arranging these things for my personal delight. Bicycling around a bend, I would see a chuckling brook spanned by an arched stone bridge, then a hedgerow with a stile over it, then a little farther an antique haywain parked in an orchard. Every foot of this land was steeped in history. Near our base there was an old Saxon church, St Swithin's. It was a thousand years old and still being used for worship. There were many such churches scattered throughout this part of England. The parish church in Kimbolton was registered in the Domesday Book, the census ordered by William the Conqueror in 1085. Catherine of Aragon spent the final years of her exile in nearby Kimbolton Castle. This was the country of John Bunyan, the great Puritan preacher. He had preached in all of the glades and hamlets hereabouts and had written his great allegory *Pilgrim's Progress* in Bedford Gaol only a few miles away.

At that time I had a passion for the English landscape painter, John Constable. Constable has been able to capture the beauty of the English landscape as no other artist has. His paintings do not exaggerate. There are still many areas in England where these lush landscapes may be seen. Curiously enough, I never felt depression here. As soon as I was away from the base and out in the countryside, I was transported to another realm.

I was quite taken with the country inns and pubs and never intentionally passed one by. These were venerable institutions, nothing like saloons. They were homey places, family-oriented. Misbehavior was not tolerated in them. I eventually learned to appreciate the English ale and beer, served unchilled and came to prefer them to the American, probably because they were much more potent. Their lager was phenomenally good. All of it had much more of a malt taste than our own.

There was always a plink-plank piano and the Limeys and Yanks liked to gather around it and sing the old World War One songs: "Long, Long Trail", "Tipperary" and "Pack Up Your Troubles." "Roll Out the Barrel" was a standard but the most popular of all was "Roll Me Over in the Clover." At least three or four times an evening there would be bawdy renditions of it. The Yanks were as fond of it as the British. There were at least a hundred verses, each describing more graphically a new violation of the unfortunate lassie, the heroine of the song.

These were the best times of all to me. I loved to sing and I loved to drink. I remember the blazing logs and the hearty camaraderie of these places. It was not difficult to believe that I was set down in the time of Dickens, for these places had in no way changed from those times. Many of them were hundreds of years old.

Many of my friends felt that the English were a backward people, slow to accept changes and new ideas. This was precisely what I liked about them. I was a traditionalist; so were they. They held on tenaciously to their enduring monuments. The British had a sense of history and were fully aware of the greatness of their past. They did not demolish old churches and other historic landmarks to make way for junk food places, gas stations and other forms of visual pollution. This was all to the good as far as I was concerned. They did not compromise with the quality of life in this respect and I hoped they never would.

Some of our people were quite vocal in their criticism of English institutions and I for one was greatly embarrassed when it occurred in my presence. I was quick to apologize for the rudeness of my countrymen. The English merely ignored these few loudmouths. They never attempted to defend their customs and way of life; indeed, they had no need to as far as I was concerned. I think it is significant that in our own country when we want to give something a touch of class, we give it an English name.

Chick's Crew, Ben Smith

The Bar

The barroom's eight foot bar was expanded to twenty feet and a portable bar of six feet was utilized at parties ... Over the bar a large blue bomb, deactivated of course, was hung with an illuminated window that proclaimed "closed" whenever the base was alerted for a next day mission. The secrecy of the message was lost upon the attendees of the barroom.

The barroom was also equipped with several one-armed bandits of the shilling and tenpence variety. Adjusting the machines to give a generous return to the users did not make the suppliers of the machines overjoyed. However, in spite of the generous payoffs, the machines provided revenues really not needed for the club's operating expenses. Unfortunately, as with all good things, gambling fever infected several of the devotees of the club, who not only squandered their own pay but also borrowed funds for their habit, necessitating banishment from the club by the CO.

The club was infrequently used by most of the flight personnel during their combat tour. Alcohol and flying do not mix very well. Again, there were a few exceptions.

The limited supply of spirits allowed issuance per night of only two or three bottles of whiskey, two or three of wine and a keg of beer, plus soft drinks. The availability in the bar of Gaymer's Cider, made in nearby Attleborough, was akin to champagne and when mixed with beer was called "arf and arf" by its users. It made the beer much more potent. A radio and record player were wired to speakers in the three wings of the club and offered background music and news to those in the reading room and the barroom. Records could be borrowed from the base "Morale Officer" and his choices could be foisted upon all assembled. The only disruptive choice was the rendition of Ravel's "Bolero", whose repetitiveness was rather trying and seemingly interminable. It was quite a contrast to the likes of those devotees of the swing era music. Most popular was "I Walk Alone" by Marianne McCall and Louis Prima, No.1 on AFR (Armed Forces Radio) for twelve weeks.

The first dance at the club under new management featured the excellent base band, whose services were in wide demand. Through the cooperation of Lieutenant A.R. Sheperd (Shep), the manager of the officer's mess, rations were set aside for several weeks before the dance date.

A list of the "good family girls" was wheedled out of the Red Cross in Norwich and formal invitations were mailed to them. The event was epochal. The dinner participants were also touching in their open-eyed amazement at the prodigious piles of food served up in typical GI portions. None had seen so much food at one time during the many years of rationing. Some were seen to surreptitiously place the one pound blocks of butter into their purses. No one could blame them. Hopefully, our generosity was not construed as another example of American braggadocio.

Needless to say, the event evoked widespread acclaim. The next dinner dance brought forth "visitors" of various types from the London area, invited by enthusiastic fliers on leave. Some were described as "Piccadilly Commandoes," or "Marble Arch Rangers."

It was said, in jest of course, that the announcement was made that all unauthorized personnel would have to clear the base after one week past the close of the dance. Some persons believed it, others ignored it. Subsequently, with stern admonishment by those in charge, the problem evaporated.

The presence of then Major James (Jimmy) Stewart about this time on the roster attracted a general and some of our "little friend" fighter jocks from the groups that gave 2nd Air Division their most welcomed attention – combat flight coverage. This dance ended at a reasonable hour but the celebration continued, less the female attendees, until the wee hours of the night. The group sing-along and the excellent piano boogie-woogie of Sergeant Ginsberg were just the palliatives needed by the war-weary participants. The unexpected death of President Roosevelt cancelled the last scheduled dance. Fortunately for the club and its manager, it was a blessing in disguise since a rowdy element threatened to "tear apart" the club in celebration of the group's removal from combat status ...

... As a result of a meeting of the governing committee in the declining days of active duty it was decided to distribute the surplus funds to the club members, all officers on the base. This was accomplished by issuing one bottle to each member, with signed acknowledgement. This listing, along the letter of commendation issued to the manager, is still proudly kept among his fond memories of combat – and his tour in the officer's club.

In Search of Peace by Michael D. Benarcik

Alcohol

Combat aviators are known as notorious drinkers. We did drink. Combat flying is a very high tension producing activity. Our flight surgeon recognized this fact and encouraged the use of alcohol. After each mission, we were served a double shot of straight bourbon for medicinal purposes. Not having eaten since early in the morning and with empty stomachs, the effect was quite pronounced. At the "O" Club, beer known as "half and half" or mild and bitters was sold by the pint. It took some time to get used to noncarbonated warm English beer. Scotch whiskey with water and gin, mixed with many things, were common. No American beer or bourbon at the bar. Those of us who drank excessively slept the night before a mission; others did so intermittently. Ten minutes on pure oxygen the next morning, you were clear as a bell and ready to meet the day's challenges.

As a military man, one needs to know two people well; the supply sergeant and the mess sergeant. Each evening when the bar closed, I would walk through the mess kitchen. I was looking for leftovers to take to the hut. I usually found bread, cheese, cake; etc. Thanksgiving had been a snowy day with lots of good food and drink. Leaving the bar and wandering through the kitchen, the mess sergeant had a whole turkey left over. He insisted that I take it to the boys at the hut. He wrapped it up in a pan; I got on my drunken bicycle and headed for the hut. Bicycles operate poorly on packed snow. The first turn I came to my bicycle went one way, my turkey another, ad I was totally disorientated. I crawled to the hut and nobody believed my story. We found it all the next day beside the road in the snow.

Once a month, we had a party at the officers club. Eight or ten trucks were sent to the neighboring villages to pick up the young ladies that were eager to entertain or be entertained by those daring combatants. Americans seemed to fascinate these gals. Many of them would love to have married an American and come Stateside or as they would put it, move to the colonies.

A good meal was served followed by dancing and a floorshow. One show that I remember particularly was a takeoff on Carmen Miranda. This person wore the loud gaudy and revealing dress to a tee. Head decorations included the entire fruit world. Her dances were perfect imitations, exotic, provocative and exuberant. After her performance, a major on the Wing General Staff made a hard play for her. We watched this with the knowledge that the lady was not a lady but a very young MP from another outfit. When the major had pressed luck as far as the MP could stand it, he was told the truth about the disguise – what a surprise with much embarrassment. Parties needed hoaxes like this. It rounded out the life style of combat fliers of airplanes, alcohol and sex.

USO shows came to us in the hanger, about once a month. Bob Hope, Glenn Miller and many more, a host of comely young gals with each entertainer. The shows were clean and much fun with GI participation. For an hour or two, we forgot that we were scheduled to fly tomorrow. A touch of home or something familiar always seemed to lighten the stress load. Glenn Miller played our base just a few days before he was lost.

Special parties that lasted all day were the 100th mission and 200th mission party. We were stood down by Wing on those special days. Visited by upper echelon brass from 8th Air Force and British civilian dignitaries. The day was filled with parades, athletic events, good food, drink, dance and endless flying stories. Just another way to make us feel proud of our accomplishments and motivate us to continue to do better. Recognition and the personal touch by the higher up developed a form of camaraderie that exists to this day.

Colonel Robert H. Tays, pilot

Movies

One of the more hilarious aspects of military life was attendance at GI movies, i.e. standard Hollywood movies shown at theaters on military bases. There were also military training films shown a lot, but that's another story. The worse the movie was the better we liked it. The typical Grade B movie was what we liked best. The "show" associated with these movies was the comments by the audience. While always good for a lot of laughs, those at Rackheath were truly hysterical. The theater was a large Nissen hut, perhaps 100ft long. About 20ft or so at the back was raised a couple of feet and was reserved for the officers. Hanging from the ceiling just in front of the officers' section was a small platform for the projector and the hapless projectionist. He had a ladder, which he used to climb up to the platform, which he then pulled up and stowed on the platform during the showing of the film. This served two purposes. It prevented the audience from stealing the ladder, thereby marooning the projectionist on the platform. It also prevented the audience from reaching and inflicting bodily harm on the projectionist. The arrangement did not, however, stop the audience from throwing things at him and generally harassing him to the point of total exasperation. Fortunately (for us) film breakage and other malfunctions were the norm. When this occurred everyone began shouting obscenities at the projectionist. Again, fortunately for us he had absolutely no sense of humor and would start yelling back at the audience, advising that the film would not proceed until everyone quieted down. He would then fold his arms and stare straight ahead, making no effort to fix the problem. At this point the theater was total bedlam with the air filled with assorted garbage. Fortunately he never learned and could be guaranteed to respond each time. Obviously, when a rare good picture was available, the audience was a model of decorum. With the more common B pictures the place was a total zoo.

On one memorable night, an actor in the film accidentally killed a young lady, whereupon he more or less looked at the camera and spoke the world's greatest straight line, "What'll I do?" As might be expected, the audience had a number of rather carnal suggestions – one of the better being that he might consider doing something before she got cold.

There being a number of Red Cross girls and nurses present, a senior officer arose and said the film wouldn't continue until the culprit identified himself. After a rather lengthy and deafening silence the officer gave up and said to get on with the film.

The same theater was used for the showing of training films as a part of the daily regimen called "ground school". The theory was that the air crews when not flying should attend some form of training. The real purpose was to keep the flying personnel out of bed or in town. Since everyone knew this, it became a point of honor not to attend ground school if humanly possible. Initially, attendance was to be ensured by use of the honor system. When it became obvious that the number of actual attendees fell far short of the number that should have been there, they instituted a procedure wherein the airplane commander (pilot) would answer for his crew with something like "Crew 8 all present and accounted for". In actuality, the pilot would attest to the fact that they were all there whether they were or not. If the pilot wasn't there someone else would usually speak for him. When it became obvious that the number of attendees was still noticeably insufficient, they then ordered that each crewman stand up and give his name and crew position. No problem. Two or three crewmen would show up with a collection of hats; half standing at the proper time with a different hat and calling a different name and position and using a variety of voices. As might be expected, the roll taker really didn't care and went right along even if he caught on to the game. Some of the guys were really good, throwing on jackets, scarves and hats to present a different appearance each time. It finally got so that the training session was largely taken up by the roll call. If they did finally get around to the film, which we had probably all seen a dozen times, as soon as the lights went out everyone promptly fell asleep.

It was all good fun and no one really cared one way or the other since the primary purpose was really to keep us out of bed or out of trouble.

Ronald D. Spencer

In the early days of powered eggs and Brussels sprouts, we carried our mess gear to the club. Beer was served from a barrel on a rickety table, using our mess kit cups. At the end we had a fine club, linens, silver and all the rest, which we paid for, but it was never so welcome. We even built our own movie theatre, using materials bought from a bombed-out movie house.

Colonel William 'Bill' Cameron

Getting "knocked up" (a British term for getting awakened) was almost always well before dawn. Remember that this was England at a latitude further north than any part of the lower forty-eight states. It was winter and not too far away in time from the winter solstice. So dawn came late and nightfall came early.

The pre-mission breakfast was always good, including eggs and bacon or sausage, cereal, juice, fruit and bread and rolls. The philosophy might have been a little like that applied to the last meal of a convict about to be executed. No Spam for breakfast! This was saved for dinner, along with Brussels sprouts, Brussels sprouts and Brussels sprouts.

Our pilot, John Belingheri, observed that, although one got real eggs when scheduled for a mission, the fare was powdered eggs otherwise. Those on a mission were awakened very early, maybe 2am, with breakfast shortly thereafter. When not on a mission, wake-up was around 6am. John liked real eggs but not the dried variety. He had a standing request that, if either of the other two crews in our hut was to fly that day and our crew was not, then they would awaken him so he could also get the good breakfast. Then he would go back to bed! I guess I am a bit different. Getting to sleep longer is almost worth having to eat Spam (or worse) for breakfast!

John L. Stewart

Dear Folks:

I hope I can concentrate above the uproar of the "post-pay day" crap game. Money means nothing to these guys. A pound is $4.03 but since it's a single piece of paper, it's treated the same as a dollar bill, especially in a crap game. Consequently, "small fortunes" change hands overnite [sic]. But the boys have to relax some way. They are all, to some extent, "flak-happy" and now I shall risk the fury of the censor and discuss a common subject in the barracks. Flak – the root of all evil and woe. If the Air Force occupies Germany after the war, pity the poor German who lets it be known that he was in any an anti-aircraft battery during the war.

I'm sure you saw it in Memphis Belle. It's just a puff of black smoke. You see thousands ahead of you and fly right thru them. The more you see, naturally, the more worried you are (if you have sense enough to worry). But the ones you the see will never hurt you. You'll never see the one that rips into your wing or your engines or fuselage. Or possibly into one of your crew.

Sometimes it's accurate and sometimes not. I'm very glad that you saw the Memphis Belle. That is the most accurate picture of what we do that could possibly be shown. But believe me every mission isn't that bad. Still ships are lost and the only "good" mission, to me, hasn't been flown since I've been here. That will be the one when none go down and no one is killed. It's mostly up to us. I read somewhere that those who fly in combat take their jobs much like steeple-jacks and coal miners. If you know it thoroughly and fully realize the disaster of being careless, or not being alert, then you don't worry. You get the feeling that it's up to you ...

Bill Ligon

Recreation

One obvious advantage we had in serving in England during the war was the fact that you lived in a highly civilized country with, relatively speaking, all of the amenities. Off the base that is. Outside the gate we had pubs, buses, taxis and within five miles or so a city of some 200,000 people. Thus, we had access to just about everything that wasn't rationed or in short supply.

When most of us hit England, the first place usually visited was the local pub. We had one just down the road which was and still is called The Green Man. Its staple was warm beer, or more to the point room-temperature beer which in the fall and winter could be pretty cold. All pubs had the duty dartboard with the locals usually playing. In a crowded pub I thought you stood a good chance of getting a dart in the ear. The pub's clientele was typically male and female of all ages. Singing in the pubs was fairly common. I never got over elderly women loudly singing "Lay me down, roll me over and do it again", a popular song in England at the time. I realized that English pubs really had no counterpart in this country, being more like a social club than a bar. I found most Americans tired of the pub scene before long and sought other entertainment. Another pub, a little farther away, was called The Cottage, pronounced Cot-age by the locals. The East Anglian dialect was one I had never heard before. They seemed to swallow the second syllable or something. I think the Yorkshire dialect may be somewhat similar but I'm not sure. When we went to the Cottage we always rode our bicycles since we weren't much into walking in those days. The ride home in the blackout from the Cottage often resulted in some nasty scrapes and bruises from collisions with other bicycles and miscellaneous obstructions. Being half in the bag didn't help.

Norwich was the obvious destination of choice if you wished to make more of a night of it. The so-called liberty run (Army trucks) left for Norwich around seven as I recall and returned somewhere around eleven. Most used the trucks since they were free if pretty spartan transportation. The typical British double-deck buses had a route, which passes by the base so you could take those if the schedule was appropriate. If you really wanted to splurge, you could take a taxi but I don't ever recall taking the taxi either way. I did walk back to the base once but I don't recall the circumstances.

Norwich, being a good size city, had a lot to offer, subject to shortages of course. It had a legitimate theater, a movie theater a big dance hall called the Samson and Hercules (better known as the Muscle Palace), a large outdoor market, a castle (mentioned in Robin Hood), the duty huge cathedral, some restaurants, but best of all a Red Cross club where you could stay over night and most important, get a hot bath, a true luxury to us. Most of the troops sampled all of the various spots when they first arrived, with the novelty wearing off after they'd been there awhile. The liberty run was a pretty cold, uncomfortable ride which was also a deterrent.

Walking around Norwich in the blackout was an experience. The English painted the curbing at crosswalks white, which helped a little, but you could kill yourself bumping into things, tripping over the curbing or getting lost. Bumping into people was rather common. Finding your way in the blackout or the fog was difficult. If you had both, it was murder. I recall coming out of the Red Cross club one morning in a fog the likes of which I had never seen. I started across the street and became disoriented and ended up walking down the street and couldn't find the curb. I ended up walking in the opposite direction and had no idea where I was. And all I had done was try to cross a twenty-foot street. On one very foggy night, I was coming home on the liberty run when we literally bumped into one of the red double-deck buses. It was crawling along with the lady ticket taker walking along about three feet in front with a flashlight guiding the bus driver. You couldn't see anything ten feet from you. We all decided we had never seen anything quite like it.

Since the war, I've heard a lot about Americans being invited into English homes; however, at the time I didn't know of anyone that was. It was never my impression that the English people were particularly warm to the Americans – with the exception of a lot of the girls who were drawn to them because of the money they had to spend. This obviously didn't apply to the older English women.

By the spring of 1945, most people hung out in the club on the base as opposed to pubbing or going into Norwich. Also, by that time, the officer's club had so much money in the treasury that they began handing out free beer and sandwiches later in the evening. That was enough of an incentive to stay on the base. Another was the occasional party where girls were brought in from town in a bus or buses. The big problem was getting them off the base after the party. Our base was pretty straight in that regard. But some bases were notoriously lax. On one, I was told, they put up a sign on the following Monday saying that all women will positively be off the base by Thursday – I guess to get ready for the following Saturday night's influx. A not unreasonable request we thought.

One of our hut-mates visited another base and on Sunday morning was in the latrine shaving when a couple of girls walked in and started brushing their teeth with soap. They quickly accepted his offer of a little toothpaste.

Parties at the club usually produced a fair amount of food and drink, obviously one of the incentives for the young ladies to come to the parties. Also, it was warm in the club, a rarity in wartime England. A specialty at the parties was often "Moose Juice", a concoction of medicinal alcohol and grapefruit juice. It tasted like straight grapefruit juice and thus was rather insidious. It got me one unforgettable night. I remember drinking a couple of cups of the stuff and not much else till I awoke the next morning with a terrible hangover. I had no recollection of how I got home. I was very ill on the way as everyone let me know. We had to fly a practice mission next day. I told Kilar he was on his own and slept it off in the tunnel under the flight deck. I steered clear of Moose Juice thereafter.

About half or two-thirds of the way through the tour you were supposedly treated to a "Flak Home" so-called; an estate somewhere in England where you could relax and recover if necessary from battle fatigue. We were never given the opportunity. We did get the week off but most of us went to London. I recall becoming bored within three or four days and returning to the base. Such as it was it was home at the time.

One thing that I always found intriguing was the dichotomy of our lives. During the day you could be deep in Germany exposing life and limb and that night be all dressed up and sitting in a theater in town watching a very good stage show. Sitting all around you were people who had spent their day in the office or some other mundane place. I'd look at someone next to me and think that while they were shopping that morning in the corner market, I was standing four miles over Brunswick at fifty below zero with the flak banging around – wild!

Ronald D. Spencer

On a bright July afternoon another pilot and I set out from Halesworth on our bicycles to visit friends at Bungay. When we got on to the long straight road that runs between the two little towns we saw two girls on bikes ahead of us. Now there was an opportunity to get us a little female company on our trip so we set off to overtake them. We pedalled as hard as we could but those girls stayed way ahead of us for miles. In the end we had to admit defeat and that English girls were too fast for us Yanks!

Co-pilot Bud Chamberlain

Stationed at Attlebridge I was frequently on my bicycle whenever we had a stand-down. How rich was that part of England, with each village offering history and literature of centuries past! A former student and teacher, I grasped every opportunity to get off base and satisfy curiosity. One day my CO, Colonel Pierce, told me he had seen a sign on a house that identified it as the Chaucer House, in the village of Bawdeswell. With everything under control in the operations center, I biked out that evening and found the owners of the house in their back garden. Mr and Mrs Lloyd Lewis welcomed me into their fourteenth-century home, which had purportedly belonged to Chaucer's uncle. That evening marked the beginning of a wonderful friendship which was to last for forty years. Both Lloyd and Adeline Lewis were gentle, well-educated people – he an engineer and she village schoolmistress. They opened their home to me and my friends, a place where we could enter the quiet of that medieval village and their clay-and-wattle house, to have a cup of tea and hours of good conversation, a time and place where we could pretend for a while that there was no war that demanded our attention and efforts. I was introduced to people in surrounding homes and halls that I would not have known except through Mr and Mrs Lewis. Lloyd Lewis died in '51 and Adeline came to our California home for her first American visit. Later, she spent another winter with us. We maintained a correspondence for forty years, our fine friendship enhanced by each well-crafted letter. My memories of that period of war in the ETO will forever be warm.

Henry Bamman

When off duty we travelled around locally to sample whatever was available. We heard that Jack Ross was probably the first Yank to visit St Neots. He was stopped by a Bobby and was asked to show his identification papers. Jack did and the Bobby said, "Quite frankly I didn't recognize the uniform and had to check you out. You are the first Yank I've seen."

A town not smothered in Yanks ... Bud Wurm and I had to check this out. We hit several pubs and wound up at an English couple's wedding reception. As with many occasions when with Wurm you wind up in unusual places.

I was talking to a couple when there was a loud commotion in the hall; somebody had fallen down the stairs. I went over and found Bud at the bottom of the stairs giggling. He wasn't hurt and we went back to partying. We had a great time and wound up at the Home Guard's barracks where they offered us beds and a cup of tea. Hungover the next day I urged that we get back to the base. Bud said, "Wait, I have to do something."

I asked, "What ya gotta do? He said, "Clean my shoes ... I got sick and I threw up in my shoes."

"Why your shoes?"

"I didn't want the Home Guardsmen to think I was untidy."

W. J. 'Red' Komarek

That afternoon, who should show up unexpectedly but the Bob Hope Special Services Show with Frances Langford, Jerry Colonna and Jack Pepper, their guitarist. They put on a terrific show that did us all a world of good.

Captain Franklin 'Pappy' Colby, pilot

The Norfolk Broads

A decision was made for all of us to take a train ride to the vacation resort coastal city of Great Yarmouth, located twenty miles east of Norwich, adjacent to the North Sea. I insisted that I buy the tickets. I approached the ticket window asking the agent for six tickets to Great Yarmouth. He gave me a set of tickets, which I paid for. When I got back with the family, they almost had a fit; the agent had given me second-class tickets. I thought nothing of it but I was quickly informed that officers only travel first class. I insisted it made no difference to me, but Mr Colman and the others were more insistent than ever. They finally convinced me that it would be an insult to the officer corps and an embarrassment to them if I did not exchange them for first class. After complying with their requests, we boarded the train for a most pleasant ride and wonderful day at the seashore and on the boardwalk. Of course none of us went swimming.

One of the many nice customs I enjoyed in England was that a person could not travel far in any city without coming to a "fish and chips" stand. For a nominal charge, the vendor dispensed a very tasty, as well as nutritious "quick food". The chips were potatoes … cooked in the fish grease. On this outing to Great Yarmouth, we ate our fill of fish and chips out of newspaper, as well as other foods.

One evening, I left the Colman house knowing that they planned to spend the following day at the river camp. I informed them that I had an early-morning practice flight and to be on the look out for my plane to overfly the camp. The next morning, I told pilots Peritti and Palmer what I wanted. They agreed that if I'd lead them to the site, they would fly low over the camp. As soon as I pointed out the exact building along the riverbank, the pilots revved the motors, getting them out of sync' so they made a loud noise. I could see Margaret and the rest of the family standing in the yard, waving at us. Then, Peritti did his thing: he banked to the right in order to re-cross the river, then turned back towards the cabin, which stood perhaps 100yd up a slope from the river. Rather tall trees were about the building, but the campsite was in plain view amongst the trees.

Lili Marlene headed straight towards the camp with the family still out in front, waving at us. We were diving straight at the cabin and the trees, but at the last conceivable instant, Peretti and Palmer pulled up just in time. I saw the Colman family throw themselves on the ground, as they were sure it was all over for them. Because we had other things to do, no second pass was made, much to my relief. We returned to the base in the early afternoon. As soon as I could, I caught the truck to town and cycled to the Colman house, arriving about suppertime. Their eyes were still as big as saucers. We had given them either the biggest thrill in their lives or the worst fright; to this day I'm not sure which. The buzz job dominated the conversation for the rest of the evening.

There was a mutual love and respect between the Colman family and myself. I was happy when my combat tour was complete but sad also knowing I would soon be transferred to the ZOI. My last visit with the family was in the middle of October 1944. Neither they nor I had any doubt that we would meet again after the war. At the same time I was leaving England, my brother-in-law, Claude Boydston, arrived. He was the pilot of a B-17 Flying Fortress crew and the husband of my second-oldest sister. I wrote to him to ask if he would visit Margaret and the Colman family. He did visit several times while he was with his bomb group. He told me later that he really enjoyed the Colmans but felt a little foolish taking Margaret to the movies, as he did once or twice, being as she was so much younger than he was. I appreciated what he did.

John McClane Jr, navigator

... Decided to go take a look around Great Yarmouth. We took a noon train and came back about 8:55pm last night and had quite a good time. First thing we did was walk along the waterfront. The beaches are all closed off now with barbed wire and pillboxes and since the beaches are mined, it's a poor place to go anyway. From Britania Pier we walked south on the big, wide walk for several blocks. It was quite a resort area in peacetime as the postcards show. There were two enormous dance pavilions, one all glass and several amusement places including a big roller coaster. The sign I've ringed on the card advertises trips to Ostend on the Belgium coast and coach trips, probably to Paris. I took some pictures I hope turn out good. Then we went to see a show before supper. You may have seen it ... it was called Rose Marie with Jeanette McDonald and Nelson Eddy. I enjoyed the singing ... then we had a real good supper; chicken and ice cream in fact, in a restaurant there. By then it was time to catch our train back. It got kinda rainy then but I didn't mind, tho', it was too late to write by the time we got home at 11.30pm. That seems to cover the day Vonny. We want to go to Cromer if it warms up and lay out in the sun on the beach since they've been cleared now of wire and mines. Might even go swimming.

Captain Ralph H. Elliott

Before Christmas, the Watkins crew flew one practice mission to test some new equipment or procedure. It was a beautifully bright fall day in East Anglia. At the close of the mission, we were over the Norfolk Broads, an expanse of lowlands that only recently, in a geological sense, emerged from the North Sea. It was in fact a resort and pleasure area dotted with windmills, lakes and a network of interconnecting canals. On this particular day it was also dotted with pleasure yachts. Tom thought it would be great fun to buzz the broads and perhaps rock a few yachts from our following draft. Of course, it would also be fun to skim the lake or canal, pretending to be a hydrofoil, head straight for a yacht and pull up at the last moment. We might even see the "Gaw Blimey" occupants hit the water.

I stood in the doorway to the pilot's cabin and watched – very nervously, because I would have pulled up sooner than did Tom. After perhaps fifteen minutes of this "great fun", and probably also much bloody cursing on the water, Tom wearied and set course for home – to begin, along a long straight canal, again testing our capacity as a hydrofoil. Ahead loomed a low arched stone bridge over the canal. Tom saw the bridge all right and pulled up in time to clear the bridge, but not the few strands of telephone wire that he did not see in time and that were suspended above the bridge. There was a sharp twanging snap as we headed home in a nervous, embarrassing silence, fun being over.

A low-winged Flying Fortress would have fouled its props in the wires, but, our Liberator's props at the high-wing level were not fouled; rather, the lowest part of a gear-up Liberator was the pair of ten-inch prongs extending from the very bottom of the fuselage and holding a radio antenna.

Tom later reported two inquiries into our experiences on the Broads. One was from the ground crew chief of our plane: did Captain Watkins wish him to report the strands of wire caught on the radio antenna? Captain Watkins did not. The second inquiry was via telephone from 8th Air Force Command, not to Tom but to our base command – the tail markings on each Liberator were coded to its group and base. As Tom told it, our command made no real attempt to reprimand anyone and possibly not even to learn which crew had done the deed.

After all, what brass was brassy enough to punish heroes who might not give a damn anyway? Would the brass wish to have one of its top crews stood down for even a short time? Heavens, no! The war had to be won and the bloody Yanks certainly could pay for repair of the telephone lines with nary a strain on the pocketbook.

Bob Shaver

It is Christmas 1944 and l am in the land of Dickens – real inns before me, real beefsteak, real ale drawn in pewter, open fireplaces, huge old oaken beams in the smoke-seasoned rooms filled with warmth and good cheer even though the country is in its fifth year of war.

I am stationed in a small Suffolk village that could have come right out of the pages of Dickens or off the front of a Christmas card. My bomber group of B-17s with the 8th Air Force is stationed just north east of London where we are engaged in flying long-range bombing missions to major cities in Germany. I am a teenage aerial gunner who has flown bombing runs through flak, clouded, fighter-infested, dangerous skies over Hitler's *Festung Europa* (Fortress Europe).

The oldest crewman in our team is twenty years old, the youngest seventeen – none of us is eligible to vote.

Now it is Christmas Eve and I am going to St Mary's Church. I haven't been to church since being in England, but tonight, my third Christmas away from home, I feel I must be there. St Mary's is over 500 years old – unheated except for coal stoves and unlighted except for hundreds of candles burning around the inside of the church and on the altar. There is a deep snow on the ground and it is lighted by the gleaming candlelight shining through the frosted, stained glass.

As I leave [sic] the church I notice that it is filled with soldiers and civilians – except for one seat near the front. I make my way to this place and there is a music folio lying on the seat. I pick it up and hold it. The soldier in the next chair looks questioningly at me. During one part of the service the choir is to sing a special anthem. I did not know this. As we are all in uniform it is hard to distinguish which was the choir. I had taken the seat of a choir member who had not shown up for the service.

At the appointed time for the choir to sing, the soldier next to me nudges me and I stand up when they do. We sing beautifully, "Silent Night, Holy Night", in that ancient place of worship. Then quietly file out into the winter night, back to our drab, cold barracks, but with a warm glow of a beautiful Christmas celebration in our hearts. It is a memorable one for me. I had never sung with a choir before ... and could not read music.

The next day [this actually happened some time later] our crew was shot down over Nuremberg, Germany, and imprisoned for the duration of the war, but I had the special memory of that blessed night to carry me through the trials to come.

Walter 'Boots' Mayberry

Barnardo children would have had a much poorer Christmas had it not been for the big hearts of the 8th Air Force men. The members of the 94th [Bomb Group] welcomed 145 children. They were provided with a bountiful dinner and greeted personally by Colonel Castle. The men of the 94th had been saving gum, candy and cookie rations for this occasion. They had also collected and contributed money to finance the party and all the necessary adornments. While in London on pass they had been buying toys, which they secretly tested for proper performance and to satisfy the whims of each age group. Maybe all of them reverted to childhood for a time. The men had requested Christmas decorations from home and received good response. Committees were formed. Christmas carols were played by the base band. Folk tunes and trick fiddling by a corporal from Kentucky and a wonderful rendition of "White Christmas" by Corporal Planisek of Cleveland, who the night before had been peeling potatoes. The Ordnance Section Chief awed the children with a flashy rendition on his accordion, which was followed by tap dancing. Then the children's choir and morris dancers entertained the men. There were skits and cartoons and finally Father Christmas. These Americans had talent but more than that they had big hearts. It was hard to say who had the most fun, the kids or the Yanks! After the entertainment Father Christmas called the name of each child, who received a gift from under the brilliantly lit tree. In each child's surprise package was a radio. Colonel Castle then presented to each of the Homes assorted games and athletic equipment. The base band played "God Save the King" and "The Star Spangled Banner". Fifty men from every section of the base had served on special committees and helped in the programme. It was a total effort that came right from the heart.

Lalli Coppinger

How they roamed the local villages, looking for the rural pubs, which they very much enjoyed. They bought anything that looked like a bicycle and learnt to ride. I remember them coming from the pub riding single file, wobbling all over the road and shouting at each other, so it was quite easy to know they were coming.

                                                                    J. Gogle

Bicycling was a major pastime. English 'cycles were issued to many of the ground men. The aircrews felt free to borrow. "Borrowing" became so bad that on one occasion all 'cycles were called in by the MPs and their numbers checked. Many were then returned to their original owners.

                                                                Allan Healy

Can you imagine a gaggle of eighteen bike riders charging down those narrow Norfolk roads, in daylight or dark? I can assure you it was not like a Hell's Angels act – it was more like a Wild West scenario where the cowboys came to town after months on the trail and stormed the Longhorn saloon. Nevertheless, these Yanks were totally accepted and – I dare say – appreciated.

                                              Myron Keilman, 392nd Bomb Group

Bicycles were the main means of transport for the American airman. Three were riding on the bicycle, one on the handle bars, one on the seat and the other one standing on the back wheel spindle, legs akimbo. Coming to a bend in the road the man steering could not get the cycle around the bend owing to the man sitting on the handlebars. They hit the high curb a mighty bang and all flew off the cycle. The one on the handlebars must have been an acrobat. He shot over the hedge doing a somersault and landed neatly on his feet. They were funny old boys.

                                                                David Bacon

9

London Times

Well first the bloody Jerry's got to find London in a blackout, then he has to find Neasden, then he has to find number twelve Cheltham Court and then I'll probably be down at the pub havin' me pint.

At Audley End Station he bought a ticket for Liverpool Street Station for his first 48-hour pass to London and squeezed on the 5:15. There was standing room only on the trains, a condition which would have prevailed even if the Britons had put their newspapers down. At first the soldier didn't know West End from The City, so he queued up for one of those faded blue cabs that sit up high and gadabout like a maiden aunt come vis-à-vis with a long-lost lover. Later, when it was ruefully discovered that a British pound sterling is not equivalent to a dollar bill green, he learned to ride the Underground, savoring the names of the stops as he went ... Ealing Broadway ... Knightsbridge ... Marble Arch ... Chancery Lane ... Elephant and Castle ... Charing Cross ... Oxford Circus ... Piccadilly Circus ... East Acton ... Bank.

On the first trip he started out to do all the historic spots, like the haunts of Dr Johnson, Goldsmith and Rare Ben Jonson. He viewed the Blitz scars but was forbidden by the censors to write home about them. He sauntered through the ineffable Piccadilly Circus, capital of America-in-Britain, Leicester Square, the Strand and tiptoed through Westmister Abbey. He took a gander at the Mother of Parliaments and set his watch by Big Ben. He progressed along Birdcage Walk to Buckingham Palace to see the changing of the guards. He whistled up a taxi, the approved method being a trumpeted *tax-hee*.

"Take me to 221-B Baker Street."

This archness is old stuff to the driver, but he drives there anyway. The fare found neither Dr Watson nor Holmes at home, which is probably elementary anyway. Probably out getting the usual 7 per cent cocaine pick-me-up.

If he were an officer, he had more or less had it insofar as sightseeing went. On subsequent 48s he headed straight for the Jules Club on Jermyn

Street, or to any of a most formidable array of places he was able to establish himself in. It's just possible that he proceeded to a lecture on the early history of the Belgian parliament but if a quorum were needed, it was best to start searching at the Cracker's Club – that dingy little Piccadilly hole with the smell of a "Y" gym through which half the Allies' fighter pilots passed and wrote their names on the walls – and wind through the Studio Club, Lansdowne House, the Garter, Wellington, Embassy and Astor Clubs.

Ah, but the enlisted man on furlough – he covered England like the dew covers Dixie. He was an authentic grassroots plenipotentiary. He was everywhere and stood short nowhere. With less money to spend but with just as much time off as officers, the enlisted soldier saw twice as much of the country and knew its people that much better.

In Piccadilly Circus, about Rainbow Corner, you couldn't see even the big "Bovril" sign for the American olive drab. They walked about with the girls of many nationalities on their arms. White-helmeted MPs – a source of ceaseless delight and fascination to Englishmen – stood in the entrances to the Underground, which blew its dank breath into the street and lay in wait for GIs with unbuttoned blouses or one more mild and bitter than they could carry. Through the incredibly congested Circus the lavender-and-old-lace cabs would rage, packed with Americans. You could tell the new arrivals because they rode in clusters of five to eight with the top down, waving a bottle of Scotch and causing the Limeys to remark, "See? The Americans are the reason spirits are in short supply."

Night would fall and Piccadilly would assume the shape, which will always be a flashing memory with those who did time in the ETO. The blackout was rigid, or at least it would have been had it not been for thousands of GIs hurrying about with their torches (Limey for flashlight). You could tell an American from any other in the dark because their flashlights were larger and more powerful. From Lower Regent Street, they made Piccadilly look like a jar of fireflies in a closet. The Leicester Square theater queues would grow even longer, reaching down Shaftesbury Avenue almost to Piccadilly. At first blackout the celebrated "Piccadilly Commandos" would begin walking the night, as much a part of the scene as the doorman in front of the Regent Palace Hotel. Inappropriately, the famous statue of Eros, God of Love, was crated during the war. They were more an institution than a facility and few GIs (I speak for Debden) permitted themselves a conclusive encounter. They were as alert as a bell captain and aggressive, approaching everything in olive drab with a parroted American slang greeting which was ridiculous when conveyed on a British accent. Their honorariums were enormous (and downright incredible when they walked under a light). But they were an integral part of Piccadilly's teeming, fetid pageantry. A Debden corporal wrote a song, "Lilly from Piccadilly", which the ETO sang.

Soon the soldier began to feel at home, the first sign being that he spent two days in London without gawking at the barrage balloons loafing over the city. He got caught in air raids and learned to tell the big ones from the little ones by the whistle. He became allergic to exposed lights and blacked them out with reflex action. He began counting British currency as easily as US. There was just one thing whose hatefulness never diminished, the weather. Every day he felt as though his skin had accumulated another layer of mold.

Isn't there some Kipling about "single men in barracks don't grow into plaster saints?" Anyway, there were 1,500 officers and men at Debden, for the most part high-spirited American males between the ages of 20 and 30, some 3,000 miles removed from home and trying to forget the fact. Some arrived as virtuosos of the secular life, while others maintained the pretense until they got the hang of it.

The American Male At Debden, Grover C. Hall Jr

"Brandon, Lakenheath, Shippea Hill, Ely, Cambridge, Audley End, Bishop's Stortford, London."

There was the time you stood from Thetford all the way to London, your feet numb in the draughty corridor, the windows steamed so that even the bleak Suffolk landscape was hidden in the November curtain of cold. There was the jerking, stopping, backing, starting and there was the inevitable twenty-minute stop at Ely. You cursed the heat-lever over the seat; it never worked. But then it was April, a half year later. You left your overcoat behind in the belly-tank crate that served as a wall-locker, stuffed some shaving articles in your musette bag and hopped the 5.50 or the 9 or the 11 o'clock bus from the MP Gate. You were taking off on a "48 to London." It was spring and you felt eager.

No tickets now at fourteen-bob round-trip. In April '45 you began getting reverse lend-lease in travel warrants to any point in the UK. You waited on the platform for the train to pull in from Norwich, buying a *Daily Express*, "*Sketch*", "*Mail*", "*Post*", or "*Illustrated*". Then you read the signs, "There'll Always Be Mazawattee Tea" and watched a Thetford farmer herd two goats off the Bury train through the passengers. And you looked over the local civilians, the British officers and the scores of American airman, a few of them with all their gear starting the trip back to the States.

Local trains from Swaffham and Watton arrived with school-kids in shorts and high wool stockings, clutching their books like the school-kids in all countries. The British Indian soldiers looked up from the freight cars they were unloading and silently watched the trains. Thetford is a small town, but its station carried life in and out by day and night. Girls from Knettishall, Scotch [sic] officers in kilts, GIs starting on pass clean-shaven and returning un-pressed, unshaven and unwell; goats, dogs, bicycles and boxes of aromatic fish.

And there was the morning a few months after D-Day when your train was an hour late and then you saw why: A hospital train steamed in to pick up a score of US wounded, casualties headed for the States. There was no ceremony, no coffee and doughnuts or brave smiles. The wounded stared back at those who stared at them, their eyes dull and tired ...

You sat in the compartment and slept most of the way. That is you sat when there was a seat, one of the eight that could be crowded into each compartment. Opposite you was a minister who smiled in a kindly, professional way; three gunners from the B-17 field near Bury, invariably sleeping; two civilian women next to you reading a cheap-covered book and holding boxes and babies; a civilian smoking steadily, his pipe acrid and penetrating, tobacco shreds sprinkled unnoticed on his well-worn overcoat.

Again you read the signs in the train ... "If danger seems imminent, lie on the floor", advised the poster next to the water-colour of the cathedral. "It is dangerous for passengers to put their heads out of carriage windows," warned the message over the door with the window you opened by working the heavy leather strap.

'48 To London', 359th Fighter Group History

On my trips to London I got to know the Underground system very well. Sometimes I'd see Britishers standing around on a platform looking lost. I'd go up and offer to give directions. Got a kick out of the look on their faces when a Yank told them which train to catch.

Art Swanson

After our first taste of combat, we decided to take off a couple of days and visit London see some sights and enjoy ourselves. We didn't think it unusual to be on duty seven days a week while in England, but we did enjoy the occasional two-day pass awarded us when flying would slack up a bit. We made several trips to London, which was about 100 miles away and we could make the trip by train in about four hours when there were no unusual delays. The GI food on base was not too bad, but we really enjoyed the various types of food offered in the British restaurants. On one occasion, we decided to celebrate and have a feast at one of the nicer Chinese restaurants in London. Most of the crewmembers were there and we ordered several different Chinese dishes with all the trimmings. These were served more or less boarding-house style so that our large table was well laden with continuous servings of Asiatic delicacies as we leisurely enjoyed the many courses offered, savoring every bite. This was one of the most tasty meals I had in England and all of us enjoyed our banquet that night.

1st Lieutenant (later Captain) Alvin D. Skaggs, pilot, 448th Bomb Group

... The austerity that is London's in wartime is one of the Yank's first impressions. It is marked in the dress of the women who are not in uniform. It strikes home in the sameness of the food and the shabbiness of furnishings, which can scarcely be repaired, much less replaced, in a city fighting for its existence. There is little complaint, because the austerity is fairly rationed, as is everything else. London is full of guests and these make a point of insisting they share the deprivations with their hosts. Long before the Yanks came, there were guests from many other lands, refugees who asked nothing more than food, shelter and a chance to work and fight with the British for the liberation of their own peoples ...

The winds of London blow chill and wet. Slanting in the wind is a sleety rain, too thin really to be a rain, yet not quite light enough for fog. It is a day on which hardened soldiers wear their trench coats buttoned tight about their throats; they shiver in their woolen uniforms and even war-scarred Tommies in battledress plod about miserably in their baggy pantaloons.

... There are other matters in wartime London that bother your complacency. For instance, there is a small tailor shop situated in a battered section of The City where six hundred acres of devastation mark Hitler's neap tide of conquest. The place is owned and operated by an Englishman, one of those Uriah Heeps made forever despicable by Dickens. I was there because slim-legged, redheaded Tracy had told me the story. I wanted to see for myself.

Tracy's husband, an officer of the Royal Navy, was one of those who give the story point.

This tailor was liberal with officers in the forces. A Royal Air Force man could always get a new tunic, even a loan of a few quid on a chit. The Royal Navy had priority on similar loans and outfittings. The Army, on the other hand, unless a man were bound for the Middle East, Hong Kong, Burma or some equally bloody front, was a very poor third on the list. This tailor had a nose for news and for action.

At first I couldn't understand Tracy's attitude. The tailor would trust officers, especially officers doing hazardous duties, for money or a new tunic. Wasn't he then a prince, a right guy?

The answer is a grim one. When Royal Air Force, Navy or Army officers are killed in the line of duty His Majesty's government sees to it that their current bills are paid. The enterprising tailor need have no fear that one of them will die in an unpaid-for blouse. It's good business to have the English officers on your books, especially in time of war. Load the boys up with clothes. The tailor can't lose.

But the little tailor has cross-stitched his seam, for officers of the Royal Forces no longer patronize him. His business smacks too much of grave-robbing ...

I'll never forget standing on the balcony watching, with a fine show of unconcern, the barrage from the main batteries blocks away. Suddenly the guns almost beneath me let go. There was an indescribable roar and I found myself sweating forty feet away in the hall, where I had leaped like a startled gazelle.

My nerves tingled. To unaccustomed ears it had sounded like at least a four-thousand pounder. I shamefacedly returned to my vantage point and a few moments later a high-altitude gun let go, equally near by. Its coughing whoop once more sent me ducking for the hall. I was glad none of my inured British cousins were on hand to view my performance.

For every Englishman of his stripe there are hundreds like the workingman with the Lancashire accent who gave me his lighter.

Cigarette lighters are at a premium in wartime London. Matches are scarce and the means of lighting cigarettes are precious. Since the beginning of World War II, the manufacture of such luxury items as lighters has been a thing of the lush past. They are a valuable possession not to be carelessly laid down on a bar and left behind.

One afternoon I walked down Oxford Street with a cigarette dangling from my lips, unlighted. My lighter was at home, forgotten.

Working in the street at an open manhole was a typical British laborer using a huge blowtorch. He was dirty, with the grime of his trade ground into his hands, but solid. He saw me and came over.

"Man," he said, "you've traveled a long way to be without a light. Here, man, take this."

He proffered a lighter made of two Victorian pennies welded together, with rude flint and steel fittings soldered in place. I took the lighter, put flame to the cigarette and tried to give the homemade instrument back. The Lancashire man was insulted.

"No, man. That's for you. You've traveled too far without a lighter. That's for you, man."

I protested. I had no desire to take the man's handiwork without paying for it. I tried to buy it. The Britisher flatly refused the return of the tiny instrument.

A passing bobby intervened. "Take it," he said. "He wants you to have it. It's a gift. Take it." I looked the tall policeman in the eye, finally understanding, and accepted the gift with thanks.

As I walked away, the bobby fell into step alongside.

"He's a strange 'un," he said. "But maybe you can understand it. He works on those mains all the time, even during the Blitz when plenty of them were aflame. His family was wiped out while he was tending his mains. He likes Americans."

And the homemade lighter which I treasure is his gift to all Yanks.

On the other hand, there are profit-seekers in London as in every other big city during wartime. Whether it be Paris, Berlin, Tampa, New York or London there will always be men who ride the skyrocketing prices to fill their own pockets.

Fresh from experiences with the rent hogs of the States, you are amazed to find the same swine here. They think nothing of asking twelve guineas a week for a dark monstrosity of a flat.

No one questions paying nine shillings for a meal in a restaurant that would be banned under the laws of hygiene in other times. The restaurants have less food than they have customers and you don't have to eat there unless you wish.

The gouge is on in London in many ways, but it's no more severe than in Washington DC, or for that matter any small town near an army camp.

I well remember the little town in Arkansas, center of Second Army maneuvers back in 1941. In this hospitable spot, a hamburger sandwich and a bottle of coke cost soldiers of the 27th Division fifty-seven cents per copy. The local merchants charged forty cents for the ten-cent sandwich, fifteen cents for the nickel coke; and then had the guts to add the two-cent state tax.

Soldiers of the last World War – "retreads", First Wing calls them, when they enter service again – remember the same situation in London and Paris in 1918, but mostly in Paris. Captain Jack Kofoed of Miami, Florida, a retread, recalled the Parisian speculators who tried to "do in" the Yank on leave from the trenches.

"To get even with 'em," Kofoed recalls, "we used to pass United Cigar Store coupons as legal tender, until the natives finally got wise."

But this is London and the Yank doesn't feel too bad about the prices.

"They've taken plenty from the Jerries," says First Wing; "maybe they need some change. And what's money for, except to spend?"

To soldiers returning after a quarter of a century London is new in her own way.

"It's like meeting a half-remembered girl," Captain Kofoed told me. "London has aged. The smashed façades of the houses, gaping windows, fire-scarred stores are the wrinkles and baggy flesh of her countenance. You aren't shocked by these changes in the West End, but when you get into The City and see block after block leveled to the ground, it's like having a strong light turned on the face of the girl you had almost forgotten. And seeing all the wrinkles and bags in hideous detail.

"Yes, the first impression is that of age. You don't sense it at once, but underneath this façade of age lies a quality of youthful resistance in the presence of trial. London stared deep into the glaring eyes of *Der Führer* and told him to go to hell. She suffered the consequences of her daring, but she took it like a lady."

This then is London Base Command, with all the facets of a big city in the war zone – sordid, sometimes funny, but most of the time gallant and courageous. Perhaps London has bedraggled skirts. Her hair may be awry and the stencil of horror has cut deep in her face. But essentially she is a *grande dame*. She accepts her shabbiness like a true patrician and extends her hospitality to her cousins from across the wide-reaching western ocean.

... Even as the German visitation upon London left its marks, so will the Yanks leave theirs. There will be a few scars, but much of fond remembrance. The Yanks of London have poured more cement into the Anglo-American mold than the top-hat diplomats and good-will ambassadors have been able to concoct over the years. True, it took a little while for the mold to set. A Yank, even one from Flatbush, is a hayseed when away from home. He is inclined to wear a defensive shell of condescension. The Englishman is sensitively undemonstrative in the presence of a "foreigner." At the beginning they were as standoffish as two distant cousins. That the relationship improved steadily is due largely to that sudsy leveler of man – the public house.

When First Wing gets a twenty-four-hour pass it follows a well-established procedure. It takes off its half-knee mud boots, dons its creased "pinks" and comes to London Town, its pockets comfortably stuffed with pound notes. Flying pay – fifty percent on top of base pay – adds up to a lot of sterling. A man gets no chance to spend while on station. He deals on a cash basis for his cigarettes and rationed bar privileges. His mess bill runs a dollar a day or less. So provident officers and men build respectable balances at the

London banks, which obligingly permit them to open checking accounts. Sending money home necessitates a major operation against red tape and cash balances have little attraction for combat crewmen, considering the uncertainties.

London is therefore the accepted "target for tonight" and the beneficiary of First Wing's sprees. Never completely subdued by the Blitz, London's nightclubs, theaters, cafés and hot spots are brilliantly lighted and tightly packed behind their blackout curtains. They flourish under the fertilization of pound notes which the profligate Yanks look upon casually as dollar bills. Actually, the pound represents a bit more than four bucks American, earned the hard way, at the most dangerous occupation invented by man or devil.

Graying, enfeebled waiters, about the only staffers left by the war in the West End bistros, scurry nightly in frenzied haste, growing young again under the largess of American tips.

Over the question of tips the Yank-vs-taxi-driver feud flourished. The cabbies are the best of all the public servitors with whom the Yank does business. They are a shabby, sullen, but efficient brotherhood of specialists. To get a hacking license in London the cabby applicant must do months of tour by bicycle until each of the winding streets and mews of this sprawling city are mapped perfectly in memory. Then, from behind the wheel of his conventional black cab, he must demonstrate over and over again to exacting police inspectors exactly how to reach given addresses from varying starting points without a single wrong turning or yard of excess haul. The London cabby is a postgraduate who knows not only how to find his way around, but who is conscious of all his prerogatives and insists upon their fulfillment. His sixpence tip is part of the pay scale, an accepted formula. The Yank is a generous tipper, but he objects to being reminded, or having the recipient fix the amount. The feud brought together two positives and the dispute was a long one, vigorously waged. Cabbies conditioned the unorthodox would-be passengers by passing them up on rainy nights. The feuding ended as soon as the Americans learned the sixpence tip was a part of the fare, though unregistered on the meter. Typically, they made their surrender generously.

Cabbies the world over are smart folk, perhaps because they are good listeners. "Dad," a wizened, crafty old skate who works out of a cab rank near the Park Lane Hotel, a favorite airman's hangout, gave me quite a shock the first time we met.

I hailed his cab, bound for the West End. "Portsea Hall, off Edgware Road," I told him.

"Roger!" responded Dad.

The acknowledgment thudded home and I asked questions at the end of the ride.

"I met one of your blokes, an Air Force bloke," the cabby explained. "He told me 'Roger' meant 'OK.'"

At an airfield "Roger" is the established acknowledgment when radio and intercom messages are understood. It is: *Little Beaver* to tower; taking off on number-three runway. And the tower control answers, "Roger," if all is well and the pilot's intention is clear. Similarly, if the tower gives instruction by radio to an air-borne bomber, the pilot signifies his understanding of the order with the same cryptic word. "Roger" sounded very strange and out of place on the lips of a London cabby.

The London Front, Major John M. Redding & Captain Harold Leyshon

Once a month we were given a two- or three-day pass to London. And this was an interesting episode, because London was blacked out and was constantly being bombed. The Germans were sending over their buzz bombs, which had just enough fuel to go just so far and then would head down to the ground, which is why they were called "flying bombs." We were in a hotel one time and a wing of that hotel was hit by a flying bomb. It scared the hell out of us and in fact, after that, I decided I would rather go to Cambridge. Both because it was a university town and didn't involve a long train ride and, also, because I didn't see any sense in going to London and risking being bombed. We usually wound up at Dorothy's, a dance hall on the second floor of an old building in Cambridge.

We did get to see Piccadilly and a bunch of other sights of London, although I must admit I wasn't in London looking for sightseeing. We would look for bars and good food and we would have tea at the Ritz where we could dance. It was just getting away – from the bombing and planes going down and from that kind of stuff.

August Bolino, navigator, 388th Bomb Group, Knettishall

One time, in London by myself looking for a good place to eat, I went into one of the major hotels. As I went by the doors there were a couple of our MPs walking up and down the street. I sat down and was about to order when a waiter comes over and says, "There's an MP who would like you to join him." Well the first thing I thought of was the two MPs I'd seen out there, so I said I don't want anything to do with MPs and if they want they can come and talk to me. The waiter went away and didn't approach me again. I had my meal and left. I got to wondering why an MP should want me. It was only later that someone suggested that the MP was a British Member of Parliament. I've often wondered what I missed and that I might have left a bad impression of GIs' courtesy if it was a British politician.

Wilbur Richardson

On pass, we stumbled on this London pub one afternoon and found it to be an excellent stop. Just think, in the land of warm beer this pub had iced lager on tap. After quite a few of these lagers, we were advised of it being closing time (pubs closed in the afternoon and would open again in the evening) we climbed the stairs from the Dive Bar section and wandered away. Not knowing what else to do we went to a cinema (movies) and took a short nap. Later when the pubs were opening up again, it was unanimous to return to the Chandos. Not having the foggiest idea in which direction we should go, we hailed a cab and told the driver of our dilemma. "Aya, Mates, I know the place, get in."

Four of us piled into the cab and we were off. And off we were. We rode around and around, not knowing one street from the other. Finally after what seemed like a long trip, we pulled up in front of the Chandos, happy to have found the place at last. We tipped liberally, thanked our driver and down the stairs to the Dive Bar we went. In conversation with our new found friends, two Irish barmaids, we told them of our adventure. The two looked at each other and asked again what cinema we went to. I said the one featuring *Gone With the Wind*. Both laughed and the redhead said, "That cinema is only around the corner and up the street!" I asked the guys, "Any of you remember what the cabbie looked like?"

It was worth it though, finding what was to be our home away from home. Pop Johnson owned the Chandos assisted by his missus and peaches and cream complexioned daughter, Iris. We soon became very good friends with the family and most of the times heading back to base broke, we'd borrow a couple of pounds and a bottle of whiskey from Pop and pay back on our return.

As with any popular public meeting house, the Chandos had its regular clientele. Our group included Lang, Wolf, Wurm and me. The other members consisted of Whitey, Tin-Can and Frank, members of a Canadian Halifax bomber crew, Ruby, a lady of the night, Doc, a Canadian Army sergeant and the Irish Barmaids ... especially the barmaids who at times had to say, "Sorry no Scotch, but would you like a glass of ginger beer?" Which when served strangely tasted like Scotch.

Word soon got around the base about the iced lager at the Chandos and shortly thereafter you could always spot a friendly face in the place. This pub had a famous convex-shaped bar in a downstairs corner. Famous I say because it had carved into it names and initials of patrons from both wars. Doc was proof of this, his initials were there from WWI and he was back for seconds. All of us made our own marks both in the bar and adjacent wall with Pop Johnson's blessings. What Pop didn't condone was singing and dancing as he had no license for those two activities, only allowed was drinking and talking. We, on the other hand, sang only when we were drinking and danced only when girls were around. Pop would come down to the Dive Bar, admonish us and when no one paid attention he'd throw up his hands and return upstairs. I don't recall one fight in the Chandos although we came close to it. I was standing at the bar with Jimmy Haggerty, a fellow tail gunner, talking shop, when this guy inches into the conversation and tells about his war service. Now a guy by the name of Haggerty and a guy whose mother's maiden name was Mahon are not what you would consider empathizers with a guy who was telling of his exploits during the trouble in Ireland in the early twenties. He served in what the Irish nicknamed the "Black and Tans". Since we detected no remorse in his stories, he hurriedly left the scene as Jimmy and I argued as to which of us should take him outside. It seems Scotch and iced lager stirs up the Gaelic genes. Mostly the mood was festive. An elderly woman coming in to sell flowers and would leave without her flowers that we'd buy and give to all the ladies present ... a patron with a sad tale would pocket a few pounds ... drinks and compliments were handed out all around. This was a fun place for now ... the damn war had to interrupt it from time to time.

The Chandos, W.J. 'Red' Komarek

Our crew had been in the ETO for six weeks now and we had our baptism of fire, completing three combat missions. So the time came for our first pass, leave or furlough. The custom was for each crew to get a 48-hour pass once a month, a break from the seven-day-a-week combat grind. And almost inevitably, they would head for bombed-out, war-weary, shabby London – like lemmings head for the sea. That was where the crews unwound, forgot the war for a couple of days, bolstered their morale and cemented their camaraderie.

There was little if any distinction between officers and enlisted men on the crew of the *La-Dee-Doo*. There was a mutual respect and we were on a first name basis. Each man had an essential job to perform for the good of all and our lives depended upon it. In the air, especially in combat, the pilot's word was law and there was no disputing it like in the Hollywood movies.

Altogether, most of our crew went on pass to London about four times. The first thing we did on our initial trip was to engage two ancient but meticulously preserved World War I-vintage taxis to take us on a tour of London Town. Two jovial Limey taxi drivers honked their way through the London traffic and confusion and gave us a poor man's historical tour of a city that was old before America was discovered. The sites included Westminster Abbey, Christopher Wren's magnificent St Paul's Cathedral (about the only building left standing in the bombed-out center of London), the famous London Bridge and the prestigious government buildings. And all the while we kept our eyes and ears pealed for the V-1 robot bombs which came over at irregular intervals night and day. We usually stayed at the Regent Palace Hotel overlooking Piccadilly Circus in the heart of London. All the windows had been blown out of one side of the building and were replaced by wooden shutters. However, the main ritual on each pass was the gathering of the crew for a sumptuous (for wartime England) spaghetti dinner at an Italian restaurant on Charlotte Street in the industrial area. Berterelli's was the best-kept secret of 388th bomber crews in World War II. Our 10-man crew would file into the restaurant to the curiosity of the Limey patrons, put three tables together, place a bottle of Chianti on each table, then systematically attack a five course meal or so, as smiling Italian waiters in frayed tuxedos flitted around filling glasses.

Another vivid memory of London consisted of the evenings we took the Tube (or underground subway) to the enormous dance hall known as Covent Garden, an opera house dating back to 1732. There, on the concrete subway floors in full view of passersby, whole families spread out their blankets in preparation for a night's sleep. These were the bombed out poor of London and they had been living like this in the subway for several years since the London Blitz.

The train rides from Thetford to London enabled us to view the quaint beauty of the small towns and rural countryside of England. The deep-green hedgerows, rolling fields and slow-flowing streams of East Anglia were scenes out of 18th Century pastoral paintings.

All too soon our two-day vacation from the war would come to an end. We would return to combat somewhat hung over, but dedicated to our rendezvous with our duty and our destiny.

The Year I Can't Forget, James E. O'Connor, co-pilot, *La-Dee-Doo*
crew, 388th Bomb Group

... A city of pomp and splendour, a panorama of history, theaters, restaurants, some of the best pubs in England ... and plenty of girls. You could go to a dance in Covent Garden and find a ten to one ratio of women to men and fifteen to one of women to Yanks ... For the less adventurous, there was the Red Cross Rainbow Corner Club. The neighborhood had a questionable reputation, being in Piccadilly Circus and frequented by ladies of the night dubbed "Commandos". The club was a big help to the GI. Fred Astaire's sister, Lady Cavendish, who was a regular volunteer ... writing to servicemen's families and a host of other activities. She even got a bottle of Scotch for us ... well it was for Jack Lang; she didn't trust the rest of us to deliver it.

December, W.J. 'Red' Komarek

The ride to London was scenic as long as the sun was still up, but was very monotonous when lights were turned out and blackout curtains drawn.

We pulled into Liverpool station in a heavy downpour. I followed the crowd into the London subway and finally found my way to Piccadilly Circus, which I knew to be near the Regent Palace Hotel. First I noticed the great number of people sleeping on the subway platforms far underground. A HMS Navy boy said they'd been doing it for years, taking the same bed every night. Frankly, I couldn't see how anyone could sleep a wink in the great rush of air and noise that announced the approach of each train.

A light rain had just been over the city when we arrived. Signs announcing the all clear were posted on the entrance to the subway.

At Piccadilly Circus things looked a bit hopeless. Rain was still falling and you couldn't see three feet in front of you. I bumped into someone and asked hurriedly where the Regent Palace was located. The "someone" turned out to be another officer in the same predicament. We teamed up and finally found the hotel but could get no rooms. I asked directions to the nearest Red Cross and took off in that general direction, hoping by inquiry every fifty feet to arrive at my destination, the Red Cross Reindeer Club on Clifford Street.

Here it might be well to tell that while wandering aimlessly like that in London, I remembered stories of "Piccadilly Circus Commandos" and, in fact, on all sides of me heard them plying their trade as I passed. Consequently, I was not surprised when suddenly I felt someone walking beside me. It was a girl and a very wet and weary one I could see when the dim light of a passing car lit up her physiognomy. She began conversation – I kept right on walking. Then I asked her where the Reindeer Club was – and surprise! She said she knew and would lead me to it if I agreed to hail a cab for her. Sure enough, she led me to it through puddle and over curbstone, talking all the time, swearing about every other word and even trying occasionally to grasp my hand. I tried to figure her out. She didn't wear that nauseating perfume women of the streets usually do, though her voice was husky, as if she were sick. I asked her what she was doing out at that time of the night alone and what she did for a living. She answered that she had just left a party and that she was a nurse's aide, off duty until Saturday. I had doubts.

At the club door stood a taxi, so I hailed it, then thought I'd go along just for the ride – take her to where she was going, then come back and hit the hay. Don't know why I did it because there certainly was nothing to see in the blackout and this girl was certainly not an attraction.

The driver amazed me with his familiarity of the dark streets. He turned every which way before arriving at Russell Square, where the girl left the cab.

I had guessed right about her. We hadn't been on our way half a minute before she tried to convince me smoothly that I'd be more comfortable if I came home with her ... "of course, it'll cost you," she said. Again I don't know why, except that my curiosity is like that of nine cats, I asked her price. Four pounds. So I began haggling like we did with the natives back in Morocco. She got angry finally and when we reached Russell Square, after calling me a "nice boy" she cussed unhealthy-like and left the cab.

I woke up late the next morning; nevertheless, before noon I had completed a whirlwind tour of the main items of interest, namely, the Houses of Parliament, Westminster Abbey and Buckingham Palace. Alongside Parliament I gazed at Big Ben, but didn't hear it chime. A guide led me through the Abbey, showed all the graves of famous scientists, poets, statesmen and kings I'd read about from the first history class on. I walked alone through St James's Park, along a pond filled with paddling ducks and herons, to Buckingham Palace ... Then to Grosvenor House officer's mess and on my way to the Tower of London, where a tour had been arranged for soldiers. I stopped off on the way to listen to a band concert on the steps of St Paul's Cathedral and then went inside for a quick look before going to the tower. Saw where a 500-pounder had landed inside the Cathedral during the Blitz. Quite a bit of damage.

Along Cannon Street, leading to the Tower, I had the opportunity to see what great damage the Blitz had done at its worst. An area, blocks wide and long, had been completely devastated, not even a chimney left standing. The Jerries must have laid their heavies there. Grass grew in what had once been warehouse cellars ... All the while I saw these never-to-be-forgotten places, I wished with all my heart that someday I might again see them all again with Mary. There's nothing like appreciating both the sights and the light in her eyes at the same time – that's appreciation. Alone, I could see but do not share, nor appreciate.

... I slept late Friday morning, wandered around London trying to find something to buy and finally headed back to the base on the 3:40pm train, on which I met Dike and Miller looking appropriately dissipated. They had had several real deals, methinks. Champagne with all the trimmings. I was surprised to learn they had found time to go on a sightseeing tour at all.

Claude V. Meconis

London during these months was one of the worst crowded cities of the world and one of the most fascinating. It was full of people during the weekdays and on weekday evenings. It was even more crowded on Saturdays and on Saturday evenings it was almost bedlam, especially in those parts of town where Americans on leave congregated. I always thought of London as the hub of the world in those days. Here was not only the throbbing heart of the British Empire but here too was the capital-in-exile of half a dozen other nations. Here the strategy and plans were being conceived, from here the vast armed forces were being marshalled and directed and on London were the eyes of the world. Battered and dirty, worn and scarred, it swarmed with scores of different uniforms and it spoke in a hundred different tongues. No matter where you were going in the United Kingdom, you had to go through London and no matter how long you stayed you never saw it all. London was the Babel, the Metropolis, the Mecca. London was It.

The centre of London on a Saturday night was Piccadilly Circus. Here was a microcosm of the whole – a combination of crossroads, entertainment centre, restaurant centre and meeting-place. Here was a bawdy, rowdy anthill that moved in three dimensions and on four levels and in a dozen different spheres. You could not see it all at a glance – it was a shifting kaleidoscope that only now and then came sharply into focus and then blurred again, leaving fleeting images on the mind. Piccadilly had everything.

It had soldiers, sailors and airmen in uniform, looking for fun. Americans, British, French, Canadians, Norse, Poles, Belgians, Czechs, Dutch – you could run down a roster of Allied nations and find all their representatives here in a moment or two. The Americans surged in a never-ending tide around the Rainbow Corner – milling their way in and out of that mammoth beehive, in search of friends, food, dancing, of an hour's sleep before a train left, or of a bed for the night.

From the Rainbow Corner the Americans flowed out and around the Circus. Some were in search of restaurants and theatres. Some were in search of bars and beer. Some were looking for girls.

The girls were there – everywhere. They walked along Shaftesbury Avenue and past the Rainbow Corner, pausing only when there was no policeman watching. Down at the Lyons' Corner House on Coventry Street they came up to soldiers waiting in doorways and whispered the age-old questions. At the Underground entrance they were thickest and as the evening grew dark they shone torches on their ankles as they walked and humped into the soldiers, murmuring, "Hello, Yank." "Hello, soldier." "Hello, dearie!" Sometimes they were drunk and then they would stand and shout at each other and sometimes come to blows. Around the darker estuaries of the Circus the more elegantly clad of them would stand quietly and wait – expensive and aloof. No privates or corporals for these haughty demoiselles. They had furs and silks to pay for.

Down in the Circus, standing on the kerb, were the men who pretended to sell newspapers. "Poybeeb! Poybeeb!" they shouted, "*News ... Standard ... Star!*" But if you walked close to them you could hear them mumble about something else they were selling and if you asked them for a newspaper, they turned and growled, "G'wan beat it!" There were other salesmen, too. There was always a man who came up to you and offered to sell you a bottle of whisky, for four pounds or more. There was the man who could take you to a "bottle-party" where you could drink and dance as late as you pleased. And there was the man who would buy your fountain pen.

The people surged everywhere. At the Newsreel Theatre they look at the framed pictures on the billboard for a moment and then went in to pass an hour. At the Brasserie across the Circus they looked askance at the burly doorman and ducked in for a quick meal. At the shop across the street there were huge sandwiches of meat pastes – or was it fish? At the "Swan and Edgar" corner two ATS police girls stood with red bands on their hats – prim, austere, guardians of the gentler sex in uniform. Bobbies, too, moved among the crowds, their coalscuttle hats standing above the heads of the people. In pairs and in fours the white-helmeted American police patrolled the streets and the girls whispered at them "Snowball!" There were frowsy women who lurched along in a private dream, muttering to themselves and beggars playing the violin for pennies at the theatre queues; there were people standing in the streets shouting at taxis that would not stop.

There were little bars and public houses down Denman Street and Dean Street where the prostitutes drank and got drunk and forgot their profession, to wander home alone to their little rooms in the alleys back of Tottenham Court Road. There were the shiny, brightly-lighted restaurants in the hotels where bands played and the atmosphere was sultry and the waiters were dressed in black and the bill was large. Up on the roofs of these buildings there were lonely men and women standing on fireguard waiting for the sirens and the bombs that might follow them.

Down below the ground, too, the activity is intense. On the first level of the Underground there are swarms of people moving in all directions, people waiting by the telephone booths and pondering the ticket-machines. This is where you kiss your girl good night and where the sailors burst into song and where the military police stop soldiers and ask to see their passes.

As you take the long escalator down to the second level there is always someone sitting on the moving steps and always a Canadian soldier who is lost. And then the third level where the wind blows dust in your face and more steps to run down and then the fourth level, hundreds of feet underground, where the trains run to Watford. Here is Pat in her grey smock, with her back to the tracks, hands in her pockets, running the show. "Stanmore Line! All stations to Stanmore! No, this is not the Watford train! Hurry up, please, there! Step lively now! Mind the Doors! Mind the doors, please, there! Stanmore train! Last train to Watford is 11.37. Hurry up, please!"

Pat stands there by the hour, being shoved and pushed and yelled at and not too tired to have her little joke. "Austerity travelling there," she shouts. "Move right down in the cars, please!"

There's the tall, blonde girl in an evening wrap who suddenly breaks into an operatic aria down in that windy tunnel! Everyone stops to listen and when she finishes they all applaud – even the austere old British colonel! And when the Watford train comes at last, there's a fellow in the car playing a violin. Just playing it for music, not for money. And when he leaves at Baker Street, a sailor comes in and starts to sing. He dances up and down the aisle, favouring each passenger with a tune and a smile and soon everyone is singing together. "I'm Just a Little Sparrer", we all sing. And "Dear Luvverpool!" and "I Belong to Glasgow" and "Nellie Dean." We all sing, the moustached nun in spats with the silver-topped cane, the labourer with the smudged face and the burlap bag on the floor between his legs, the four sailors and the French soldier who doesn't know the words, the sentimental middle-aged lady and the little fellow with the big pipe. They all sing, all but the lovers in the middle seat. They just sit and hold each other tightly, the girl looking up at him dreamily, lost in clouds. They hear nothing, they are far away – this RAF pilot and his girl.

But back in the Circus, up on the surface, there is life still. It is getting late now and the other sections of London are quiet now except for an occasional footstep but there is yet life in old Piccadilly. There's a commotion down towards Leicester Square and a shout is heard, coming closer up Coventry Street. And then into sight comes a strange group – two Bobbies and struggling between them, his arms flung out as if he were being crucified, a wild-haired, pale young man. He flings his head from side to side, he kicks out his legs in all directions but the Bobbies have a firm grip and they move slowly across the Circus. As the writhing figure moves, he bawls at the top of his voice, "*Communism! Communism! Communism!*"

A voice at your elbow says quietly, "Whut oi'd loik to know is – is he for or against?"

As the bars and public houses close there is a brief flood of people again. This is the second of three tides. The first came when the theatres emptied their crowds at half-past nine. The "Closing Time" crowds are the second. And the third will come an hour later with the rush for the last train home. After the last trains leave, there are still a few girls walking the streets, still a few maudlin groups of soldiers – like-as-not lost, like-as-not unconcerned about it – progressing with determination toward some uncertain goal. In the dark shadows of Air Street a soldier leans against a doorway and goes to sleep. Down in Great Windmill Street a late lingering girl, quite drunk, tries to convince a timid airman to come home with her – for seven quid.

Now and then the pale blue glow of lights moves though the streets and disappears to a chorus of "*Taxi!*" from all sides. Piccadilly Circus is almost through for the night now. There are a few night clubs open, if you have the money and know where they are. But they are hot, noisy, cheap – their music is bad and the liquor that you must buy by the bottle tastes like the bottom of a tanning vat.

The Circus is almost quiet now. In the distance a pale grey "S" hangs from the doorway of a shelter and the tiny lights on the avenue click from red to green but the rest is darkness. The wind blows scraps of paper and refuse across the pavement and in the distance you can hear the piping note of a policeman's whistle. On the corner of Shaftesbury Avenue are two sailors and two girls singing. One of them has an oil lantern in his hand. He walks out into the precise middle of the street, swinging his lantern from side to side and he urinates.

This is London at war, this is England – or a small part of it – with its hair down. Piccadilly – dirty, maudlin, tumultuous – fascinating, obscene.

Good night, Piccadilly – time to call it a day.

London After Dark, Robert S. Arbib Jr

During a trip to London we went into a hotel named Grosvenor House which at the time was owned by Lord and Lady Townsend. Because of the blackout it was necessary to carry a flashlight, which the British called a "torch". This rather elegant lady, who was Lady Townsend, admired the American flashlight, which I promptly gave to her as a gift. She then took me to the desk clerk and advised that any time I wanted a room the hotel would accommodate me. Thereafter, any time I came to London I would bring her lemons and oranges, which the British hadn't seen for years.

As a result of this meeting she would invite me and some of my friends to her Sunday afternoon tea dances which featured the fashionable young women from some of the more classy families. I also became her favorite in that I would stand in the receiving line with her to greet Allied officers. Being located only fifty miles from London; the trip to town was only about one hour, so ... my social life improved with the addition of the Sunday dance. It tickled me to greet generals and other high-ranking officers with me being a first lieutenant. Because of the relationship I was always seated at her Ladyship's table. One of my friends, Lilburn "Buck" Rogers, met his wife through the Sunday tea dance. I think that Lady Townsend was amused by my friends and me and I also served as a buffer.

In the three years since I left Chicago, the association with educated people and the new social contacts with sophisticated people left its mark on me. The air force uniform was a pass into anywhere. In the pre-war years I would have never ventured into some of the places that I now was at ease in. In short, they would never get me back on the farm after I'd seen "Paree".

Edward Laube, 306th Bomb Group bombardier

On 1 February our crew received a 72-hour pass to London and Virgil, Pete, Shorty and I caught the train out of Norwich to London, about a four-hour trip because of the numerous stops made along the way. The coaches, considerably smaller than those in the US, consisted of individual compartments with seats facing each other and doors opening directly onto the loading platform. In other words, there was no aisle going the length of the coach and no way to go from one compartment to the adjoining one – also, no access to a rest room!

In London we took a taxi to the Piccadilly Circus area and began looking for a hotel room, but there were no vacancies. Hoping we could find a room if we got away from the Circus, we began walking. It was now dark and we knew nothing, of course, about London. One thing I did know: I did not want to spend the night walking the streets of London. Then, as we went down a side street, we saw a "Rooms for Rent" sign and knocked at the door to inquire. It was a home owned by a couple who furnished board and room for long-term renters, but since they had four empty beds in a large room, they agreed to put us up for the night. Somehow the place reminded me of something out of a Horatio Alger Jr novel, many of which I had read when I was in grade school, for the inmates looked as if they belonged to the same time period, the early 1900s.

After getting settled, we hurried to the Palace Theatre and arrived in time to see a stage production, a musical comedy entitled *Something in the Air*. As an all-English production, it included no songs familiar to us but provided an enjoyable evening. Unlike our theaters, waitresses circulated through the audience during the intermission, serving refreshments and taking orders for drinks.

The next morning we ate breakfast with our hosts, since it was included with our night's lodging. About a dozen other renters and we all ate together at an extra long table. I still had the feeling of the early twentieth century, for the men wore stiff white collars and black business suits.

We spent the remainder of our leave taking in as many of the landmarks as possible, most of which were included on a taxi tour that cost six shillings, the equivalent of only $1.20 in American money. Of all the places we visited, Westminister Abbey impressed me the most as I walked around reading inscriptions on blocks of stone in the floor and walls, many of which marked the graves of people about whom I had studied in high school history and literature courses. I thought about what a different perspective Americans have on age compared to that of the English – what was old in the US was almost recent history in England.

Staff Sergeant Dale R. VanBlair. Sergeant Virgil Carrol, engineer and top turret gunner, was later returned to USA after being hospitalized with bronchitis. Albert 'Shorty' Spadafore was KIA on 8 March 1944

... Our crew received weekend passes and Pete and I took the train to London on Friday. This time we were able to rent a room at the Regent Palace Hotel by Piccadilly Circus for Friday and Saturday. That evening we went to see *Life on the Mississippi* with Frederic March, a film based on the Mark Twain book with the same title. The film had lots of Twain humor in it and Pete and I frequently found ourselves laughing a second or so before the English. They seemed to be just a little slow to react to his type of humor.

We had been back in our room only a short time when we saw the beam of a flashlight shining on the outside of the one window in our room. A Bobbie or an air raid warden on the street below was calling our attention to our failure to pull the blackout shade. London was frequently being hit by buzz bombs at this time and we had no more than gone to bed after pulling the shade than the air raid siren began sounding. We dressed and went down to the ground level, where we waited for about three hours before the all clear sounded. When the same thing happened Saturday evening, we decided to take our chances and remained in bed. Even though we heard one hit a few blocks away, we chose our beds over the lobby of the hotel. We figured the odds were at least a thousand to one against one hitting the hotel.

Thousands of Londoners spent their nights in the "Tube" or "Underground," as they referred to their subway system. They brought blankets and slept on either cots with wire springs or the walkways. When Pete and I took the Tube back to the hotel late each evening, we found hundreds of people sleeping there. I developed a great deal of admiration for these people who could spend their nights under such conditions and then put in a full day's work. Although the Blitz was long since over, German bombers still put in an occasional nuisance appearance over London and other cities. When I saw the evidence of the damage done during the Blitz, I could only marvel that the Londoners' morale did not break. The whole area around St Paul's Cathedral, for example, was practically leveled, as were many other areas. On a later trip to London, I found that the top floor or two of our hotel had been destroyed by a buzz bomb.

When Pete and I returned to Hethel Sunday afternoon, we learned that we had missed some excitement. A few German fighters had managed to sneak in as some of our planes were landing following a mission, shot up two or three and strafed the field. What an opportune time to be on leave!

Staff Sergeant Dale R. VanBlair

During my first trip to London in June or July 1943, my friend Hoffman and I arrived at Liverpool Street station. We noticed a red phone box on the platform and thought it would be a good idea to phone Rainbow Corner, the servicemen's leisure center at Piccadilly Circus. We wanted to find a bed and breakfast place for the night.

It was during the time when four pennies, the big ones, were required. I knew that much about the phone box, but little more. After I gave the number, having inserted four pence, someone spoke through the receiver saying, "Press button 'I' (pronounced eye) please". Open-eyed, I spotted "A" and "B" but no "I". I pressed nothing. "I cawn't hear you" she says "Press Button 'I'". There is no "I". She thinks I've done it and says "Speak louder please, I cawn't hear you". I do ... she still can't hear me. My friend Hoffman says, "Let me get in there. I'll make her hear me".

But he had no better luck than me, though he yelled so loudly that many people stared at us. Most everyone was in uniform of some kind.

In disgust, having pressed button "B" to retrieve the four pennies we started walking along the platform. We did not know that in England some people pronounce "A" like "I"!

And then it happened! An experience I've remembered for over forty-seven years. Not all those platform people were passengers. A man came up to us and said, "Say, have you gentlemen been to Petticoat Lane?"

"Why, no we haven't" we said.

"Today is your lucky day, because I just happen to have the last two tickets to Petticoat Lane" he babbled. "Tell you what, I'll let you have them for half a crown each".

' I turned to my friend and said, "Do you think we ought to go?"

"Yes" he says "the last two tickets. Aren't we lucky?"

Since this was our first time off base, we didn't know how much half-a-crown was. "Hold out your hand" I said, "He will know how much to take". He did. To this day I don't know how much he took but we were certainly taken.

"Now then" he said. "Walk up those stairs, turn left and you'll soon see Petticoat Lane".

We did and soon saw what we took to be a marvellous display of merchandise and wares of many shades and varieties. Walking up to a woman stall holder I said "who collects these tickets?"

"What tickets?"

I gave them to her and she read, "'Admit one to Petticoat Lane'. You've been had. No one has to pay to walk down this street."

Jim Johnson

I went to London on all my passes. My first pass was spent trying to find my way about London that I knew only from history and geography courses in school. London in 1944 was a quiet but working city. The worst of the bombing was past but there were V-1 buzz bombs and fairly regular strikes by the V-2 rocket.

The "Tube", as the London underground railway was called, was the most memorable and wonderful technology for people that I encountered in my entire stay in England. The trains and stations were amazingly clean, given the circumstances ... the ends of some subway lines came to the surface in residential areas and I enjoyed seeing the suburban homes with their small gardens. On one trip I rode up the escalator behind a mother and four or five-year-old daughter. I gave the little girl an orange I brought from the base. She curtsied and said, "Ta", turned to her mother and asked, "What is this mama?" The mother said with tears in her eyes, "She has never seen an orange before".

On another trip I transferred at Victoria Station. In the main concourse was a square glass showcase with a beautiful bunch of grapes. The sign said, "£4 per pound". At home grapes were probably ten cents a pound. No wonder the grapes were displayed behind glass fit for diamonds with spotlights. Obviously, not many people ate grapes in wartime England.

Madam Tussauds wax museum was the first wax museum I had ever heard of let alone seen. It was a revelation to see historic people displayed in dress with props of the period. I was scared out of ten year's growth when the 1900s Bobby I was examining closely walked away! Roosevelt,

Churchill, Shakespeare, Nelson and seemingly every hero and villain in European history were there, so life-like you expected them to speak to you. A few theaters were open with live performances. Those I went to were in the Haymarket and Piccadilly areas. I saw *Charlie's Aunt, Arsenic and Old Lace* and another or two … the first I had seen with professional actors. They were very well done. Also in the Haymarket was the "*Théâtres Plastiques*". Their format was still scenes of mostly historical or literary themes with live nude posters. The one thing that kept them from being closed as an offence to morals was that the nudes were not permitted to move, from "lights up" to "lights out", a minute or so for each pose. There were museums to see. I went to the Victoria and Albert but I was not interested in museums at that point in my life. I enjoyed strolling the city streets. Piccadilly Circus was a disappointment. I had heard of it from the day I got to England as the place where everything happens. Perhaps it was but it wasn't what I was interested in. It was a motor car circle with a boarded up lump in the middle, covered with handbills. The next biggest attraction was a huge sign advertising, "Bovril, Important for Nursing Mothers and Adolescent Girls'. (Bovril is an iron supplement). Trafalgar Square was unusual because wooden planking did not cover its statue, an obelisk.

I went to Hyde Park Gate and to Marble Arch to see the soapbox orators and their ever-present hecklers. By walking around one could get harangued on subjects from anarchism to vivisection. I wasn't interested in the subjects but in the institution itself. The hecklers were more fun than the speakers were.

Other officers at Station 104 told me about the TOQ (Transient Officers Quarters) at Prince's Gate, Knightsbridge and the Officers' Mess on upper Grosvenor Street. During my January stay at the TOQ the maid, a pretty girl, one of the few with beautiful teeth, came in with swollen red eyes. She said she had just found out that she was pregnant and had been waiting to tell her American fighter pilot fiancée. He had been killed in action yesterday. She, of course, could not claim support because of "Non Fraternization Rules" intended to avoid just such problems. If he had been around to get married or even acknowledge the girl, there would be no problem but a pregnancy and no legal paper was a disaster.

It tore my heart out, but I could do no more than cry with her.

After the mission of 10 November 1944 the 8th Air Force flew no missions until November 16. On the 17th, our crew was given a 62-hour pass. Pete Scott, the co-pilot and I, took the train for London, as did the rest of the crew, except that Pete and I had similar feelings about how we wanted to spend our pass, neither of us being interested in liquor. Pete and I headed for Madam Tussauds Wax Museum then strolled in the area of the Haymarket and Leicester Square. (Pete who was 21 and the youngest on the crew was good-looking with blue eyes, light curly hair, about 5ft 10in tall and possessed a warm, friendly and very engaging personality). While walking, we were accosted by two quite young girls. They invited us to their homes. Pete went with one of them but I went to see *Charlie's Aunt* in the Haymarket theater, while the young lady sought her fortune elsewhere, a decision later to have an enormous impact on my thinking about life, the war and my part and place in them.

These appeared to be schoolgirls but since school was finished at sixteen they might have been working girls. Pete said he was going to see how far he could go and not go all the way. The girl's mother welcomed him into the home then served them tea in bed the next morning, certainly an unusual situation to my naïve way thinking. Pete said there "was no part way".

We were on the alert list for 21 November. At briefing that morning they said "Hamburg!" I began to sweat immediately. We had been there on 6 October but that time we fooled them. The entire 450 planes of the 2nd Air Division divided up into ship formations and came in on many targets from every direction under the sun. Even so, every single flight had flak guns tracking them individually. Those Hamburg gunners were good; 150 targets and everyone had a few guns giving it undivided attention. We heard that the bomb results were not too good on that occasion. Now, we were going *downtown* in the standard bomber stream.

1st Lieutenant Walter F. Hughes, 93rd Bomb Group

It was November 1943 and a very foggy night. The occasion was one of my first visits to London and we were returning on the train. The word "Bovril" appeared at one of the stations. Nothing else was on the sign. Another GI said to me "It's a bad fog, really bad, he's going round in a circle. We've been through Bovril twice before!"

We did not know, being foreigners, that Bovril was a drink!

Jim Johnson

We had money; glamour and the devil-may-care attitude, which came from knowing that every day might be our last. When we came overseas, we had several built-in advantages. I had deliberately decided not to get engaged to Joanie before leaving the USA. This was partly because of the possibility that I might not come back, but I must confess that it was also because I did not want anything to cramp my style.

We did not get many weekends off – about one a month – but when we did, we sure made the most of them. The place we always headed for was London. The town was really buzzing and absolute heaven for an American flyer. In order to cut a dash, Captain Paul Swift and I had our uniforms especially made by Gieves & Hawkes, with the wings on our jackets embroidered in gold and silver thread. This was much against regulations, of course, but we thought we could do anything and get away with it. I also commissioned Cartier to copy my navigator's wings in platinum and diamonds as a present for Joanie. These were the only wings of this type they ever made. We were always able to reserve the same apartment near Piccadilly Circus but we spent very little time there. We would go our separate ways, then meet up at some club or other with the new girls of the moment. I would take Shelagh Macaulay to Claridges, where we always had the same table; then on to The 400 – I suppose the chic-est club in town – to dance and we would end up at yet another club. We belonged to all of them. The fact that the city was in blackout was no problem to us. It just heightened the fun and games.

On one occasion, we could not get our regular apartment. There was a help line for officers who could not find accommodation, so we called it and were given an address: The Cavendish on Jermyn Street. We spent two nights there and when I went to settle the bill the lady who seemed to be in charge refused any payment. She said American flyers did not pay in her place. Rosa Lewis was her name. When my cousin, Dorothy Cooper, heard where I had been staying she was shocked and told me never to go there again. It was nothing but a brothel! Apparently, Edward VII had financed Rosa to buy the Cavendish. He much admired her and also her famous cooking. He would take his favourites there, where he had his own apartment. Her rule was that you paid when you left but if you were on hard times, your bill was put on to someone else's account, who happened to be in the chips. We had no inkling of any of this. It would hardly have made a difference if we had.

Even when we could not get to London we found ways to enjoy ourselves. Swift and I were able to buy two almost-new motorcycles for practically nothing as the English owners could not get fuel because of rationing. We had unlimited petrol and had great fun touring the countryside in our spare time. I must say, this really impressed the local girls and we thought we were the Don Juans of Norfolk. The fun did not last long; our motorcycles were confiscated and locked in a motor pool never to be seen again. High Command told us in no uncertain terms that they had better things for us to do than fall off motor bikes.

Hard Luck And Back, Paul Arbon, lead navigator, *Virgin on the Verge*, 561st Bomb Squadron, 388th Bomb Group

London was the only destination for the first time off in England. My seventh and eighth grade teacher in school in Bennington, Kansas, was an Englishman, Mr Johnny Barker. He was an excellent teacher and a stern disciplinarian. He was also a little unorthodox. (He retired as a Professor of English at the University of Colorado.) At that time, Prince Edward had abdicated the throne to marry a divorced American woman, Wally Simpson. Edward's younger brother George was then crowned as King of England. We listened to some of the ceremonies on the radio. We also spent a several weeks studying the history of the English Empire [sic] and, more specifically, its government. As a student in a small central Kansas school, I had no idea that I would ever have the opportunity to actually go to the very places where these historic events had taken place.

The crew had three days off and we all traveled together to London. An Army 6 x 6 took us to the train station in Bury St Edmunds, the closest station to the base. It was a typical English train. The doors to each compartment, which could seat eight to ten, opened from the side. It had a coal-fired engine so smoke and soot were still a problem. The train ride was uneventful but pleasant rural scenery until we approached London. The damage inflicted upon the city by the Germans' indiscriminate bombing during the Blitz became readily apparent, and it hadn't stopped. Instead of bombers, Germany was now using its terror weapons, the V-1 buzz bomb and the V-2 rocket. We had seen many V-1s as they flew over the base in the evenings on the way to London. It made a distinctive pup-pup-pup sound. You only got concerned when the sound stopped. Then it was time to find cover. The V-2 was a high-altitude rocket carrying a high-explosive warhead. It traveled faster than the speed of sound. Therefore there was no warning. These too were aimed for London. Rather than demoralizing the English people, they seemed to stiffen their resolve. They went about their business as if everything were normal. We knew that these attacks were continuing but we were going to London anyway.

It didn't appear that any parts of the city had been spared. Everywhere you looked you could see the devastation. Spaces where buildings used to stand were still filled with rubble, although most of the streets had been cleared and repaired. I could see what the bombing had done and was still doing to London. This was the result of an unprovoked war. There was no question in my mind that Nazi Germany must be stopped. The only way to stop them was to defeat their army. I was helping to do just that by bombing their manufacturing facilities and destroying their communication and transportation systems.

The city itself seemed dark and shabby, even in the daylight. All of the buildings undamaged by the bombing were dark and gray-looking. Most of the buildings were four or five stories tall and built right next to the street. On the roofs were rows of chimneys, as there were very few buildings with central heating. Most are heated with stoves and fireplaces. Coke is the primary fuel and produces a great deal of smoke and soot, hence the amount of pollution in the air, the dense fog and the discoloration of the buildings.

The train pulled into Victoria Station. It is a beautiful old building, with its wrought iron and glass-covered loading and unloading area. The station was filled with a milling mass of humanity, each person intent on their individual destination. Most of them were in uniform – US, British, French, Canadian – it seemed that all of the Allies were represented in the crowd going and coming. We officers checked into a nice hotel while the enlisted men all elected to stay at the American Red Cross billet. It was located in a large building just off of Piccadilly Circus. The first order of business was to find a good restaurant that did not look like a mess hall. We did, but in a way, it was a disappointment. The shortage of food was evident from the selections on the menu – forget the sizzling steaks; but the food was well prepared and tasty and a change from the mess hall.

London was a fascinating city to a kid off a Kansas farm. It was huge, busy and dark. The black taxis with the driver sitting outside and their sliding doors and circular seating were everywhere. Incredibly, they had a very short turning radius and could make a U-turn almost anywhere. They, along with the double-decked busses, generally had the streets to themselves, except for the military vehicles. Few private autos were seen as the scarcity of fuel limited their use. However, some of the English were very ingenious and fueled their autos with a coal gas. There would either be a large bag on top of the car containing the gas, or it would pull a trailer with the gasbag and a connection to the car. Unmanned barrage balloons were flying over those parts of the city containing the important government buildings as protection from low-flying enemy aircraft. At night, the city was totally blacked out. No lights showed and all traffic on the streets drove with hooded lights – just small slits in covers over the headlights. The wartime conditions did not stop the traffic on the streets, in the Underground (subway), or on the sidewalks. London was a busy city, people on the go everywhere.

The first day, Walt and I visited the historic sights. We went to the Tower of London even though the royal jewels were not on display. Like so many other valuable and irreplaceable items, they had been removed to a safe place for the duration of the war. Westminster Abbey, the site of the coronation I had listened to on the radio, was the highlight of the trip for me. It is a beautiful building and steeped in history. It embodied all of the things that we were fighting for. We also saw Big Ben towering over the parliament buildings, the source of government from which our country developed. I saw Buckingham Palace, where the royal family resides when they are in the city. It is surrounded by its high wrought-iron fence and located near the center of the city, a short distance from Hyde Park with its orators' corner, where anyone can get on a soap box and promote whatever subject is near and dear to their heart. A stop at Trafalgar Square and St Paul's Cathedral rounded out an unforgettable day.

London was much more than just historic sights. Joe was from Baltimore and he enjoyed going to the Vaudeville Theater. One afternoon we attended a performance at the famous "Windmill". "We never closed" was their motto, referring to their staying open all through the Blitz. While waiting in line to get in I was amazed at the sidewalk entertainers. There were cockneys with their coats covered with buttons working the crowds and speaking a dialect that was almost impossible to understand, young girls selling flowers, mimes and street performers with their colorful costumes. War seemed a long way away. It was a different world from anything I had known. It was also my first introduction to live theater. The music was lively, the comedians were corny and we forgot why we were in England. There were three or four nude young ladies on the stage for almost every number. It seemed that women could appear nude on the stage as long as they didn't move. As I said at the time, "I'm not in Kansas anymore."

The officers' mess at Grosvenor Square was the best place to eat but it was segregated by rank. Lieutenants and captains were in the largest lower area. Field grade officers ate on a raised level and general officers had their own space. Anyway, the food was good, plentiful and the price was right. After-hours clubs flourished. For the equivalent of $2.00, you could join a club for the evening. There was usually a band with a singer and, most importantly, mixed drinks could be purchased. There was a shortage of men in London, so opportunities to meet members of the opposite sex were always possible. The English lament was that the "Americans were overpaid, oversexed and over here".

Then there were the street girls. They were everywhere and available, for a price. You couldn't walk in the Piccadilly Circus area without encountering them. The usual approach was "All night for five pounds, Yank!" A wave off brought a response, "How about going around the corner for a quickie! Only a pound." The entryways and phone booths on the side streets could often be filled with a couple completing a transaction.

Three days in London wasn't very long but it was an unforgettable experience; then it was back to the base and on with the war.

Dean M. Bloyd

... I tried to buy a handkerchief since I seemed to be coming down with a cold and in my haste I forgot to put one in my pocket yesterday. However, ration coupons are needed to buy cloth goods and I didn't have any coupons, so I couldn't get a handkerchief. A middle-aged lady was standing nearby while I was trying to buy the handkerchief. She wore a very attractive wool tweed suit. The cloth looked like it was at least a quarter of an inch thick and brand new. I spoke to her saying, "Lady, that beautiful tweed suit of yours must have cost you at least one year's worth of ration coupons."

She laughed and replied, "Oh no I didn't spend a single coupon for it. I bought it eight years ago."

Lieutenant John Howland, a 381st Bomb Group navigator on a visit to London, 5 Feb 1944

Surely it is a mystery that the fame of the beauty of the Englishwomen has not spread around the world – for it is a beauty rarely equalled. But no one talks about it, no one advertises it. The English beauty clothes herself in coarse tweeds of unflattering cut, she ruins the lines of her legs with "sensible" flat-heeled shoes, she condescends to comb her unsurpassed locks but that is about all. Yes – you have heard that she has a beautiful complexion but it is the women of France, the women of Spain, the women of a dozen other countries whose very mention has always set the imagination afire. You must look past her modesty in dress and past her obvious and perverse desire for anonymity and conformity and you find yourself saying, "Now, there's a girl who could be beautiful – if she only gave herself a chance." And when you have said that a hundred times you become aware of the secret fact – the unmentioned discovery – that English womanhood is beautiful after all. But not for you, not for the casual bystander – not to be advertised – not to be displayed, except for the initiate invited within the gates of the private English garden.

Thoughts On British Character, Robert S. Arbib Jr

London was really the major attraction when you got a three-day pass. The train ride took three or four hours. In London I would stay at a Red Cross club near Piccadilly Circus. Like the one in Norwich, it had rooms and baths at very reasonable prices. Being close to Piccadilly, it was in the heart of a lot of activities, particularly theaters. A wartime favorite was the Windmill Theater, which took great pride in the fact that it never closed during the Blitz. It was sort of like a US burlesque but with better comedians. It was at that time that I found that English comedy could be very funny. I occasionally went to a stage show in one of the other theaters. One that I still have the playbill for was entitled *Sweeter and Lower*, starring a youngish Hermione Gingold, a very funny lady indeed.

One of the better haunts in London was the Grosvenor House, which had been turned into a very large and sumptuous officers' club. Located on Park Lane, around the corner from Oxford Street, it was a great place to go, with food, drinks and music in a very nice setting. It was a very popular hangout at the time. I've gone into the place recently, but can't recognize a thing.

Sightseeing was a common pastime in London with many famous places to see. Buckingham Palace was a must, as was Westminster Abbey. Somehow I never knew about Harrods at the time. I used to stroll through Selfridges on Oxford Street, which I considered their Macys.

At night, the hookers came out in force. "Bed & Breakfast" was what they were usually selling. The term obviously has a different connotation today. Prices reached their peak on payday and declined to bargain rates just before the next one. The payday asking price was usually around £10. This was a truly princely sum, about $43 dollars (about $600 today). I expect that the negotiated price was a lot lower. With a legitimate office job paying about $20 a week, you could see why a lot of the girls were drawn to the trade. In Piccadilly, you'd get propositioned about every ten feet. The standard question for anyone returning from London was "what are the latest quotations?" It was somewhat of an academic question since few of those I knew ever partook – a lot of talk, but not much else.

I once went to Madame Tussauds waxworks. I was impressed with the quality of the various figures, but the thing I remember most was an old woman sitting on one of the benches scattered about for the visitors. I think she was holding an umbrella and a couple of packages. The big question was, was she real or wax? I've seen people sit down next to her and not realize that she wasn't real. I had to watch her for quite a while before I decided she had to be wax.

Unfortunately, after a time even London ceased to interest most people. I think most of the troops tended to be more interested in finishing their tours and going home. In short, the novelty had worn off.

Ronald D. Spencer

... While Piccadilly Circus was usually the starting point for the American airmen, the entertainment avenues of those London times led in many directions. At the Ambassador Theatre, throughout the war, was a music revue that was perhaps the favourite of the Americans. It was called, at various times, *Sweet and Low*, *Sweeter and Lower*, and *Sweetest and Lowest*, and featured music, comedy and dancers. Perpetual star of the productions was Hermione Gingold, who was such a favorite that she came to America after the war and had a great success on Broadway and television ... The years of 1943–44 found the production of almost half of Shakespeare's canon on the boards in the West End, including the major pieces – *Hamlet, Macbeth, King Lear* and *Midsummer Night's Dream.* George Bernard Shaw's *Arms and the Man, Androcles and the Lion, Pygmalion* and *Candida* were also in production, along with Henrik Ibsen's *A Doll's House* and *Hedda Gabler.* The American playwrights were much in evidence in those years – Robert Sherwood, John Steinbeck, Thornton Wilder, Eugene O'Neill, Cole Porter, Maxwell Anderson and, in late November of 1943, Irving Berlin brought his all-soldier revue to London.

The perennial London attraction of those times, Noël Coward, continued to beguile his audiences with *This Happy Breed, Private Lives, Present Laughter* and, later, *Blithe Spirit.* The American servicemen, not always accustomed to live theater, came in large numbers to the West End where they especially liked the shows of Ivor Novello – *Perchance to Dream, The Dancing Years* and *Arc de Triomphe.* The theaters were sold out many times and always crowded with the military uniforms of Allied nations and London civilians. London's eclectic theater life in those war years of 1943–44 also included productions of *The Vagabond King,* the *International Ballet, The Merry Widow* and Sigmund Romberg's *The Desert Song.*

The war documentaries, Noël Coward's *In Which We Serve* and *London Can Take It,* with a commentary by the American journalist Quentin Reynolds, played to large audiences in the movie houses. In the early stages of the war, older Hollywood movies like *Destry Rides Again,* with Jimmy Stewart and Marlene Dietrich, were shown. Later, newer movies like *Goodbye Mr Chips, Mrs Miniver* and *The Wizard of Oz* began to appear on the London screens. I shall never forget one London night seeing the movie based on the Ernest Hemingway novel, *For Whom the Bell Tolls* – and the next night having a drink at the Dorchester bar with Mary Welsh, the *TIME* war correspondent who introduced me to the famous author. Hemingway was in the ETO as a correspondent for *Collier's* magazine. Mary later became Hemingway's fourth wife and widow.

London dining places favored by the American airmen included Simpson's in the Strand, Mulatta's in Half Moon Street, The Savoy Grill, Prunier's and Café Royal, just off Piccadilly Circus. The favourite was Rainbow Corner ...

                                                                    Starr Smith

The next morning we rode the Underground to Madame Tussauds, the world-famous waxwork exhibition founded by Madame Tussaud in 1760. Hundreds of wax models of historical and contemporary celebrities are displayed here and their life-like appearance is most uncanny. After touring the exhibition, we decided to walk back to Piccadilly but were in doubt which way to go. A doorman was standing with his back to us a few feet away, so Bob stepped over to him and requested information. On receiving no response, Bob tapped him on the shoulder, only to discover that he was talking to a wax dummy.

Staff Sergeant Dale R. VanBlair

On a "forty-eight" in London, I left a party at around 11.30pm to go back to my hotel. Found there was a real bad fog, couldn't see your hand in front of your face in the blackout. Asked a taxi driver to take me back to my hotel but he said with the dimmed lights he had he couldn't see which way to go. So I volunteered to lead the way until he could. Started off walking with one foot on the kerb and the other in the gutter. Ended up walking the whole two miles back to my hotel with this taxi following. When we got there the driver wants full fare and I never even got into his cab!

Calvin Hill of the 364th Fighter Group

The place to go in London to dance was the converted opera house near Covent Garden. It was here that I first took the floor with a British gal. All was going fine until another girl tried to cut in, grabbed me by the arm and tried to pull me away. I'd been told the English girls were shy and reserved and here's one trying to pull me away from another! Embarrassed, I just held on to the girl I had, said "How do you do", and kept dancing. My partner's immediate reaction was offence. What was I doing not taking the other girl? I was bewildered until it was explained that this was a ladies' "Excuse Me" dance. When a girl tapped your shoulder you changed partners.

Al Zimmerman

Gee but she was pretty and nice and decent. We met on my second pass to London and got along well, all things considered. Neither of us knew much about tragedy or about human beings who had grown up so far apart. Our fourth date was to be a mini-anniversary. She didn't show and I phoned her home again and again, but couldn't make the connection. I took the Tube to south London, then a cab to the address she had given me on our last date. The cab stopped at a street barricade and I stepped out. As I turned to face the cabbie said, "I don't want to take your money, lad. But I must live too, you know." I paid him and followed his instructions on how to get to her address past the "construction" site. Where there had been a row of connected houses was now a jumble of debris – she was gone, her family was gone and their neighbours were gone. These quiet peaceful God-fearing people were all gone. Gee but she was pretty.

Pretty Girls, Bob Oberschmid

First Wingers soon discovered that any single-fisted drinker can hold a prodigious amount of the wartime low-proof whisky, when and if he can get it. Industrious elbow bending and free spending produce the desired effect in time, however. First Wing does not come to London Town to eat. Generally speaking, the food served at American bomber and fighter stations is as good or better than can be had in the high-priced London restaurants. The pub, therefore, is a subject of careful research. Soldiers stationed in London generally adopt a particular pub, which they call their "local." There the barmaid learns to ration the always-scarce supply of spirits among casual customers so that her favourite "regulars" may get one or two shots anytime they drop in.

At the Sprinting Horse, for instance, one group of habitués discovered they could save a good number of shillings over the week by patronizing their local for lunches washed down with big glasses of lager. It was cheaper than the officers' club, the food was about on a par and by regular patronage you could establish your shareholder's interest in the bottle of spirits that generally lurks well out of sight behind the bar. The "Horse" provided a darts board and shove-ha'penny board, over both of which the regulars could compete for drinks. One day the proprietress moved in a familiar pin game fresh from some juke joint back home. It had been remodelled only to the extent of accepting the big British penny and it looked garish in the ancient burnished oaken interior of the pub.

It was in this pub that a colonel with a slightly nasal twang told one of the memorable stories of First Wing.

"There I was in the nose of the damn plane, sweating out a bad one. We lost sixteen ships that day. Rough day. We got hit by flak and the bombardier was knocked down by a piece of iron in the arm. Believe me, I was scared stiff – didn't know what to do. Finally, I got up enough gumption to get out my first-aid stuff and jab him with some morphine. This damn kid looks half dead, blood all over the place. But he puts his good arm under his head, looks up at me very seriously and says, "You know what, colonel? I don't think there's much future in this racket."

Major John M. Redding & Captain Harold Leyshon

'See Sadler's Wells opera *The Barber of Seville*. Sit in "Pit Stalls" for four shillings' (about $1.00). In wartime Britain, evening showtimes are at 6 to 7 o'clock and shows let out at 8 to 9, just when the bars are closing and the sidewalks being taken in ... This is particularly frustrating when on leave; we are not ready to go to bed when it is still daylight. We meet a couple of Londoners in a Lyons café and learn about "Ricks", a bottle club. For innocents, bottle clubs are private, membership only, late night bars similar to those found in areas of local prohibition in the States. "Rick" provides membership cards at the door and we enjoy the rest of the evening ... the buzz bombs do not bother us as much that night.

Bill Wilkinson

One of the things I liked was railroad trains. I liked the English railroads. They were just real neat. The cars ran smooth; they were fast; everything worked good. Seemed like better than ours. But the only chance that I got to ride a train was when we went to London. I only went twice while I was there. London wasn't a bad town but it was tore up. Terrible! I slept in a hotel right off Piccadilly Circus and you'd hear the sirens starting to go off. I was never there during a bombing raid but you'd hear the buzz bombs coming. One time we left the hotel and went down the subway to shelter. The other time we just stayed in bed and let 'em go. I was glad that I never went back down there because a lot of people were killed in the subway when they got a direct hit. It burst a huge water main and most of the people drowned. They were just jammed in like sardines – women and kids and soldiers – everybody.

Sergeant Robert 'Bob' S. Cox, mechanic, 466th Bomb Group

After the first few trips to London, we always arrived at the Liverpool Street railroad station, as it was the end of the line from that part of England. Whenever you move by rail in England you have to go to the proper station to start from. For quite some time we had heard rumors that there was a famous pub across from the station called "Dirty Dicks" and that you had not seen London until you dared to enter into its doors and have a drink of beer or liquor. Finally a friend of mine and I decided to take up the dare and see what it was all about. It was an eye opener when we did.

Once inside we quickly learned why it was so famous. The bare ceiling joists were covered with cobwebs, cats, skeletons and all sorts of dust-covered items. The same held true for the walls – it was dust, dust, dust and cobwebs all over. The only places that were cleaned were the back bar, bar, tables and floor. When you finally got up enough courage to order a drink after the initial shock, once the drink was set on the bar you quickly covered it with your hand the way the others were doing. After sitting there for a few minutes, you learned why. Without notice, a chunk of cobweb overloaded with dust would break off and gently float down toward your drink.

Being curious, we asked why the pub was in such filthy condition and the bartender told us the story. It seems that an owner named Dick back about two hundred years was about to be married to a beautiful young lady whom he dearly loved. On the appointed day, she mysteriously died of an unknown medical problem. This was too much for Dick, who made a vow that he would never again clean the pub. This started a trend, which lasted for many decades, being tradition-bound as only the English can be.

One good thing on Dick's side was that he was smart enough to serve a variety of the finest beers and liquors in the British Empire. People from all over went there to enjoy their favourites and the word spread throughout the world. We were not able to find this variety due to war conditions, but to enjoy what they had to offer was a challenge one will never forget. After all these years I can still see that pub in its unique condition. Knowing English tradition, my guess is that it still is in business. After all, who would upset such a crowd pleaser?

Dirty Dicks In London, Ron Kabitzke

"There was a buzz bomb alert one night ... I was in a hotel with a crew buddy who had been wounded in the knee. It was still bandaged and stiff, so he couldn't bend it. When the sirens sounded we could hear these buzz bombs coming over and we were trying to decide whether to pull the blackout curtains and head for the shelter. We had the lights out, of course. I said, "Nah, no point in that. The engine always cuts out before the thing goes off." Well, this was one of the new ones, a V-2, I think, where the thing just suddenly dipped its nose down and exploded. Fortunately it was far enough away so that it didn't do any damage where were. I closed the blackout curtains and turned around to talk to the fellow I was with. Couldn't find him. I turned on the lights and called, "Where are you?" "Down here", he said from under the bed. Believe me, from where we were standing there wasn't enough room for anyone, even without a stiff knee, to drop down and roll under that bed. But he did it and I'll never know how.

Walter Wallace

Big Ben, Houses of Parliament, Westminster Abbey, Buckingham Palace, Tower of London and St Paul's Cathedral were the sights to see. It was dinnertime when I finished and I took in a movie afterwards. It was *A Guy Named Joe* with Spencer Tracy, Irene Dunne and Van Johnson, a good "flick" that I'd already seen three times before.

Seated next to me in the theater between two beautiful girls was a staff sergeant. And since it seemed somewhat out of balance, I offered to help out and was, surprisingly, welcomed.

Afterwards the four of us stopped in a pub for a few drinks and to socialize and then – another pub and then ...

It was peer pressure. I didn't even like the taste of alcohol, especially straight and without the sweetness of some kind of soda pop, but that's the way the girls ordered it and that's the way they drank it. And was the Lieutenant not going to match them drink for drink?

Some people were talking in what sounded like a cave or tunnel, because of the echo. They had a problem. They didn't know what to do with a drunken lieutenant. They didn't know where he'd come from nor where to return him. I wanted to ask if I could help, but my face was numb and my voice didn't work. That's all I could recall.

I don't know what kind of a room it was. I was in a bed, but it wasn't a bedroom. It was as large as a warehouse or maybe a dance hall. It was empty and unfurnished, except for two beds: the one I was in and another at the far end of the room.

My clothes were lying on the bed and alongside on the floor. I definitely did not feel well, but forced myself to get up anyway and I got dressed. It was almost noon and I recalled I had to catch the train back to base, but I seemed to be moving in slow motion, had no idea where I was, nor how I was to get to the train station, wherever it was.

Out of curiosity, I walked to the opposite bed that was occupied by two beautiful girls. Oh, yeah. I recognized them from – last night. The way they were embraced I felt they must be in love. So, quietly, I left them in peace and headed back to war.

London Town, Lieutenant Truman J. 'Smitty' Smith, co-pilot, 385th Bomb Group, Great Ashfield, Suffolk, May 1944

I met a Lieutenant Walter Furia at the KPM, the Kensington Palace Mansion, a hotel for American officers. He was a high-energy hotshot bombardier asking in the lobby if anybody wanted to join him for a steak dinner.

Now that was something I could relate to, even though I couldn't remember how long it had been since I'd had a steak. With wartime restrictions and rationing, steak was a rarity ... I asked Furia where we were going to get the steaks. He produced a business card someone had given him that gave the address and we went for it. It was a respectable little restaurant and steak was on the menu. I thought it unusual that the clientele was only American, but then we Americans do have an appetite for steak. So we ordered and while waiting, went to the washroom down the hallway and near the kitchen.

I asked Furia, "What stinks so bad back here?"

"I hate to tell you Smitty, but I think we made a mistake."

"How so?"

"You obviously have never experienced it, 'cause you could never forget it if you had."

"What's that?" I asked.

"Horse meat. That's what they're cooking in the kitchen. We're going to have horse steaks."

"Maybe *you're* going to have a horse steak," I said, "But this cowboy from Oklahoma ain't gonna eat no horse."

I don't know what they did with the steaks we didn't eat, because we left, concluding that with all of the shortages that they wouldn't even be serving good horse meat, but probably some nag that had died from old age or disease and had been re-routed from the glue factory.

Boy, it sure did *stink*.

Truman J. 'Smitty' Smith, London, May 1944

... After flying our first few missions, our first 72-hour pass came due. John and I went to London to see the sights of a big city in England. It was about a two-hour train ride from Norwich. After arriving, we felt our best bet would be to flag down a taxicab so we would at least have someone who could answer our many questions about London. The first thing was to find a "good" hotel. The driver suggested that a good hotel would be the Savoy. This sounded fine to us, so that's where we went.

When we walked in we knew it was all first class. The crowd inside were all generals and colonels. I had never in my life felt so much like a buck private as I did at that point: two 21-year-old kids, lowly second lieus not knowing up from down, mingling with all this top brass. I think our stay at the Savoy was less than three minutes.

Back on the street again we asked someone who looked like a native where a nice cheap hotel was. Up the street a bit was the Strand Palace, not necessarily cheap, but it was surely more our style.

There, in our private bathroom, we had our first introduction to a bidet. I looked it over and asked, "What the hell is this for?" John didn't know. I don't think we ever did figure it out. At that time we didn't even know there was such a word as bidet.

The next day we found out about several American Red Cross clubs nearby. These were hotels for the US military. They were clean and completely adequate, plus they served free coffee and donuts all day and night. The Red Cross is an organization that has to be well respected. How well we would realize this in the future! There were seventeen Red Cross clubs scattered around London and their main headquarters, Rainbow Corner, was just off Piccadilly Circus. We chose the Jules Officers' Club, which was on Jermyn Street near Piccadilly where most of the action was.

Our first full day in London was spent sightseeing. We took the standard bus tour to acquaint ourselves with the city. We saw it all: St Paul's Cathedral, the Tower of London. Big Ben, Albert Hall, Buckingham Palace, the changing of the guard and lots more.

The first craving we had, believe it or not, was for a good steak dinner. From local advice, we learned of the White House restaurant a few blocks from Piccadilly. We had a great dinner there, with wine and the works. It was expensive but well worth it. It was the best meal we ever had in Europe, in fact, the best since we had joined the military.

After dinner we decided to take our first stroll along Piccadilly to see if what we had heard was true. We walked from the White House to Piccadilly. We came up a side street and with my first step around the corner and onto Piccadilly; a girl grabbed me right in the crotch and then kept right on walking. What an introduction to Piccadilly and London! We continued our walk and when we got to Piccadilly Circus there they were, the Piccadilly Commandos, all those girls we had heard about. I've never seen so many women as aggressive as they were, displaying some of their wares right out on the streets. But this was their business; it was how they earned a living. They liked the Yanks; after all, a second lieutenant flyer earned $225 a month, whereas an RAF flyer earned only about $50 a month.

Every time we went to London there were a good number of Nazi V-1 and V-2 bombs exploding. We could tell when a V-1 was about to drop nearby. They flew like airplanes and we could hear the motor chug chugging along. When that chugging stopped, the bomb was about to hit the ground, so everyone would run for bomb shelters, which were usually underground rail stations, known as the "Tube". With the V-2 there was no warning whatsoever because it was a rocket-type missile. When we went to the cinema and tried to absorb the movie, every few minutes a V-1 or V-2 would explode nearby. We just never knew when one might land on the theater. That's the life the Londoners lived for a long while.

While we usually stayed at the Jules Club, for some reason we were at the Reindeer Club one night. John and I were awakened from a sound sleep by a huge explosion, which sounded as if it were right next-door. There was no damage that we could see, so we went back to sleep. The next morning we found out the bomb had hit near Selfridges's department store about two blocks away. We went to see it. The bomb had hit squarely onto a pub right next door to Selfridges; it was completely demolished. The store was damaged, but not beyond repair.

Only once did John and I venture to another city besides Norwich and London. We spent a 72-hour pass in Cambridge, the university town. I don't know what inspired us to go there. It was unlikely that we were thinking of our higher education there after the war was over. Again, more sightseeing, visiting the university, some good eating and pretty girls.

Major Frederick D. 'Dusty' Worthen

... Having experienced all kinds of difficulty in trying to get accommodations in London on previous visits, I was surprised at the ease of checking into the Savoy.

I asked for a room as close to the ground level as possible, since I had a "phobia of heights". The desk clerk looked at the wings and ribbons on my tunic. He paused, no doubt wondering if I was "having him on" as they say and assigned us a room on the second floor.

I was surprised at the availability of choice due to the normal shortage of rooms. However, the explanation came in answer to my question to the bellhop, who was showing the way to our room.

"Which way do they come from?" I asked him as we climbed the stairs to the second flight, which the British considered to be the "first storey," since it is the first storey above the ground floor.

He knew without clarification that I was asking about the buzz bombs and replied, "You can see 'em coming."

"We don't want to see 'em coming!" I responded.

But that was it. That was why it was so easy for us to have gotten a room. We were on the side of the hotel facing the attack of the flying bombs. That entire side of the hotel was probably vacant, except for expendable Yankee airmen.

What a treat it was. The room was extremely large with unbelievable luxury and grandeur. *Mirrors!* The walls and even the high ceiling were totally covered with mirrors. In scale and detail, everything was dramatized artistically from the crystal chandelier to the golden handles of the doors. One side of the room was entirely covered with a heavy drapery that was more like a magnificent tapestry.

I didn't open it to check the view, which according to the bellboy overlooked the Thames. However, I did tug on the drapery and guessed that it must weigh several hundred pounds – at a cost of thousands of pounds Sterling.

[John] Shea produced a bottle of Scotch from his travel kit and wanted to celebrate on the spot. I suggested we go out for the best dinner we could find and if we got lucky, maybe we could go to a stage play.

Well, it didn't quite work out that way. Maybe it was better?

We couldn't get tickets to the theatre and the best dinner fare seemed to be mutton or fish. I detested both. This was probably because I'd been raised on beef and potatoes back in Oklahoma.

However, Shea and I did find some worthwhile entertainment at the Windmill Theatre. It was vaudeville that did not lack quantity nor quality of near-nude beauty queens. While it was a variety show of comics and many acts it was the backgrounds that were so gratifying to behold. Nudity was not forbidden as long as the models did not move. So they were just there posing in the nude. This of course beat the hell out of any pin-up picture I'd ever seen.

There wasn't a bad body in the bunch. What made them more provocative was their ecstatic poses and their silence – certainly more restful and recuperative than anything offered at the Flak House. I even forgot to remind myself about the war.

I felt really good and relaxed.

Back in our room I was asleep before Shea could pour himself a drink.

Oh, me. What a wonderful sleep it was, like being lowered into a deep dark well and I felt so comfortably calm and dreamy …

… Yet – I was *awake*!

Nobody could have slept through it … The sound of the blast was deafening! I was in the midst of Dante's Inferno!

At first I could only see brilliant red! My body and bed were jolted as if I were in a colossal earthquake. The sound blast almost knocked my teeth out of me!

Red! Red! Red!

The colour amplified and multiplied from one mirror to the others, crashing into itself!

The heavy tapestry-drapery extended horizontally into the room; held there by the force and persistence of the blast. And when it dropped back in place, there was total darkness.

Wow, I thought. *That* was a *close one*!

… There was no flying glass because any glass the window had already had been blown out previously.

That's why the Savoy had vacancies on this side of the hotel …

With the drapery drawn and the darkness in the room, I slept until almost noon, awoke with a great hunger and called room service for breakfast.

This was living.

All I had to do was to look in any direction – even overhead – and watch myself in a mirror enjoying the luxury.

My only regret was that I was alone and didn't have anyone with which to share such good fortune. And while I had been playing the role of a loner to keep from getting hurt from the loss of a friend, it was getting to me. I was *lonesome*!

Wouldn't it be great to have just one of those beautiful girls from the Windmill with me right now, hmm? I wouldn't even have to know her name. In fact it would he better to not know each other. That way nobody would be hurt when I did get shot down or blown up.

So if I had just one of those beauties – *one*? Why just *one*? Didn't the Air Force have a reputation to uphold?

"Yeah! You fly-boys have it real tough; plenty of money, running around London with a girlie on each arm."

Well, why should I disappoint them, or myself?

I decided that the time had finally come to enjoy myself.

By four in the afternoon, from the audience in the Windmill Theatre, I was shopping the stage for *two* companions.

The menu – no – the program identified all of the performers on the stage by name and photograph.

Within an hour I had made my selections and was at the stage door with a note and a generous tip for the doorman.

Would Ruby and Peggy do me the honor of joining me for dining and dancing at the Savoy?

Who could refuse such an offer?

As I paced back and forth on the sidewalk outside of the stage door, I wondered why it took so long for a response. It made me feel uncomfortable. Maybe I was being auditioned and I was sure that they must have consulted the doorman for his opinion of me, this kid from a small town in Oklahoma.

Maybe it was a mistake. Lacking experience, I wasn't qualified to fulfill any expectations of just one girl, let alone two. My self-confidence dropped to zero and I regretted having committed trying to bite off more than I could chew.

Another thing that made me uncomfortable and self-conscious was the damned hotel key I had in my pocket. It wasn't really the key, but the ball; a bit smaller than a baseball, chained to the key. This was obviously done to encourage leaving the key at the desk of the hotel instead of taking it with you.

Well, I had taken it with me, thinking to save myself the embarrassment of asking the desk clerk for my key in the single company of two girls. Now I was stuck with it – a huge bulge in my pants.

So, shuffling back and forth outside of the stage door, it occurred to me that I was wearing my battle blouse, which did not have a skirt on it to cover me below the waist. There was no way to disguise that fact that I did have a large bulge in my pants.

Here I was, one of those horny American pilots parading outside of the Windmill Theatre with a lump in my pants.

It took quite an effort to grapple for the key-ball-chain in my pocket. It had dropped in easy enough. But with my hand around the ball to retrieve it, the fit was too tight to get both the ball and my hand out of my pocket.

I almost panicked until I was able to get just the key out and then pull the ball out by the chain. And just in time.

The stage door opened and a rather short female wearing a bulky sweater, sunglasses, no makeup and a scarf about her head emerged into the afternoon sunlight.

She was not very attractive and my opinion must have reflected on my face. For as I walked over to her she said, "I'm not what you expected, am I?"

"Well?" was all I could say, because she certainly did not look anything like I had seen on the stage.

"I am Peggy."

She was short – shorter off the stage – and in spite of the scarf, I could tell she was a brunette. Peggy was the brunette and Ruby was the tall blond.

"Ruby and I will meet you upstairs in that pub over there across the street within thirty minutes," she said, leaving me juggling my key-chain-ball.

All's bad that starts badly.

I had a dream ... It was a fantasy that was coming to life ... A handsome young Air Force officer leaving a pub with a beautiful babe on each arm. It was the stuff that myths are made of. But in reality, what in hell can you do with two girls?

There was no doubt that I was in over my head and I felt as awkward and unnecessary as a second nose on my forehead.

Arm in arm we strolled toward the Savoy hotel, each girl with a little bag with a change of clothes for an evening out. We had formalized the date in the pub. They would have to change into something more suitable. I offered them my room at the Savoy, so they had stopped at the theatre for whatever they thought was necessary.

I was trying to think of a subject we might discuss to get better acquainted and to brighten our new relationship when Peggy asked, "Are we going to spend the night together?"

Such straightforward honesty caught me totally by surprise. I had no idea what was going to happen. I had never spent a whole night with even one girl. I had never even kissed a girl on the first date.

"Well-I-I, ah, maybe not tonight." I mumbled, "Maybe some other night."

"I'm a virgin, you know." Peggy said.

"No, I ah-h-h – didn't know that", I responded.

What else could I say? Why was she telling me this anyway? The fact that Ruby made no comment gave me even more to think about.

I was glad that Shea had left me his bottle of Scotch. It gave me something to do while Ruby and Peggy enjoyed refreshing themselves in the regal atmosphere of my mirrored cube quarters.

However, I was not a Scotch drinker. In fact I was not a drinker. Bourbon and Coke was about the limit of my experience. I had not even acquired a taste for beer. This was okay with me because bottles and throttles didn't mix, be it in airplanes or automobiles. Alcohol had killed more people in one way or another than all the wars.

Even so, having a drink appeared to be the thing to do while trying to entertain not one, but two young ladies. The part I was trying to play, as a suave, dashing, rakish American combat pilot, demanded a devil-may-care

Many impressive country houses were made availiable for 8th Air Force servicemen as 'Flack Homes'. Above is Coome House.

Keythorpe Hall.

Left: Hurry up and wait. (Bill Cameron)

Below: P-51D Mustang *Little Joe* in the 357th Fighter Group at Leiston. (USAF)

Right: The chorus line of *Tonight and Every Night* from the Windmill Theatre, sitting on the wing of Duane Beeson's P-47 Thunderbolt, *Boise Bee*, in the 4th Fighter Group at Debden. (USAF)

Below: Chow line at Duxford. (78th FG)

A 389th Bomb Group crew studying navigation maps at Hethel before a mission. (Charles Nigrelli)

Leisure hour. (Charles Nigrelli)

Sergeant Gordon Winkler, a young B-17 gunner in the 350th Bomb Squadron, 100th Bomb Group who shot down two Messerschmitt 109s. (TAMM)

James Stewart and Clark Gable, Hollywood movie stars who flew B-24 and B-17 missions respectively in the 8th Air Force. Gable, who had appeared in several movies and had won an Oscar for his role in *It Happened One Night*, made in 1934, voluntarily enlisted in the USAAF on 17 August 1942, aged 42, following the death of his wife, actress Carole Lombard, who was killed in an air crash while on a bond tour. By July 1944 Stewart had been awarded the DFC and the Air Medal. (USAAF)

Above:
Sweating
them in at
Molesworth
in late 1944.
(USAF)

Right: Damage
to the tail
of a 100th
Bomb Group
B-17G caused
by an enemy
fighter that
deliberately
rammed the
Fortress on a
mission in April
1945. (USAF)

Sergeant L.F. Teetman, a B-17 gunner from Brooklyn at Kimbolton all smiles with coffee and a sandwich after the mission on 31 December 1943. (USAF)

Fighter tactics. (USAF)

Crew of
Buckeye Belle
in the 384th
Bomb Group
at Grafton
Underwood.
(USAF)

303rd Bomb Group crew at Molesworth in June 1943, their tour completed. (USAF)

London on VE Day. (TAMM)

London on VE Day. (TAMM)

personality. So I gagged myself on the Scotch and tried to appear casual, as if I was in my element.

I'd offered the girls a drink when we first entered the room and they had accepted. I apologized that I didn't have any soda or ice; just Scotch. However, it made no difference to them. Scotch was fine. They didn't even want any water with it. Just Scotch. "How much?"

"A half-a-glass would be fine."

My God! A full bottle looked to hold only maybe four full glasses and Shea had used up a fourth of it. At a half-a-glass for each of us, there might be enough for only two drinks each. But then, I knew I wouldn't drink a half-a-glass. Maybe the girls wouldn't either and the bottle could last all night.

Well, that's what I thought until I saw the girls put it down as if it was water and they were dehydrated.

Americans, for the most part, drink to get drunk. From what I'd seen of the British, they just seemed to drink as if it were nourishment. I concluded, therefore, that the bottle would not last the night; and wondered if *I* could last the night.

We socialized with small talk about the big and elegant room. Was it Baroque or Georgian? I didn't know and I didn't care. I could only wonder how I was to perform. What was the game we were playing, anyway?

To be honest, it had to do with sex. I had been attracted to it, but my experience was definitely limited in the sport.

Lieutenant Truman J. 'Smitty' Smith June 1944

When in London, I tried to get a room at the Cumberland Hotel near Marble Arch, which has 9ft-long bathtubs and great big beds. A good hot soak and a night of uninterrupted sleep is number one on my agenda. I discovered a Chinese restaurant in Piccadilly Circus, two storeys up in a building just behind the huge Bovril sign. Not as good as Wo Fats in Honolulu but considering the circumstances, not bad. And I didn't see a single cockroach anywhere.

When I visited the parents of a pen pal in London, I was wearing only my DFC ribbon. The lady of the house was a confirmed "Monty" fan, which was okay with me because I thought he was a great general if for nothing else but that he identified with his men and they loved him for it. General Patton had this quality as well. They were a couple of prima donnas. Anyway, while she talked, she seemed to be eyeing my DFC. The lady finally broke through her British reserve and asked me what the medal represented. When I told her it was the Distinguished Flying Cross, she fairly gasped. I didn't have the heart to tell her that our DFC was a much lower-ranking medal than the RAF DFC, which was more akin in rank to our Silver Star.

Just outside of Hyde Park, I happened upon a group of people who were listening to a soapbox orator on a street corner. It turned out he was a WWI British Army veteran who was giving the US military what for because when US soldiers arrived in England they already had at least three

medals and had yet to confront the enemy. He was referring, of course, to
the American Theater medal, the European Theater medal and the Good
Conduct medal. He proudly pointed to the single medal he wore for four
years of service on the western front.

... On the way to Simpson's restaurant, a V-1 flew over at about 400ft
altitude doing around 400mph. Its noise was nerve-wracking (even more
so than the air raid warning London Klaxons) reminding me somewhat of
a pack of motorcycles racing by. It passed over us, its motor stopped and
it began a 180-degree turning dive to the left, exploding a couple of blocks
away. My admiration for the British people has increased a good deal since
I arrived in Britain. They walk about as though the "*Vergeltungswaffen*"
do not exist.

Abe Dolim

Had quite a time awful drunk out. We stayed in a place called King's Palace.
Some joint, except that half of it had been blown off by buzz bombs. A lot
of loose women live here are running in and out of your room constantly.
Moved out the next day to the Howard Hotel, uptown; extra nice place
– beds a foot thick and a great big bathroom, which we fought over all day
and all night. Paid £18 for a quart of Scotch, but it was worth it. Walked
around Piccadilly half the night, fooling around with the Commandos
– swell time. Ate dinner in the ritziest places we could find and paid a
small fortune for taxi fares.

Bill Campbell

The accommodations were difficult to come by, the ones you got were not
very good and the Blitz was no fun. Stage shows and movies were good
and the food at "Willow Run", the junior officers' mess at the Grosvenor
House was the best (and cheapest) in town. We did some shopping, ordered
custom jodhpur-type flying boots made at Bunting's, battle jackets at
Stone's, and lenses for my movie camera at Wallace Heaton's.

On a couple of visits there I had interesting chance meetings. One was
very fortunate. Father Frank Sullivan, a Jesuit priest from back home, had
become a lieutenant commander in the Navy Chaplain Corps, stationed
in London. I enjoyed seeing him again, but the real bonus was that the
Navy supplied him with generous rations of cigarettes and whisky and he
didn't use either, but offered me his rations whenever I could make it to
London. Whereas on our base we were rationed various unheard-of brands
of mongrel cigarettes, he could get "Luckies" or "Camels" in any quantity
for the same price of fifty cents a carton. Our base officers' club was paying
$18 a fifth for no-brand Scotch diluted to half strength; Father Frank could
get a fifth of any brand for one dollar! He got Johnnie Walker Black Label
for me. The Navy really took care of its own.

Another chance meeting was embarrassing, particularly for the one met.
During an air raid, my flight surgeon, Spivvy (Captain Seymour E. Spivak
MD), and I reluctantly obeyed the Air Warden's instruction to go down

into the Underground, which was always jam-packed with bodies, smelly, damp, and dimly lit. After much stumbling over sleepers, knitting ladies and crying children, we squeezed into a small opening on a backless narrow bench against the wall. As my eyes adjusted to the dark, I saw that sharing the bench to my immediate left was a "Piccadilly Commando". Even closer to her on her left was an American, his uniform amorously draped around the "her". Curiously, I poked my head forward to get a peek at the uniform wearer at the same time that he wanted to get a look at me, the intruder upon his scene. There we were, almost nose to nose and both incredulous. He had been a senior officer in my cavalry regiment in the late Thirties! We knew each other; I had met his wife and had given riding lessons to two of his children. Our eyes remained fixed for what seemed an eternity with neither acknowledging the other. He suddenly blinked, grabbed his girl friend, and they stumbled off into the dark.

Another time when in London for a couple of days of major dental work, I was billeted at the Dorchester with another dental patient, a colonel from Patton's armour. After dinner and a late show, we were on our way back to the hotel, griping about the strict curfew rules making it too late for us to get a drink, when to our surprise we came upon a bar that was still open. It was crowded with uniforms inside and a larger group outside trying to get in. It was unheard of for any bar, any day, any place in the UK to be open "after hours". There was a policeman standing right there. We asked him "How come?" He said he tried to close the place down, but couldn't with "those people in there." We asked, he answered: "The Prime Minister's daughter and the President's son!" Sure enough, we could see Sarah Churchill and Elliot Roosevelt at the centre of a very festive group inside.

Spivvy and I had the same interests – some good meals at "Willow Run", some shows, points of historic interest and no pub-crawling. Getting decent accommodations in wartime London was a problem. The rumour with Americans was that hotels there, particularly the better ones, gave preferential treatment to British forces. The darker side of that rumour was that if you did manage to book a room, it would be on one of the top three floors – which proved most vulnerable to Blitz bombing!

Spivvy stopped by my office one day and suggested we take a couple of days in London. I preferred Edinburgh or nearby Cambridge. I was not too thrilled with London's V-1s and V-2s and the closet-sized rooms with water closet down the hall we'd been getting there. It wasn't that much of an improvement over what we had on base. My senior clerk, Sgt Brosseau, overhearing us, interrupted and asked where we'd like to stay in London if we had a choice, and ventured he might get a reservation for us. I gave him a disbelieving look, but having known him to pull rabbits out of a hat before, listed the Savoy as first choice and the Dorchester as second. He went back to his desk in the outer office and reappeared a few minutes later with a Cheshire grin and the pronouncement, "You have a room at the Savoy for two nights. When you check in, remember to use the English pronunciation of your rank and name. Knowing some chicanery was involved, I asked how he managed it. Switching from his natural

Brooklyn accent to a very believable English one, he had represented me as a "Left-tenant colonel in the Eighth" not specifying whether it was the famed British Eighth Army, or our Eighth Air Force, and followed with the English pronunciation of my name.

When Spivvy and I checked in at the Savoy, while feeling a little apprehensive about participating in Brosseau's deception, I said to the clerk very positively, "You have a booking for Left-tenant Colonel *May-uh-nee*. He checked his file and said "Yes, I do", then with a delayed but sizable double take, "But you are an American." I refrained from using any of several sarcastic replies that came to mind, said nothing, and stared him down. What he had said was out of surprise, but realizing I might take offense and create a bit of a row unbecoming the quiet dignity of the Savoy, he nervously summoned a bellman and sent us off to the lift. When we got to our room, the most luxurious we'd seen since we left home, and were feeling very pleased with ourselves, we ordered up a couple of Scotches – each. Next on the agenda was a hot bath in one of the Savoy's giant-size cast iron tubs! As we savored our drinks, letting the hot water flow, we were about to flip a shilling to see who'd get first crack at the tub, when there was a gentle knock on the door. It was a man wearing a cutaway coat, identifying himself as a house detective. He said he had passed our room several times and heard the water running continuously. He asked if we were aware of the restrictions on the use of water for bathing because of its need for fighting Blitz fires. He also wanted to check to see if we had exceeded the three inches allowed for a tub. He turned off the faucet, pulled a ruler from his pocket and plumbed the depth. Sure enough, we had substantially more than doubled the allowable, then, despite our vigorous protests, he did the unthinkable – he let that precious hot water go down the drain until it reached the three-inch level on his ruler!

"Rules, you know."

London Trips, Lieutenant Colonel James J. Mahoney

We stayed overnight in a servicemen's place, kinda like our YMCA. I think we all enjoyed the feeling of clean white linen sheets instead of woollen blankets we had back at base. Fish and chips spring to mind – we ate lots of those, they were so good. I guess the newspaper gave them that good taste, but I have never eaten them since.

We did the usual things, visit the historical places like Westminster Abbey, Madame Tussauds and rode the subway, I think you call it the Tube, can't think why. We did visit a pub or two, but I was not impressed with English beer, I am sure it was watered down. I know several of the other guys took pleasure in the seamier side of the nightlife, but that never appealed to me. I was too young and innocent to be bothered with such things and besides I had got a sweetheart waiting for me back home.

Apart from Piccadilly and the surrounding area, we never did go for the usual stuff in London. We checked into the Rainbow Club first. We would book a room, although we hoped not to use it, but this was a sort of place for the GIs in town. They had a bulletin board where you could check to see if any of your buddies were in town and John and I always put our name up. We didn't have any buddies off base that we wanted to find. We did it just so that it looked like we belonged.

I remember meeting a lady of the night around the Circus, a sweet young thing; she came from Scotland. The night we met we had just got back to her room when the alarm sounded. She was terrified and shaking with fear. I remember we got under her bed and I put my arms around her and held her tight all night. For some strange reason I felt really good in the morning – sweet thing, I will always remember her.

Nineteen-year-old Rufus Webb, air gunner

At Rainbow Corner there was this lovely lady in an American Red Cross uniform who sat at a desk in one of the rooms. A sign on the desk read "Have Adele Astair write a letter home for you". Adele Astair was the sister of Fred Astair, the famous movie tap-dancer. She was also Lady Cavendish, having married into British nobility. I was one of the fascinated guys who went over to ask her to write a letter home for me, but I really did it so I could stare at her; I think she had the most gorgeous set of legs I've ever seen in my life.

Al Zimmerman

Not all the London sightseeing is done at night. The blackout is disconcerting to fun-seekers who like to sample numerous haunts in a single evening. The midnight close-down of subways and the thinning of the always-scarce taxis by late evening stymies the gadabouts. So the average American soldier stationed outside London, as most of them are, sets aside most of the daylight hours of his leave to see the sights.

He is an unflagging tourist and one who will return home with a fair smattering of what the guidebook recommends, plus a number of things it fails to mention. One of his favorite spots is oratorical row in Hyde Park. It has enjoyed a revival since the Yank came to town, not because its oratory has improved but with hundreds of Americans swelling the audience, additional hundreds of British attend to watch the Americans kibitzing. The Yank, loquacious as he sometimes is in pub and bar, has made no move, as yet, to take over the speechmaking rostrums from which the sorely heckled, weather-beaten orators debate mostly politics, religion and the war. The war and the soapbox oratory is new to the Yank. Give him time.

With the first days of spring great patches of greensward in this vast park were appropriated by baseball-crazy Americans. Sundays saw dozens of softball battles going, with thousands of interested Britishers crowding the sidelines and outfield without regard for foul or line drive. Harassed outfielders and grim GI umpires attempted to shoo the crowds off the playing field, but the Londoner took his stance firmly, umbrella or stick in hand and pretended not to hear the warnings. Many a baseball will bounce off many a decorous bowler hat before the Yank departs for the sandlots of home, but the Britishers will have enjoyed a close-up of the crazy Americans at their game of "rounders". After all, why should he move from his vantage point on the first base line? Didn't he and his forebears roam this park long before the Americans came?

The razzing chatter that goes up from the fielding participants in an American baseball game interests the Londoner as much as the antics of these soldiers who smite furiously at the ball and then sprint madly around a squared footpath. The British call it "barracking," but the term doesn't half describe the insults and epithets hurled by the Yanks at their opponents at bat. On the sidelines of the baseball lots that dot the landscape at Hyde Park, these truly English-speaking people are learning something of English "as she is spoke".

The exchange in language lessons is mutual. The officer who dated the British miss, promising to meet her at a stated hour on the first floor of the Palais Royal waited for an hour and gave up in disgust, only to discover she had waited just as impatiently for him on the first floor above the street level, which is a second floor in the USA and always will be a first floor in England. "Vegetable marrow", popping up intriguingly on a menu is your old friend boiled squash. Slacks are bags, but an "old bag" is what it means back home. Tenpins are ninepins and bowling is skittles, with or without beer, which usually is lager. A sedan is a saloon car and a Jeep is a Jeep, though you can't get a lift in one, literally or linguistically, a lift being an elevator. A telegram is always a wire, though a wireless (never radio) message is a "signal". A long distance call is a "trunk" and when you're connected "you're through" – too often literally "through."

Military traffic on telephone circuits in London has rendered service equally as difficult as in Washington, DC, which is adequate description of a sad state of communications affairs. The telephonic techniques of the American user and the London operator not only differ but suffer in accent translations. A classic telephone story around American headquarters in London concerns the harassed general's aide who, sweating profusely over a priority call, demanded desperately of the London operator: "How's about it, dearie? Do I have to marry you to get a connection?"

In the early days of the American headquarters in London, the motor pool was staffed by attractive young women who wore snappily tailored olive drab and overseas caps pinned jauntily onto careful coiffures. Many of them were wealthy, some from titled families. High-ranking officers, on inspection tours of troop installations and supply depots scattered over the face of England, found themselves making long, tedious trips, of times in blackouts, with slim fragile-appearing women doing the hard work. Military etiquette ruled that a colonel or a general may not drive; indeed no officer, as a rule, may drive a vehicle in the European Theater. It was an uncomfortable arrangement to the American mind, not yet accustomed to seeing women employed in every military chore except actual combat. Male drivers were added to the pool after the experience of one general and his girl driver.

They were driving home across a lonely moor after a day of almost nonstop visits to various military installations. At a place on the road where bushes bordered both sides, the tired girl embarrassedly suggested a brief stop, parked the car and hurried off to one side of the road. When she returned to the wheel, somewhat red of face at keeping the General waiting, she mumbled brief apologies, looking straight before her and drove off. It was not until she parked the car an hour later in front of the general's headquarters and turned to tender him the trip ticket for signature that she discovered he, too, had taken advantage of the brief stop, but had been left behind and compelled to spend the night upon the gusty moor.

Major John M. Redding & Captain Harold Leyshon

The local public telephone system run by the GPO (Government Post Office) required some education. After one deposited an assortment of strange coins into a noisy metal box, the operator would ask what number you wanted. If you were lucky, after a couple of minutes and a new variety of noises you might reach your party and start a conversation, whereupon the operator would come back on the line and ask "Are you through?" in "Yank", this meant "Are you through talking?" (The operator was asking whether your call had gone through to the intended party.) Upon hearing the GI's anxious "No", the operator would disconnect the call with a "Sorry, I'll try again." A few of repeat performances of this misunderstanding left most inclined to pull the phone from the wall and express some nasty thoughts about the GPO.

James J. Mahoney

The telephone system is a constant bafflement. Not merely for the complexity of Button A and Button B but for the unpredictable results obtained from manipulating these gadgets and the familiarity with which he can converse with the unseen operator at the other end of the line. Accustomed at home to hear nothing from these impersonal, stylized voices that is not strictly business, he is amazed and often delighted to get advice, consolation, humour, back-chat and philosophy for his two pennies, even though he might fail to get though to his party. And strong rumour had it that in rare cases, if he knew the right words and the right sequence of questions, he might even get the age, colour of eyes and hair, approximate size, name and lastly a date with the smiling voice at the switchboard. This, definitely, was not the American way.

There was the evening in April when I was in Berkshire and tried to get a call through to Suffolk. It was a lovely soft spring evening and the girl at the switchboard was in a friendly, communicative mood appropriate to the season and the weather. She took my number, told me there would be a wait because the lines were so busy at this time of night and then, feeling that I should not stand there for minutes at a time holding a dead receiver, "Beautiful night, isn't it?" she ventured.

"Yes, it certainly is."

"I suppose you're calling your girl now aren't you?"

"Yes, I am. How did you know?"

"Oh, all the fellows are calling their girls at this time of night. That's what keeps us so busy. I can always tell when it's a young American voice there'll be a girl waiting at the other end. I suppose she wishes you were there in Suffolk?"

"Yes, I think she does."

"Well, she'll be glad to hear you. But she'd be happier far if you were there. It's a lovely evening. There's going to be a moon later. Ah, now here's your call coming through. You're only allowed six minutes, remember."

"Only six minutes?"

"Well, we'll make this a long six minutes tonight, just as a special favour."

"Thank you! Thank you!"

No, this was not the American telephone system.

First Impressions, Robert S. Arbib Jr

We were in London from Sunday night through Wednesday morning. Stayed nights at one of the Red Cross clubs. Most of them are pretty nice, have bunks with sheets for a change. Had a little trouble finding our way around the subway system (Underground to Londoners). It seemed the most convenient and fastest way to get around, though there are plenty of double-deck busses and antique taxies. Monday afternoon we took a taxi tour of some of the high points – an hour-and-three-quarters ride, with fifteen whole minutes in places like St Paul's Cathedral and Westminster Abbey. We saw the palace, parliament, No.10 Downing Street, etc. The most amazing thing is that every building on the list escaped destruction during the 1940 Blitz and the buzz bomb era. Of course some were hit, but there is no extreme damage on them. After the tour it began raining and rained most of the time until we left.

That night we ate in a good hotel and had a nice meal that wasn't too expensive, but I don't imagine many Englishmen could eat there often. You don't need too much money to get a decent meal in London. And some places really try to do things up lavishly. Think service is much better than it is in the States during the war. Of course, in most places there are lines to "sweat out" before you get in, but they aren't too bad.

Then we went to a dance and I met a Canadian leftenant (lieutenant) who is on sick leave after being in the hospital for a wound suffered in France. He was in civilian clothes and I took him for an American, since he didn't talk like a Limey. He told me about things at the front and in Canada. Really a swell fellow. Decided the Canadians make almost as much as we do and the Limeys make about half as much as we do.

Most of the art galleries and museums in London are pretty bare because the valuable things have been removed for safekeeping. Tuesday night I went to a fairly large London theater and saw the play *Arsenic and Old Lace* ... It was really funny. They serve tea and cakes between each act and allow smoking throughout the whole performance – sort of different.

Got to talk to a lot of soldiers and civilians here and there. Met one American at the Red Cross, who is from New Orleans, but who married a Polish officer in London and expects to live in Poland after the war. Many Londoners talked about the blitzes, the 1940 one and the present buzz bomb one. An English girl told me what a Victory Roll was. She said during the 1940 Blitz the outnumbered RAF planes ("Never had so many owed so much to so few", Churchill) who did such a good job of defending London and England would fly over the city each day following a German raid. Each RAF pilot would do a number of rolls for the number of planes he shot down the night before.

Not many people sleep in the subway stations now though. I only saw a dozen or so, altogether, while I was there.

London Pass, 8 October 1944 Frank H. Spurlock, Radio Operator,
466th Bomb Group

Went to one of England's oldest cities, Winchester, Sunday. It is about forty miles from London. Looked up a third or fourth cousin who is with American Red Cross. Took a tour of the city. There is a huge cathedral built in 1078. Also a boy's school founded about the same year. It is for boys from about ten or twelve years old to eighteen. Children can go to public schools until they are about fourteen and then they have to pay to go to school. This is a private school, of course, but over here they call them public schools. The boys in Winchester School, upon graduation go to a university, such as Oxford or Cambridge, if they meet the high requirements. The students wear a peculiar looking straw hat which is their school symbol, or rather the thing that shows what school they attend. Strictly a tradition. The ones who are there by scholarships wear robes, the others don't. On Sundays they all wear dress coats with swan-cut tails. We saw where they eat and were shown some wooden trays used there years ago when plates were not in use. We were told that they put soup in the center of the tray surrounded by the other food to keep it from running off the tray. The soup would be eaten first, then the other food.

On the way back to the Red Cross from the school we passed the house in which the novelist Jane Austen (*Pride and Prejudice*) spent her last days.

Monday I toured the Parliament buildings. The first hall we looked at was built about twelfth-century and housed the first Commons and Lords and the first law court in England. Then we went through the newer buildings, which are all connected. They were built under Victoria during the 1890s. The House of Common chamber was destroyed during the 1940 Blitz. We saw where it had been. Commons now meets in the House of Lords chamber and Lords meets in an adjoining hall. To vote, the Commons members go out one side or another according to whether they are voting yea or nay.

The tower the Big Ben is in was built around the sixteenth century. The clock has been up only a comparatively short time. It was put up by a well-known watch and clock firm, Bensons. So the name, Big Ben. The big hand is nine feet long and the short one is six feet long. One of the clock's bells weighs four tons. The Thames runs alongside the Parliament buildings. Its course was changed so that the buildings could be built where they are.

After the tour I walked about a half block to as close as I could get to the well-guarded No.10 Downing Street. It is in the shadows of some big government buildings and is a dirty looking three-storey building with a British flag on a pole on the front of it – the only distinguishing feature. About a block from the Scotland Yard headquarters.

Monday night I went with another American to see *Blithe Spirit* by Noël Coward, which was good. It has been running in London for four years.

Several days before I went to London, a rocket hit the annex of one of the biggest department stores, Selfridges. Americans have offices in the Annex and several Americans in trucks outside were killed by it. It just happens to be about four blocks from the Red Cross club that I usually stay in when I'm there.

To London Again, 15 December 1944, Frank H. Spurlock, radio operator, 466th Bomb Group

... *Left about 1.15 and got there about 5.30 I guess. Saw lots of English scenery and it is beautiful. All of it! The stone and brick houses just amaze me ... They are so different. Real pieces of artistic masonry and so old and well put together. Went thru lots of towns on the way. Guess Cambridge was the biggest. Think I'll stay there next time and see the University. Farmers all out in their fields – many girls and women among them. 3 horse-hitches seem to be the common style here. Plows, discs and seeders even. They have many, many canals and streams here ... all sorts of boats in them. Every family along it has a private "dock". And a boat or two. Some of the boats are quite nice and almost as wide as the small canals it seems. Oh that green grass and blue water go well together ... I haven't seen a spot in all rural England that wouldn't make the ideal resort spot ... no kidding. Everything looks so well kept up and "refreshful". Can't believe people live in such surroundings the year round. Saw a gypsy band encamped along one such stream. About two dozen wagons that looked to be fresh from a circus or something. So pretty and masterpieces of design and carvings. All colours – and small and trim sorta parked in a big clearing ... with bright clothes on the line. Quite a sight! The hay-stacks look like the thatched African houses you see in books ... They make sort of a roof of bunches of hay thatch ... And same shapes as huts – Funny.*

Ok we're almost to London. The train grinds on ... its getting quite hazy now ... big smokey city and evening approaching. On the outskirts I find myself picking out the bombed-out spots. Just imagining what the Blitz must have been like! Oh so many buildings ... even blocks ... completely gone. They've done a marvellous job of removing the debris ... just whack off the side of the buildings so falling stuff won't be a hazard ... And clear up all the rubble. You can't believe such a large city could have so many "spots" like this within. It's terrible! And we thought we knew what war was! No I'm afraid we don't! Can't! I hope ... And they're not freed of this destruction yet, nope. Buzz bombs and rocket bombs still come in every day. We heard some each day – some close, some far ... But all taking lives and making a mess of things.

Unloaded at Liverpool Street station ... Quite different than any of the

big stations in the US. One large roof over it all, with viaducts of stairways up and over the tracks ... small buildings at the end of the tracks and under this roof too are the news stands, ticket agencies, etc – all quite dark and smokey. Out on the street we hailed our first British Cabbie. Gee, they're quaint little jobs. So small and peculiar, mostly all black ... driver sits alone on right side ... No other front seat, then the window pane between him and the back seat where you ride. Austin makes most of the cars, small and hearse-like in appearance ... look about 1930 models – hm! Drove the 3 of us out to the Princess Gardens (Red Cross) hotel for 2/6 (2 shillings and sixpence) ... about 52 cents and we put up for our pass. Pretty nice place tho' our dormitory style room (5 beds) was away up in the "pigeon loft" it seemed. Quite a hike! Ate our supper there and went out to see the town a little.

Next day (after enjoying a good sleep on soft beds for a change till noon almost) we went to the Grosvenor House for dinner. A huge place ... Feeding only Officers now ... A <u>thousand</u> a setting (about 12 settings per meal). Quite an impressive sight. That many Officers – mostly Americans ... Went to big tea dance in the Grosvenor House Tea Room ... Found a couple attractive "items" and managed to enjoy the tea & sandwiches too. Felt just a bit dumb tho' ... When this kid can attend teas and dance to soft music with strange people – in the middle of the afternoon – well! Tom and Greening "sicked" me on a beautiful number in black (found she's a stage stand-in on vacation ... her story!) And then they left to imbibe a little "hard to get" spirits. I ended up taking a gal (Mary Collin) to supper at the Jr Officers Club. Then went to a couple of dance-halls – drinking parlors (everybody has his mild or bitters (beer) or gin or something here). And had a fairly enjoyable evening ... Still get along being a "T-Totaller" as they call it. Took the gals home by cab (saves getting lost and isn't so expensive anyway). Wandered down to Piccadilly Circus to see the nightlife about. It's even worse than I'd heard – you'd think they were bartering for butter and eggs.

Oh yes, before the tea-dance we'd gone to an artist's supply shop and Don & I invested a little over a pound a piece on pastels and paper etc. We're pretty well fixed up now to become real artists – ahem! Tried 'em out too and think I'll have lots of fun. Wonderful what material can do even with poor hands on it. Will drop you a few samples from time to time.

Stopped in the National Art Gallery just for atmosphere after our purchases ... thence across the street to what I call "Pigeon Square" (Trafalgar Square they call it, you know, the spot where they feed the pigeons). Had our pictures taken doing just that ...

Next day – afternoon (I never interrupt my sleep for nuthin) I went for a sight seeing tour on my own while T and Don had dates with their acquaintances of night before. Took my pastel crayons (or chalks ... whatever you call them) and a pad with me to get a pic of the Thames and some good background. Got a cabbie and said, "London Bridge". Told him my mission etc. Ended up letting him take me almost everywhere ... regular tour ... just we two. Saw St Paul's Cathedral, original Cheddar Cheese manufacturing place, Tower and Tower Bridge (went over it) and *back across the London Bridge ... he was pointing out bombed places etc ... Then Bank of England, Buckingham Palace, lots of famous arches etc ... Then Houses of Parliament and Big Ben and I left him at Westminster Abbey. (Cost – with big tip 10 shillings ($2.00) cheap! I was more than impressed with this place, as you can imagine. Such a huge solid, divine looking and atmospheric place inside. One place I automatically reached for my hat without ever thinking, as I opened the door. It is wonderful. I was just a bit undecided about whether my walking on such as famous as Isaac Newton and oh so many others (poets, writers, everybody) was OK or not? But some places the* <u>whole</u> *floor is "headstones" so this reassured me ... I think of probably 3 big thrills there:*

1. The sight down the length of the main corridor ... Such design, architecture and strength in its columns, with the hue of gray, the stench of age and the "keyhole" beams of lights radiating thru those high portals ... reflecting on the hallowed dust of the ages ... Truly a serene picture, heart-taking and God inspiring. The ceiling is so high I can't say I remember ever getting a look that far up ... It's warmly dark yet cool in the place ... So quiet and big.

2. The inspiration I got just climbing up to one of the main pulpits and thumbing a few pages of the huge old Bible there ... Always open. The print is half an inch tall ... I could just imagine the sermons preached from behind such a Book.

3. The two-huge-bronze candelabrums ... One telling the story of the New Testament ... The other main characters in Old Testament. Too bad none of my souvenir books I bought picture them for I thought they were masterpieces ... The "souvenir seller" there ... a bald headed "pope-ish" looking fellow (Scottish) ... had this remark about some of the famous busts etc. being removed. "Yes, they've taken Shakespeare's, – one of the Kings Chairs is gone ... 'bout all of importance that's left is me." *The way he said it! – Hah. Several sections of the Abbey are now blocked off from view ... are internally braced with sandbags against the bombings. The Houses of Parliament nearly have been grazed by a bomb in the Blitz.*

Well, after leaving the Abbey I walked along the Thames to a spot where I might find suitable for a sketch. Found what I was looking for atop a relatively small bridge but as large as most car bridges in the States ... Just newly constructed between their new concrete Waterloo Bridge (downstream) and the Westminster Bridge upstream. I sketched a quick one of this bridge and the House of Parl and Big Ben in the background. Wasn't too well pleased with my work for the pastels are a little <u>thick</u> *and messy compared to the Conte Crayon (which I should have used) but I did enjoy the experience. After all I had never sat astraddle a beam over the Thames and tried to record such scenery as Westminster Bridge and Big Ben tho' I've seen photos and stuff of such historic spots all my life. So, it was worth it! To* <u>ME</u> *– anyway.*

Walked along Victoria Embankment (along River) to London Bridge ... wandered thru town till my feet ached – gave up, got a cab and back to our hotel for evening supper. Walked uptown after supper ... rode the Underground R.R. to Piccadilly Square and met the Radio Op. and nose gunner (Bob & Ed). (Oh yes, just thought, I didn't tell you did I, that this afternoon I walked thru Hyde Park ... Saw the city's ack-ack set-up ... also some Americans (Air Force office workers) soldiers on parade & drill in the Park ... just exercise I guess).

Now – back to evening. While still talking to the boys their dates came up with a <u>spare</u> that I condescended to going with (hah!) She wasn't so bad (The boy's dates were really keen gals ... looks too). But I still like my pickin 'em the best ... anyway. We saw the show "Tonight and Every night" with Rita. Well – it's a good show on England's morale, courage and doings ... until you've been in England and then see it in England – with an English gal for a date ... And then your just a bit disappointed in the Hollywood Producer ... This English gal hated to see the Blitz pictured. She almost shuddered to think she had to be reminded. She found the accent quite fake and a few other things. But other than that – good! Bah! I know I would have enjoyed it in the States, but here, not so much!

After the show we hit a little restaurant "The Yankee Doodle" With a real live jukebox in it ... ate rabbit – and then after a little wandering around – gave up for the night, our last one there. Came home next afternoon after picking up our week's rations (candy etc.) at the Officers PX in London ... Then big train ride home. Tried my pastels out on a "memory-scene" of the mountains. Got home about 11.30 ... After stopping at Kings Lynn for an evening of show and waiting for bus back. Really an OK 3-day pass.

I was very much interested in London wartime measures in evidence. I had no idea how a large city would or could get prepared for the Blitz and all they've gone thru. First of all it's very dark at nights still (yet relatively light compared to Blitz days, I understand). Just a dim-out in effect now ... That means a tiny hooded street light about every two blocks and hooded traffic lights only showing light ... that's all the lights there are in London – except cabs use very dim lights ... and bicycles. Stores are mostly wooded up in front, sandbags still in evidence against some store corners, banks and places where the underground stores have light coming that the sidewalk. Everything in the windows has a ration value tag as well as a money value ... almost <u>everything</u>.

Air-raid shelters are numerous – some just within stores for daytime use. Then many shelters along walks etc. Water tanks are erected at various places ... some bombed out blocks have the whole ¼ of a block filled with water in case of fires ... I couldn't imagine what the life-preserver and grappling hook were doing on the side of a board fence until someone told me it was for use when there had been water there ... That drunks wandered off into it now and then, hm. Downtown and everywhere fire zones are carefully and conspicuously marked. Everything about their life seems regimented and orderly nowadays ... People seem happy, out for the Yanks' money and as unshaken about V-bombs as if they were firecrackers of a July 4th.

Was shocked with what I saw in the Underground R.R. tunnels ... at the stations I mean. They're all filled with beds in tiers and people ... all ages sleeping there ... living there ... some have a satchel of belongings ... others nothing but Govt. provided blankets. Can you imagine it? I couldn't! Old *people – trying to sleep in a busy, noisy R.R. tunnel ... lights on and people standing all around. How I feel for those homeless probably many, many familyless people ... and they aren't few in numbers either! It puts some of the fighting blood in you – I say! Like a cabbie tells me "these buzz bombs and German tactics on cities aren't war ... it's bloody murder!" ... and he's right. It's merciless – and swift ... and no one is safe from this terror.*

I guess that's about all ... oh I could tell you how the women do with (or without) things US gals would cry for. Shoes, hose, dresses, very old styles and scarce (socks, I mean and shoes). Should see the way they stuff their handbags with oranges when they eat out at a US Officer's mess place with you. Just little things mean so much to them. You're reminded of "snipe-shooters" and "garbage-grazers" in the States – but they're proud here and I sorta feel plenty lucky to think my folks and gal friend at home can have the nice things they have ... But I'll sure tell off anyone now that "cries" in the States about rationing – or "I don't have a thing to wear" ... Not meaning I ever expect any of you to – but I've seen people. You know gang; we've been a long ways from war ...

Closing with an overall backward glance at London ... A huge, old city of tradition and unique beauty in its age and consequently different style. She has no skyscrapers – but she's big ... streets like spokes on huge wheels ... many wheels side by side. Buildings, each one a masterpiece of architecture and design (old and smokey) ... People friendly and warm ... conversation a pleasure ... their lingo a killer for a new ear. They speak simply ... don't seem too highly educated (which they're not) yet they're very flowery and courteous in their speech and manners. Streets teem with uniforms ... all nations and countries, nothing but cabs and trucks and buses and streetcars for transportation on top ... plus their magnificent speedy underground. We saw it in beautiful spring weather ... but still a bit hazy at sundown and early morn. (They say). The buildings & streets are very close ... narrow streets and "alleys" most of them in under bldgs etc.

Saw a horse-drawn milk wagon ... and a pedal-car milk deliverer, milk-bottles have small – almost pop bottle size tops. Piccadilly Circus reminds me of a huge football bowl (or stadium) in the States. A semi-circular street with bldgs solid joined on both sides and about that high (8-10 stories) ... With just about one or two breaks under a bldg here and there for a street every distance of a about 3 blocks in the states. Peculiar arrangement just a solid curved line of stores of both sides of the one street – main part of Circus. Oh yes – I didn't know what or who the song "Rose of Charing Cross" was. I do now – it's a street in London. Hm – also Leicester Square of song fame ... great education – this travel – Huh!

Wait'll I write you of our mission (8 hrs 50 minutes deep into Germany) where we crossed Rhine, Danube and I saw Alps close ... next "edition" perhaps – Huh! Love all, Walt.

London Log, 1st Lieutenant Walt N. Cranson

There is a certain type of doll found in London called the Piccadilly Commando. A typical commando would be named Legion and her middle name would be Host and her last name would be Lots or Many or Thousands and she'd probably be wearing a sable cape.

When the dusk begins to grip the streets, the Commandos come out of hiding and head for their respective theatres. The top operators wander along the edges of Hyde Park and past the Grosvenor House. There are dark-eyed French girls in the eddies along Bond Street, but most of them are in and around Piccadilly.

They ease along the avenues and they're always willing to talk, sometimes for quite a while, if business is flourishing and they think they won't lose anything by it.

You couldn't pick a typical life story.

She might have been born in the south of France, or maybe in a bower of heather in the Isle of Skye.

About all you can say is she was born.

Maybe her father drank flagons of ale and threw the empty flagons at her. Maybe her mother made love with the ironmonger and didn't pull the shades. Maybe her sisters read unclean books.

If she went to school it was probably casually and she probably spent most of her time looking out the window at the dandelions, or but behind the hedges with the little boys.

She can see in the dark and she can hear the casual white feet of an MP a block away.

She and her sisters come from every battered city in Europe and she can whisper her sales-talk in a dozen languages, including Braille and Indian Sign, but she is at her best in the tongue of the Yanqui.

She is part of the night of London, part of the magic, part the ugly loneliness. She fills in an hour or a stray ten minutes or any part of a night. She is someone, when all that is needed is someone. At least she is a human being.

She may be a hard-eyed bitch in the dawn and she may put you away without pay for months, but when the mist is in your brain and the war is yesterday and overhead and probably to-morrow, she is the princess of darkness.

Some day the Yanks will go home and the bit-of-love for five pounds will deflate like the barrage balloons and her phase of lend-lease will unofficially terminate.

Maybe she'll marry a shell-shocked tank driver who'll take her home to Detroit, or maybe a flak-happy bomb-aimer and go back to the Isle of Skye.

She might make a dutiful mother and an excellent cook. And the past might fit into the past as merely an interlude and grow over with time and be almost forgotten in time.

Or maybe one gentle spring morning the Bobbies will fish her out of the river and no one will care whether her name was Legion or Host or Thousands, whether she plied her trade along Bond Street or in the soft shadows of Piccadilly.

Commando, Bert Stiles. Stiles was co-pilot on 1st Lieutenant Samuel Newton's crew, then 2nd Lieutenant John W. Green's in the 401st Bomb Squadron, 91st Bomb Group at Bassingbourn. While he was flying a 35-mission tour, 19 April-20 July 1944, Stiles wrote the classic, *Serenade to the Big Bird.* Stiles completed his bomber tour but instead of returning to America on leave now due to him, he asked to be transferred to fighters and he moved to the 339th FG and to P-51s. At age 23, he was shot down and killed on 26 November 1944 while escorting bombers to Hanover

In a moment of danger the British always seemed to come up with a laugh. I was sitting in a London movie theater watching Ginger Rogers in *Lady In The Dark.* The hero had just taken the heroine in his arms and we knew the inevitable kiss was not far away. At that moment the unmistakable engine noise of a V-1 flying bomb could clearly be heard and then ceased abruptly, meaning it was on its way down. Immediately a voice from the balcony yelled out: "For God's sake *kiss her* before it's too late!" I don't know if it was the laughter or the explosion of the bomb that shook the building but plenty of dust was stirred up.

Blackout Capers, John Lusk Moore

Near Hyde Park two aircrew officers are walking back to their hotel. Paratroopers on leave from the Normandy beachhead are very active. As the officers approach a building entryway, they hear a loud unmistakably Yank voice says, "Five pounds! Whattayagot a diamond-studded snatch?"

Abe Dolim

Deke and I decided to take in a movie at the Rialto and then hit a few pubs on the way back to the Red Cross club. After leaving the last pub, we walked along, single-file, with our left hands barely touching the walls of buildings. That was the only way to walk at night in London because of the blackout. It was so black that it was impossible to see your own hand right up in your face. I heard Deke grunt as he bumped into someone and then I saw the red tip of a burning cigarette. A female voice said, "Hi Yank, are you lonesome? I'll take it around the corner, standing up, for a pound-ten" (at that time, one pound, ten shillings was worth $6.30).

Deke declined. We took a cab back to the Red Cross club.

The next morning, I decided to go back to the base. Deke said, "I think I'll stay a couple of more days and make like a tourist in London." The *Royal Scot* took me back to Peterborough just in time for high tea. Having some time to kill before the bus arrived from the base, I stoppedin the Idlewild Restaurant for tea and little sandwiches ...

William L. Cramer Jr

Two-day passes were regularly given out in the 8th Air Force. Most of the guys were too bent on chasing girls and raising hell to spend their passes in truly rewarding activities. England had so many rich experiences awaiting us in its scenery, culture and history. London, of course, had its share of culture and history, but girls and nightlife are what led to the overwhelming number of two-day passes being used in London. The trains from Norwich to London and return went by two different routes and required three or four hours each way because of numerous stops. They were always overcrowded with servicemen seated and standing everywhere and they were always tedious ordeals.

I went with the guys only once to London on a two-day pass. Three of us took a room in the Savoy hotel. One of the fixtures that puzzled us was a bidet. Someone knew that it was of French derivation, but none of us had seen one or knew how it should be used. We didn't much try and repaired to the cocktail lounge, which was mostly deserted. We ordered drinks and then one of us recognized bandleader Glenn Miller, who was with a male companion. We went over to talk and were invited to sit down and drink with them. I remember none of the conversation, but I do remember that he autographed my "Short Snorter Bill", a ten-shilling note worth $2.00, which I have lost. Not long after this chance meeting, Glen Miller was presumed killed during a flight that never arrived at its destination.

Everyone had to visit Piccadilly Circus, of course, a great hub-like intersection in the middle of London that radiates streets in all directions. To American servicemen and to any serviceman in general, its main attraction was symbolized by the statue of Eros, the Greek god of love, rising above the fountain in the center of the circus. Under Eros' spell thousands of innocent young American boys fell as war casualties to the charms of the many English night ladies and ladies of other nationalities, who took up station there.

The ladies stood in secluded doorways or walked along the street. The innocent boys needed only to stand still a moment, which was all the opportunity the ladies needed to discuss their charms with their open-minded male audiences. The London Bobbies were all very understanding and considered that their duty had been sufficiently discharged if they urged a too-long-standing group or couple to get along with whatever they were planning, which seemingly the Bobbies knew not. "No loitering, please", or "Move along now, please."

Of course, there were at least two kinds of prices to pay if an innocent boy, struggling nobly to abide by what would be his mother's advice, nevertheless became overwhelmed by temptation. The first price ranged from £4–£8 ($16 to $32) for a whole night of bliss. This was not too unreasonable a price for overpaid Yankees, particularly not if the selected lady were English rather than French. The former were said to have significantly larger and more pleasing breasts than the latter. One presumed that they were more or less equal in other critical aspects.

A second kind of price was paid after return to base, its exact means depending on whether the innocent fallen boy were Catholic or anything else. If Catholic, confession was mandatory, but it was easy, as we heathen

Protestants thought. The Catholic chaplain would ask the young victim how much he had paid and then promised absolution if he donated an equal sum to the Red Cross. We Protestants thought this to be a very easy expedient because, of course, no vestige of a burden of guilt remained on the conscience of the Catholic boy. It was as though the padre said, "Pay up, you sinner and now go ye forth cleansed of your sins and sin no more, but if you do, be sure to come back with another contribution."

It was not quite so easy being Protestant, because some burden of guilt remained on the Protestant soul. There was no Protestant system for purchasing forgiveness. Or so uncharitable Protestants were inclined to think!

Actually, the padre was judged to lead a high life himself, considering his position. A regular Army chaplain, he seemed to have to prove himself tough. He drank with the boys, he cursed with them, he got down on his knees and shot craps with them, he smoked a cigar and put on the best of poker faces with them at cards and on a challenge he flew a couple of missions as a waist gunner with Tom Watkins. In the ready room before his flock boarded carriers to their planes, he stood on a stool and yelled, "All right, all you fish eaters, get over here and get down on your knees! Pray like hell, sinners all!"

There was the slightest suspicion that the padre could be so profligate with his drinking, poker playing and crap shooting only because not all of the tarnished pound notes earmarked for the Red Cross actually got that far. I did not agree, however. The Red Cross club in Norwich was far too well stocked with free doughnuts, coffee, games, reading and comely hostesses as to suggest anything but purity on the part of the padre. Indeed, I recognized that there was an unexpected benefit to my not being Catholic that I had not previously counted. Conscience be hanged! I savoured free Catholic doughnuts.

The Catholic boys paid still another price, however, same as that paid by all the Protestant boys and Jewish boys (a few, surely?) who fell as casualties of war under the spell of Eros: worry about dreaded VD. Oh, there were tests and cures all right, but if a boy was recognized a second time in the testing laboratory, the needles were rumoured to become much longer, thicker and duller.

Two Prices for Piccadilly Circus, Bob Shaver

I met Hilary at a dancehall just off the Haymarket, not far from Rainbow Corner. At first we were afraid of each other. She was very shy and not sure of Americans, as many English girls were at the time. She walked me back to my Red Cross club, would kiss and then beg one of my American cigarettes if I had any. She also insisted on eating fish and chips as a late night snack. Hilary clung to me. She always wore a raincoat, or a slicker as they say and wool sweater against the dampness of the London nights. I recall taking a taxi or two with Hilary and making rather passionate foreplay in the cab while we raced through the blackout. I had one of those overseas caps that kept falling off and she took it from me, clamping it on her head and pulling one edge of it down over one eye. Once, she said to me: "Do you want me to show you around?"

I was puzzled by this and replied, "Around where?"

"Around my old neighbourhood," she replied.

"Okay," I said, rather casually.

We got into a taxi. I didn't know where I was going but the night held promises far in excess of my poor anticipations. I had visions of some romantic hideaway in Southwark. I was young; the night pregnant with promises and Hilary snuggled against my olive drab tunic. I could see her face in the moonlight; a complexion that shone in the darkness like the silver path of the moonlight on the Thames. She became very passionate in the taxi, flinging her body hard against mine and kissing me so vigorously that I lost my cap. She started undoing my jacket and shirt. I took this as a sign that some sexual adventure was about to begin and this increased my anticipations. As was the custom of English girls, she called me "love" over and over again.

As a consequence of her lusty approach and her constant embraces, my arousal was reaching breaking point and I asked the cab driver to stop so we could get out. However, she persisted in going to a place she had designated to the driver. All this while my passion was mounting more and more and I had visions of the most lusty kind.

We had gone through an air raid warning earlier in the evening, but by this time there was a strange peace over the city of London. There had been nightly raids on the city for several days. It was such a bright moon that night the bombers could easily be seen by the ground batteries.

By this time the cab had gone through the blacked out streets to the vicinity of the Elephant and Castle. I imagined a secluded hideaway of a lover's nest where we could complete our lovemaking in privacy. For many nights in wartime London I had been forced to sleep in a Red Cross club in a large barracks-type room with cots among many men. Now I had visions of sharing a bed with Hilary.

We finally stopped and Hilary gave the signal for the driver to let us out. We found ourselves in the middle of one of those old eighteenth-century squares or parks surrounded by row houses. It was past midnight by now and the moonlight filtered through the trees and spangled the grass in the park. Hilary and I sat on a park bench and the first wisps of the famous London fog began to drift across the moon and creep over the grass. There was a long silence as we merely sat. Then, breaking the silence, she spoke.

"I used to live here," said Hilary, pointing to a gap in the buildings now filled with rubble. "It was bombed out in the Blitz."

She began to sob. As the tears filled her eyes, I kissed her.

We sat there until the first faint twinges of dawn showed in the eastern sky. I couldn't leave her so we spent the night in that park, huddled together in the damp fog of a London dawn.

8th Air Force sergeant

About every two weeks we were given a three-day pass to do as we pleased and relieve the tension of combat. London town was our destination on almost every occasion. Good old London. Staying at the Jules Club operated by the Red Cross for four shillings per night, we had a good base of operation to see London – one block from Piccadilly Circus and some of the best hotels and bars in town. The tourist impulse would have us visiting the well-known landmarks, edifices and places known to world travellers. As the day wore on, high tea was taken at one of the hotels. This was very formal and awkward at first until the proper protocol became a way of life. This was followed by a theatrical production with a late dinner at the Exhibition Club – always something different, exciting and something to look forward to.

All activities during the night hours were in total blackout conditions. Strange and frightening at first, but Fergie and I, carrying a small torch, found our way. I remember asking a bobby one night for directions to get some place and he answered, directing us to this street, then that street and on and on and he finally said,

"Yank, bear straight ahead and you cawn't miss it."

The confusion was caused by the fact that streets frequently change names every block. We found our destination.

While attending the theatre, there would be an air raid alert posted. People would leave the theatre and go to air raid shelters. Fergie and I would go outside and witness the splendid aerial show – hundreds of search lights crisscrossing the sky searching for enemy bombers or fighters with English or American fighters in pursuit. Grand as the stage production was inside, the show outside was thrilling enough to prevent us from seeking protection in an air raid shelter. Money cannot reproduce this epic drama in the sky for movie producers. As the all clear siren blew, we returned to finish the show. Somewhere during all of this we found another drink … airplanes, alcohol and sex.

Then off to the after-hours Exhibition Club off in South Kensington – three floors with an English pub at ground level, an American bar and dining room second floor and a South Seas tropical club room top side. A fine spot to relieve combat tension eating, drinking and wenching.

Yes, we visited Harrods, the Bank of England, Madam Tussauds wax museum, Hyde Park, Governor's House, City Hall of London, 10 Downing Street, Trafalgar Square, St James Park and all the government buildings. Flyboy on pass gets around by taxi, yes, to see it all.

Next day back in the air to who knows where until after briefing.

Robert H. Tays

What at place! Guess I'll be back again soon as the next pass comes along. Stayed in the nicest hotel in Piccadilly. I don't know how they charge so little. In England they serve breakfast at no extra cost in all the hotels. For 2 days in a swell room and breakfast $7.60, or $3.80 apiece. And if you put your shoes outside the door at nite [sic] they pick them up and shine them – no charge. Of course, some things are very expensive tho. I saw *in the paper where an ex-soldier was jailed for stealing a peach. The price was $1.10 apiece. You can have nice portraits tho for low cost. I'll have some pictures made soon.*

Wednesday. Saw For Whom the Bell Tolls *last nite. I don't know if I've ever seen a more beautiful picture. The technicolor wasn't overdone and I'm convinced more than ever that Ingrid Bergman is the most beautiful woman I've ever seen. And to top it all a brilliant actress – as good or better than Bette Davis. There's no one to compare with her.*

As a nation, the United States is sometimes called a melting pot. I can tell you now that as a city London is every bit as much a melting pot as the US. And there is no racial trouble in London. I've seen more races here than anywhere in America. Especially Asiatics. There are many East Indian and Javanese in the Dutch Navy. Many mixtures of Indian and Chinese blood and quite a few different Africans, too. Moslems, Egyptians, Moors, Negroes, Riffs and about anything you can think of. And, all the nations of Europe are represented, whether Allied or Axis.

I could spend 6 months in London and find something of interest or mystery, something still new to me.

Bill Ligon, who went to London for the first time in August 1944; on the 29th he wrote and told his folks all about it. Other trips to London followed

We'll be going to London in 3 or 4 days I guess. Think I'll spend most of my time in the lobby of the Regent Palace and watch people while I listen to the orchestra that is usually playing. That doesn't sound very interesting, but, believe me, it is. You might be surprised at what you could see.

Just got back from London again and just got the package this afternoon. It was sure good to see all that stationery. It looks like I'll have enough for the duration. And of course I hope that isn't far off ... Well, London's about the same as ever. I guess you heard about the lifting of the black-out soon. I guess the place will really come to life at night then. But it's by no means dead at nite now. But there's nothing blacker than a London black-out.

On this trip I took in a little culture. Went to Westminster Abbey where all the kings are buried, London Bridge, the Tower of London, St Paul's Cathedral and Hyde Park. St Paul's is the largest and most beautiful church I've ever seen. The area around it is all bombed. It was struck by a 1,000 pound bomb, but thru an act of God the bomb went thru and never exploded. The damage was very little.

Hyde Park is the biggest attraction of the day I guess. They have a big zoo with a more natural surrounding than the one at home. You could spend a whole day there. Then there is a large lake with beautiful flowers, bridges and row boats. Lots of the soldiers relax by rowing around the lake in the afternoon. The park itself seems to be half as big as Oak Cliff. But the best part of Hyde Park is the speech makers. Free speech isn't known in any part of the world as it is in Hyde Park. There are soap box orators everywhere and never without some sort of audience. There are fanatics in

*every field. Religion, politics, science, morals, culture – anything. Any one
who speaks will have an audience. They won't applaud if they agree or
jeer if they disapprove. They only listen intently. That's the way the English
are. They are eager to hear what you have to say but very reserved in their
own opinions. If I had the time I think I'd spend the day in Hyde Park
and listen to the speech makers. Some of them have good ideas and some
bad, but they are nearly all amusing. I suppose you could preach fascism
in Hyde Park and nobody would bother you, so long as you didn't insult
the King of England.*

    *They have large state registers in the Red Cross clubs in London. I was
running thru the Texas section the other nite ... The war news continues
to look good. You asked in the last letter if I was flying on missions – yes,
I am. I can't say how many, but I have to fly 35 before I can come home,
Unless of course I get home when the European War is over and I expect
it to be before I get 35 missions. I was sorry I didn't get to see Son, but
I'll bet Aunt Dolly will be glad to see him home again. He'll get at least
30 days at home plus some time at a rest center ... I read in the paper
that they had cut the production of the B-24, but I didn't think about the
Dallas plant. The article only mentioned the Ford plant at Willow Run
which I noticed today is having the weekly strike ... My arm is tired so
I'll quit. Write soon.*

    Love Bill

10

'Keep Your Tears For Him In After Years'

Do not despair
For Johnny-head-in-air;
He sleeps as sound
As Johnny underground.

Fetch out no shroud
For Johnny-in-the-cloud;
And keep your tears
For him in after years.

Better by far
For Johnny-the-bright-star,
To keep your head,
And see his children fed.

'For Johnny', John Pudney

Johnny's Death

I never knew him. He fell in battle when I was three. He gave me his
name and his Irish heritage and little more; but perhaps, in the end,
that is all there is to give. I remember feeling his loss but at age three
I could not comprehend the enormity of it. Most of my knowledge
about him was as seen through the eyes of others. They remembered
that his well-to-do family spoiled him (he drove and wrecked a
Cadillac convertible during the Depression years when many Americans
considered themselves lucky to eat!). He took flying lessons and,
when courting my mother, would "buzz" the church when she was at
services. All would run out to see Johnny disappear in the clouds in a
biplane.

... Here then is the last mission, on 5 January 1944, of the B-24
American bomber crew 38 of the 713th Squadron, 448th Bomb Group

and the last desperate hours in the life of Staff Sergeant John E. McGlone Jr, gunner and staff sergeant, USAAF.

The target for today would be Kiel. The crews suffered the usual Army game of hurry-up-and-wait, as they were delivered to their planes by trucks and then nodded off, huddled in their flying suits awaiting take-off. Finally, the plane began its lift-off and cleared the end of the runway and the treetops. They climbed through the blinding overcast for thousands of feet before the nose gunner, Bob Hudson, observed that the overcast was beginning to thin out. Soon they broke through the clouds and reached the dazzling sunshine to see before them a huge fleet of bombers assembling for the raid. Two hundred and thirty-five aircraft were to attack Kiel, 131 B-17s from the 1st Bomb Division and 114 from the 2nd Bomb Division. From his left waist gun position, Johnny watched as the planes climbed, circled and struggled to attain their assigned positions.

The 1st Division had been designated to lead the raid, but somehow a group of B-24s had gotten into the forward position instead of the B-17 group. They departed the English coast over Cromer and headed out over the North Sea. The clearing weather revealed whitecaps on the ocean below. It looked cold and ominous. The long flight eastward over water kept them out of German territory as long as possible. An in-flight 360-degree turn by the B-24 group failed to correct the group alignment and the B-24s would be the first to go in over the target. The entire formation turned 90 degrees to the south for the downward thrust toward Germany. "Clyde" Maxton scanned the sky above his top turret position, John McGlone and Hank Gautier watched from the waist positions, while Malcolm Crow looked rearward through his sights at the trailing American bombers. The territory below was German-occupied and the plane began to receive hostile fire. Bob Hudson in the nose position was the first to see the bursts of flak as they approached the islands off the northern coast of Germany and the Jutland Peninsula. The Germans were beginning to get the range. The planes themselves were so high they could not be seen with the naked eye, but the German anti-aircraft gunners were aided by radar and range finders which made them deadly accurate.

Almost an hour of flying time remained before they reached the target when Major Squyres' plane (*Maid of Tin*) was hit by flak and went down. The loss of a squadron leader was a bad omen. (The pilot, William Ferguson, Kenneth Squyres and all the crew were killed). Tension mounted and stomachs tightened as flak bursts increased about them. From his waist gun position, Johnny could see the "little friends" who were escorting them that day.

As they approached the target area, the utter chaos of aerial combat blinded all reality. They were now squarely over the Third Reich and approaching a heavily defended industrial city. The flak that had been previously experienced was a minor annoyance compared to that which was about to be thrown at them. Hundreds of German gun positions were now plotting their course and fighter squadrons of the *Luftwaffe* were scrambling to meet the invaders. To make matters worse, one B-24 group was forced to make two runs over the target. This double jeopardy would cost lives. Forty per cent of my father's squadron would be shot down in the next few minutes. Aside from the deafening roar of four engines in an uninsulated bomber, the additional noise and confusion were almost unbearable. Gunners became excited and hollered into the intercom as they saw German planes approach or witnessed the loss of a fellow bomber. The noisy clatter of machine gun fire almost drowned out the sounds of exploding flak nearby, but no one failed to hear the rattle of metal against the side of the bomber from a near miss. Soon to this confusion would be added flames, explosions and screams of pain. They approached the target at high noon.

The first to die was Robert P. Hudson, in the nose-gun position. Prior to the final approach over the target, the bomber could take a certain amount of evasive action to avoid the flak but for the last two minutes of the bomb run, it had to fly straight and level for the bombardier to sight on the target. Lieutenant Leonard Feingold was in the nose area just behind the nose gunner, leaning over his bombsight, when the bomber was hit. A burst of flak took away the nose turret and with it the life of Bob Hudson. Feingold was undoubtedly rattled at the sudden appearance of a gaping hole where only moments before there had been a friend and fellow crewmember. The wind whistled through the bomber with tremendous force, scattering maps, charts, papers and people about.

Feingold regained his position over the sights and opened the bomb bay doors. The weather was clear and visual bombing was possible. At exactly twelve noon, the bomb load was jettisoned on the enemy city. Pilot Lieutenant James E. Curtis and co-pilot Donald Clift, with the bombs away, could now begin to take evasive action and perhaps escape, even with the nose blown away. But it was not to be.

Seconds after the bombs were dropped and with the bomb bay doors still open, another burst of flak hit the plane, entering through the open bomb bay doors and exploding in the mid section, setting the aircraft on fire half way between the radio room and the waist gun positions. First one engine and then a second was hit as the mortally crippled bomber dropped out of formation and began to lose altitude. Sergeant Eugene Higgins, the radio operator, was having his own private hell dealing with the flames in the radio room. He reported to Curtis that the whole ship was on fire and the pilot sounded the alarm bell, a signal for all to hear that it was time for those who could bail out to do so. The co-pilot was trying to help Higgins put out the flames and at the same time reopen the bomb bay doors as an escape route. Clift lost consciousness in the process but later reported he had seen that Higgins was badly burned, without a parachute on and still struggling with the flames in the radio room.

Meanwhile, in the rest of the plane, all was confusion, noise, burning and death. The book says that the plane was hit and exploded, but there were several minutes between these events, minutes which must have seemed like an eternity for men about to die. Lieutenant Feingold was last seen with a parachute on, crouched over the nose wheel opening, ready to bail out. Others in a similar position, Curtis, Clift and Moore, survived even the explosion of the plane, when they were thrown clear, but not Lieutenant

Feingold. He never made it to prison camp with the other officers. In view of Larry Maxton's report that some were killed on the ground, it is easy to conclude that Feingold made it out of the ship but could not make it past Nazi hatred of Jews. With the name Feingold on his dog tags, he was the last person who needed to be bailing out over German territory, but he did and was never seen alive again. Ominously, German burial records show most of the crew buried on 6 January 1944. Feingold was not buried until 13 January. The stricken plane was travelling at hundreds of miles per hour and the difference of a few seconds or minutes in bailout time could make a great difference in where one landed. If the landing was near a regular army unit, a person might he treated roughly but fairly, whereas a landing near some farmer who lost sons in the war might end fatally from a pitchfork or scythe. A survivor on another plane lost over Kiel that day told me that the town where he landed was governed by a raving lunatic of a Nazi who would certainly have caused an American's death, but he was away that day and the other villagers treated him with sympathy. It was a draw of the cards.

It also made a vast difference what kind of parachute one was wearing (or not wearing). Lieutenant Curtis and the other officers aboard the plane had been wearing back pack 'chutes as they went about their business of flying and navigating the plane. All survived save Feingold. The enlisted men had chest pack 'chutes which they carried with them and had to put on before bailing out. The few seconds involved in this procedure apparently spelled the difference between life and death for at least some of the men. The official reports are filled with comments stating that the crew did not have time to don their chest 'chutes. In a few minutes it would not have mattered anyway, for German fighters intent on finishing off the crippled bomber now attacked them.

Staff Sergeant John McGlone reported the coming attack over the intercom. "Fighters coming in at six o'clock low".

The official report of operations, written two days later, states that the bombers were subject to heavy attacks by 100 enemy fighters, mostly two-engine aircraft. Jim Curtis later described their attack as "savage". In order for Johnny to see them approaching from six o'clock from his left waist gun position, he had to be looking at an extreme angle and upward from his side position. His final thoughts are known to God, but one can imagine a grim determination as he sighted through the cross hairs and down the long barrel of his single, .50-caliber machine gun at approaching death.

That he was still alive and at his gun position surprised the pilot, who thought that all the crew had already bailed out. Perhaps Crow in the tail and Gautier at the right waist were sighting at the same approaching planes as Johnny, since their bodies were later found with the wreck. Maybe they were already dead. Johnny was certainly wounded and may have been the last gunner left alive in the slaughterhouse that had been a B-24. Either he couldn't, or wouldn't, get out and since McGlone sighted and reported the coming fighters, it may be presumed that he made his last best effort to blow them to hell. In the next few seconds, McGlone's fight *in extremis* would be over. Those last moments are shrouded in the confusion of the uncontrolled roar of damaged engines, the chatter of machine gun fire, the choking, oily smoke and the twisting gyrations of the dying plane undoubtedly seen through dazed, bleary and pain-wracked eyes. Then, in a blinding flash, all was over. Johnny's soul was freed with the speed of light.

He and the others had gone to their God, like soldiers.

The plane crashed in an open field near Krempechide that was used by the German Army for maneuvers. The next day, Nazi soldiers cleared the wreckage and found the bodies of the gunners who "rode her in", McGlone, Gautier, Hudson, Crow and Maxton. Curtis, Clift and Moore had escaped the burning plane. They were thrown clear by an explosion and had been able to parachute to safety, or at least to the relative safety of PoW camp *Stalag Luft I*, where they spent the rest of the war. Two were still missing, Higgins and Feingold. Their bodies, "carbonised" as the local Bürgomeister later stated, would eventually be buried with the original five. Later, mortuary reports would describe crushed skulls, missing limbs and bullet-riddled bodies.

In 1949, Johnny's remains were brought home to his final resting-place in a national military cemetery. The mementoes began to accumulate. The flag that had covered his coffin, the Purple Heart, a certificate attesting to his valour and now his name etched on a headstone. None of this fooled his mother. She carried the pain for the rest of her long life. They had killed her darling boy ...

'Flight To Eternity' by Dr John McGlone Jr

They'll never take my son again
Johnny, I swear this to you!

'Johnny, I hardly Knew Ye' (Irish Folksong)

PETE

There is a subtle response to the drawing back of the curtain in the briefing room and the announcement of the target. If the target is lightly defended, the breath is let out in a quiet sigh. If it is perceived to be very tough, there is an intake of breath and involuntary body movements that create a quiet rustle, which, added to every person's anxiety, creates a tension that can be physically felt, almost as the building itself groaned. November 21 1944 was a mission of the second type.

I remember the Intelligence Officer that morning:

"You will be in range of 446 guns (each gun can fire three shells a minute). You will be in flak nine minutes before 'bombs away' and three minutes afterward." The briefing officer gave us the course: up the coast off the Friesian islands, between the coast and Heligoland, cut sharply toward Bremen then directly east toward Hamburg. After "bombs away", a right turn to the south, then veer east around the city, north up the

Danish peninsula, left out over the North Sea, north of Heligoland and back to England.

We followed that path that day. As soon as we turned in from the sea at Cuxhaven we could see the target a hundred miles away, not a cloud in the sky to hide us from the gunners. That was a real shock and raised our anxiety level a few more notches because visual aiming by flak batteries greatly increased their accuracy. It took a long time to get to the initial point, but it wasn't long from there to the flak. On heavily defended targets like this one, sometimes the flak concentrated on one group for a long time to get better results from tracking, then they might skip a group and pick up the third. We were the third in this line-up. Before we came under fire the flak was so thick that the lead group disappeared behind the curtain of smoke ahead. Too damned soon we were in it. It was thick; bursts came between me and the ship I was flying, an eternity to the drop point.

Bombs away and we started a slow right turn. At that moment there was the most terrific explosion I have ever heard. It was so loud that all the other senses were overwhelmed, even sight; the whole world was one tremendous crash.

I glanced at Pete [Pete Scott, the co-pilot] and at the same time he looked at me, apparently unaware that he had been hit. I saw nothing in his eyes except surprise – no fear, no pain, nothing else. Then he began to slump into the control wheel, forcing the plane into a dive. I think I called the crew and told them not to jump. Then I tried to set up the automatic pilot. It wouldn't work so I let it dive; stood up between the seats and pulled Pete out of the controls; tried to keep the plane flying with one hand on Pete's wheel while holding him in his seat with the other. I couldn't find where he had been hit; there was no blood, so he couldn't be hurt bad, maybe just knocked out. But I felt his heart beat become irregular almost as soon as I got hold of him. I called someone from the bombardier's compartment. Then with Ecclesfield's help we disengaged Pete's radio, electric power, oxygen tube and safety belt and pulled him from the seat and laid him on the flight deck. Most of this time the ship was flying itself so we were a long way from the group; in fact we never saw it again.

We had lost a lot of altitude, from 22,000 feet to 18,000 feet, so we threw on the power and prayed fighters wouldn't hit us. At the Kiel canal we could see a six-gun battery firing. That scared me because we were so low. We took violent evasive action and somehow got through without further damage.

I guess my psyche wouldn't let me accept that Pete was dead. I had Eck keep oxygen flowing in his face all the way home.

Conway climbed into the co-pilot's seat to help with the piloting and landing. Eck radioed in a report of our troubles while I put the ship in a very shallow dive and pushed the airspeed up to 240mph.

Over the base, Ralph shot emergency flares but no one saw them. They had not yet received the message that Eck had radioed to Division. I parked on the taxiway near the tower and asked the tower where the hell Doc and the ambulance were. Doc Steinbock came right out then and saw that Pete was dead. We then lifted him out of the plane. There was no one to take the plane to the hardstand so as near crazy as I was, I had to taxi around the field and park it.

We had beaten the group home by forty-five minutes so the tower assumed that we had aborted the mission before reaching the target. The radio message was not received until after we landed and they failed to see our flares. Therefore, no one realized we were in need of help. This just about drained my last reserves of sanity. Fortunately, Doc sent someone with me to get me through debriefing and on to the hospital.

On the flight home my face and right arm had begun to burn. Fine particles of Plexiglas had gone through my oxygen mask and clothing and penetrated the skin. Conway climbed down from the top turret and flew co-pilot because he knew the instruments and had a private pilot's license. He got a bad windburn from the air blowing through the hole in the window where the piece of flak that killed Pete came through. The No. 3 engine had some holes but kept running all the way home.

Dr Steinbock said that even if Pete had been on the operating table when the flak went through him, they probably couldn't have saved his life because it clipped off the right subclavian (arm) artery very close to where it branched from the Aorta and he bled to death in less than a minute. The reason we couldn't find a wound was that the hole was inside the angle of the Clavicle on top of the shoulder, a very small spot the flak vest didn't cover. The piece of the shell that hit him was nearly three-quarters of an inch square and an inch and a half long. It exited through his back and went through his packed parachute, coming to rest inside the canvas cover. *What an enormous power!*

[Many years later Ralph Hendershot, bombardier, recalled vividly. 'Before we left the hangar area for our plane, Pete was sitting in the concrete with his back resting against the building and saying how tired he felt and wished he didn't have to fly that day as though he was being warned of the danger ahead for him. Then when we got back from the mission and helping remove his body from the bomb bay compartment, how the blood seeped from his clothing in the process.]

How am I to tell of Pete's death, the death of a friend, but more? We worked together long enough that I knew exactly how he would respond to whatever problem occurred. I knew I could trust him in any situation. When Doc Steinbock climbed out of the ambulance and up to the flight deck, he examined Pete for about one second and shook his head toward me. I knew I had to accept that he would no longer be with us. Even then I realized I must have been half-crazy even to hope there would be any other answer. Pete's heart had stopped before we got him onto the flight deck. I had felt it flutter the last as Lou and I unfastened him from his seat. I wonder about the feelings of Ralph, Conway, Eck and the others when I ordered that the emergency oxygen be forced into his face and that his body be left on the flight deck. I was totally unprepared to face the possibility of death of any of our crew. I had twenty more missions to fly. *Where could I find the courage!?*

The next day I heard that Doc was seeking a volunteer to accompany Pete's body to Cambridge. I was deeply hurt that he had not asked me first.

I had forgotten that regulations required a person of equal or higher rank to accompany the body and Doc, when I didn't request to go, assumed that I would probably rather not. Fortunately, we got together.

The day was beautiful and the long ride in the ambulance was the first I had made through the English countryside. We drove a mile or two beyond Cambridge then turned off into a grove of trees alongside the road. Just beyond the grove was one of the neatest cemeteries (Madingley) I had ever seen. Under the trees were the chapel and other buildings, then sloping down to the northeast was the cemetery. Beyond the small stream in the valley bottom, the land rose again green and quiet.

I stepped out of the ambulance and walked toward the chapel to complete my duty. About half way there, a group of German prisoners was cleaning leaves from the path. As I approached, their leader called "*Achtung!*" The men came to attention like bits of spring steel. I was absolutely stunned. I could not bring myself to return salute for if I could have found a club, my reaction would have been to start swinging. The chaplain jumped to my side and said I should ignore them. My hand shook so badly that I could scarcely sign my name when we reached the chapel. I worried the whole return trip about why in those few seconds I had felt such enormous rage.

The funeral was held two days later. The group provided us with a hard-riding, cold 6 x 6 truck to travel to the cemetery. Besides the whole crew several of Pete's new friends from the other crews went. We left the base at nine o'clock in the morning and traveled hours in bitter cold weather. We gathered a little way down the hill where each of us in his own way, then collectively, with the chaplain, prayed God to keep Pete near. There in the United States Cemetery at Cambridge, with the Stars and Stripes flying top cover, Peter Scott was buried.

Pete's death robbed me of our invincibility and replaced it with guilt over his death and fear for the lives of the rest of the crew that I led into danger.

                              1st Lieutenant Walter F. Hughes, 93rd Bomb Group

The first thing every combat crew member did upon arriving at Polebrook air base was to get a bicycle, usually by buying it from someone going back to the States. We all got on our bicycles and I was appointed the leader, since none of them had yet been off base.

Our first and only stop was at my favorite pub, the Rose and Crown, in the town of Oundle. I introduced the crew to John, the owner, and we had many beers. John brought us all sandwiches of freshly baked bread with corned beef, cheese, sliced onion and hot British mustard. He told his new customers, "This is your mate's favorite and maybe you chaps will enjoy it. The next time you stop by you may see "Bill's Sandwich" on my menu."

The crewmembers, one and two at a time, met and left with local girls. The girl I had dated a couple of times was John's youngest daughter. However, she attended school in a nearby city and was only home on weekends. I was not scheduled to fly the next day, so I played darts with John and drank ale.

John taught me the fine art of drinking ale. The necessary items are a stein of ale, a roaring fire in the fireplace and a poker. The poker is left in the fireplace until it is red-hot. It is then inserted in the stein until it stops steaming. I never did learn if the heat of the poker caused a chemical change in the ale, but it was one fine drink.

After closing time, I stepped outside and noticed that the cold air did not have the usual sobering effect on me; in fact, just the opposite. Missing my bike the first time I reached for it told me I was in trouble, but I mounted it anyway and started pedaling for the base. I almost made it, but just prior to reaching the main gate, my bike decided to leave the road and we fell into a hedgerow. I decided it would be too difficult to get out of there in the dark, so I just slept there all night. My big, heavy GI overcoat and the alcohol in my system were probably the only things that kept me from freezing to death.

Early morning truck traffic on the road woke me the next day. I got out of the hedgerow, back on my bike and headed for the base – with quite a hangover.

After a three-day stand-down, mission No.9 for me was to hit the railroad depot and marshaling yards at Hamm. It was to be a radar bombing mission, so it gave me a chance, as a bombardier, to use what I had learned about radar bombing at RAF Hawkinge. Although the crew and I had the same number of missions, it certainly had not taken them as long to get theirs completed. No enemy fighters were seen and flak – even over the target – was inaccurate.

After landing, we had a short mission interrogation and I headed for the air crew mess hall for dinner and then to the officers' club. At the bar I saw a friend, Pete [Hagen], who was the co-pilot on another crew. Pete suggested, "Let's challenge my pilot and navigator to a few hands of bridge." As usual, Pete and I beat them and we won a few dollars. After the card game, Pete said he wasn't scheduled to fly for several days. I then suggested that we go to London and spend some of our bridge winnings. It was agreed we would meet for breakfast and then head for London.

The base bus took us to Peterborough, where we caught the *Royal Scot* for London. We arrived in London late in the afternoon and I asked Pete, "How about getting a room at the Red Cross club before we start hitting the pubs?" Because it was always very difficult to find your way around London at night in the blackout, Pete thought that was a good idea. We had no trouble getting rooms and Pete told me, "I'm going to call a couple of girls I know at the American Embassy." The girls agreed to meet us at the Red Cross club for dinner. Since a dance was scheduled there that night, we decided that was preferable to pub hopping.

I went to our room to get some rest while Pete roamed around the lobby area. Awaking late and suddenly, I jumped out of bed, splashed cold water in my face, put on my uniform and headed for the dining room. Pete was already there with the girls from the embassy. After making my apology to everyone for oversleeping, we had a very enjoyable dinner with pleasant company and then moved into the ballroom for dancing.

Sitting at a nearby table was Fred, the ball turret gunner on the crew I went to Schweinfurt with on my first mission as a new second lieutenant. He was sitting with a Canadian sergeant and two girls in RAF uniforms. I excused myself to go over to say hello to him. I didn't know it before, but Fred had a split thumb on his right hand, which operated like two separate fingers. He could pick up things with his thumb. While I was standing at the table, Fred was going to pay the waitress and picked up a pound note with his split thumb. She took one look at it, let out a shriek and would not go back to that table the rest of the evening. That night Fred had met Elbert, a Canadian gunnery sergeant from the RCAF who had a split left thumb that was just as dexterous as Fred's right one.

Before I left their table, Fred had to tell everyone within hearing distance that I shot down a German fighter during the mission we were on together. There was some applause and shouts of "Good show!" from several RAF guys that were near enough to hear Fred.

Pete also heard Fred's remarks. "You didn't tell me you shot down a German fighter," he said.

"What's there to tell? I'm a trained aerial gunner."

The rest of the evening, we could not buy a drink at our table. We never did see who was sending the drinks over, but any time we got up to dance we had fresh drinks at the table when we returned. We finally decided to just relax and enjoy the free drinks because we were not able to find out who to thank for their generosity.

Later in the evening, Fred and Elbert got on the crowded dance floor with their dates and they both used their split thumbs to pinch girls dancing nearby just to hear them scream. Probably the only other person in the club who realized what was going on was me. I began to laugh so hard at each screech; I had to tell Pete and the girls about the two split thumbs. They thought it was hilarious. Now every time a girl screamed on the dance floor, everyone at our table had a fit of laughter. That caused everyone around us to start laughing. We all agreed that we had never before been in a place with so much screaming and laughing at the same time.

The ballroom was about to close, so we called a cab and took the girls to the apartment they shared. When we returned to the Red Cross club, Pete and I stopped in the restaurant for some tea and tarts before we hit the sack. Before we left, Fred and his friend from the RCAF joined us. They really were a couple of clowns. Fred started out showing us how he stirred his tea by holding the spoon in his thumb. Elbert had to top him by holding his knife in his thumb and cutting a piece of toast. Everyone in the restaurant gathered around the table to watch the dexterous thumb feats.

Pete and I slipped out and went to our room. We had flipped a coin earlier to see who would have to climb into the upper. I lost. It did not take either of us long to drop off to sleep, but about two hours later there was one hell of an explosion. The whole building shook, windows broke and I was knocked out of the upper bunk onto the floor. My crash landing was on my rear end and it really caused considerable pain for a couple of hours. It was a good thing I was sleeping when it happened; I probably would have broken an arm or a leg trying to break my fall if I had been awake.

Pete and I got dressed and went downstairs to see what had happened. We learned that one of the German V-1 rockets crashed into an apartment building just a block away. The rocket did a tremendous amount of damage and killed fifteen people who lived in the building. I decided I was ready to go back to flying combat.

Back in our room, a chambermaid had brought each of us four blankets because most of the windows had been broken out and it was even colder than my night in the hedgerow. At breakfast we talked about how the brave English people – men, women and children – had been going through that kind of brutal destruction and death for the past three or four years. After breakfast we packed up, checked out and headed for the train to take us back to the base.

William L. Cramer Jr [Pete Hagen, a big Texan, was co-pilot of the B-17 when he and Cramer were shot down on 21 December 1944 during a mission in support of the ground troops in the Battle of the Bulge. Both men survived and bailed out but Hagen was shot by a German guard while attempting to escape. Hagen killed the guard by bringing the butt of his own rifle down on the guard's head repeatedly]

The 23 March 1945 mission was to Munster, one of the hottest little flak towns in Germany; only fifty guns but I think they were all old master sergeant gunners. This day they were right on us. We were flying deputy lead on the right wing of the group lead, Lieutenant Powell's crew. The group commander was 330 Squadron CO, Major Biggers, with whom I had so much trouble after Pete's death. (Biggers was transferred into the squadron fresh from a desk job in the States. He didn't believe in battle fatigue. He called it "goofing off" or just plain cowardice. After we got back from Pete's funeral at Cambridge we were informed by Biggers that there was no such thing as combat fatigue and that we would get no flak leave. I said that we were in no condition to fly without the leave and he retaliated by placing us on the next day's mission. We took off on December 1 on a mission that was cancelled; Doc Steinbock got into the act by grounding the crew for combat fatigue. We were sent on flak leave. If this were the end of it I would not complain but not two months later after a rough mission, his 5th, where no one was injured, Biggers applied for and got flak leave. He became increasingly flak happy.) That trouble continued to flare regularly. I thought he was small-minded, mean and vindictive. I hated him.

Within seconds of "bombs away" the lead ship blew into a million parts. The biggest parts I saw were an outboard wing panel burning on its way down, a wheel and one engine. The fireball was so big we flew right through it. I have no idea why pieces didn't hit us and knock us out of the air too. Strange as it seemed to us, three men, two in the nose and one in the waist of the ship, lived through the explosion and were captured. As with the girls in London where Pete did and I didn't and Pete died on the next mission, I took Major Biggers's death as a warning from God. I was never to hate anyone again. My hate might be a factor in something bad happening, as it did to Major Biggers, and I didn't want any more of that kind of responsibility hanging over me. Flying through the fireball that killed people we talked with every day increased the psychological pressure and drove me further from developing close friendships.

1st Lieutenant Walter F. Hughes, 93rd Bomb Group

As I pedalled my bicycle around the corner of the briefing block and started coasting down the hill towards the living sites, the cool English breeze filtered around my shoulders, so I zipped my leather jacket all the way up. "No use catching another cold" I thought.

I put my hands in my pockets and coasted slowly down the grade, feeling proud that I could ride a bicycle "no-handed", although I had been doing it for more than two years now and it had become a habit. Maybe deep down I just liked to show off a bit while coasting along.

It was about 10am. The ships were out on a practice mission and wouldn't be back until afternoon. There was nothing else doing, so I though it would go over to the dispensary and see Doc Pete about those pills I was taking. At least it was something to do.

As I coasted along, I looked about and noticed the sun breaking through and making big bright splotches in the blue-grey of the English sky. "Might clear up yet", I thought, as I noticed a couple of P-51s zooming across the horizon in tight formation along with some Forts and an RAF Lancaster, each following his own course. I decided it wasn't bad day at that.

I looked down and watched the front wheel of my bicycle wobble and turned. Just a habit, I guess. Sometimes I would almost be run into – because of my watching the wobbling instead of looking where I was going.

Suddenly, I became aware of a strange sound but I paid no attention to it because there were always aircraft in the sky and one gets tired of looking up at them. Then I heard a captain, who had been riding a few feet behind me, shout in a startled voice, "Look at that ship!" I jerked my head around to look over my shoulder and saw the captain pointing his right hand, almost at me, as he struggled with his left to keep his reeling bicycle under control. He was all but falling.

This startled me and I snapped my head around to look up into the sky ahead of me. I didn't believe what I saw! I realized suddenly that I was also about to fall from my bike and I grabbed for the handlebars and brakes as I zigzagged all over the road, my heels digging at the pavement to help me stop while I kept my eyes fixed on the distressed ship in the sky.

It must have been at 800 feet and half a mile away. It was in a flat spin. A Flying Fortress in a flat spin! Spinning like a boomerang, falling straight down and dropping like a rock. It was almost level, with the nose pointed slightly down. It spun around one, two, three times in about as many seconds. Each time it went around I heard the thundering, throbbing roar, as if the engines of a dozen Forts were all wide open and still screaming for more power. Rrrunumrnm! Rrrunummm! Rrrunummm!

I still couldn't believe it. Maybe I was dreaming. I wished to hell I was. Thoughts flashed through my mind: "It was impossible, but I am looking at it and hearing it ... it should blow up when it hits ... maybe it can pull out at the last minute ... out of sight now behind the dispensary; maybe they bailed out ... but the engines were wide open ... God have mercy on them ... no explosion yet; maybe I *am* dreaming!

"No! There it is!"

A belch of black smoke shot skyward like a giant fist thrust up from hell with orange and red flames seething and darting through the column. I now knew I wasn't dreaming.

I felt so helpless as I watched the exploding fire. "Fire!" I thought and I turned around and shouted to a fellow, who had been walking along the road, "Go tell the fire department!" But I saw that the captain behind me was already running to the firehouse, which he had just been passing. I thought, "Well, there is nothing else I can do now."

I had only come about 200 feet down the hill since I had first heard the shout behind me. Just a few seconds had passed. It all happened so quickly and was hard to believe, but I could still see the ship spin around in my mind and the roaring of the engines echoed in my ears. I realized that my mouth felt like the inside of an old trouser pocket. I closed my mouth; it must have been open all the while.

I was still on my bike, going very slowly now and thinking, "I may as well see the hole in the ground," so I started pedaling toward the huge fire, because I was now at the bottom of the hill. An Englishman was walking on the road toward me and he looked at me as though I was a clown trying to do stunts on my bicycle. He must have thought me quite crazy, but he didn't know what had happened because the crash was behind him and he hadn't seen it ... I pedalled up the hill as the fire truck raced past me. Then a Jeep with MPs whipped by and zoomed around the corner and out of sight. An ambulance that had been coming toward me had stopped and the driver was looking puzzled as I pointed to the smoke behind him. Then he started to turn around as two more ambulances raced by after the fire truck.

On I went up another hill. I was panting and out of breath by now. Maybe I could flag down a Jeep, I thought, because they were racing by in a steady stream, but I gave up that idea, because there was no chance to stop them. "Just keep on riding, a few minutes wouldn't make any difference anyway ..."

... And there it was.

A big crowd was there already; must have been about 200 people. The MPs were busy keeping them fifty feet from the fire. I walked over and got as close as I could to what was left. Still standing defiant and erect was the unmistakable Fortress tail. A few minutes ago it was silver and flying proud and high in the air. But now it was blackened from the oil smoke and wrinkled like a huge washboard stuck in the ground. There was a big gap at the front of the tail where it had been joined to the body of the ship.

The rudder had been torn from the fin at the top and its smoking skeleton flopped in the wind like an old palm branch. I could still make out the numbers and the letters on the tail, but who cared about numbers now.

The wind changed a bit and the smoke was coming toward me so I walked up in front and watched the boys work with the foam hoses.

You couldn't tell it was an airplane. The highest part, except the tail, was squashed to about four feet, compared to about twenty feet the Fort' would ordinarily stand. The No. 1 engine wasn't burning, but the rest were still blazing. The firemen would stick a hose right inside the half-buried cowling and the fire would stop. Then they would squirt at something else and in a few seconds the engines would again sprout a fan-shaped orange fire, and again they gave it the foam treatment. There were about four Yank fire wagons working and three or four RAF trucks either working or getting ready to work under the direction of a flight officer. A WAAF driver looked very unconcerned as she leaned against her fire truck as it pumped foam onto the debris.

I walked to the left of the ship and looked around. The left wing, still burning, had been torn off and was lying at a crazy angle, pointing to the rear. Only a few ribs were left to burn, along with the main gas tank, which smoldered, belching out gray stinking smoke. I watched some men working with grappling hooks and asbestos gloves pull out something from the vicinity where the rear door had been. There was no door there now, nothing except a pile of smoldering rubble about a foot high. I saw what it was now. It had no head, but part of the arms and legs were outstretched and bent in strange directions. It was difficult to see it more clearly, for it was still covered with bright orange flame and dirty grey smoke. An RAF man brought up an asbestos blanket, covered the body, then shot a lot of CO_2 under the blanket to put out the fire.

I turned and walked away, almost stumbling over a body lying on a stretcher and wrapped in a gray blanket. I turned away, not caring to look closer.

I kicked at a large oxygen bottle lying in the grass, hardly scratched, bright yellow and looking out of place. A few feet away lay half of another bottle, scorched. It had been blown in two. Litter covered the ground everywhere. An officer's polished low cut shoe lay undamaged ... a smoldering parachute was scattered about ... part of a burnt yellow dinghy boat ... half a blue split dinghy paddle ... some flight instruments with their faces bashed in.

I walked over to the side of Captain Max, the Engineering Officer.

"What do you think?" I quietly asked.

He shook his head and answered, "I don't know."

I thought awhile, then said, "One of ours, isn't it?"

He said, "Yeah, fifteen men on board, I think. Hope they all had on their dog tags."

I agreed and walked away.

There was very little fire now and I walked up close to what had been the nose. It wasn't burned. Flight instruments and flattened objects of all sorts lay about. The once-round top of the nose section lay flat and wrinkled on the ground. A blackened steel radio whip antenna stuck defiantly straight up and vibrated slightly in the wind. The instrument panel and the control columns weren't where they belonged in the cockpit, but were lying, bent in strange shapes, on the ground about ten feet forward.

I looked at the cockpit more closely. The top of it was gone and it was all out in the open, heaped up higher than the rest of the surrounding debris. I just stood there looking. Everything was covered with whitish-brown foam from the fire hoses and it molded everything into one large mass of almost indistinguishable objects. My eyes suddenly stopped wandering. Yes, it was the co-pilot still sitting in his seat; his body could just be made out as it protruded from under the blanket of foam. It was sitting upright, with no head on its shoulders, its right arm at its side and its left arm raised and bent as if to protect a face that wasn't there. The arm was very badly burned and still smoldering. Leaning against the co-pilot's seat was another form; the engineer. He was at his post between the pilot and co-pilot, his body horizontal, looking like a smoldering potato sack, crushed against the debris. Then I picked out the form of the pilot, lying on the floor of what had been the cockpit. A bent arm without a hand that protruded above the foam covering was all that indicated that the shapeless form had once been a man. I had seen enough and turned away.

I passed some local women jabbering wildly. They wondered if there had been any women aboard. How could they think of such things, I wondered, and in a few minutes I heard the rumor that the plane was full of women – it traveled like a plague. I noticed some majors and captains had heard it and they were fuming mad, for they knew there were no women. The men on board had been their friends.

The fire was almost out now and, as I walked around near the tail, I watched some MPs and GIs chop with axes at the tail gunner's position, which was squashed almost flat. The GIs pulled trash away then finally the body came out and was quickly laid on a stretcher and covered by a blanket.

The smoke wasn't so thick now. I had been standing in it and stench was just terrible. The mixture of burning oil, high octane gas, rubber, metal and the pungent odor of burnt flesh made me lightheaded and I began to feel feathers in my stomach, the wet sticky kind, so I avoided the smoke. I walked around a bit and watched the NFS (National Fire Service) that had finally arrived with their tank of water and some ladders on a flat truck. God knows what they would do with ladders here, but they made ready to transfer water to the empty foam trucks. This took quite a while and some of the fires started up again, including the one engine that refused to be put out. Finally, after several minutes of cranking, the little two-cylinder pump engine coughed and started and the pumping began I guess, for I didn't wait to find out. I had seen all I cared to see and started for the hole in the hedgerow.

Some other men were leaving and I tried to get a ride back but all trucks and Jeeps were full so I set out across the barley field, through clover and along the hedgerow, back along the lane and across the turnip field with the farmer still cultivating and completely ignoring rest of the world. I picked up my bike and started off; passing some civilians who had stopped their car and got out to watch the fire. They wanted to ask me something, but I went on by. I wasn't in the mood for talking

It was now noon and chow time but I still had feathers in my stomach so I went to the barracks and listened to the radio.

The following morning I pedaled out in the country after my laundry and on the way back I stopped to see the wreck again, for it was just a few hundred feet from the road. I learned this after having walked over half-a-mile of fields the day before.

I leaned my bike against a gate, slithered through the hedgerow and saw an old man in a tweed coat with a crooked cane and oval shaped spectacles loudly describing to the MP how it all happened, while making sweeping motions with his arms and cane as he talked.

All was quiet now, except for the old man. A few things smoldered and the stench was still very pungent. The wreck had been pulled apart to look for bodies. The wheels had been dragged about a hundred feet apart and they rested there on their assemblies like giant black sunflowers. I walked over and examined one. The tire had burned; must have been synthetic, for it still held its shape and looked like a sponge.

The MP came up to me, for the old man had left and offered to show me something interesting. I went with him and as we arrived at the tail he asked me if I had ever seen brains before. I shook my head no, trying to figure out what he meant. I understood quickly when I looked at the tail gunner's position. It was covered with dried blood and two small piles of brains lay there with insects buzzing about them. I said nothing and turned away. The feathers had come back.

I walked through the wreck and noticed a lump of something. It was a parachute, melted together by the heat into a glob of nylon. There was a radio set about two-thirds the size it used to be, just crushed together by a terrific force. I picked up part of another radio; it wasn't burned, but the insides rattled like gravel in a can when I shook it. Going up to where the cockpit had been, I looked about me. There were long lengths of bare wire tangled up in everything, with some instruments or boxes dangling on the ends. Everything was bent or crushed. There was nothing in its original shape. The engines had all dug a furrow about six feet long, which was now full of oil and water. Only the top half of the engines could be seen. The prop blades were bent and twisted in peculiar artistic shapes and planted crazily in the ground in front of each engine. As I walked through the litter on the ground toward the nose section that had been dragged to the edge of the clearing, I noticed a crushed canteen, the top half-missing, laying close to a scorched GI shoe. I couldn't see if the shoe had anything in it, for it was still laced up and I had no desire to find out. As I approached the nose section I saw a bent machine gun on the ground. All sorts of instruments dangling from wires. The throttle column lay on its side with all the knobs and throttle handles broken off. All this was under a wrinkled piece of metal about six-feet square that had been part of the ship's skin. I noticed something red and looked closer and saw several rows of little red bombs painted on the metal to indicate flight missions over Germany and then some black and yellow swastikas for fighters shot down in air battles. I don't know how many there were for the metal was torn across the rows of little red bombs.

I had seen enough and started for the hole in the hedge, slithered through and got on my bike and pedaled off. As I rode down the lane towards the road, a farmer said, "Good morning." I acknowledged with a nod and he went back to hoeing his beans.

The wind blew hard against me as I pedaled down the road, but I hardly noticed it, for I was thinking:

Fifteen men. God have mercy and let them, somehow, guide other troubled flyers to safety. For the fifteen dead men are the only ones who know why the gallant lady of the sky had foundered.

A few days later there was an article in the *Yank* weekly paper about the crash. It quoted a general of the 8th Air Force Command who said, "It is impossible for a B-17 to be in a flat spin."

The general was wrong. I saw it.

Witness to Tragedy, Captain David K. Elliot. 388th Bomb Group B-17 which crashed near Bury St Edmunds on 31 March 1945 on a Trolly mission to Germany killing all five crew and ten passengers

Twenty-one, Forever

You always wanted a little blond girl. "Look at that dollbaby blond", you would say as we strolled hand in hand down Larimer Street, walked quickly to the bus stop in Harlingen, or ducked our heads against the wind in Casper. And after I had looked jealously about, you would chuckle teasingly and point with your chin, "See that babe, right over there?" And I would see the child. "That's what we'll have, a little blond girl. When I get back."

Like the fireplace to hold a six-foot log and the scaling of Long's Peak, it was an important part of "When I get back." I never thought to ask how you expected a black Irishman and a brown-eyed redhead to produce a blond. I was just happy you had such a positive attitude about coming back.

And now here we are, my brand new blond daughter, as close to you and me as we can get. It's very peaceful here. There's a busy quiet. The water spray whirring; the lawnmower droning. With my back to a headstone, my recently slimmed body cross-legged in the summer grass, the fragrance of flowers is in my nostrils; an uncertain honeybee is circling my head, while my baby sleeps in my lap.

I had faced the fact you might not return. It paced beside me as I followed you from camp to camp and when you were really gone the endless miles of land and sea away, it moved in and lived with me, leaned over my shoulder to peer at the mail and departed only when it could say, "See, I told you so."

Months later when the lieutenant with the young face brought your body back I behaved as I had promised myself I would, careful not to snap at anyone. I conducted myself like a proper mourning widow even if some of your disapproving relatives didn't think a proper widow would be there on the arm of her second husband and six months gone with child. I behaved, that is, until one of your second or third cousins from down Thermopolis way sniffled and forced your courageously dry-eyed mother to agree for the nth time as she stood there with her arm around my thickening waist that yes, it was nice you were buried where there was such a wonderful view of the Tetons and that's right, you had certainly loved those beautiful mountains.

"I most certainly hope he isn't down there, in that God-awful hole," I said before I could catch myself. The very idea gave me nauseating claustrophobia. I took a deep breath to control my queasiness, avoided looking at your mother. Understanding, patient, she deserved the Gold Star she wore proudly. My child stirred and mixed me up further: You gone, me here, carrying another's child – I buried my face in my hands and burst into tears, Jake helped me to our car and drove me home.

You'll like Jake. Really, you will. He thinks like you. Physically, you are exact opposites. You: lanky, dark. Him: short, sturdy, fair. He came back from the Pacific area. When he talked about it infrequently, I saw how he would look as an old man. Women grow up fast in wartime, too. You were gone and I was 21, then 22, 23, well on my way to fading into an undistinguished twilight like a tragic maiden of the south keeping hopeless vigil for the sweetheart who had ridden off to the war between the states. "As long as there's anybody left on earth who loves me, I'll not be dead", you said once. It was night, almost our last night together, something we suspected but did not know for sure. There in the darkness we spoke haltingly of God, His plans and our beliefs. Haltingly, for such things did not come glibly to our tongues. Like so many of our agnostic generation we were reticent about speaking familiarly, lovingly of God and His Beloved Son as our Victorian forefathers had been about the details of sex. I clung to your words and heard impatiently all the good intentioned bromides and clichés designed to rouse me to living again, from your mother's insistent "Life must go on, darling," to Jake's patient "Time heals all wounds."

I can't explain the change exactly. I know when it came. One day I was a fading young widow dedicated to anachronistic black. The next day I was ready to live again and declared myself by going out and buying a scarlet dress. For, you see, it was my 24th birthday and I had looked in my mirror. Then I had put the usual fresh flower, a pink peony this day, before your picture and really looked at you, not at my memories.

"Why, you are only 21", I said aloud. "You'll always be 21. For all eternity." I sat down slowly. I had made a momentous discovery: I would never be 21 again.

It's time to go now. The bee has found the yellow roses I brought. I can see Sake's and my '39 Chevy coming from town – your mother is driving it. She didn't say a word at the hospital when I asked to come here before going home with my baby.

I can't be 21 forever, or even 26, like Jake. But I have managed that dollbaby blond. You would consider it the more important achievement.

You and Jake. For along with my five-day-old daughter, I am carrying another war department telegram. The words are the same, but the name is not yours – this war.

Margaret Hawkes Lindsley.

On 6 February 1944 2nd Lieutenant Glenn Folsom and his crew were assigned to the 66th Bomb Squadron, 44th Bomb Group, at Shipdham. After a period of training and practice missions and flights, they flew their first combat mission on 2 March, followed by a second on the 5th. When the mission slated for 7 March was scrubbed, several crews, including Lieutenant Folsom's, were given practice flights to sharpen their skills. This crew did not carry a full complement and flew with only seven men – a bombardier and two gunners were apparently not needed on this flight. During this training flight, a P-47 pilot for reasons known only to him apparently began simulated attacks on Folsom's ship. Somehow, either due to his manoeuvres, or because he over-shot, or perhaps prop wash caused him momentary control. The result was a collision that tore off one wing of the B-24. Staff Sergeant Raymond McNamara stated that when he looked up, he saw the B-24 fly on for a few moments, saw one of the wings tear off and then the plane winged over, crashed and burned. The P-47 also spun down, partially disintegrating and crashed. There were no survivors from either aircraft. The tail gunner, Sergeant Hazen E. Hawkes, from Drummond, Idaho, had married Margaret shortly before leaving for overseas, would not live to see his daughter.

The Freckleton Disaster

On 23 August 1944 1/Lt John Bloemendal was doubling as a test pilot and officer of the day at Base Air Depot 2 at Warton, Lancashire SE of Blackpool. That morning, as Bloemendal and his three man crew flew B-24 Liberator 42-50291 over the Lancashire countryside, an unusual and severe storm approached BAD 2 with extreme turbulence and heavy rain. In the Trinity school in the little village of Freckleton adjacent to BAD 2, a mixture of local children and many who had been evacuated from London to escape the Blitz were hard at their studies. Bloemendal crossed the River Ribble at about 1,000 feet. He was heading north, opposite his base leg. It was 1040 hours.

Across the Lytham Road in a snack bar (nicknamed "The Sad Sack") a handful of GIs and RAF types were having a bull session with some civilians who sought refuge from the storm. They looked out the windows as the rain began to fall. The B-24 ploughed on toward a landing in about five minutes. The crew watched the darkening clouds ahead as the rain began to splatter on the windshield. It was 1043 hours.

Suddenly a terrific bolt of lightning split the clouds. The sky seemed to open up to release a deluge of rain. Violent turbulence buffeted the plane. This was more like a tropical hurricane than the English weather that the GI's had so often cursed. The village streets were running with torrents of water. No such storm had been seen by the men of Warton since its opening as an American base in mid-1943.

Instantly a massive downdraft clutched 291 and literally threw her 1,000 feet to the ground. The fight for control was useless. The time span was too short for the pilot to react, even if the gust had released its grip. There was scarcely time to register fear in the hearts of the crew before the ship slammed into the ground. The nose turret ground into the school as the plane flipped onto its back. The main gear crashed into the sidewalk, the ball turret bounced to a stop in the middle of the road and the tail turret ploughed through the snack bar. The clock on the wall of the classroom stopped at 1045.

Robert Nelson, the town bobby, was in his home at the village police station repairing a chair. His wife, Doris, was happy for the noise he was making because it helped drown out the sound of the crashing thunder. The phone rang. It was a special constable: "Bob, come down. There's a plane on the school." Pulling on his uniform, he rushed from the house. Flames were visible, rolling down Lytham Road. He turned to his wife and told her to go back. Mrs Nelson saw the huge plane on fire and thought: "They teach us about Heaven and Hell – and this is Hell." Nearly 3,000 gallons of 100-octane had cascaded over the demolished classroom and was flowing down the road, making the village center a sea of boiling flames.

A village witness said, "The rain during the thunderstorm was amazing. We've never seen rain like it before or since. Yet, when it stopped it was a most beautiful summer's day, so lovely and tranquil." The storm was so concentrated that less than a mile away in the base tech. area mess hall, men were not even aware of a storm so violent that it had uprooted dozens of trees in the vicinity of the school.

Rescue work was started immediately. As the four- and five-year-old children were freed from the debris that covered them, they were taken to the base hospital for treatment. For the thirty-five children who perished it was only their second day at school. Only three of the infants escaped alive. Two teachers, six other civilians, four members of the RAF and six USAAF personnel in the snack bar plus the crew were also killed. It was the day Paris was liberated but the men at Warton and the villagers were scarcely aware of it.

A local citizen later recalled: "We did what we could to comfort the bereaved parents while the little bodies were taken to a storage room by the Coach and Horses public house. Everybody was just frantic but the Americans came and took over and helped everyone."

Rescuers worked on into the night, with the aid of searchlights. Sections of the B-24 were removed to the base salvage yard. As one nacelle was being raised for loading, flames erupted from it and shot twenty feet into the air. By the 25th bulldozers had cleared the area and the death toll had been established at fifty-six, including Bloemendal, Technical Sergeant Jimmy Parr and Sergeant Gordon Kinney, who now rest at Cambridge.

On Saturday the 26th the child victims of the crash and one of their teachers, twenty-year-old Miss Jenny Hall, were buried in the Holy Church yard in the common grave dug by American soldiers. General Hap Arnold cabled from Washington and directed Brig. General Isaac W. Ott, Commander of Base Air Depot Area, to represent him at the funeral. Servicemen from Warton acted as pallbearers. Wreaths were built up into a mountain behind the communal grave, which forms the shape of a cross.

Today it is covered by rose trees and bordered by memorial vases, many of which simply bear the names of individual children. In a nearby playground, built by the men of Warton, stands a block of rough stone with the inscription "This playground presented to the children of Freckleton by their American neighbors of Base Air Depot No.2 USAAF in recognition and remembrance of their common loss in the disaster of August 23rd 1944."

David G. Mayor, BAD 2

BILL'S LETTERS

Thursday 14th September 1944   England
Dear Folks:
... We finally got a ship of our own. The name is Dozy Doats. Don't ask me why 'cause we didn't name it. It has 36 missions without any trouble.

I guess my worries are over. The Germans have already sent up the flak with my number on it and it failed. It tore thru the skin of the ship behind me and hit me in the back, but by the time it got to me it was too spent to do any damage. It stuck in my flying suit. It wasn't as big as the hole in the ship so there must have been another part that broke off when it came thru. I have the piece with me and I'm going to bring it home and show it to you. Flak doesn't make a clean hole like a bullet. It's just a jagged hunk of metal and makes an ugly hole.

But what happens? When you get back down to low altitude you take off your oxygen mask and show everybody what happened and laugh! You laugh loud and long. You land and show it to the ground crew and laugh some more! We all do that. I tell you we're all crazy as hell. I can't see a thing funny about it but you laugh just the same. Maybe it's relief that makes you laugh. I don't know. But I'm beginning to think that it's perfectly natural.

Well, time to go to bed. Might have to get up early in the morning.
Write soon.

Love, Bill

[On 27 September 1944 Bill Ligon and the rest of Lieutenant Everett L. 'Ike' Isaacson's crew in the 548th Bomb Squadron, 385th Bomb Group, at Great Ashfield, Suffolk was awarded the Air Medal but Bill made no mention of it in his letter dated Thursday 29 September]
Dear Folks:
It's been so long since I wrote anybody I don't know where to start.

We've had it pretty tough this week and I haven't written any letters in 5 days.

The big Group party is coming up in a couple of days. Should be quite a celebration. They say Glenn Miller will be here along with Jimmie Doolittle and the other big shots. Today a small circus arrived on the base. Not as big as Ringling Bros but still a circus ... I saw in Stars and Stripes that they are getting ready to ring the Victory bells in the U.S. pretty soon. They must be crazy. I agree with Ernie Pyle. The war will probably go into the winter and early spring. As far as we're concerned over here it's already winter.

I could tell you some interesting things I've heard about the group Son was in, but it wouldn't go right now.

If Hitler's main purpose in using the buzz bomb is to scare people, he's doing a damn good job with it. You should see one of those things at nite. Of course, everybody runs out to see them anyway. As one Englishman told me, the Yanks in London run out in the street to see them while the civilians run for a shelter. It's always the civilians who get hit ... Food is still good – in fact we're supposed to have a bunch of steaks for the big party. All the guys get a shot of liquor when they come in from a mission. Most of them take it before eating and are so tired it almost knocks them over ... Got kicked up another stripe – Ike got promoted to 1st. Lt. too.

Guess that's all for new. Time for lites[sic] out. Write again soon.

Love, Bill

Saturday September 30   England
Dear Folks,

Well, here it is payday and the big gambling hall of the 548th (our barracks) is going full swing. Just got back from the show where I saw "Lifeboat" again ... Well, the big party comes off tomorrow, Glenn Miller, etc. There will be 1500 girls here from somewhere. Should be quite a spree ... That's all for now I guess. Write again soon.

Love Bill

Wednesday Oct. 4   England
Dear Folks:

Just got back from London again. Same old place. The bombs have almost stopped and everybody is coming back to the town. All the trains are crowded with people coming back. But trains leaving aren't so crowded. Of course there's still danger and the government tells them not to come home but that's like telling Americans not to travel in wartime.

I hope you can read this. This English ink isn't so good and I can hardly read it myself.

Oh yes – it's 8:00 at nite here and the first game of the World Series is just starting. We bought a good little radio in London. The radio we had was taken by the crew that owned it when they went back to the States.

We are the "big wheels" in our barracks now. That means we have more missions than any other crew – I meant to have my picture made in

London, but didn't get around to it. Saw a new picture in town "Greenwich Village". It was very colorful but boring with Don Ameche, Vivian Blaine, William Bendix ... The big party went off all OK I guess. Glenn Miller played all the good music he's ever put on records – Doolittle was here. They had a big dance lasted till 2:00am and the next morning we staggered down to the train and went London. The only thing wrong was that it was too cold. The outdoor concessions were a little uncomfortable.

We had ice cream in the mess hall today. The second time since I've been over here.

Be sure and let me know how Texas and Oklahoma come out in their big game. I was glad to get the clippings about Sunset beating Adamson 7 to 0. How did the game with Waxahachie come out?

Had a swell time in Hyde Park last nite I was in London. I went there at 5:00 in the afternoon and didn't leave till 12:00. What a place. One old lady who preaches there is me biggest attraction. She has about 8 teeth and a dirty old gray coat. She's against the war. Her line goes something like this – "and if you boys had any manhood you'd get out of those uniforms and preach the word of the Lord. You know, when I started preaching I had a chance to go to America and convert the wayward Yankees, but the Lord said 'Hyde Park' – and behold! he's brought the Yanks to me."

Anything you wish to discuss will get an audience in Hyde Park. A lot of them are very intelligent people, too. What took my time last nite was a talk with a Lieut. from the battle in France, an English nurse and a Canadian. We talked for about 4 hours. After we started – maybe 10 minutes after – we'd quite an audience. Nobody raises their voice in any discussion, but the people are just interested in what the other fellow thinks. You can be very blunt and brutally frank and nobody gets mad. And you can bet the way some of the American soldiers talk should make anybody mad. Hyde Park is freedom of speech in its broadest sense.

Well, that's all for now, I guess. Write soon.

Love, Bill

DMD119 44 GOV=WASHINGTON DC 23j1004PMC 1944 OCT 24 am 9 40
MRS MINNIE R LIGON
**409 SOUTH POLK ST DAL=
THE SECRETARY OF WAR DESIRES ME TO EXPRESS HIS DEEP REGRET THAT YOUR SON STAFF SERGEANT WILLIAM Y LIGON JR HAS BEEN REPORTED MISSING IN ACTION SINCE SIX OCTOBER OVER GERMANY IF FURTHER DETAILS OR OTHER INFORMATION ARE RECEIVED YOU WILL BE PROMPTLY NOTIFIED=
          J A ULIO THE ADJUTANT GENERAL.
     THREE HUNDRED EIGHTY FIFTH BOMBARDMENT
                    GROUP (H)
              Office of the Chaplain

                                      A.P.O. 559
                                      18 October 1944

Mrs Minnie R. Ligon
409 South Polk Street
Dallas, Texas

Dear Mrs Ligon

Since we have received word that your son, S/Sgt. William L. Ligon, Jr,
18177067, has been reported missing in action, we wait anxiously for
some report. The men of the Air Force, such as your son, are rendering
untold service to their country and mankind. We pray through the love of
God for William's safety and return because he was a fine young man, a
good soldier and a man of good character. I know you are proud of him
and in these hours of distress we extend to you our deepest sympathy and
prayers.

May I point out to you a great passage of scripture and I pray that it
may strengthen you. As the Psalmist said, "I will lift up mine eyes unto the
hills from which cometh my help. My help cometh from the Lord which
made the heavens and the earth. The Lord shall preserve thy going out and
thy coming in from this time forth and for evermore."

William's Commanding Officer, Lieutenant Colonel George Y. Jumper,
the Commanding General, Eighth Air Force and the men of this station
extend to you our deepest sympathy. If I can assist you at any time, feel
free to call upon us.

   Sincerely,
   (signed)
   JAMES O. KINCANNON,
   Chaplain (Capt.)
   Group Chaplain

D.LA687 48 GOVTWUX WASHINGTON DC 9 143P 1945 FEB
9 pm 1 36
MRS MINNIE R LIGON
409 SOUTH POLK ST MD DAL

REPORT NOW RECEIVED FROM THE GERMAN GOVERNMENT
THROUGH THE INTERNATIONAL RED CROSS STATES
YOUR SON STAFF SERGEANT WILLIAM Y LIGON JR WHO
WAS PREVIOUSLY REPORTED MISSING IN ACTION WAS
KILLED IN ACTION ON SIX OCTOBER OVER GERMANY
THE SECRETARY OF WAR EXTENDS HIS DEEP SYMPATHY
CONFIRMING LETTER FOLLOWS+
   J A ULIO THE ADJUTANT GENERAL

B-17G 42-97079 *Dozy Doats* flown by Lieutenant Everett L.
Isaacson, was one of eleven Fortresses in the group that were shot

down on the costly raid. Isaacson, 2nd Lieutenant Filbert F. Dye, co-pilot, Technical Sergeant Howard C. Ryan, radio operator and Staff Sergeant Joseph M. Mandarano, tail gunner, were also KIA. Four men, including top turret gunner Technical Sergeant Irvin W. Poole and ball turret gunner Staff Sergeant Joseph M. Matuszak, who wrote this letter to Mrs Ligon, survived and became PoWs.

> *531 Madison St,*
> *Wilkes-Barre, Pa.*
> *June 29, 1945*

Dear Mrs Ligon,

I wish to express my deepest sympathy to you upon your son's failure to return from his duty.

I cannot ever forget his overwhelming energy and desire to do his best at all times. William was a man of refined character, a true soldier and a real gentleman. He never did fail, whether it was on the ground or in the air. He came through all his endeavors as a man of distinguished ability. In company his presence was ever prevailing. His upstanding ideals will not easily be forgotten. I looked up to him and valued his advice to the greatest extent. He did his job to the greatest perfection. I am proud to have served with your son.

On the sixth of October while we were on our target over Berlin, our airplane was attacked by German fighters (FW 190's and Me 109's). There were somewhere between 300 and 400 of them. We didn't have a chance. They let loose with all they had. Our bombay, radio room and waist were hit and caught on fire. William was still in the waist. He still was there when I bailed out. The airplane exploded in the air when the fire reached the gas tanks and oxygen system.

The Supreme Sacrifice was made for his men so that someday they would return and live as they once did. His sacrifice will live forever in the eyes of his fellowmen. He died in order to accomplish his duty to his country.

Closing now, I remain sincerely yours,

Joe Matuszak

Bill Ligon was buried in the village cemetery at Buschow, Brandenburg, Germany, but later disinterred by the American War Graves Registration personnel and moved to the American cemetery at Neuville-en-Condroz, Belgium. He was reburied in Dallas, Texas on 15 June 1949

11

Brief Encounters

On the evening of Wednesday, 12 May 1943 we saw a truck with a white star on it come down our road, followed by another and then another. We ran outside and began to count them. We were very excited and amazed; they just kept coming and coming, with the dust flying up behind them. From our garden we watched the boys get out, while the roadway beside the house became one great mass of khaki, kit bags, helmets, mugs and blankets. The Yanks had arrived!

The base was not finished and many of them had to sleep in tents. They had no water or lighting for the first few days and some of them brought their tin helmets to get water from our house. At mealtime they had to march up to the mess hall. We could hear them singing and whistling, banging on their mess kits as they went along.

They were not allowed off the base for the first two weeks, so many of them roamed around our house and farm. We tried to make them understand our English money and gave them our English newspapers to read.

When they first arrived their uniforms looked so much alike to us that we did not know which were officers and which were enlisted men, but we soon found out who was who and what all the various bars and stars meant. It was queer for us to see stripes stitched on upside down.

It was some days before the first planes arrived, which we learned were called "Flying Fortresses" or "B-17s". The boys began flying practice missions every day and then they began the actual bombing raids. We used to watch them take off and count them. Then we waited for their return and counted them to see if they were all there. There were not many bombers to go out in those early days of 1943. On 12 August about 160 went on a raid. This was considered a great number then, but was only a fraction compared with the hundreds and thousands that were to go out in the following years.

All through the night there would be planes warming up, but we soon got used to that. In the morning when they began to taxi out the sound changed.

I remember being awakened about 4.30 one morning by the roar of the ships taking off. It was still quite dark and I could only see them by their lights. Others were going up from airfields all around and the sky was filled with hundreds of colored lights. As dawn began to break I heard our cowman calling in the cows and everything began to wake up all around, while way up above the ships were getting into formation. They would circle round and round, gaining altitude before starting east toward the coast. Then, the planes gone, the base would wake up to the work of the day.

We generally knew when the boys were returning from a raid, for two or three fighters would arrive and fly around, then we would hear the bombers coming. They would come right over our house in perfect formation. Then away would go the flares and the planes would begin peeling off to land. We never felt at ease until they all had landed. We called those boys "our boys," and their ships "our ships". Many a time we knew that some of the planes were missing and we could see others with holes in them. On Sunday, 10 October 1943 our boys raided Münster. Nearly all the planes came home rather badly shot up and several were only flying on three engines.

Thursday 23 December 1943 the Americans gave a party for all the schoolchildren in the district between the ages of five and eight. It was held in the Red Cross club on the base. The children had a wonderful time and I know the boys did too. The boys saved up their candy rations so that every child could have something to take home.

The year 1944 became a year of continuous missions. Day after day the boys went out and night after night the fight was kept up by our RAF.

The 571st Squadron was just across the roadway from our farm and we got to know almost everyone in it. Soon after the boys arrived names began to appear on the doors of the huts. There was "The Sleepy Lagoon", "Ye Olde Pig Sty", "Consumption Center 3rd", "The Dog House" and several names of night clubs.

At harvest time the boys used to ride on our empty wagons and some of them came and helped us in the fields. They were interested in our farm and our work and the neat way we made our stacks. We exchanged ideas about farming in America and England.

Our shooting days puzzled the Americans. I remember the first shooting day we had in October. We were walking across the fields, about nine of us all lined out, to frighten the birds from in front of us and over the hedge where the men with guns stood. The boys all came dashing out of the huts to see what was happening and climbed up on the fences and concrete blocks to get a better view.

Almost every evening there would be a game of baseball going on. We never could make out why they had to make so much noise while they were playing. We English may get very excited over some of our games, but I do not think we ever do quite so much shouting or cheering. They played volleyball and throwing horseshoes, too, but they did not make so much noise over these games.

I must not forget to mention all the dogs that lived on the base. There were dogs everywhere, big ones, little ones, all colors and every kind, chasing trucks, riding in Jeeps, following the boys to eat and always around somewhere.

The Germans were sending buzz bombs across all during the summer, winter and spring of 1944. We hardly missed a day or night for quite a long while without having at least one over. Most of them went past us and crashed inland, being aimed for London, but several came down very close to the base, damaging houses.

The boys had to fly twenty-five missions before they were sent home and later it was raised to thirty, then thirty-five. When one crew left a new one moved in, so there was always a continual coming and going; boys going on flak leave, some going on pass and others returning. The train from Framlingham to Wickham Market was always packed. They made jokes about our train, as it is only a small branch-line train, with three coaches and a small engine. It amused us to see the boys get on when they first came. They clambered on from both sides and some even rode in the engine – they just seemed to swarm onto it like a bunch of ants, but they soon learned the right way.

Many of them also learned to ride bicycles and we thought it awfully funny to see some of them learning. They mostly landed on their knees with the bike on top of them. When they could ride quite well they carried others on the crossbars and one often saw two or three on one bike. They found it difficult to remember to cycle on the left side of the road.

We always knew when it was eleven o'clock, for there was a daily tannoy test – "Report any failures to Extension 1-0." Shortly after that the boys all went to eat and the roadways were packed – truck loads and Jeeps, too. It was surprising the number of persons who could ride in one Jeep.

At five o'clock a bugle was sounded and the colors were lowered. Everyone was supposed to stand at attention and salute, but if they were anywhere near the barracks they made a dash inside and shut the door.

Many times, during the night, we would be awakened by a voice over the tannoy announcing "This is a red alert! All personnel take cover!" The sirens would start up in the villages near the base and then in the towns farther away. They filled the night with that horrible wailing. The boys would come out of their huts to see if there was anything exciting going on. They generally made a terrific amount of noise, shouting, singing and throwing stones on the huts to sound like the noise of bombs coming down.

Every Tuesday afternoon was gas-mask practice and they had to go around driving trucks and Jeeps and cycling with the queer-looking masks on.

The boys liked to tease us. There was always something being said about our "limey" weather and they teased us about the way we talked and tried to copy us. It sounded funny to hear them say "I cawn't." I expect we were just as funny when we tried to talk through our noses like them.

On 23 August 1944 a big party was held to celebrate the 100th Mission, although the hundredth mission had been flown some time before. Hangar No.2 was beautifully decorated with bracken, with bales of straw around the side to sit on and a great many blue lights. There were thousands of persons there from neighbouring villages, British service girls and American WACs. Glenn Miller's band played for the dance.

The 200th Mission party was held on Sunday 8 October with civilians again invited to attend. The afternoon began with a religious service, followed by a football match and then an open-air performance by a variety show from London. In the evening there were four dances to choose from – at the officers' club, the Rocker Club, the combat mess and the Red Cross.

VE Day was officially announced on 8 May 1945. In the evening bonfires were lit, blackouts torn down and lights turned on everywhere. The American boys were restricted to the base, but they made up for it by making all the noise they could, blowing whistles, motor horns, sounding the sirens and fire alarms and sending up hundreds of colored flares. The tannoy would announce (in a very stern voice) "There will be no more flares sent up on this base!" and straightaway about a hundred more would go off. The searchlights all along the coast were making V signs in the sky, the guns were banging and around we saw flares and rockets from other airfields. It was a wonderful feeling to be free from Jerry raids and to show our lights again!

On 13 May the 300th Mission party was held. The hangar was beautifully decorated, this time with parachutes of colours hanging from the roof. There were thousands of persons invited again, the entertainment consisted of variety shows and dancing and we ate with the boys in their mess halls.

On 29 May we saw the review of the 390th and all attached units on the runway in front of the control tower. This was the last parade and the last time they all appeared together. Practice missions were still kept up and night flying was started. Then the boys flew food over to the starving people the countries which had been occupied.

In June the boys who were to fly home began to get ready and after several delays they finally got away, the last one going on 26 June. Quite a lot stayed behind, to go home by boat after the tasks of cleaning up and packing were complete. On Thursday, 2 August the 570th and 571st squadrons left, and on Sunday 5 August the 568th and 569th. They went shouting and singing and waving. We could hear them as they went along the road to the station, until they got farther and farther away, then everywhere became silent. The Yanks had come – and now they were gone!

I shall always remember that vast contrast when they left. One moment it was all noise, shouting, trucks starting stopping and then dead silence, with everything deserted. I walked back home across the runway. There was no one in sight; it was just as if everyone had fallen asleep. We should never forget the 390th, the boys who had come so far from their homes in America, many of them never to return. For more than two years they lived in and were a part of our countryside and we missed them sincerely when they were gone.

An English girl who lived in one the farms on the Base at Station 253, Framlingham (Parham)

What do I remember of the Yanks? I remember being called from my bed in the middle of the night by a noisy crew in a Jeep! Then hurriedly climbing into my uniform and dashing out into the dark streets, finding my way up an embankment on to railway tracks and desperately searching the sidings for an ambulance train. At this stage of the war I had joined a team of sisters, nurses and orderlies working on a casualty evacuation train. The war was nearing its close and we were on loan to the American Army to help ferry the wounded who'd been flown back from the fighting in Germany. My "ward" consisted of a milk van which had been adapted to carry thirty men. The "beds", in tiers of three, were stretchers attached to the sides of the van. There was no heating in the cold and very little ventilation in hot weather. We had no windows. At the end of the ward there was a paraffin oil stove on which we could boil water, but if the train went round a bend too quickly, the stove would catch fire and whatever I was doing in the ward had to be left and I ran to help extinguish it. It was far from luxury for badly injured men. In fact it must have been agony – but I do not recall one single complaint from them.

Food was a bit scarce but we always kept enough tea to give them an early morning cup. How well I remember their reactions! We could never get used to the fact that tea was not welcome – especially in the morning!

I look back and remember some very sad times, but always, whatever the circumstances, the wonderful sense of humour of those GIs shines through. In pain and discomfort they had a lovely caring attitude towards those who were caring for them. It is quite unforgettable after fifty years and I feel that I was very privileged to have worked among them. It is hard to find adequate words to describe their courage – though the memories come tumbling back to me as I write.

Audrey Tallboys

It was awfully cold. We just had coal stoves and they would have orderlies who always had a fire going in the little stove when we got back. One time we couldn't make our field, but we were in England and we took a secondary landing at a Royal Air Force base. They were really funny. It was raining and we landed in the mud. The wheels went down into this mud. So we notified our base where we were, we're safe and all that. They would get the plane out the next morning and we'd fly to our base. And, lo and behold, those wheels and the whole nose of the B-17 must have been half covered in mud and slop. This little Englishman had a little half-ass tractor and he pulled up. In this English accent he said,

"Gentlemen, I'm gonna get your plane out."

We looked at him and said, "You're gonna get this plane out of this mud with that tractor?"

"Oh, no problem, no problem."

So we all stood back and he hooked the thing on and he gave it one with that tractor and the whole damn motor of the tractor came out.

Staff Sergeant Robert L. 'Bob' Schroeder, top turret gunner/flight engineer

Out of the darkness walked a strange chap in USAF uniform with both RAF and USAF wings. His chest was splattered with combat decorations and he sported a long handlebar moustache. In a crisp British accent he introduced himself as Flight Officer Vance Chipman, mentioning that he had just been transferred to the 25th Bomb Group. He would be assisting in Mosquito pilot training. I noticed that his mouth was watering while staring at our drinks so I poured him a stiff one. After several drinks together in the officers' club, we began to call each other by our nicknames. His was "Chip" and I was "Tip".

Several weeks later I was going to London on leave. The little train left Watton about 2pm for its fifteen-mile trip to Thetford, where connections were made with the 4pm express train to London. The general procedure was to wait in the pub directly across the street from the Thetford railway station. The pub owner always made sure we Yanks never missed the train. Chipman was in the pub and on his way to London also, so we teamed up for the journey. By the time the London train arrived we were in "great shape", boarding the train with more than an adequate supply of Scotch and ale. I guess we made a big splash upon arrival at Liverpool Street station. Getting a hotel room in London was almost impossible. I had made friends with the desk clerk at Russell Square hotel and he was able to arrange rooms for "Chip" and me.

We wound up in some pub that night and having a great time. Suddenly, I thought my ears were playing tricks upon me as "Chip" had dropped his British accent and was speaking in a strong Russian voice. He had everyone in the pub believing he was a Russian pilot sent over to help their American and British allies. All night I wondered just what game Chipman was playing. The next morning I went to his room to awaken him. To my amazement, he began to speak with a typical American mid-western accent. I asked him point-blank, "Just where in hell did you come from?" Laughing, he replied that he was a former racetrack driver from Chicago. He had joined the Royal Canadian Air Force when war started in Europe.

At breakfast that morning we agreed to meet in the hotel pub at opening time. At 11am I was there, but not "Chip". About thirty minutes later, in he strolled with a monkey on his shoulder. "Chip" explained that as he was walking past a pet shop, this monkey saluted him (or so he thought). The monkey seemed to be searching for a long lost friend. Chip bought the monkey for £20. For the remaining two days that monkey accompanied us on a tour of pubs, causing quite a commotion I must admit.

Upon return to Watton, the next evening at dinner some chap seated next to me asked if I knew anything about some monkey romping through officers' BOQ. The Group CO, Colonel Leon Gray, was on the warpath. It seems that the monkey had gotten into Colonel Gray's quarters and opened tooth paste, shaving cream, talcum powder, etc. and decorated his room in a most non-military manner! He added something about Colonel Gray was looking for "Chip" or "Tip" and that was enough for me!

I left my food, quickly eased out of the mess, mounted my trusty bike and dashed off to the safety of the Flying Fish pub. By closing time I had regained my courage and rode back. As I passed the Manager's Office there was a familiar voice – Smitty, who asked me to come into his darkened office and to watch the show in the bar. Chipman was sitting at one end of the bar drinking Scotch, with the monkey perched on his shoulder. "Chip's" personal pewter mug was filled with ale. The monkey would jump down, take a large gulp of ale and leap back onto "Chip's" shoulder – much to the amusement of the bar patrons.

The next thing I knew, "Chip" was having a duel with fire extinguishers with some high-ranking officer. Men were dashing out of both doors so I got the hell out of there, too. The following day, while visiting the "Flying Fish", I heard rumours about what happened. One was that the monkey had set off a flare somehow and "Chip" used a fire extinguisher to clean up the mess. Many 25th Bomb Group pilots were soaked in an acid/soda bath in the process, plus some damage was done to the club furniture. Colonel Gray banished "Chip" to a thirty-day residence in a pup tent erected on the lawn in front of the officers' club!

Vance Chipman was later shot down flying a secret "Mickey" mission and was a German prisoner. After his liberation and return to Watton, "Chip" told me he once tried to escape by stealing an Me 109. He was recaptured before he could start the engine.

Ralph Tipton, 25th Bomb Group

One briefing I recall was conducted by Colonel James Stewart, who was then Group Operations Officer. He enlivened the proceedings with his dry wit and acting ability. Flight-line ambulance duty was assigned on a regular basis and each medical officer took his turn at meeting the returning aircraft. As the returning bombers approached the base, a red flare was sent up by the crew if there was a mechanical or physical problem aboard. As soon as the aircraft was landed, the ambulance went to meet it for evacuation and/or treatment of any injured or dead crewmembers.

One occasion in the spring of 1944 German planes followed our returning bombers and attacked them as they approached the English coast and then proceeded to strafe the air base. Captain James Munsey and crew were hit in this attack and their aircraft was set afire; however, Captain Munsey was able to keep his ship airborne until he was able to ditch it near the shore. Munsey and his co-pilot Lieutenant Crall were killed but Lieutenant Leon Helfand, navigator and Sergeants McClure, Cole and Lax survived.

Some residents of a small English village near the ditching site assisted the survivors to shore. Lieutenant Helfand had received burns to his face and hands and was taken to a small dispensary or hospital near the ditching site.

The next day late in the afternoon or early evening, I was sent with an ambulance and driver in search of this small coastal village in order to return the survivors to Old Buck. Due to the blackout, the English maze of small roads, "turnabouts" and lack of road signs, we finally found our objective in the wee small hours of the morning. We picked up Lieutenant Helfand and returned to Old Buck.

Lieutenant Helfand had received his "Purple Heart" in more than one way, for the British people who treated him had applied a generous portion of purple Gentian violet dye to his burned areas.

... Occasionally as medical officers, we had to travel with ambulance and driver to the cemetery in Cambridge to carry our dead to their final resting place. On one such occasion as our ambulance travelled down one of those narrow English roads with high thick hedges on either side, the hedgerows suddenly erupted and a P-47 hurtled across the road in front of us and came to rest on the other side the road. The ambulance driver stopped and I ran to the P-47, which was still intact and upright and climbed up on the wing. I was looking into the cockpit when the pilot opened the canopy and looked at me. He apparently was unhurt for he spotted the caduceus on my blouse and said, "Doc, how in the hell did you get here in such a hurry?" He apparently had elected to make a belly landing after his fuel ran out.

Frank J. 'Doc' Pickett MD, medical officer at 'Old Buck' from 19 April 44

One summer evening, 15 July 1944, Mary Hovells and her husband, a chief air raid warden, who had lived at School Farm, Ilketshall St Lawrence, since 1935, were getting ready to visit some friends. Mary's husband was standing on the lawn. She was looking out of the window, talking to him. She says, "In the distance I saw a cloud of smoke and then suddenly, the blast reached us. It blew my husband over and I felt as if I had been hit in the face. My hair, which I had just brushed, was blown all over the place. The blast also blew open the front door, broke a pane of glass in the front window and sucked a big pane of glass out of the scullery at the back." At the time she did not know that the bomb dump at Metfield airfield nearby and 1,200 tons of bombs had exploded, killing five American airmen and destroying five B-24 Liberators. Other aircraft were badly damaged. The distance between St Lawrence and Metfield is only a matter of a few miles as the crow flies, hence the damage to St Lawrence.

Mary recalls another summer evening, returning home from a visit to some friends in Spexhall. It was beginning to get dusk. She says, "I got on my bike to ride home, having some young chickens to shut up. A lot of American bombers were coming home from a raid. As they came in with their landing lights on, a German fighter flew in with them and was shooting them down. It was terrible to see them crashing down in flames."

Another time, while hoeing sugar beet in one of their fields, Mary witnessed another disaster involving an American bomber. The B-24 Liberator, heavily loaded with bombs and fuel, was taking off from Metfield and was having trouble gaining height. "We could see it coming down and thought it was going to fall near us. I must confess that we did a hasty dive into a nearby ditch. Luckily for us, it skimmed over us and fell with a terrible crash in a field about a mile further on. But of course the poor crew were lost in the crash."

On one particular bright night Mary Hovells heard what she thought was a tractor. She thought it strange hearing a tractor at that time of night. Looking out of the window she saw the glow from a V-1 Doodlebug pilotless flying bomb. To Mary the "pop-pop-popping" noise sounded like a Field Marshal tractor.

Mary's husband was in the Royal Oak pub at St Lawrence one evening when a Doodlebug came down. When the engine of the Doodlebug stopped it was the signal to take cover, for this was when it would come down and explode. Upon hearing this everyone in the pub took cover. Mr Hovells ran outside and dived into a nettle-covered ditch. Another man thought he might get some protection standing behind a telegraph pole. Mrs Hovells doubts that it would have offered much protection, as the man was much wider than the pole. Luckily, the blast from the explosion missed them by going in a different direction. Mary Hovells was at home this night and took cover in a passage in the centre of the house, hoping that if the house were destroyed it would be the safest place to be. She was very surprised by the lack of an explosion. "Just like a beer bottle going off", were her words.

Dick Wickham

From time to time, aircrew members were invited to homes in the area to share food and talk. The practice was enhanced on a day like Christmas. The co-pilot and I signed up and were invited to the vicar's home in a nearby hamlet, available by local bus. We knew that rations were in short supply so we took with us what we could: candy, cigarettes, and two cans of fruit (obtained by devious means). The dinner table held us, the vicar and his wife, two early teen children and a niece by the name of Carol. She had recently been widowed, thanks to a shell fragment in Italy. Her home was in Cornwall, but her late husband had been stationed in the Rackheath area. After we flew the last mission of the war, 25 April 1945, Carol and I made a trip to Cornwall. We both knew this was an interlude helping her to overcome grief and helping me to keep my head on straight. Cornwall is steeped in history ... residents spoke a Celtic language of their own. Phoenicians searching for tin were the first to land there. King Arthur with his Knights of the Round Table founded a castle on the rocky cliffs of Tintagel. Carol and I had a drink at the historic Jamaica Inn, which is also the title of a famous book by Daphne du Maurier. I must admit that Carol was not my exclusive companion at dances and elsewhere and certainly not when boozing up at the club or with this purpose in mind at some pub. But the times with her are fondly remembered. Some attempt was made after the war to maintain contact, but this effort gradually declined and ceased when she remarried.

'Carol', John L. Stewart

There was the time when Snyder and some others were visiting our barracks and the putt-putt bombs would come over – "putt, putt, putt". The conversation would stop, everyone would listen to see if it fell before reaching our location or putted on past and then stopped. This particular night, the putt-putt stopped directly overhead. Everyone scattered. Even though it was serious, it was real amusing, for one great big old boy tried to crawl under the lower bunk. The board rail was probably five inches from the floor, so, of course, he could not get underneath there and it looked so silly to watch him head butt his head and continue to try to get under the bed!

Emmett D. Seale

Characters

In life we tend to remember the more flamboyant people that we have been associated with as well as those with particular idiosyncrasies. All others in time fade into obscurity. The air forces, being voluntary, at least as far as the flying personnel were concerned, tended to attract a somewhat more adventurous type. Some were drawn by the perceived love of flying, some probably to avoid the possibility of hand-to-hand combat, some because of the more glamorous uniform, some because of the additional flying pay and some I'm sure to ensure that they would be able to sleep in a bed at night and not on the ground someplace.

In any case, characters abounded and served to make life interesting in what at times was a very boring existence. In our hut we had more than our share. The standout was The Captain, also referred to as Moogle. Somewhat older and more senior than the rest of us, he had spent a lot of time in the States as an instructor pilot. In fact that was how we first met him, i.e. as a B-24 instructor pilot. The Air Force had begun tapping these people in the summer of 1944 and sending them to combat as crew members; in Moogle's case as a first pilot or airplane commander. A very fine looking individual, he looked a lot like Dennis Morgan, a well-known actor of the time. Although he did pull rank on the rest of us now and then, he was basically a very friendly and funny guy. He saw humor in most things, as did most of the rest of us. He never referred to the B-24 as anything but "The Big Ass Bird" and was fond of describing in some detail the many problems he had trying to fly the thing. He painted a picture of complete incompetence, which was obviously not the case. He liked to describe very graphically the problem he had attempting to urinate into his flak helmet at altitude with the temperature at forty or fifty below zero while wearing about four inches of clothing. He would act out the procedure while sitting in a chair or on his bunk.

Moogle apparently had a very doting family back in Pittsburgh who sent him copious quantities of food in care packages. My strongest recollection involves biscuits and a variety of cheeses. It was my first introduction to biscuits. He liked to spend his evenings at the club, returning late to the hut ravenously hungry and a bit under the influence. He would open up his pantry, then look for an eating companion. When Moogle ate, everyone ate – or else. If you happened to be asleep, you'd be awakened to find him trying to push a biscuit and cheese in your mouth. After awhile I found it wise to quietly eat it. He was tenacious and wouldn't take no for an answer, pulling rank if all else failed.

The high point of his many escapades came when he was arrested and confined to the hut by the MPs. It seems he was attracted to a young lady at one of the Saturday night dances at the club. When the time came to take the girls home in the bus, he accompanied her onto the bus and refused to get off when told to by the MPs. They then tried to forcibly remove him, at which point he slugged one of the MPs. They then returned him to the hut to sleep it off. He remembered none of this the next morning and prepared to head for town, probably to find his date of the previous evening. Finally, with great difficulty, we convinced him that he was under house arrest and would be considered AWOL if he left. Fortunately, it occurred at the end of his tour so they decided to confine him to the base until he left for home with no other penalty.

Then there was Araskog who led the daily entourage to the mess hall for lunch and dinner with his usual call – "They're gonna feed 'em now!" à la feeding time at the zoo. It was a daily ritual. He too was a very funny guy who found humor in just about everything.

And Buckshot, who came from a ranch in Montana or Utah or somewhere out that way. Apparently they did all their own canning and used to send him innumerable cans of beef, venison and chicken. He was very generous and shared it with all of us. We realized that we had a real-life cowboy in our midst who looked the part with a very leathery complexion and typical western drawl.

Radar, who predated the *M*A*S*H* show by many years, was a married navigator who sent most of his pay home to his wife and kept only a pittance for himself. Unfortunately, he was a confirmed gambler who went to the club every payday night and promptly lost the little money that he kept for himself. Thus, he spent the rest of the month lying on his bunk and grubbing cigarettes, never going anywhere. To add to his woes, he was involved in a crash on Christmas Day 1944, which took the life of his pilot and co-pilot. They crash-landed in Belgium and Radar and some of the other crewmembers tried desperately to pull the two pilots from the burning wreckage, but were forced to leave them despite their pleas ... After that, he spent a lot of time staring into space.

He obviously felt that he had abandoned them and that it was at least partially his fault.

Then there was George, a former West Virginia coalminer with a monumental inferiority complex. For some reason he took his feelings out on one of the pilots in the hut (killed at Christmas). The pilot had come from Syracuse, New York, always pronounced Seery-cuse by George. He seemed to equate Seery-cuse with Palm Beach or Southampton, accusing the pilot of acting like a big shot because of his snooty hometown. He also liked to go to London whenever he got a three-day pass, invariably returning late the night of the third day very drunk and very obnoxious. We finally decided to get even one night when we'd about had it with him. First we removed the fuses from the electrical box in the hut thereby killing the lights. We then placed a number of pieces of angle iron under the straw pallets that served as a mattress. We then short-sheeted the bed, all got into our bunks and waited. Right on schedule he came crashing into the hut and tried to turn on the lights with no success. In the blackout, the interior of the hut was like ink. He then started cursing all of us and tried to find his bunk in the dark, falling all over the place. He finally found his bunk and tried to climb in clothing and all but was stymied by the short sheeting. He then gave up and lay down on the whole mess, angle iron and all, the angle iron clanking away. All the rest of us are almost choking trying not to laugh out loud. Almost immediately he fell asleep and started to snore. When he finally roused up next morning he wouldn't even speak to us. What we didn't know the night before was that walking down the road to the hut area in the dark and the rain, some guy on a bicycle ran into him, knocking him down, scratching and bruising him up thoroughly and tearing his uniform. Thus, he was in a particularly foul mood when he hit the hut.

In the next hut to ours lived an intelligence officer generally referred to as "Flak and Fighters" Barrett. One of the mission briefing officers, he typically tried to scare his audience to death by his dire predictions of all the flak and fighters that we would probably encounter. A typical statement went something like "You can expect attacks from a force of as many as 500 fighters along your route to the target today". He also liked to comment on the hundreds of flak guns along the way and in the target area. Barrett was probably in his 50s and came from Hartford, Conn., where he had worked for an insurance company. He regaled us with stories of his good job, fine house, big Buick etc., etc. He did make it exciting, however.

Another classic was our second squadron CO, who quite candidly admitted to being scared to death on missions, especially when he had to have lead responsibility. While most shared his concerns, most managed to hide their feelings pretty well. One of the most hysterical incidents of our tour was the day the major had to fly the weather ship which would usually take off at 2am or so, climb up to the area where we were to assemble and call down the weather conditions. On the day in question, the weather was terrible and he finally found the cloud tops at about 20,000ft. About the time he got there his radio went out so he could send but not receive. About the same time he got to 20,000 they decided to scrub the mission because of the weather. While they kept calling him to tell him to land, he couldn't hear because he had no radio. To compound his problem, his navigator had forgotten to bring his maps so didn't know where they were or how to get down. The situation went on for hours. Meanwhile we're all back in bed with someone coming into the hut periodically to advise that the major is still circling and still pleading for some help. We were convulsed every time. He finally made it down somehow but was the butt of jokes for a long time. He never lived it down.

Another prize was a flight surgeon who had had a medical practice in Elizabeth, New Jersey. He would show up at briefings in the middle of the night with his tools of the trade; three or four used tongue depressors in one pocket, a throat spray bottle in another, one pants' pocket full of aspirin and the other full of Benzedrine tablets. We all maintained that the doc could have handled open-heart surgery with the four items. If you asked for aspirin or Benzedrine you always got a little lint and tobacco along with it. The most noteworthy characteristic though was a slight speech impediment. He had a lot of problems with his Ls, coming out more like Ws. Thus, in his first aid lectures he would discuss bweeding, ahtewial and capiwawwy. We loved it. He could have passed for Mr Magoo.

And Goodrich, another intelligence officer who lived in a small room in the next hut. We all decided that he was, in today's parlance, gay. He was always inviting guys into his room to share his copious quantities of food and to share the warmth of the place, having one of the more efficient oil burners. We never really knew if he was gay but we all sort of assumed it, perhaps a little unfairly.

Another character was the club officer who we considered flak happy, a term used for those who had had some bad combat experience(s) and was grounded for psychological reasons. He played the piano, not too well, but with great gusto; leading all of the profane singing that was common in the club. He at least kept the atmosphere lively. One of our hut-mates came back to the hut one day after a visit with the club officer. He said the club officer was talking to him when he suddenly stopped talking while looking out the window. He then grabbed his 45 automatic, opened the window and started blasting away at something. It turned out to be a large rat that was sitting out on the grass. Apparently a poor marksman, he emptied the clip, slammed the window and began cursing that he had missed. Flak happy I guess he really was.

One of the more flamboyant types was a captain known throughout the base as Captain Tannoy for his loud foghorn voice. An apt name, Tannoy being the name of the manufacturer of the many loudspeakers scattered around the base. The loudspeakers were cast metal with the name Tannoy molded into the horn. I never knew his real name.

But the classic was a pilot whose favorite expression was "Heil Hitler, just in case we lose". I probably heard him say it a hundred or more times. Unfortunately, he and his crew were shot down and killed or made prisoner. In any case, a couple of days after they were shot down the pilot was heard on the German radio extolling the virtues of his captivity and how well he was being treated. Our reaction was, "Jesus, he really meant it all along."

Ronald D. Spencer

I'd flown with many bombardiers, most of whom usually said: "Let's get the hell out of here," after "bombs away", but one fellow I'll never forget said very quietly instead: "Die you bastards!"

Like love, hate is a very personal emotion.

Abe Dolim, navigator

As it turned out, St-Nazaire was Spook Bender's last mission. He'd lost a lot of weight and was usually shaking like a leaf. Who could blame him? All he could talk about was "all them Focke Wulfs" and "all that flak". It was about this time that Bill Lindley and Spook went to see a movie in the nearest big town, Ipswich. They sat in the first row of the balcony but the projectionist made a big mistake when he showed the latest newsreel before the movie, with nothing but German fighters attacking B-17s of the 8th Air Force. Spook went slightly berserk. He crouched down behind the rail of the balcony and kept screaming for his gunners to "Shoot! Shoot! Shoot!"

Bill managed to calm him, got him outside and then they took a taxi back to Horham ... Bob stayed in hospital for a rest and they finally sent him home to the United States. He suffered a massive heart attack a few years later and died. He was only twenty-five years old.

Don Merton, co-pilot, 336th Bomb Squadron, 95th Bomb Group

Right after we landed General "Hap" Arnold and a party of high brass arrived at the field and the general gave the boys a pep talk. I was real surprised to see Clark Gable, the movie actor, in a captain's uniform and later found out that he had gone on five raids and earned his Air Medal. He was well thought of by everybody and was going back to the States ...

Captain Franklin 'Puppy' Colby, pilot

We flew on Captain Calhoun's wing and Clark Gable flew with him and handled the radio hatch gun. Claude Campbell, my pilot, could quite easily see the Hollywood film star grinning at him over enemy territory.

Howard E. Hernan, gunner

Everyone had nothing but praise for Stewart, for here was a man with nothing to gain and everything to lose taking such risks over the best-defended targets in Germany.

> Harry H. Darrah, talking about James Stewart, movie star

On a mission to France he flew *Wham Bam,* our assembly ship, over the normal "race-track" course around the Group's homing beacon, "Buncher Six". Then he pulled out to the left about a quarter of a mile and flew on ahead to allow the lead ship to take over. However, contrary to procedure, he stayed in this position: all the way into France! Finally, the major turned *Wham Barn* around and came home, much to the relief of his crew.

He said: "If anyone breathes a word, I'll kill ya."

Colonel Ramsey D. Potts, the Group Commander, probably wanted to know where he had been for the past six hours!

> 1st Lieutenant (later Lieutenant Colonel) Bernard H. Fowle, lead navigator, 734th Bomb Squadron, interview about Major James Stewart; film star and 453rd Bomb Group Operations Officer

The tall, slender, boyish-looking pilot walks in a somewhat effeminate manner and you really have to look closely to see that he does indeed shave. He wears the only fur-collared summer flying jacket in the squadron and is one of the few who keeps his grommet in his dress hat. But he has been in the outfit long enough to have brought back shot-up bombers a couple of times and has recently been wounded – not seriously, however. Those of his friends who know him well know he has a doting mother and five older sisters – that's all.

> *The Graceful Pilot,* Abe Dolim

The most popular man in the squadron is the generous navigator from Oklahoma whose mother sends him Southern fried chicken packed in lard in a three-pound Crisco can about every ten days. The other lucky stiff is the kid from the Bronx who quite often gets a whole salami from his girlfriend back home. One time the salami arrived badly mildewed and everybody moaned as he chucked it into the trash bucket. One of the guys plucked it out of the bucket, got his trench knife and pared the salami. Then he sliced it into ¼in-thick pieces, stuck a couple of them on a fork and began to toast them over the pot-bellied stove. No sooner had the aroma wafted around when a mad scramble began for the remaining pieces of sausage.

> *Ol' Buddy Winter 1944–45,* Abe Dolim

One could walk into a room full of airmen and in a short time pick out with considerable accuracy who held what position just by observing the mannerisms of those present. Navigators were easy to sort out. Just look for a hypersensitive guy, someone who can't hold still one minute, an eager beaver asking questions unrelated to the interest of anyone else. It helped to be a little odd, but I loved the job.

1st Lieutenant John W McClane Jr, navigator

Mail Call was one of the most important events of the day. Everyone's mail was addressed to an APO number in New York and the Army took care of getting it delivered to us. Presumably, our families did not know where we were, or specifically, what we were doing. Letters from home were eagerly anticipated. Packages were even more welcome than letters and especially if they contained homemade cookies. My wife wrote almost every day and writing a letter to her was usually the last thing I did each evening. I used the V-Mail. It was a single page that was folded and made its own envelope; also, the message space was limited. It was just enough to let your family know that you were still all right. We were restricted to what we could write. We could not tell them exactly where we were, although they knew that when I left the States, I was headed to the 8th Air Force. Anything that could be useful to the enemy was prohibited. I'm sure that it was the same for the loved ones at home as it was for us over here. Usually what was contained in the letter wasn't nearly as important as just getting the letter. Everyone needed to know that their loved ones at home had not forgot them.

All outgoing mail had to be censored. The censoring task was passed around among the officers. Periodically, each one of us would catch that assignment. We would come back to the hut and there would be a box of outgoing mail on our bunks. I didn't like censor duty. It made me feel like I was eavesdropping. Some of the letters were very personal, containing detailed descriptions as to what the wife or girl friend could expect when they got home. Most of the time, there was very little that had to be blacked out, but on occasion, someone would get carried away and describe in graphic detail the horrors of a buddy getting shot up over the target and trying to take care of him on the way home. Those kind of details always got deleted.

Dean M. Bloyd

The air echelon, including the maintenance crews, were a close-knit group and felt themselves a cut above the Perimeter Defence Squadron whose soldiers were actually camped in the woods on the eastern end of our line at Thorpe Abbotts. Their purpose was to protect us against marauding aircraft, but many of us were worried against the possible danger they presented to our own welfare since they were not necessarily crack-shots. Some of the men were not overly impressed with their judgement. Some of the linemen undoubtedly knew that the defence crew were, from time to time, filching chickens. These were subsequently cooked over an open fire and undoubtedly were delicious. However, as to be expected, the farmer complained to the police. Of course, our heroes knew nothing about the missing chickens, but then Scotland Yard was called in with a bloodhound. Lo and behold, that smart dog took off on a trot and led these modern-day Sherlock Holmeses right to the spot where the feather and chicken bones were buried. It was a dark day for our protectors, but a triumph for British justice.

Bill Carleton, Engineering Officer

MURDER AT THE HALL

The 3,000-acre Honingham Hall estate was located at the south-eastern corner of the 466th Bomb Group base at Attlebridge. Sir Eric and Lady Teichman lived in the large Elizabethan Hall on the estate. A former Consular at the British Embassy in Chunking, China, Teichman was recognized as an outstanding expert on China, especially Chinese dialects. During the Blitz children from a London orphanage moved to a building on the Honingham Hall estate. During the early evening of 3 December 1944 Lady Teichman called the base. She was greatly concerned because her husband had not returned after leaving the house at 1600 hours. It was unusual for him not to return before dark. About thirty men joined local constables to search for him and military police were sent by car to Honingham Hall. The search continued until about 2330 hours. Early the next morning Lady Teichman, a practical nurse and the chauffeur found the body of Sir Eric in heavy underbrush about 500 yards from the hall. Sir Eric had been shot in the head. Examination of the spent slug found in Sir Eric's clothes revealed it was from a 30-caliber carbine, the kind issued to all ground men on the base.

The base was sealed and personnel were interviewed. Each man was required to bring his carbine with him so that the serial number could be checked against the records. On 5 December officers of the Army's Criminal Investigation Division (CID) arrived to assist in the questioning. One of the kitchen helpers went to the Orderly Room to tell the 1st Sergeant that he had information on the killing. The informant said he had seen Privates George E. Smith Jr and Leonard S. Wojtacha leave their barracks with carbines in their hands on Sunday afternoon. In the morning of 6 December two Scotland Yard detectives arrived and they examined the two carbines. Smith's gun had been recently fired. Both guns were test fired and the slugs were recovered. Wojtacha finally broke down and told what he knew. Smith was confronted and he confessed to the crime. They had gone to the woods on the estate and fired off 100 rounds between them. Sir Eric told his wife he was going to put a stop to the shooting so near to the house. He came upon the men and Wojtacha started to walk away when Sir Eric said, "Wait a minute young man, what is your name?" Smith was facing in their direction and holding his carbine at his side with his finger on the trigger. When Sir Eric was about thirty feet away, Smith said,

"Old Man, don't come any closer."

Sir Eric didn't stop and Smith fired from his side, not lifting the weapon. Sir Eric was killed instantly, the bullet entering his jaw and coming out the back of his neck.

At his General Courts-Martial in January 1945 Smith (28) was found guilty of the murder of Sir Eric Teichman and sentenced to death by hanging. Lady Teichman appealed to headquarters to spare Smith's life. She also appealed to General Eisenhower, who also denied the request. Finally she appealed to US Ambassador Winant in London. All her gallant efforts failed. Smith was hanged at a US Army Disciplinary Training Centre on Tuesday 8 May.

12

'What Time Would You Like To Be Knocked Up In The Morning?'

A "flak shack", that delightful, full-fed, pleasant English country estate, helped to cure both operational and flying fatigue.

Allan Healy

Surprise, surprise! Seems I had just joined a crew that was ready for the "flak house." That's the term used for the R&R (Rest & Recuperation) home. I did know some of the prior missions were rough on them. They had already lost their radio operator and co-pilot. This Ludwigshaven mission was the last straw.

The flak house was a mansion in a town called Lymington. It was called the Walhampton House Rest Home. It was owned by Lady Naeson. We were sent up by plane. It was a huge place, almost like a palace; big enough for sixty airmen on R&R. The first thing they did when we arrived was to have us strip off our uniforms right down to the underwear. Civilian clothes were issued to us and, believe me, they sure felt strange. We were free to come and go anywhere on the estate. All kinds of recreational things were available to us.

Here I was with a crew after one mission and I didn't even get to know all their names after all that we had just gone through. On other one-time missions with other crews, I sometimes never even saw some of them. There was a big lake to go canoeing on and a big gym nearby. We were there for ten days.

George E. Kistner, extra gunner and radio operator, 388th Bomb Group, Knettishall

The briefing on 9 May 1944 for Liège, Belgium, indicated it was to be a fairly easy mission, with good fighter cover all the way but moderate to heavy flak at the target. Intelligence was right except that the flak was light over the target, but extremely accurate. A shell burst just twenty feet from our right vertical stabilizer, sending a piece of shrapnel through the tail turret, killing our tail gunner, Staff Sergeant William "Bill" E. Jackson. It was after this mission that Crew 64 was given a week's rest at a home (Moulsford Manor) in southern England.

Captain Skaggs: "The rest home on the Thames River, outside of London, was a wonderful invention. When the bosses decided that a crew was sufficiently combat weary ("flak happy"), they allowed the crew a few days' rest and recreation at one of the rest homes. We didn't think we were really that bad off, but finally agreed to take off a few days from combat to join the other "flak happy" troops. We were really pleased to find that our rest home was a renovated mansion on a large estate. There were two to four men assigned to comfortable bedrooms. There was a nice dining room and lots of recreation facilities. The American Red Cross and their British counterparts managed and staffed the rest home. We were not allowed to wear uniforms. In fact, we were issued an old pair of blue jeans, a shirt and a pair of tennis shoes and that is all we had to wear while we were there. Recreation facilities included tennis, golf, horseback riding, punting on the Thames, British croquet and many kinds of club games (checkers, dominoes, cards, etc.). We were particularly delighted with one special treat – breakfast in bed most any time we wanted it from about 6:00am to 9:00am. This was served by one of the waitresses, who would knock on the door at the time we requested the night before. In establishing this time, however, it did take us awhile to get accustomed to the British use of the English language when the young lady at the desk would ask, "What time would you like to be knocked up in the morning?"

1st Lieutenant (later Captain) Alvin D. Skaggs, pilot, 448th Bomb Group

Some of the boys were developing the equivalent of "shell shock", in spite of all our doctor's efforts. The nervous strain of continuous raids had been more than some of them could take. It raised the very rough command problem as to how long these lads would still be fit to fly a combat mission, especially the pilots whose nine-man crews were trusting him with their lives. I finally had to go to Colonel Castle about one pilot who was rapidly coming "unstuck" as the British say and they sent him to the "Rest Home" in southern England. He didn't like it and I felt real sorry for him, but Colonel Castle agreed that it was no longer safe to send him on combat raids.

Captain Franklin 'Pappy' Colby, Squadron Commander, 94th Bomb Group

It's January in England, so sun just rising is rare and welcome. Breakfast smells like bacon and eggs. Apparently the grapevine knew it too because half the house is up for breakfast, twenty or so combat flyers disguised in sweaters, slacks and sneakers. Plans are afoot for golf, tennis and shooting skeet in the back yard, but the loudest conversation and most uproarious kidding center around the four who are going to ride to hounds in a country fox hunt. On a rainy day there's almost as much activity at Coombe House – the badminton court in the ballroom is our chief pride. But nevertheless the Army calls it Rest Home. It looks as English as the setting of a Noël Coward play, but even as you approach the house you discover that actors and plot are American. You meet a girl in scuffed saddle shoes and baggy sweater bicycling along a shaded drive with a dozen young men. You'd guess it was a co-ed's dream of a college house party – not a military post to which men are assigned and where girls are stationed to do a job. We have so much fun that we usually forget it and so much the better, because the house party is a successful experiment to bring combat flyers back to the peak of their efficiency.

There are four of us here, American girls sent overseas by the American Red Cross. Never in our wildest dreams did we expect such a job. At first we felt almost guilty to be having such a good time. I was talking about what a picnic it was to one of the boys. "That's the way it should be," he said with authority. When I looked again I remembered that he was a Medical Officer who'd been at Coombe for six weeks. That was odd in itself because most of them are flight surgeons who come from their airfields to stay for a week. That gives him the chance to see at first hand what we're doing and gives us a medical officer in attendance. In the course of our conversation I found out that he was Captain David Wright, Psychiatric Consultant for the 8th Air Force. He had spent his six weeks in careful observation to decide the value of rest homes. "Coombe House and the others like it," he said, "represent the best work of preventative medicine in the ETO. Very definitely I can say now that rest homes are saving lives – and badly needed airmen – by returning men to combat as more efficient flyers." Statistics (which cannot be quoted for security reasons) show that a remarkable percentage of men who finish their missions have had a chance to be in rest homes sometime during their combat tour. "There isn't any one word to describe the varying states of mind of combat flyers when they are just plain tired. Tired because it's hard work flying a P-38 or navigating a B-24 or shooting out the window of a Fort. Tired as anyone is after intense mental and muscular strain – intermittent it is, but lulls in between are not long enough or quiet enough for the flyer to get past the let-down stage before he plunges up into danger again."

At first the Air Force ran these rest homes alone. After two had been established, a large part of the responsibility was transferred to the American Red Cross to make them as un-military as possible. Army quartermaster outdoes itself on food and "Cooky" in the kitchen cooks it to perfection. Fried chicken, steaks, ice cream and the aforementioned eggs are regular items on the menu and they're served by pretty waitresses. Irish Mike and Cooky and all the rest of them are another of the contributions of the Red Cross which disguise the technical and military nature of Coombe House almost beyond recognition, and we four American girls show no obvious solicitude for anyone's morale. We turn down an invitation to play bridge if we want to dance with someone else. We wondered about that, too. "The natural impersonal friendliness of Red Cross girls who set the atmosphere is a huge factor in making these houses 'home'," says Captain Wright. "Lack of Army demands and freedom from regulations help create the free and easy tempo of the place. The whole feeling is one of such warmth and such sincerity that men come away knowing they have shared an experience of real and genuine living the first and frequently only time while they are over here."

No one means to imply that fun and gaiety and sleeping late in the morning are requisites of the ideal life, certainly not the Red Cross, nor the Army, nor even the men themselves. But here in Coombe House is tangible evidence that youth and laughter are not forever lost to men who cross the Atlantic to fight a war that shocks them. It is a reminder of the way of life that gave them their strength, of families at home that gave them faith in themselves. As Captain Wright puts it: "Their efficiency by the time they return to their fields has been developed by making them individuals again, men with feeling, stability and a renewed sense of belonging to the world they knew, in which familiar things and people still exist for them." That is why now, less than five months after the Red Cross began shaping a rest home pattern, the results in terms of rehabilitating flyers are, to me, almost unbelievable. Certainly I am convinced that the Red Cross is playing a key part in saving lives and even money and none of it would have been possible without the Red Cross.

Flak Happy Isn't The Word For It, Ann Newdeck

My rest home was at Coombe House, near Shaftesbury in Dorsetshire, England, where even in late December and early January the weather was wonderful. I recall only bright, sunny days and crisp, cool air, sometimes with a touch of morning frost. By four o'clock teatime we were able to eat our sandwiches and jam tarts on the lawn without coats. Coombe House was a large impressive manor house of an English estate that was lent for our purposes and seemed to be managed by the Red Cross, whose hostesses, at least, were our main contacts.

The manor was set amidst gently rolling hills overlaid with a patchwork of woods, pastures and fields. The countryside was green and even many of the trees and shrubs held their foliage. The manor once had a large stable of horses, which then was reduced to a few horses for our riding pleasure. Our other diversions were endless, consisting of tennis, ping-pong, badminton, softball, touch football, hunting, bridge, poker, being lazy and more – a visit to ancient Shaftesbury, where I saw the movie *Four Feathers*.

I decided to go rabbit hunting one sunny frosty morning, checked out a 12-gauge shotgun and began my trek along the edges of coppices and up and down hedgerows. I had no luck with rabbits but did have luck of an unexpected kind. A farmer wearing boots to his knees, trousers tucked into the boots, a worn tweedy jacket, woollen billed cap and a pipe approached me along a hedgerow.

"Aire Ye fahretin' 'long 'edge?" he asked.

I was nonplussed. I did not then know that the English used domesticated ferrets to send down rabbit holes when hunting. Besides, that regional bloke used a broad "a" rather than a broad "e" in pronouncing "ferret." I was sure that he said, "Are you farting along the hedge?" I wondered if he thought that the fumes would defoliate his hedge – evidently I had wandered off the estate and onto his farm.

"I don't understand what you said," I stammered.

Back came, "Aire Ye fahretin' 'long' edge?" This time it dawned on me that he might mean "firing along the hedge," both ferrets and farts being farthest from the realm of possibilities in my mind.

"No," I assured him, "I haven't fired a single shot."

This time the farmer was nonplussed, considering that I was carrying a loaded shotgun, obviously was ferreting in this colloquial manner of speaking and hadn't answered his question directly. He pulled a moment on his pipe, peered at me with raised eyebrows and then,

"Weel, then, please be off wi' Ye. Don't 'low fahretin' 'long 'edge."

I reversed my course and returned to the manor house without farting even once.

Fahretin' 'long 'edge, Bob Shaver

Everything over there was the "King's." The ferret, rabbit, and pheasant were a few of the many and the only ones I cared about. You could eat the rabbits and the pheasants. The ferrets were nice if you had seen almost nothing but Nevada desert. The best way to catch a rabbit was to get a ferret (a weasel-like animal), then tie a line on his neck, run the rabbit down his hole and then send the ferret down after him. He would bring the rabbit out and then all you had to do was to get the rabbit away from him. However, getting the ferret was a problem and so we had few rabbits. We even tried shooting flares down the hole in hopes we would smoke the rabbit out. But this didn't work too well. The flare was so hot it would cook the rabbit and that was the end of that.

Getting a ferret wasn't too hard. He would come up close to the hut and a trail of breadcrumbs would bring him in. A rabbit was something in the pot. Just don't get caught. Remember, you were fooling with the "King's" property. No rabbit or pheasant would mean round steak or Wieners, fried Spam, liver, and cabbage at the mess hall. Fortunately, I liked them all and so I ate well.

Rabbits And Ferrets, John Belingheri

Rest Homes Used by US 8th Air Force Personnel

	Opening Date	Developed Capacity
Stanbridge Earls, Romsey, Hampshire	03/01/1943	30 officers
Palace Hotel, Southport, Lancashire	19/02/1943	50 officers & 100 EM
Moulsford Manor & Bucklands Hotel		
Wallingford, Berkshire	13/05/1943	25 officers
Coombe House, Shaftesbury, Dorset	20/09/1943	50 officers
Walhampton House, Lymington, Hampshire	17/02/1944	50 enlisted men
Aylesfield House, Alton, Hampshire	15/03/1944	25 officers
Phyllis Court, Henley-on-Thames, Oxfordshire		
Roke Manor, Henley-on-Thames, Oxfordshire	10/04/1944	25 officers
Pangbourne House, Pangbourne, Berkshire	01/05/1944	30 officers
Spetchley Park, Worcestershire	01/06/1944	45 enlisted men
Furz Down House, Kings Somborne, Hampshire	26/06/1944	25 officers
Eynsham Hall, Whitney, Oxfordshire	22/07/1944	65 officers
Keythorpe Hall, Tugby, Leicestershire	26/07/1944	30 enlisted men
Erbington Manor, Chipping Camden, Gloucestershire	05/08/1944	20 enlisted men
Knightshayes Court, Tiverton, Devon	06/10/1944	40 officers

I was sent for a "flak furlough" at Coombe House shortly after the Brunswick mission of 11 January 1944, when we lost eight B-17s. We were in such bad shape our flight surgeon, "Doc" Miller, went along with us! He too was getting "flak happy" riding along with his boys.

Cliff Hatcher, pilot

The day for my discharge from the hospital finally arrived. That forty-five days had seemed more like a year. As I was taking my hospital clearance papers through the necessary steps, a nurse handed me special orders for one week at the Spetchley Park flak home. Then she took them back as she said, "Lieutenant, let me check on these orders because combat-wounded patients are supposed to receive two weeks of R&R."

I told her, "Don't bother, nurse. My commanding officer misses me so much that he and the doctor decided my wounds only deserved one week of R&R." The poor nurse must not have realized I was joking because she was shaking her head and looking sad as I got on the bus.

In town I took the train to the city of Worcester. At Worcester I boarded a bus that took me to Spetchley Park. That gorgeous estate was set in a beautiful, tranquil English countryside. Many buildings, stables and retainer quarters made up the manor, but the focal point was a stately early eighteenth-century manor house which contained many artifacts that probably dated back to the very early days of the manor. The lawn surrounding the main house looked like a putting green. The formal garden at the back of the estate, which ended at a crystal-clear lake made a spectacular setting. The very generous owners of the estate had made it available for 8th Air Force combat crews to get a little rest from the rigors of flying combat.

At the registration desk, I learned that the administration of the manor was under the auspices of the British Red Cross. There were three very attractive British Red Cross hostesses and one of the girls, Joanna, told me, "There are only eleven combat crew members here at the present time so you will not be crowded." I must have appeared amazed to learn there were only eleven people in a place that could easily have handled 100 people in comfort. She explained, "Other titled British people have turned their manors over to the British Red Cross for the same purpose, so there really is no need for crowding."

Joanna called a footman and asked him to take me to find some country squire clothing and to get me settled in my room. It had been over two years since I had worn anything but a uniform. After a shave and a bath, I put on the tweeds laid out for me. That heather aroma and soft comfort caused my whole body to completely relax. It seemed so strange that the locale, the friendliness of the people and the wonderful soft tweeds could have such a soothing effect on my body and on my mind.

Lieutenant William L. Cramer Jr, 351st Bomb Group, Spetchley Park Manor. He began his career with a bomber crew flying B-17s in the 351st Bomb Group when he was nineteen years of age. A few days before his twenty-first birthday he returned home after completing thirty-seven combat missions with the 8th Air Force. He was shot down five times, wounded twice, became a PoW after bailing out of his burning aircraft during a mission during the 'Battle of the Bulge.' He was able to resist daily German interrogation for three months while blindfolded and with his hands tied behind his back with rope. By killing his guard one night he was able to escape. After a period with the Belgian and French underground he was returned to American control so that his nearly gangrenous head wound could be treated. With a ninety-day R&R leave and over $3,000 in back pay in his pockets, he arrived home. His homecoming was marred by the fact that his family and friends all believed he had been killed on a bombing mission

My father worked on the estate at Furzedown near the village of King's Somborne in Hampshire for four owners, the last being Colonel and Mrs Firbanks. They bought Furzedown just prior to the war. During that time the farm was rented to a Mr Silegman and my father transferred from the farm to the extensive gardens which were around the house. The two younger gardeners were called up for military service and were replaced by two Italian prisoners to work with my father. The house was rented to the American Air Force as a rest and recuperation home for their pilots. The Firbank family lived in the servants' quarters. The produce grown in the gardens was sold to the Americans and to the local shop in King's Somborne. One thing I remember was a game the pilots played which was to take some item from the house, i.e. the matron's slipper, when they left and fly back over the house and drop in onto a large round rose garden on the front lawn. On one occasion a Liberator pilot hit a tree top and it fell onto an asparagus bed which had taken many years to get to perfection, much to the disgust of my father. He did receive a letter of apology from the pilot concerned.

Gerald Deacon

On 10 September 1944, between my twenty-ninth and thirtieth missions, orders were cut for our crew to take official combat leave. The enlisted men were ordered to a rest home near Pangbourne, Berkshire. The four officers were to proceed to Roke Manor. These were official 8th Air Force Rest Homes established to let the combat personnel wind down. All of our crew traveled together to London. There we separated for the respective rest homes. Charlie Peretti, Burr Palmer, John Wargas and myself arrived at Romsey, Hampshire, on the 14th. A vehicle with a driver was at the train platform to take us to Roke Manor, located approximately fifty miles southwest of London. What a magnificent structure the manor house was, three floors high I'm sure with an attic where the domestic help lived when the house was occupied by a wealthy landowner in peacetime. Located atop a moderately high hill with a large grassy knoll lawn, which was beautifully manicured, the house commanded a splendid view of the countryside below. It would be safe to estimate there were between thirty and forty rooms, the largest being the grand reception and dining area. Wealth and opulence were manifested everywhere.

A reception committee of young ladies attired in attractive civilian dresses greeted the four of us. It was apparent from the first encounter that their duty was to make us feel at home as if the war were non-existent. We were escorted to our room and given the admonition to chuck our military uniforms in favor of civilian clothing, which had been selected on the way. After being acclimated to uniform dress for so long, the sight of seeing each other in multi-colored, checked and stripped shirts and trousers was almost too much. Our stay was only going to last seven days so we had to make a quick adjustment to our new environment. One of the rules laid down on arrival was that we were not to talk about the war or combat. I can't recall a more pleasant week in my life as the stay at Roke Manor.

The food was excellent and served family style. The girls were obviously chosen for this task not only for good looks but also for personality and the ability to be a good conversationalist. If laughter is the best medicine, then the cure from combat jitters was assured. I never felt at any time during the war that I would become a victim of combat fatigue and I never saw any signs in our crew, but there were men among us who were obviously on the verge of a breakdown. I specifically recall, from personal encounters, two such individuals that fitted this category but there were probably more that I never suspected. How much a week's respite from the stress of combat flying helped I'll never know, I only know that I personally enjoyed the break.

Aside from the organised activities such as baseball, table tennis, croquet etc., time was set aside to relax on your own. Lounging in an easy chair, listening to music on the phonograph accorded a great deal of relaxation for me. One of the records was Dinah Shore's rendition of "Please Give Me Something to Remember You By." At the time I had a strong attraction for my English girlfriend, which caused me to wish she were there.

John McClane

After the Schweinfurt raid we got to go to a rest home run by the Red Cross which was much needed. The officers went to Stanbridge Earls while we went to Moulsford Manor. We were treated royally and got to wear civilian clothes. There were butlers, waiters and maids to take care of us.

Howard E. Hernan, air gunner

On the staff were the most beautiful American and English Red Cross girls I had ever seen. Perhaps they looked more beautiful because we had just come off combat flying duty. We had flown quite a number of missions. Constance was the typical English beauty, complete with the alluring accent of the British and the complexion to fit. She was the objective for a date with all the men stationed at this English manor house on a large country estate surrounded by acres of green lawns, gardens and woodlands. There were many walks about the estate that lent themselves to romantic interludes with the girls. As was common among war-weary airmen of the time, there was always one or two who boasted how they could make out with any of the girls. I became frustrated by their claims and decided it was time to do something about them.

Constance, or Connie, was a popular companion on these walks and it was not uncommon among the men to bid for the privilege of accompanying her. Since she could not accompany all the men, lots were drawn to see who would get to walk with her the following day. I drew one of the lots but as luck would have it, that day turned out to be a typical English soaker with rain and mist most of the day at intervals. Nevertheless, we did take the walk and using umbrellas we managed to walk a considerable distance in the woodland, out of sight of the estate. Half-way around I got the courage to try to kiss Connie, but this was against the rules and she let me know it. Not to be outdone, we decided that I would teach the other airmen a lesson and so it was agreed that we would stay out longer than the usual time and make it appear we had done some prolonged and heavy romancing in the shelter of the woods. It was a cruel illusion but one that delighted me at the time. How cold and damp we got sitting in a greenhouse and under a shelter to make the time pass. There was nothing whatever between us, not even an embrace. We were examples of puritan discretion. However, to make the others more jealous, Connie agreed to smear some of her lipstick (a rare enough item in wartime Britain) on my cheek to make it appear we had experienced some hot and heavy romancing. I shall never forget the looks on the others' faces when we emerged from the woodland what seemed hours later. The jealousy was so thick it was palatable.

Forrest S. Clark, air gunner

The day after Christmas 1944, my crew was sent to Knight Hays Court near Tiverton in the Land's End area. The manor house had ninety-nine rooms, well-kept by its owner, vaulted ceilings, fireplaces, a dining room, library, game room and special rooms like one might expect a knight to have. Several thousand acres belonged to Knight Hays, which were worked by its tenants and supervised by gardeners, game wardens and others. Wearing civilian clothes given to us by the Red Cross, who operated the place, we romped in non-military fashion for ten days. A herd of cattle grazed near by so the crew challenged me to ride rodeo-style. They were very docile and soon all were riding. The Texas image faded. Playing much bridge, eating well, drinking well, playing golf in civvies, the war was forgotten for a few days.

Colonel Robert H. Tays, pilot

On 6 December our Group Command granted our crew a seven-day leave at what airmen called the "flak shack." The 8th Air Force had at least half-a-dozen of these rest-and-recuperation havens for bomber crews and fighter pilots. Officers and enlisted men went to different locations, but they were all similar in quality and method of operation.

I and the other three officers of my crew went to Aylesfield House, a magnificent country home that a wealthy Englishman had built in the

1930s. He leased it during the war either to the British government, who made it available for 8th Air Force use, or to the Air Force directly.

I wrote my parents on 8 December 1944, "Aylesfield House ... is a beautiful mansion about an hour's train ride (south and west) of London ... All our needs are taken care of. We get to sleep as long as we want in nice soft beds with real sheets on them and we get very good food. Also, we have all the recreational facilities you can think of with Red Cross hostesses to help us enjoy them ... They also give us civilian clothes to wear during the day. The house is the kind you read about in books ... It's in the middle of a large estate and has beautiful grounds surrounding. There are about 25 of us (flying officers) here."

Although sleeping late was an option, we were always awakened in the early morning by an accomplished English butler, who was appropriately clothed in black formal garb. He knocked and then entered our room with a tray of fruit juices. "Juice, sir?" he would ask politely. Then, he would peel back the drapes from the large window overlooking the fields around and exclaim: "Oh what a beautiful day, sir! I am sure you will enjoy it." The day might be miserably gray, overcast and raining, but he was right. Any day I woke up in that place with those surroundings and the ambience of Aylesfield House was a beautiful day. The butler was a prop, of course, to make us feel welcome and relaxed. He could not have been cast better for the part, or a more authentic representative of what was solidly British.

Our day was completely free to do with as we pleased, even leave for some hours to go into London. If we stayed around the house, we could entertain ourselves with card games, ping-pong, hikes in the country and most memorably, horseback riding.

Aylesfield House had its own stable with ten to fifteen riding horses. Of course, such a herd required a stable master to manage and care for the horses. This man also provided instruction and guidance on riding. Good that he did, because one of our daily options was to go horseback riding. Decked out in casual civilian clothes provided by the house staff, we would assemble near the horses. Then, under the supervision of the stable master, we would get horse-borne and ride single-file out into the lanes and country roads of the area.

I had never ridden horseback before but I twice volunteered to risk it while at Aylesfield House. Without flak in the offing, nothing else seemed very risky. So one gray wintry morning I found myself high atop a relatively docile steed. I tried to practice what I had observed from watching others in this precarious position. I had the reins in my hand and thought that they controlled the horse – pull up and he should stop, put pressure an the left rein and he should turn left and so forth, similar to the controls on a B-17.

In fact, none of these common means of control had any effect on the horse. The stable master, who was proficient in this art, controlled his mount perfectly as he led us through the countryside. Most of the time the horses walked, but occasionally the riding master would put the lead horse into a trot or a gallop for a short distance. When he did so, all the other horses would do exactly what the lead horse did. I had no control over my horse at all. He knew who was boss and the boss's name was not Lieutenant R.H. Timberlake.

Nonetheless, the ride required concentration and gave the rider some exercise and a sense of achievement, so it was fun – with one exception:

The roads were muddy and looked slippery, especially for horses' hooves that had no "sure-grip" on their shoes. To make matters worse, my horse seemed to have stumble-itis. When he started to gallop following the stable master's cue, he would stumble slightly every so often as though he was losing his footing. The slippery mud and his stumbling gait led me to expect that the nag would go sprawling at any instant. So every motion faster than walk put me on ready – alert for a soft place to land if this no-control horse went down, forcing me to bail out. Fortunately, it never happened.

One other horse, I noticed, kept kicking up his hind hooves, as if to repel something behind him that he did not like. I thought at the time that his skittishness might endanger the horse and rider behind him. I found out two months later, when I was again in the hospital, that this occasional kickback finally found a mark: his hooves broke the tibia of a flying officer riding the horse behind. Flak was not the danger at the flak shack; it was horses and hooves!

Since fighter pilots also visited the flak shack for rest and recuperation, we had interesting discussions with our fighter escort comrades. One fighter pilot there was Charles "Chuck" Weaver of the 357th Fighter Group, who had trained with me in primary and basic flight training. We had a grand time together exchanging experiences. (We could not anticipate then that we would lose touch after the war, only to meet again fifty-two years later as "old boys".)

Every evening we reverted to our dress uniforms – forest-greens and pinks – and had supper served by the butler in the beautiful dining room. Of course, we talked shop to let off steam, although everyone was careful not to let off too much. Then there was after-dinner dancing and relaxation. The week was such an oasis in the desert of war that it could only pass too quickly.

Richard Timberlake, 388th Bomb Group, who was very badly injured by flak on 28 January 1945 and was hospitalized and later, repatriated stateside

In January 1945 members of our crew were sent to rest homes for a week, the four officers going to Eynsham Hall near Oxford. On Sunday the Yanks at the Hall were transported to various places of worship and the party I joined went to a small Methodist church in the town of Witney. We were ushered to seats on the left side of the sanctuary as one faced the chancel. There was a balcony along the full length of the opposite side and in the end closest to the chancel was a group of children who had remained following Sunday school for the church service. The text of the sermon was introduced by the pastor's listing several leave-taking expressions, including "*adios*", "*au revoir*", the British expression of the day, "God bless", and what he thought was the predominant American expression, "so long". He then asked the children in the balcony which expression they thought was the nicest and most meaningful. Obviously he expected their reply to be "God bless" which would lead him nicely into his sermon. Those kids looked down at the dozen or so Yanks in their proper dress uniforms and shouted as one, "so long". Whether it was the novelty of having Yanks in the congregation or just that natural rapport that seemed to exist between the US servicemen and the British kids didn't matter, but those kids really made the day for some homesick young Yanks. We almost stood up and saluted our young friends. Needless to say, it took some adroit manoeuvering on the part of the pastor to get back on track with his sermon.

John Ramsey

13

Journey's End

There were many things that we knew we would never forget as we looked back on those two long years. The earliest days at Debach and the rain that seeped through the British tents. The British Army rations that we ate for six weeks – carrots, mutton, cabbage, rice and dates, with a liberal sprinkling of mud and live bees and rain, and how we marvelled at the stamina and health of the English soldiers who were thriving on this diet. The German raiders that slowly circled in the clouds over Ipswich and the curtains of green incendiaries that they dropped. The reveille in the inky blackness of dawn and the days out on the runways in fog and rain. Our first taste of English beer and our first visit to wartime London and the morning rides to Sudbury when the two girls waved from the upstairs window.

There were other sights that moved us: flowers and weeds growing in the empty cellars of Coventry and Bristol and Chelmsford and a hundred other towns; the classic steeple of St Bride's in Fleet Street standing above the gutted shell of its church; the silver fleets of Fortresses droning through the skies like lines from a feather brush; the tower of the Boston Stump like a white sword across the fens; the dank wind from the passing trains flapping the blankets about the thin forms of old women and babies in the underground stations; the blood red of a wheat field brushed with poppies in Hertfordshire and the sulphur of a mustard field in Suffolk; there were the dawn calisthenics in the quiet streets of Watford and the midnight meetings around the fire in the Nissen huts at Debach.

There were sounds, too, that will linger: the piper in the mist-shrouded hills of Loch Lomond and the boom of Big Ben on the BBC, the skylarks' songs as they danced over the English meadows and the lapwings' lonely cries at night in the fields around Wattisham. There was the endless drone as the RAF bombers went out at night and there were rooks cawing in the rain on a winter's day. There was the echo of steelshod shoes on the cobblestones of the villages at midnight and the lonely hum of the wind in the telephone wires. And, above all, there were sirens at dawn, at noon, in the evening and at night. Will you ever forget that mournful wailing cry of Doom?

Yes, there were the smells too. The fresh clean smell of a clover field at Debach; the heavy, sour smell of smoke and the fog of London; the smell of the sea at Felixstowe and the sickly-sweet smell of a sugar-beet factory at Ipswich; the smell of a fish-and-chip shop suddenly permeating the damp air in a blacked-out Ipswich street, the smell of beer through the rain in Reading and the smell of pipe tobacco like burning seaweed in a Suffolk bus.

Nor would we forget the people: the hard-working factory girls like Iris and the office girls like Bessie and Joan and the other workers like Winnie at the Gainsborough and Daphne with her butcher's van and like Pat at the Piccadilly underground station and the porters at railway stations and the clippies on the buses. And staunch men like Sheriff Moody and Vic of the ROC and John of the ARP and Albert of the NFS of London; like the tired miners of Washington and the slow-moving farmers of Suffolk and business-men like Vivian and Pop working in the evenings to grow vegetables and drilling on Sundays with the Home Guard; there were the grimy girls of Glasgow and the old men of Hull who had come off retirement to help unload the cargo, yes and thousands of others like them ...

Retrospect, Robert Arbib Jr

Do you remember, my girl Joan, the many evenings that I came to Sudbury during this war – and the many ways I found to come to you on Saturday evenings? There were the buses westward from Ipswich and the trains from London to Marks Tey and then the change to Sudbury on the train that went up the beautiful Stour Valley past Colne and Bures? And the train eastward from Cambridge down through Clare and Long Melford? And the bus from Wattisham that went over to Lavenham and Long Melford? And the farmers who brought me in as a hitch-hiker from Bury St Edmunds and north from Braintree. And the bicycle that brought me down through the fourteen most beautiful miles of Suffolk countryside from Wattisham to Bildeston and though Chelsworth, Monks Eleigh, Little Waldingfield and down the long hill into Sudbury?

Do you remember the spring evenings after I had moved to Wattisham, when I would set out on my bicycle and you on yours and we would meet at Little Waldingfield; and how you tasted your first beer at "The Swan" there? And how we walked around the lanes and then you waved good-bye, standing by your bike with your fair hair, bottle-green slacks, pink blouse, a picture there waving to me until I was out of sight?

Do you remember the day we went to Foxearth to collect the rent from the little cottage of your father's and how we got lost coming home? Do you remember the day we walked through the meadows when they were ankle-deep in water and how later that afternoon I met your father for the first time, standing barefoot in his living room, while our shoes dried?

Do you remember the day we walked across the meadows when the Home Guard was having battle practice and provided the comic picture of Sunday strollers in the midst of a skirmish, being chased from the field of battle by an indignant officer?

Do you remember the suppers we had at Gainsborough House and the evenings we spent watching American movies in the balcony of the little Gainsborough Theatre and marvelling over the wonders of America? Do you remember the letters we wrote each other, delivered by "special messenger" each morning and the evenings that I walked a mile or two to the telephone just to hear you say, "Hello there, Robert?"

Do you remember the country fair at Long Melford and the haunted rectory at Borley and the dances in Victoria Hall and the evening you came over to Ipswich and the day we had together in London?

Perhaps these were small incidents to you, things that you had done before, things to be soon forgotten. But to me they are moments that will never be repeated and never be forgotten. For they were new and fresh, they were flawless and perfect, they were true and good – to be cherished and loved by a soldier.

... Joan Ramsey belonged to her countryside and she was a fan of its history and for that history, and its continuity, she had an unconscious feeling. She was a product, too, of that history and she belonged to that Suffolk village and in that Suffolk landscape just as surely as the bluebells in Aga Fen or the oaks on Sudbury meadows or the most carefree skylark in the skies above those meadows. Knowing her, you felt you knew England.

For in her beauty Joan was a distillation of all the qualities that had gone into slow centuries of English breeding, tempered by centuries of English climate. In her you could see the Saxon and the Dane, the Anglian and the Norse that had come in ages past to England's eastern shores. Her hair was straight and silky, blonde with a few darker streaks; her eyes were English – large, pale, grey-blue, under long lashes. Her face was small and heart-shaped.

In stature, too, the girl Joan was English. Small shoulders, slim, high waist, straight, long, coltish legs. Even her Christian name – "Joan" – was a frequent one and her surname – Ramsey – an ancient East Anglian one. Her speech was soft and musical, her accent slightly touched with the sing-song Suffolk and the poetic turn of phrase. Her special charm was that of shy innocence – grace and a warm sensitivity, sprightly grace and a warm sensitivity.

Joan never needed a reminder that she was heir to a long history of which she was a part and a link. She lived it and in it. All around her in her world were little churches that had been standing in the same verdant lushness for seven centuries. The same cobblestones on which she rode her bicycle had marks of wagon wheels, the same inns and stage-coaching taverns were still standing and the heirs to them were still drinking their ale from pewter mugs in them. The same Thursday Market days brought the farmers in to Sudbury as they had for countless years; the house where Sudbury's famous son was born was still standing and occupied, the pink-plastered cottages still stood in the valleys and the lanes as they had always stood, the mushrooms still sprouted on the meadows at night and were gathered at dawn. The soldiers that roamed the streets at night were in new uniforms, they might be called London Scottish or American 8th Air Force but they were the same strangers who had been quartered there a century ago; and did not, could not, each Sudbury family, if it only knew, tell of sons who fought for Cromwell and, before Cromwell, for Drake and before Drake for the York dukes and before them, long before – for Queen Boadicea? And when they came home from their wars and their crusades and their sea-fights, was there not a Maid Joan waiting at the pink-painted cottage?

The Girl Joan, Robert Arbib Jr

I was now an old combat veteran; and though only twenty-one years old, I had seen enough for a lifetime. I had literally grown up in the war. More of my friends were dead than alive. A seemingly endless procession of crews had come and gone out of our squadron. Only a handful of them had completed a tour of operations. I had seen them come and go, but always on my mind was the spectre of Lieutenant Long's crew, who went down on their final sortie. The same thing happened to Lieutenant Holdcroft's crew. I was getting closer and closer to the day when my tour would be complete. Now that it looked like I had a chance to finish, I began to sweat it out. I had finished twenty-five missions and had collected my DFC. Before I completed the required thirty missions, the brass said we were going to fly unlimited missions (as did our friends, the RAF). This was so disastrous to morale that they finally relented. I actually had to fly thirty-one and was given credit for four I didn't fly. I don't know how they figured it; it made no sense to me.

Ben Smith Jr, radio operator, *Chick's Crew*

Bombing Dresden we were told that we had a chemical plant as our target, which was well defended. It was a very long and difficult mission. The 8th Air Force went to that area three days in a row with the Royal Air Force the same three nights. I have heard many stories about what happened on the ground. It must have been terrible. This must have been the first effort to bomb the civilian population, or they just got in the way of the military. German refugees were streaming west to get away from the on-coming Russians and German military were rushing east to meet the Russians. This created a transportation logjam. Many died because they could not move. Another story has it that the Allies thought that the German scientist, Klaus Fuchs, was in the area trying to escape to Russia so the town was methodically destroyed hoping to destroy Klaus Fuchs in the process. Estimates of the deaths that occurred ranges from 100,000 to 300,000. This terrible loss of life did have one significant effect: it destroyed the Germans' will to fight.

It was the beginning of the end.

Robert H. Tays

Hawaiian Love Song

By April 14 1945 I was in Atlanta, Georgia, and I hadn't seen Mary Frances for more than a year. In July 1944 I had received a letter from Mary Frances advising me that she had become engaged to my rival, the scion of a well-to-do Chicago couple who spent their winters in St Petersburg, Florida. I had never felt so low. I felt strongly this was the woman I wanted. She was attractive, intelligent, self-confident, poised, cheerful and I loved her dearly. I sent her a letter of congratulations wishing her the best of luck. Then I had second thoughts as I was determined not to give up on her. Three days later, I wrote her again telling her that I didn't give a damn how many guys she became engaged to – that we were going to be married one day soon! On 5 December I received a letter from Mary Frances and she told me she had broken her engagement to my rival, the US Navy well-heeled sailor. Naturally, our correspondence took a whole new tack. Later I discovered the breakup came about when Mary Frances and her prospective mother-in-law had a disagreement over the purchase of a hope chest and her son, the dimwit, sided with mama. God bless Mary's mother for raising a daughter with a self-esteem that won't tolerate a bully or a mama's boy. That's my kind of woman.

I was not the young man I was a year earlier. My nerves were shot. I was jumpy and not sleeping well – not that I had nightmares or anything like that – it was just that I had trouble shutting the war out of my head. I knew my survival was due much more to luck than skill, training or discipline. Mary Frances, too, must have changed. She too had seen more than her share of suffering, of death and dying – not to mention what had to be traumatic experiences in psychiatric rotation in the state mental hospitals at Chattahoochee. I couldn't wait to see her again. I received my orders from HQ Fort McPherson, Atlanta, Georgia. I'd been granted a 21-day leave before reporting to Miami Beach for reassignment. At the Mound Park Hospital, St Petersburg, Florida on April 16 I waited in the living room of the nurses' home until Mary Frances came off duty. We stared at each other for a couple of seconds, then fell into each other's arms. We whispered tender words, then in what had to be the dumbest thing I'd ever done, I did not propose marriage again but simply asked her how she felt about last year's proposal. She laughed and accepted and I felt a lot happier than I deserved to be.

On May 8 1945 we celebrated VE Day at the Chatterbox Club in St Pete, which did the best Planter's punches in the whole of Dixieland. I reported to Miami Beach on the 10th for processing, physical exams and reassignment. I passed the flying status physical but I went to see the psychologist. The captain seemed to be friendly. He invited me to sit down and said, "How can I help you?"

Boy, can he help! So I told him about not sleeping well.

He asked, "How many missions do you have?" And I knew I've got it made.

When I told him I had fifty-one, he said, "Hmmm" and then asked me if I would like a couple of weeks' rest at the local AAF convalescent hospital?

So I told him I was not too keen on Miami Beach and then he said, "Well perhaps you would prefer our St Petersburg location?"

They stopped my processing and on the 19th I was back in St Pete. Two days later I checked into the Don Ce Sar AAF Convalescent Hospital where I had plenty of time to cement bonds with my fiancée, as I would not be leaving for Miami Beach until 7 August. The medical captain who examined me asked a lot of fool questions until I realized the sneaky bugger was trying to get my number. I soon began to see I was not as well off as I thought but looking around I saw that there were some ex-combat types who were somewhat, if not entirely, bonkers.

Abe Dolim, who married Mary Frances in spring 1945

Trolly Trips

7 May (1st Trolley Mission) 6.15

11.30 briefing for a 'trolley tour' of Germany with 10 ground-pounder passengers and our 5 (skeleton crew) Quite a thrill – knowing it was being flown on the day VE day was announced (for tomorrow). Flew down to Ardennes Forest, Mannheim, Dormstadt, Frankfurt, Coblenz, Cologne, Bonn, Dusseldorf and to Brussels and home. A nice trip – flew really low! Most peculiar sight to see those big birds in every direction you looked – right on the deck! Boy, it was really the most fun I've ever had flying I believe. And such sights we saw – took some snaps too – of Cologne Cathedral etc. Swell!

8 May – VE DAY! Hurray!!

Another Trolley-trip and today I was really glad to be flying ... on such a day – to see so many miles of celebration. Took along 3 rolls of toilet paper for my celebration ... really makes confetti when unwound and thrown out in bunches. Had the boys in tail turret watch it – they could see it! Same tour as yesterday ... only flew too high today – sorta scaring the guys ... with monitor ships. Still saw lots! Circled Brussels 3 times with Count's ship ... He shooting flares and me kicking off the toilet paper like mad. (Was reported Major Player saw it all and liked it! hm) Everybody celebrating below ... Flags everywhere and people wave like mad! Took off by ourselves with Count and decided we wanted to see another big Capital celebrating, Yes, London! We found it – circled down to 400ft ... and I really dumped a lot out over Piccadilly ... Man were the streets packed, flags & bonfires everywhere. So low – could see the mob waving and climbing up on the lions of Trafalgar Sq. Home about and hour later than other guys 8.15pm. – Nice Day!

Diary entries, Walt Cranson

London assumed a new attractiveness now that the war and with it, the blackout, was over. Piccadilly Circus had long been a concentration point for 92nd Group men on two-day passes; the Hans Crescent, the Milestone, the Jules, the Reindeer, Duchess, Princes Garden, Mostyn, Columbia and other Red Cross clubs were part of the pattern of the wartime metropolis. Many a splitting headache was nursed on the 8.30am train from St Pancras Station back to Wellingborough, then to the field.

The Northampton and Wellingborough pubs continued to get attention – rather desperate attention now, when the Group was on the verge of a move. In Northampton the men went steadily to the Plough and the Angel, the Grand, the Swan, the Black Boy, the Queen's Arms and came out less steadily. The nightly liberty runs were loaded each way.

The cyclists and the thumbers continued to go to Wellingborough. Billy Burke's Exchange Hotel drew a steady patronage; drawn perhaps equally by Mr Burke's undeniable charm and his woefully weak spirits. Mr Burke, an ex-rugby star of national fame, was also a man of considerable personality and a raconteur of high degree. A great many personnel spent numerous pleasant evenings in his company. Mr Burke had one curious shortcoming and it was mathematical; he knew to the farthing what a drink cost but he was unable to count the wings on a goose.

Other places in Wellingborough which attracted interest were the Hind Hotel, an ancient and rather stuffy place dating back to the Stuart period; The Angel, The Sun, The Dog and Duck (on the road back to Podington), The King's Arms, The Cambridge, The Chequers and others.

John S. Sloan

Popular watering holes off base were The Swan at Topcroft where the innkeeper, Bert, painted names of his regulars on beer mugs. It was sad when he was forced to retire a mug after its owner went MIA.

Ted's Travelling Circus, 93rd Bomb Group History Carroll 'Cal' Stewart

The English were a nation of people who endured more wartime hell in bombings, rockets, privations, rationing that the rest of [us] never even came close to, loss of loved ones in the service and at home, being occupied by another nation's troops and still coming out of it with heads held high and an undaunted spirit.

22-year old Arthur L. Prichard, co-pilot, 467th Bomb Group

I never liked the service, or being in the service, but I will always be grateful for the training, for the leadership, for the people I met, for the opportunity to serve in England, for the hospitality of the people of England ... of London ... surrounding our base and those in Norwich. I praise God for England, for your people, for your courage as you stood together in hard times until freedom returned again. God bless you.

Paul M. Dickerson, 21-year old waist gunner, 445th Bomb Group

My stay in England was an interesting one and was quite enjoyable when

I was able to visit the various sections of the country. I have memories that have lasted these thirty-eight years I wouldn't trade. As I've heard many times from those speaking of their experiences in World War Two, I'd surely not want to go through it again but I wouldn't give anything for the experiences that I did have.

Lyndon Allen, rear gunner, 44th Bomb Group

We stood at the front gate in a row while Bob [Helmling] walked past, shaking hands with each of us in turn. "Good-byes", "Good Lucks" and "Thank Yous" were said. Bob walked off along the road and I had to turn away to hide the tears which blinded me as I walked back to the house. The end – for a time – of a perfect friendship.

Fourteen-year-old schoolgirl Primrose Henderson-Gray whose family were friendly during the war with Robert Helmling and David Grinnell of the 467th Bomb Group at Rackheath

Perhaps it would be of more interest to future historians if, instead of logs and flights and targets and bombloads, we all set down our thoughts about those times – what our daily lives were like, how we coped with the dreariness of our lives, the friends we made and some of the fun times. Because there were those and history is made up of many things.

Mary Carroll Leeds, American Red Cross

Finally the war was over. I was glad I guess, but I was confused. I didn't know what to expect in a world without war. I had to stay in the ATS until February 1946 and by that time many of the Americans had returned home and the airfields began their long road into history. I thought of moving to America where I had some relatives, but couldn't make the immigration quota from England; so I got a job in Germany with the military government.

I wanted to find out what happened to my family, since I hadn't heard anything. I searched everywhere and even made my way back into Vienna, which at that time was divided into four zones. Many buildings had been bombed to the ground, the city was in total upheaval and I learned nothing. It was years later when, with the help of various agencies, the grim picture emerged. Father, mother and brother had all been picked up by the Nazis, deported from Austria, interned and killed. I'm still trying to learn some of the circumstances.

I finally was able to immigrate to the US in 1950 on the Austrian quota. It was not without some culture shocks, however. So many American mothers with young children held jobs. I was completely overwhelmed by the abundance and variety of food and merchandise in the supermarkets and the beautiful drugstores.

I eventually married, had two sons and a daughter and became an

American citizen. We now also have a grandson and a granddaughter. Last May I returned to Vienna with part of my family, but my feelings were mixed. I expected to be sad, but having a four-year-old granddaughter along certainly put a new perspective on the sentimental journey to the old hometown. To my utter surprise, I found myself riding on the Ferris Wheel and checking out all the kiddie rides in Vienna's huge amusement park.

Other, more somber sites were put "on hold" until next time. I did manage to visit the old house and pause by the staircase where fifty years ago the storm troopers stomped up to fetch mother to her death. I want to go back again, perhaps alone, to recapture the days of my childhood and family life.

My main attitude today is one of surprise that finally, after it all, I, Frances, am leading a normal middle-class life like everyone else. The experiences of my life keep coming back to me; and when I think of my family, the war years and England, I think of how close it was – Hitler almost won. If it hadn't been for the English Channel, the Royal Air Force and the American Air Force, Hitler might have won and where would we be now?

Frances Nunnally

> *Goodbye GI, Good-bye Big-hearted Joe*
> *We're glad you came. We hope you're sad to go.*
> *Say what you can for this old fashioned isle,*
> *And when you can't, well say it with a smile.*
> *Goodbye GI, Bud. Now you know the way*
> *Come back and see us in a brighter day.*
> *When England's free and the Scotch is cheap but strong,*
> *And you can bring your pretty wives along.*
> *Goodbye GI, don't leave us quite alone.*
> *Somewhere in England we must write in stone*
> *How Britain was invaded by the Yanks*
> *And under that "a big and hearty thanks"*

The Right Honourable A.P. Herbert MP, a famous English historian

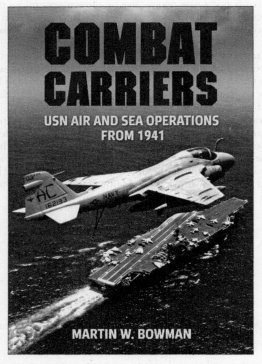